T0375650

WHOLE

EXPERIENCING ABUNDANCE IN
YOUR WALK WITH JESUS

JEFF BAUER

WESTBOW
PRESS®
A DIVISION OF THOMAS NELSON
& ZONDERVAN

WestBow Press books may be ordered through booksellers or by contacting:

WestBow Press
A Division of Thomas Nelson & Zondervan
1663 Liberty Drive
Bloomington, IN 47403
www.westbowpress.com
844-714-3454

All Scriptures are taken from the New King James Version. Copyright © 1982 by Thomas Nelson, Inc. Used by permission. All rights reserved.

ISBN: 979-8-3850-2535-0 (sc)
ISBN: 979-8-3850-2536-7 (e)

Library of Congress Control Number: 2024909791

Print information available on the last page.

WestBow Press rev. date: 6/12/2024

CONTENTS

FOREWORD

The year was approximately A.D. 28. The nation of Israel, except for a brief period of independence following the Maccabean revolt in 167 B.C., had lived under foreign rule since 586 B.C.[1] Generations of Jews had been born, grown up, and lived out their lives only to die in captivity. The people were suffering under the oppression of the Roman Empire, and wondering when God would send His deliverer – their Savior and Messiah – prophesied centuries before by Isaiah (19:20) and Daniel (9:25-26).

An inkling of what was to come had occurred about 30 years earlier, when one night a multitude of angels pronounced the following to a group of stunned shepherds:

"Glory to God in the highest, And on earth peace,
goodwill toward men!" (Luke 2:14)

And the source of that peace? None other than Jesus Himself: The Prince of Peace who came to restore a fallen and broken world. In His first clear declaration that He in fact was the Savior and Messiah to come, Jesus proclaimed:

"The Spirit of the LORD is upon Me, Because
He has anointed Me To preach the
gospel to the poor; He has sent Me to heal the
brokenhearted, To proclaim liberty
to the captives and recovery of sight to the
blind, To set at liberty those who are
oppressed; to proclaim the acceptable year of the
LORD." (Luke 4:18-20; cf Is 61:1-3)

---

[1] https://www.ancient.eu/article/827/the-maccabean-revolt/

After numerous miraculous healings, teachings about the righteousness of God, and the lofty expectations of discipleship, Jesus made a bold statement to those who had believed in Him and were beginning to trust in Him:

"...if you abide in my word, you are My
disciples indeed. And you shall
know the truth, and the truth shall make you free." (John 8:31-32)

A short time later He said this to His closest disciples:

"The thief does not come except to steal, and
to kill, and to destroy. I have come
that they may have life, and that they may have
it more abundantly." (John 10:10)

According to the Apostle Paul, the freedom and abundant life Jesus offers is seen when one is fully experiencing the fruit of the Holy Spirit:

"But the fruit of the Spirit is love, joy, peace,
longsuffering, kindness, goodness,
faithfulness, gentleness, self-control. Against
such there is no law." (Gal 5:22-23)

This suggests people who are generally content and satisfied with their lives and is more often the experience of those who are followers of Jesus than those who are not. A study by the Austin Institute for the Study of Family and Culture, for example, found there is a strong correlation between religious affiliation and personal happiness, as 45% of those who attend religious services weekly say they are "very happy", compared to only 28% of those who never attend.[2]

The researchers concluded the main factor contributing to the disparity in happiness of their respondents is the social support and sense of community of those who regularly participate in some form of religious practice. But noteworthy is the following:

---

[2] http://www.dailymail.co.uk/news/article-2886974/Study-Religious-people-happier-life-satisfaction-others.html#ixzz55JAGyKEg

- While those committed to religious practices experience much more happiness and satisfaction in life, *less than 50%* are experiencing the fruit of the Spirit; and,
- The difference between regular religious practitioners and the self-declared non-religious is only *17%*!

And unclear in these findings is whether this 17% difference is the product of a vibrant spiritual life, or simply having a stronger sense of community and social support. But Jesus promised much more than a sense of community and social support – He proposed we <u>all</u> (that's 100% of us) can experience the freedom and abundant life He offers.

While Americans do not live under the oppression of foreign rule like those 1st century Jews, it is safe to say many do not feel "free". Just as racial tensions have dominated the news the past few years, a significant number of American adults continued to suffer under the bondage of psychological disorders such as anxiety (40 million) and depression (16.1 million).[3] And when you consider as many as 165 million (60.2%) Americans aged 12 years or older abuse alcohol or drugs, it is clear many are not feeling "liberated".[4]

As you consider the declarations of Jesus and Paul, you might ask yourself: Do I feel "free"? Am I experiencing life "abundantly"? And am I experiencing the "fruits of the Spirit"? Perhaps you might consider if the following statements are true for you:

- I feel loved and valued by the important people in my life,
- I am content with my life and generally feel joyful,
- People would consider me kind and gentle,
- I rarely experience conflicts with others, and when I do am able to resolve them quickly and amicably,
- I am patient and rarely get irritated or frustrated when things don't go the way I want them to or hope they would,
- I do not struggle with compulsive behaviors like over-eating, drinking too much alcohol, viewing pornography, or shopping or gambling excessively.

---

[3] https://adaa.org/about-adaa/press-room/facts-statistics
[4] https://drugabusestatistics.org/. Data obtained 5/11/21.

Do the above statements accurately reflect how you would assess your life right now? Or are some – if not most – of the fruits of the Spirit missing in your life? It is apparent many followers of Jesus would say "no". As a result, churches throughout America have found it necessary to develop ministries that include counseling and support groups for those battling alcohol, drug or pornography addiction and other forms of mental illness, as well as for those who have suffered abuse and trauma, or divorce.

Seeing the need for a study group and curriculum for those not experiencing the fruit of the Spirit in their lives, the staff at Oasis Community Church in Phoenix, Arizona developed a curriculum that led to the writing of this this book and had all church members participating in Life Groups work through the curriculum during the Fall of 2018. From the reports we received, even long-time followers of Jesus well-versed in the Bible experienced growth and healing as they addressed and confronted issues that had inhibited their spiritual growth and sense of freedom in the past.

The Jews of Jesus' day could clearly point to Rome as their "oppressor" (Is 61:1-3) and the cause of their suffering.[5] In the same way many today may point to some system, group of people, or other factors generating the anguish that is inhibiting their ability to experience joy and contentment in their lives.

Yet as we will see, the early followers of Jesus – living under the same Roman rule and being scorned by their unbelieving Jewish brethren – experienced "gladness" (Acts 2:41-47). And perhaps this is a product of coming to realize just who Jesus is:

> "For unto us a Child is born, Unto us a Son
> is given; And the government will
> be upon His shoulder. And His name will
> be called Wonderful, Counselor,
> Mighty God, Everlasting Father, Prince of Peace." (Is 9:6)

---

[5] See https://www.history.com/this-day-in-history/state-of-israel-proclaimed. While Israel formerly became a "state" again for the first time in 2,000 years in 1948, it is safe to say the people of Israel generally feel far from free given the persistent threats they face, examples being the 11 days of conflict that occurred in the Gaza Strip in May, 2021, and the attack by Hamas-based terrorists against Israelis on October 7, 2023, that erupted into full-fledged conflict.

In this short, succinct statement, Isaiah proclaims Jesus to be the mighty and powerful God who will one day rule over all, but who even now is that wondrous counselor and father figure through whom we can experience *shalom*, or that inner peace that no oppressor can take away from us.

This is what Jesus came to bring, what He offers, and my hope you will experience through the insights you gain from this book.

CHAPTER 1

HOW DID WE GET HERE?

INTRODUCTION

In early 2021, a top news story was the "assault" of a "prolonged polar plunge" wreaking havoc across America. Over 150 million Americans were issued weather advisories and ice storm warnings, and over 50 million saw temperatures dip below zero. The townships of Cotton and Ely, Minnesota (my home state) experienced several days in which the low temperatures plunged to 50 degrees below zero. And that's without wind chill, folks!

While much of America experienced weather reminiscent of the movie, *Day After Tomorrow,* during the winter of 2021, fast forward to 2023, during which the United States and throughout the world record heat was recorded and 70% of the Earth's surface recorded the hottest temperatures ever recorded. My now-home of Phoenix, Arizona, "endured the hottest month (July) for any US city as historic heat streak comes to an end", and daily highs finally dropped below 110 days for the first time in 32 days.[6] In 2023, Phoenix recorded 54 days at or above 110 degrees, 115 degrees or more 17 days, and the low did not drop below 90 degrees for 16 straight days. Our <u>average</u> in July was 102.7 degrees, only to be followed by the second-hottest August ever recorded!

And Phoenicians were not alone. Extreme heat and droughts contributed to fires raging throughout North America and the world. An

---

[6] https://www.cnn.com/2023/08/01/weather/phoenix-us-heatwave-streak-climate/index.html

historic fire on the Hawaiian island of Maui killed over 100 people and destroyed over 250 buildings and over 2700 homes, and fires raged across British Colombia Canada, burning over 733,000 acres.

While fires raged throughout the world, other areas saw record rains and floods killing thousands of people. And along with the heat, droughts, fires and flooding, earthquakes ravaged much of the world. Death tolls of over 50,000 were recorded after earthquakes struck Nepal, Turkey, and Syria. And ominous signs were evident in Washington state as Mount St. Helens recorded over 400 quakes in the latter half of 2023. All this contributed to record costs for weather disasters in the United States as expenses exceeded $1 billion.

Yet, the suffering inflicted upon humanity by Mother Nature paled in comparison to the suffering inflicted by Human Nature. The War in Ukraine, which had captured much of the headlines since early 2022, drifted to the back pages after war broke out on the Gaza Strip on October 7, 2023, when Hamas terrorists attacked Israel, killing hundreds and wounding thousands of Israelis. As of May 13, 2024, estimated casualties exceed 35,000 casualties – of which more than half were women and children – with concern that war will expand throughout the Middle East growing.

Here in the United States, there is a growing sense of unrest and distrust. Crime rates for murder and other forms of gun violence as well as theft by organized crime groups have soared, and gun sales have almost doubled to 20,000 annually since the start of the COVID pandemic. Mass shootings (four or more) are again approaching the record of 690 that occurred in 2021.

And while Americans have always disagree about how to solve the *problems* that plague our nation, we increasingly disagree about the *facts* contributing to them. Doubts about the legitimacy of our elections – including the 2020 Presidential election that culminated in the January 6, 2021, breach of the U.S. Capitol –persist, putting our very democracy at risk.

All this to say it appears "We're not in Kansas anymore, Toto." And if the this isn't enough, add to it the emergence of and rapidly developing uses of AI artificial intelligence (AI) to create simulated (i.e., fake) versions of something real, and one can't help but wonder if we collectively are heading down the proverbial rabbit hole where we can't discern between what is fact, fiction, or fallacy – and what is "truth".[7]

We struggle to experience the peace, joy and happiness in life God intended for us because this wasn't how He intended it to be, nor how it was in the beginning. And as we long for that day when *"God wipes away every tear from [our] eyes..."* (Rev 21:4), we might remember when Jesus proclaimed, "I am the way, the truth, and the life" (John 14:6). If there's ever been a time for humanity to turn to him it seems to be now.

But this begs the question, *How Did We Get Here?* To answer this, we start with the Creation Account as recorded in the book of Genesis.[8]

IN THE BEGINNING: IT WAS ALL GOOD!

Chapter One of the book of Genesis describes the process in which God created all that exists, after which He declared it to be "good", or "pleasing" to Him (Gen 1:4, 10, 12, 18, 21, 25).[9] But the crowning achievement of His work was clearly the creation of the first human beings, as after assessing all He had done God declared His work to be "very" ("exceedingly" or "abundantly" in the original Hebrew) good (Gen 1:31).

This communicates something beyond checking off a to-do list and declaring, "Well, that's good enough". Instead, God took great pleasure in the beauty of His work. He had created His own personal masterpiece! And the proverbial icing on the cake was the first human beings created in His very image. We see this in the last few verses of *Chapter One*:

> *"So, God created man in His own image; in the*
> *image of God He created him; male*

---

[7] Noteworthy is Steven Pinker ("Enlightenment Now") and Ronald Baily and Marion Tupy ("Ten Global Trends Every Smart Person Should Know") provide evidence the world is more prosperous, safer, and healthier than at any time in recorded history.

[8] The following reflects a literal interpretation of the Creation Account. Some take a more figurative approach. See: Genesis 1: Are the Six Days of Creation Literal or Figurative? | Grace Communion International (gci.org).

[9] James Strong, S.T.D., LL.D. Abingdon's Strong's Exhaustive Concordance of the Bible. Nashville, TN: Abingdon, 1981.

and female He created them. Then God blessed
them, and God said to them, 'Be fruitful
and multiply; fill the earth and subdue it; have
dominion over the fish of the sea, over the
birds of the air, and over every living thing that
moves on the earth.' And God said, 'See,
I have given you every herb that yields seed
which is on the face of all the earth, and
every tree whose fruit yields seed; to you it shall
be for food. Also, to every beast of the
earth, to every bird of the air, and to everything
that creeps on the earth, in which
there is life, I have given every green herb for
food'; and it was so." (Gen 1:27-30) [10]

Some important points we can glean from these verses:

Point #1: God created us uniquely in our capacity to live in loving and respectful relationships with Him and each other.

God uniquely created the first human beings, Adam, and Eve, in "His image and likeness". While employing a common literary device called "parallelism" used in ancient Hebrew literature to communicate completeness, there is a lot to draw from the Hebrew words *tselem* (image) and *demuth* (likeness) used in this passage, as they refer to the physical, cognitive, emotional, and spiritual capacities God endowed us with.

Biologists have found the human brain is three times the size of that of chimpanzees, the primate closest to us in the animal kingdom. The difference is found predominately in the frontal lobe, or the area of the brain that facilitates language, self-awareness, rational thought, reasoning, comprehension, and problem-solving. These neurological advantages have enabled human beings to invent and develop the complex civilizations that

---

[10] All passages from the New King James Version (NKJV) translation of the Bible unless otherwise indicated.

have evolved throughout history, as well as the capacity to willfully choose our actions. [11]

Adam and Eve had the capability of doing two things. First, they could comprehend what God meant when He said, "See, I have given you…" (Gen 1:29). In this simple statement, God seems to ask Adam and Eve to ponder the awesomeness of their Creator, how small and insignificant they were in comparison to Him, and how He had blessed them.

Second, it equipped them with the capacity to live in loving and respectful relationships with God in the same way the Trinity of God the Father, the Son, and the Holy Spirit have existed throughout eternity. In essence, Adam and Eve had the capability of mirroring the image and likeness of God by loving Him and loving each other.

This is seen in Jesus summing up the law in the Great Commandment by "loving God and loving your neighbor".[12] We most reflect the image of God when loving Him and others.

Point #2: God has given us all we need for a satisfying life.

God was very intentional in creating an environment that would provide sufficiently that all of humanity can experience abundance in life. Genesis 2:8-9 describes it as follows:

> "The LORD God planted a garden eastward in
> Eden, and there He put the man whom
> He had formed. And out of the ground the
> LORD God made every tree grow that is
> pleasant to the sight and good for food. The
> tree of life was also in the midst of the
> garden, and the tree of the knowledge of good
> and evil. Now a river went out of Eden
> to water the garden, and from there it parted and
> became four riverheads." (Gen 2:8-10)

---

[11] http://www.brainfacts.org/ask-an-expert/how-does-the-human-brain-differ-from-that-of-other-primates

[12] Matthew 22:36-40; Mark 12:28-31; Luke 10:26-27; cf Deut 6:5; Rom 13:8-10; Gal 5:14; Jam 2:8-10.

Picture a beautiful and bountiful garden filled with foods that not only nourish healthy bodies but is pleasing to see and eat as well! A garden not hindered by excessive heat or drought, nor ravaged by bugs or disease. No striving or stressing over our ability to pay the mortgage or having enough to eat – it was all right there to enjoy!

Today we can only imagine what the Garden was like. Picture the place you most like to visit – that place where you feel most at peace and experience the incomprehensible splendor of God, and you're only getting a glimpse of it. Add to that your "paradise" is that place you rarely get to visit, while for Adam and Eve paradise was their home!

Point #3: God highly values us.

God gave humanity the authority to "subdue" and "have dominion" over all that exists on earth. This is further described in Genesis 2:15, 19:

> *"Then the LORD God took the man and put him*
> *in the garden of Eden to tend and keep*
> *it. …Out of the ground the LORD God formed*
> *every beast of the field and every bird of*
> *the air and brought them to Adam to see what*
> *he would call them. And whatever*
> *Adam called each living creature, that*
> *was its name." (Gen 2:15, 19)*

These verses tell us God intends us to be productive by using the skills and abilities he has uniquely gifted us with. Rather than a curse, work is a calling, or "vocation".[13] But, God also gave Adam complete authority over His creation as well. In the ancient Near East, the privilege of naming a child, town, or piece of land implied authority over the object being named. In granting this to Adam, God also delegated

---

[13] Note vocation is, "a strong feeling of suitability for a particular career or occupation" and "a feeling of being called by God or born to do a particular type of work". https://www.thefreedictionary.com/vocations

authority over all His creation as well – a powerful testimony to how much God valued him.[14]

While given the privilege of naming all living creatures, Adam was also given the freedom to do it in <u>his</u> time and in <u>his</u> way. No pressure of unclear or unreasonable demands or deadlines; instead, God seemingly watched Adam to "see what he would call them" (v 19).

You can almost see God sitting back as a proud parent watching His child use his creative abilities, and excitedly anticipating what Adam would come up with. And God didn't hover over Adam like a doting parent, correcting every mistake he made or telling him what he did wrong or could do better. Whatever Adam decided, "That was its name".

In this we get a picture of the perfect job and work environment. You are given complete authority of how you will get the work done, and you get to use your creative abilities as you see fit– in fact, you get to write your own job description! That's what God intended work to be, which we see in the following passage in the Psalms:

> "What is man that You are mindful of
> him, And the son of man that
> You visit him? For You have made him
> a little lower than the angels,
> And You have crowned him with glory and honor." (Ps 8:4-5)

And with God's creation of Eve, we get a sense of the first "division of labor" in which Adam and Eve worked as perfect complements, efficiently and effectively completing the work God had given them by working as equal partners (note 1 Pet 3:7).

But noteworthy is some argue in the context of this passage the Hebrew words translated "to tend" and "keep" are better translated to "worship" and "obey".[15] This suggests their work was not a "job", but a priestly duty to be carried out in reverence of God and all He had created. While granting them the authority to have dominion over His creation,

---

[14] The Nelson Study Bible: New King James Version, Earl D. Radmacher, Th.D., gen ed. Nashville, TN: Thomas Nelson Publishers, 1997.
[15] John H. Sailhamer. The Expositor's Bible Commentary – Genesis, Frank E. Gaebelein, gen ed. Grand Rapids, MI: Zondervan Publishing House, 1990.

they were given the responsibility to ensure it was properly and lovingly cared for.

Point #4: God knows our needs better than we know them, and before we know them.

In Genesis 2:20, we're told something dawned upon Adam as he was naming all these living creatures God had brought before him to name:

> *"So, Adam gave names to all cattle, to the birds*
> *of the air, and to every beast of the field.*
> *But for Adam there was not found a helper*
> *comparable to him." (Gen 2:20)*

Now *Chapter Two* of Genesis seemingly provides a chronological order of God's creative process. And if Adam was in fact created before Eve, it appears God messed up in not creating a partner for Adam. But this isn't the case, as just two verses earlier we're told:

> *"And the LORD God said, "It is not good that man should be alone,*
> *I will make him a helper comparable to him." (Gen 2:18)*

God knew Adam needed a mate comparable to him – even before Adam did! Which begs the question, why did God wait until Adam realized he was the only living creature without a partner? Well, we're not told, but a hunch is God waited to let this sink in so Adam would realize two things: 1) how alone he was without another human being, and 2) how caring and attentive God is to make sure we have all that we need.

In the ensuing verses (Gen 2:21-22), we see God creating Eve through the first recorded surgical procedure in world history. We're told God provided Adam with perfect medical care through supernaturally anesthetizing Adam so he would feel no pain whatsoever. And we're told God used one of Adam's ribs to create Eve.

The Hebrew words Moses (generally understood to be the author of Genesis) used to describe God's creation of the universe and simpler life forms such as fish and birds suggests He created it all from nothing (Gen 1:3, 6, 9, 11, 14-15, 21). It also implies God didn't need to use one of Adam's ribs to create Eve. Which begs the question, why did God put Adam through a complex surgery rather than simply declaring, "Let there be Eve"?

Well, the answer is seemingly provided in the ensuing verses, as Adam first sets his eyes upon the life partner God has created specifically for him:

"And Adam said: "This is now bone of my bones
and flesh of my flesh; She shall be called Woman
because she was taken out of Man." (Gen 2:23)

In the original Hebrew, the "deep sleep" God put Adam under (v 21) is best understood to mean a form of trance-like state in which Adam was fully aware of what was occurring, and therefore aware that God had taken the time to create a partner just like him. And the Hebrew words translated "This is now..." are better rendered, "at last!" It suggests Adam is experiencing the joy and exhilaration of having a life partner made just for him, as God intended the perfect complement of a man and a woman in marriage to be for each other:

"Therefore, a man shall leave his father and mother and be joined to
his wife, and they shall become one flesh. And they were both naked,
the man and his wife and were not ashamed." (Gen 2:24-25)

Here "nakedness" refers not only to their physical state, but their psychological and spiritual states as well. They are the perfect couple living in complete harmony with God and each other. They are at peace with themselves and each other – not burdened with the insecurities, conflicts, or doubts about themselves or each other that plague us today. There was nothing to hide, cover up, or hold back. They could live openly and freely with God and each other with the knowledge they were both acceptable and accepted.[16] Life in the Garden was literally heaven on earth. They are experiencing *WHOLENESS*.

---

[16] Lysa TerKeurst. <u>Forgiving What You Can't Forget.</u> Nashville, TN: Thomas Nelson, 2020, 79.

WHOLE

I've taken the time to explore this in depth to provide a sense of the care and concern God took in the Creation process. His motives were perfectly pure and good, and He was intentional in creating and communicating in such a way Adam and Eve would realize this. By observing the Garden's beauty and abundance and "seeing what God had given them", Adam and Eve would know God is all-powerful (omnipotent), all-knowing (omniscient), and completely trustworthy. But with their freedom came one restriction:

> *"And the LORD God commanded the man,*
> *saying, 'Of every tree of the garden*
> *you may freely eat; but of the tree of the*
> *knowledge of good and evil you shall*
> *not eat, for in the day that you eat of it*
> *you shall surely die'." (Gen 2:16)*

God had demonstrated that He not only knew what Adam needed better than Adam himself did, but He knew it before Adam as well. God was appealing to the credibility He had demonstrated by asking Adam to trust Him with this <u>one</u> command.

A GOOD THING GONE BAD

Adam and Eve had <u>everything</u> they needed to experience life abundantly. So, what went wrong? Well, note while God gave Adam the command not to eat the fruit of that one tree before creating Eve, it is unclear whether God repeated the command in Eve's presence. But we do know that Eve was aware of it, as we look at what transpires in Genesis 3:1-6:

> *"Now the serpent was more cunning than any*
> *beast of the field which the LORD God*
> *had made. And he said to the woman, 'Has God*
> *indeed said, you shall not eat of every*
> *tree of the garden?' And the woman said to the*
> *serpent, 'We may eat the fruit of the trees*

*of the garden, but of the fruit of the tree which
is in the midst of the garden, God has
said, You shall not eat it, nor shall you touch it, lest you die'."*

*Then the serpent said to the woman, 'You will
not surely die. For God knows that in the
day you eat of it your eyes will be opened, and you
will be like God, knowing good and evil.'*

*So, when the woman saw that the tree was good
for food, that it was pleasant to the
eyes, and a tree desirable to make one wise, she
took of its fruit and ate. She also gave to
her husband with her, and he ate." (Gen 3:1-6)*

The "serpent" is Satan, a fallen angel who throughout human history has done everything he can to undermine God.[17] He is described as "cunning" or "crafty" and demonstrates this in his efforts to undermine all that God has created. And he does this in three ways:

1. Satan distorts what God said.

Now we're not told how much time passed between the creation of Eve and the events described above. It could have been days, weeks, months, years – even centuries.[18] And we're not told how Adam and Eve dealt with this warning initially. Perhaps they ignored the tree or avoided it altogether. But somewhere along the way one or both – their curiosity stirred – may have thought, "What's the big deal with eating that fruit?"

I say this as we all have experienced "temptation": we're told not to do something because it's wrong or dangerous, but something in us is inclined to ignore the warning. Take, for example, observing speed limits or traffic lights. We're told, "You can't drive faster than...", and "Stop at the red

---

[17] See Rev 12:9, 14, 15; 20:2. More on Satan in *Chapter Six*.
[18] Consider, for example, the time it would take for God to parade all of the creatures God had created for Adam to name.

light", but we push the speed limits a few (or more than a few) miles per hour, or "slip" through an intersection if we don't see any cars coming.

While speed limits and traffic lights serve to protect us from ourselves and others, we may see them as needless rules imposed upon us by some authority figure whose intention is nothing more than to control us by telling us what we can or cannot do. And we resist it, because we don't like our freedom restricted, and we don't like being ordered around.

Perhaps Eve wanted to indulge in some of that fruit, but Adam said, "We're not supposed to eat that". And when Eve asked why, Adam responded, "Well, God said we'll die. But when Eve asked, "What does "die" mean?" Adam could only reply, "Uh, I don't know!"

Think about that – a life where there is only goodness and abundance. No evil thoughts, intentions or actions, and no sickness or death: Adam and Eve literally had no idea what God was protecting them from. And this is where Satan's "cunningness" comes in.

Satan – with nothing else to occupy his time – just lurking in the shadows watching and waiting for doubt to creep in rendering them vulnerable to temptation. And he chooses Eve, who seemingly heard the command from Adam rather than directly from God. Perhaps she's starting to question whether Adam got it right or wondering if maybe Adam was just making it up. And perhaps, she started to question God Himself as well.

Notice Satan distorts what God said, suggesting God said not to eat the fruit of "every" tree rather than just the fruit of the one tree, which Eve seemingly misunderstood as well as she responds, we're not to "…eat it, or touch it" (v 1). Either way, Satan shrewdly picked a time when Eve was most vulnerable. And notice rather than stopping right there and going to God to clear it all up, she keeps listening – because Satan now has her attention.

2. Satan raises doubts about who God is.

Noteworthy is an important transition of how God is referred to in the Creation Account. From Genesis 1:1 – 2:3, He is called "God", but beginning in *verse 4* He is referred to as "Lord God".[19] In our English translations of the Old Testament, He is "God", or "Lord", but in the original Hebrew

---

[19] Thanks to Andy Milich, Executive Pastor at Oasis Community Church, for contributing this insight as this was being written.

there are over a dozen words translated "God" or "Lord" – each descriptive of one of His characteristics or attributes. Here, the English "God" comes from the Hebrew *Elohim*, which means, "deity, supreme being, strength, mighty" referring to His superior power and ability to create all that exists. The English "Lord", however, comes from the Hebrew *Jehovah*, which means, "existing one, self-existing, Lord". This implies God's right and authority to rule – and to issue the command, "don't eat the fruit".

And notice beginning in Genesis 3:1, every time Satan refers to God he omits "Lord", a challenge to God's authority to rule. He is subtly saying, "Who does God think He is giving you rules like that?" Then he suggests God is a liar in proposing not only would they not die, but they surely wouldn't die, and questions God's motives in stating that by eating the fruit, your "eyes will be opened" and you'll "be like God" in knowing all that He knows.

Satan has led Eve from curiosity about the fruit to questioning not only God's authority to issue such a command, but His motives and even His very integrity in doing so. Instead of lovingly caring for them and protecting them, she is starting to wonder if God is simply holding back and keeping something from them so He can have it all for Himself.

3. Satan appeals to their desires.

This is arguably not the first time Eve was drawn to the fruit's appeal. But the prospect of not only eating something good, but "being like God" (i.e., not needing Him) and becoming "wise" (not needing to listen to Him), was too much to resist – and she ate it. And then she included Adam in her rebellion by handing some to Adam, who ate it as well.

This suggests two things. First, Adam was right there all along listening to their dialogue. And second, Adam was probably every bit as vulnerable as Eve – needing just a nudge like having the fruit handed to him – to cross the line and give in to temptation as well.[20] And it was in this very moment the reason for His command became apparent to them:

"Then the eyes of both of them were opened..." (Gen 3:7a)

---

[20] This reflects the wisdom of a principle in addiction recovery groups such as *Alcoholics Anonymous (AA)*, in which those early in recovery are encouraged to avoid the "people, places, and things" that may trigger a vulnerable person to relapse.

13

Adam and Eve now experienced what God had warned them of. Just moments before they were living in a state of blissful ignorance, having never experienced "evil", and having no understanding of what it is. But now they did, as they had become evil doers themselves.

Which begs the question, "Why was eating a little fruit 'evil'?"

Well, it's not so much <u>what</u> they did, but <u>why</u> they did it. The English "evil" comes from the Hebrew *rah*, which has a range of meaning including "calamity, adversity, harmful, hurtful, distress, misery, trouble", and comes from the root word *ra'am* meaning, "To agitate, irritate, to crash". Their actions were evil in disobeying and rebelling against God, and their motives in serving themselves rather than God. By eating the fruit, Adam and Eve had usurped God's authority, and took what wasn't theirs to have. The apostle John summed up the root cause of all the troubles of the world in this one short verse:

> *"For all that is in the world -- the lust of*
> *the flesh, the lust of the eyes, and*
> *the pride of life -- is not of the Father but*
> *is of the world." (1 John 2:16)*

God was not flexing His authoritative muscle and demanding Adam and Eve's obedience through His command to not eat that fruit. Instead, it was God simply protecting them – and all of humanity – from themselves then, and us today as well.

THE COSTS OF ONE BAD DECISION

And we can see the devastating effects of their one impulsive decision in what followed:

> *"...and they knew that they were naked; and they sewed fig leaves*
> *together and made themselves coverings. And they heard the sound*
> *of the LORD God walking in the garden in the cool of the*
> *day, and Adam and his wife hid themselves from the*
> *presence of the LORD God among the trees*

> *of the garden. Then the LORD God called to Adam*
> *and said to him, 'Where are you?' So, he said,*
> *'I heard Your voice in the garden, and I was afraid*
> *because I was naked; and I hid myself.'*
>
> *And He (God) said, 'Who told you that you were*
> *naked? Have you eaten from the tree of which*
> *I commanded you that you should not eat?' Then the*
> *man said, 'The woman whom You gave to*
> *be with me, she gave me of the tree, and I ate.' And*
> *the LORD God said to the woman, 'What*
> *is this you have done?' The woman said, 'The serpent*
> *deceived me, and I ate'." (Gen 3:7b-13)*

Here we see the devastating effects of one willful act of rebellion against God upon Adam and Eve, as well as the rest of humanity and literally all of creation.[21]

1. They traded their innocence for guilt.

They now realized that God was in fact telling them the truth, and they had rejected it. Having only known good they now had come face-to-face with its counterpart, evil. They had done wrong, <u>knew</u> it, and their once-clear consciences were burdened with guilt.[22]

2. They traded their honor for shame.

In being created in God's image, they were declared "very good" (Gen 1:31). They were given the honor and privilege of having authority over all His creation. But in rejecting His authority, they brought shame upon themselves. And they were painfully aware of it.

---

[21] See Jayson Georges, The 3D Gospel: Ministry in Guilt, Shame, and Fear Cultures. HonorShame. com, 2014. See also Charles Kraft, "What Kind of Encounters Do We Need in Our Christian Witness?" https://missionexus.org/what-kind-of-encounters-do-we-need-in-our-christian-witness/

[22] The English "conscience" from the Latin *conscientia*, or "with knowledge". https://www.etymonline.com/word/conscience

Uncomfortable in their nakedness, they scrambled to cover themselves with fig leaves. Now most images you'll see depicting Adam and Eve show the fig leaves covering their genitalia. And if these renderings are an accurate portrayal, it would suggest by eating the fruit Adam and Eve were covering up what physically and visually made them different.

What a sad development! While once completely comfortable in their uniqueness – in fact, while once celebrating how their physical differences complemented each other perfectly – they were now painfully aware they were no longer the innocent, flawless perfect beings God had so carefully and lovingly created. While still God's image bearers, they had tarnished that image, and become a "reproach" to themselves (Ps 44:13, 15).

The perfect harmony once shared between God and humanity had been severed. While once enjoying God's presence in the Garden (note Gen 3:8), they had lost that privilege:

> "Then the LORD God said, 'Behold, the
> man has become like one of Us, to
> know good and evil. And now, lest he put out
> his hand and take also of the tree
> of life, and eat, and live forever' -- therefore
> the LORD God sent him out of the
> garden of Eden to till the ground from which
> he was taken. So, He drove out the
> man and He placed cherubim at the east of
> the garden of Eden, and a flaming
> sword which turned every way, to guard the
> way to the tree of life." (Gen 3:22-24)

Banished from the very presence of God to a life of futility in a harsh environment only to die and return to the dust of which they had been formed (Gen 3:18-19). With a "do-over impossible, they experienced the anguish of human regret for the first time in history.

3. They traded their freedom for fear.

While once innocent they were now burdened with guilt. While once honorable they had become shameful. While once walking in the "power" of being affirmed as God's image bearers and having been granted dominion over His creation, they now found themselves shrinking away and desperately trying to hide from God as well as each other.[23]

Freedom had given way to fear – the fear of being "known" – a curse that burdens every human being. We have a deep-seated awareness of our inadequacy before God. While He may not "walk among us" like He did in the Garden, we know He is not only aware of our actions, but our every thought and desire as well. As a result, we "cover up" and present the best "me" for others to see, rendering us prone to feelings of isolation and loneliness.

4. They introduced "sin" into the world.

St. Augustine (354-430 AD) proposed sin is the result of a three-step process. First is Satan's "suggestion" (no harm will come from eating the fruit). Second there is "pleasure" (the fruit was "pleasant" to the eyes and "desirable"). And third there is "consent", or the decision to act on one's desires.[24] By eating the forbidden fruit, Adam and Eve had committed the first sin, and had introduced sin into the world.[25] This "sin nature" afflicts all of us like a virus or a genetic defect of the soul – something that has corrupted every generation of human beings that has been born and lived out their lives ever since.

In the Old Testament, the Hebrew word most translated "sin" is *chata*, which means, "to miss, forfeit, lack, lead astray, offend, or harm". In the New Testament, the most common Greek word translated sin is *harmatia*,

---

[23] Believers today rest in the truth there is "no condemnation to those who are in Christ Jesus" (Rom 8:1), that "if God is or us, who can be against us?" (Rom 8:31), and as a result walk with a spirit of power, not fear (2 Tim 1:7).

[24] https://wyattgraham.com/how-desire-becomes-sin-according-to-augustine/

[25] In Psalms 51:5, David writes all human beings are born with a sin nature. In Romans 5:12-19; the apostle Paul tells us this sin nature comes through our common ancestors, Adam and Eve.

which means, "to miss the mark".[26] These words communicate the idea that embedded within our nature is the tendency to fall short and miss the mark of the purity and perfect goodness of God.

We all have God-given needs innate within us to be valued and treated with dignity, to have a sense of purpose, and to experience the satisfaction of a good meal or the pleasure of sexual intimacy. To "sin" goes beyond the obvious like theft or murder to greed, pride-fullness, abusing one's authority, blaming, deflecting, and over-indulgence. It is seen in the passive failure to value and care for others through a preoccupation with satisfying our own desires, to the schemes devised to swindle or downright destroy others:

> *"Truly, this only I have found: That God made man upright,*
> *But they have sought out many schemes." (Eccl 7:29)*

5. They failed to take responsibility for their actions.

If rebelling against God wasn't bad enough, Adam and Eve compounded the problem by failing to take responsibility for their actions by simply acknowledging they had done wrong and asking for forgiveness. Instead, Adam played the blame game by pointing the finger at Eve – and even God Himself for creating her – for his decision to eat the fruit. And then Eve blames Satan. And this human tendency plagues the world to this day.

Important to realize as well is the sins we commit do not happen in a vacuum. Instead, every sin we commit is like a stone tossed into a pond, its effects rippling across and disrupting the surface of the water. By eating the fruit, Adam and Eve had ignited the spark of sin. And their refusal to take responsibility for their actions and choosing to deflect blame on others was like a strong wind that turned that spark into a bonfire. And in the following verses, God foretold just how devastating their actions would be.

---

[26] James Strong, S.T.D., LL.D. Abingdon's Strong's Exhaustive Concordance of the Bible. Nashville, TN: Abingdon, 1981.

A WORLD CORRUPTED BY SIN

In Genesis 3:16-24, we're told:

1. Relationships would now be difficult.

Human relationships are disrupted and torn apart by our conflicting desires, resulting in distrust, discord, and division. We engage in "my way or the highway" power struggles and question the motives of the most important people in our lives, generating tension and resentment within families, friendships, co-workers, and communities.

It's seen in Adam blaming Eve – and God – for eating the fruit (Gen 3:12), God's warning of the ensuing power struggles and abuse that will plague male-female relationships (Gen 3:16), and the conflict between their sons resulting in Cain's murder of Abel (Gen 4:8). It's seen in how we are prone to see our differences rather than our shared humanity – an "us versus them" mindset – that separates us religiously, politically, and ethnically, through which our desperate efforts to shed our gnawing sense of inadequacy generates the tendency to demonize "those" people by declaring them inferior and unworthy of being treated as equals. And we see this in the countless wars throughout history that have resulted in the deaths of anywhere between 150 million to 1 billion people.[27]

And it affects the depths and quality of our relationships. Instead of developing trusting and mutually rewarding relationships, our relationships tend to be more "transactional" in that they are limited to getting our needs met. But we find when anxious, distressed or discouraged, we don't have anyone we are comfortable enough with to confide in.

2. Work is frustrating.

Instead of a vocation that provides a sense of purpose and fulfillment in utilizing the skills and abilities God has blessed us with, work is battling traffic each day to carry out the marching orders of those who "rule"

---

[27] https://www.nytimes.com/2003/07/06/books/chapters/what-every-person-should-know-about-war.html. Some estimate peace has reigned throughout the world only 8% of the time in recorded human history.

over us but seem to care little about our well-being. Instead, work is more reflective of the drudgery articulated in the following lyrics:

> *You get up every morning*
> *From your alarm clock's warning*
> *Take the 8:15 into the city*
> *And if your trains on time*
> *You can get to work by nine*
> *And start your slaving job to get your pay* [28]

You "toil" in work that is boring or repetitive, doesn't maximize your skills and abilities, or burdened with the stress of meeting the ever-increasing demands you stress all year to achieve in hopes of getting a bonus, or simply keeping your job. Then the calendar flips to a new year, the slate is wiped clean, and you're starting at zero, and the demands of "What have you done for me lately?" hang over you.

Maybe you work in an environment where doubt – and even distrust – is prevalent, and your boss questions your work ethic or integrity. Perhaps you have had to carry the workload of others not doing their share. Or perhaps you're the manager dealing with the frustration of "motivating" employees trying to get away with doing as little as possible.

Rather than feeling blessed, you feel cursed – you're simply "marking time", dreaming of the day you can retire – and hoping you'll live long enough to experience it, and will have the financial resources necessary to enjoy it.

3. We are all living with a death sentence.

Implied in Genesis 2:17 is if Adam and Eve hadn't eaten the fruit of that one tree, they wouldn't have died. This suggests death wasn't our original destiny; instead, it was the consequence of not trusting God and disobeying Him. God created humans with the capacity to live indefinitely without the pain, anguish and suffering of sickness, disease, disability, death, and the sense of loss of losing our loved ones. But sin changed all that.

---

[28] *Taking Care of Business,* Bachman-Turner Overdrive, from the album *Bachman-Turner Overdrive II*, 1973.

The Bible doesn't tell us how sin corrupted our bodies in such a way that as we age, our bodies deteriorate and eventually cease to function. But it does suggest the onset of death was gradual, then accelerated in pace as sin increased throughout the world. In Genesis *Chapter Five*, for example, we're told Adam and his descendants lived over 900 years! But in time life spans became shorter and shorter to the point that by the time of Abraham, a "good old age" was 175 (Gen 25:8). And as the sin virus passed on from generation to generation, life expectancies continued to decline to the point from 1480-1679, women in England and Wales – if they made it to age 15 – could expect to live only 48.2 years![29]

But that first sin didn't only trigger the onset of physical death to human beings:

> *"For the creation was subjected to futility, not*
> *willingly, but because of Him who subjected*
> *it in hope because the creation itself also will be*
> *delivered from the bondage of corruption*
> *into the glorious liberty of the children of God.*
> *For we know that the whole creation*
> *groans and labors with birth pangs together*
> *until now." (Rom 8:20-22)*

In some way that first sin corrupted all of God's creation – bringing not only death and disease, but droughts, deterioration, and decay as well. We've all experienced the futility of pulling weeds, painting our house, or fixing our car – only to have to do it again, and again, and again. This is seemingly our reality in a life under the "bondage of corruption".

4. We are separated from God.

Finally, sin brought separation between God and all of humanity. The price of sin is death, and the curse of death is irreversible. But while Adam and Eve were banished from the God's presence, we get a hint of His grace and mercy in what transpired before it:

---

[29] https://www.ncbi.nlm.nih.gov/pmc/articles/PMC2625386/

*"Also, for Adam and his wife the LORD God made
tunics of skin and clothed them." (Gen 3:21)*

God provided them a more resilient form of covering made from
the skin of animals. God determined that despite their sin we are worth
redeeming. and sacrificed an animal as proof. And this provides a precursor
of the event foundational to Christianity:

*"For God so loved the world that He gave
His only begotten Son, that whoever
believes in Him should not perish but have
everlasting life." (John 3:16)*

We all learn early in life that our world operates on a merit system:
nothing is free, and if we want something we have to work for it. Do "good"
and you will be rewarded but do "bad" and you will suffer consequences.
Whether grades in school, or the raise, bonus, or promotion you want at
work, you won't get it unless you go out and <u>earn</u> it.

The problem is we cannot live good enough to offset the damage done
by sin. But Jesus could – and did – and by simply placing our faith in Jesus,
our guilty record is wiped clean, our shame is removed, and we have the
freedom of living freely in relationship with God:

*"For there is no difference; for all have sinned
and fall short of the glory of God, being
justified freely by His grace through the redemption
that is in Christ Jesus." (Rom 3:22b-24)*

God turns this upside down through this amazing proposition:
"Acknowledge you are a sinner, trust in My Son Jesus, and you will receive
favor." Hard to comprehend, as it contradicts everything we experience in
life, and to our knowledge is unique among all religious traditions. And it
was equally mind-boggling to those hearing it 2,000 years ago.

In 1st century Israel, Jews lived under the tenants of the Mosaic Law.
And since I will refer to the nation of Israel and her unique relationship
with God throughout this book, the following is a brief overview of the

origins and history of the nation of Israel leading up to God's issuance of the Mosaic Law.[30]

Virtually all the Old Testament centers upon God's interactions with the nation of Israel, His "chosen people". Israel's history begins in about 2166 B.C. with God calling a childless 75-year-old pagan named Abram (later renamed Abraham) to a land (then Canaan) where God would bless him with numerous descendants, where his descendants would prosper, and his name would be made "great" (Gen 12:1-3).[31]

Years later God ratified these promises (Gen 15:5-7), but with an important caveat: while his descendants would inherit a land, they would first be "strangers in a land that is not theirs... and be afflicted four hundred years" (Gen 15:13-14).[32] Abraham would also have to wait, as it was 25 years before God's promise of children was fulfilled (Gen 21:1-7).[33] It was in fact through Abraham's grandson Jacob (renamed Israel) God's promise that Abraham's descendants would become a "great nation" was realized.

Fast forward 300 years. A great famine has spread throughout the Middle East, but Jacob and his family are granted permission to settle in Goshen, a fertile region located in Egypt (Gen 41:56-47:12). During the ensuing 400+ years, Jacob's family prospers and grows into a nation of as

---

[30] To fully understand the New Testament, particularly the Gospel accounts of Jesus, St. Augustine proposed: "The Old Testament is in the New revealed, the New Testament is in the Old concealed". https://www.azquotes.com/quote/662519

[31] Gen 11:30 tells us Abram's wife Sarai (later renamed Sarah, Gen 17:15) was "barren" at that time.

[32] The reason God could not give Abraham the Land at that time was the sin of the Amorites hadn't yet risen to the level justifying God driving them out of the Land (Gen 15:16). God also promises Abraham He would judge those oppressing his descendants, who would leave with "great possessions" given to them by their oppressors (Gen 15:14). Note this promise came in the form of a *Brit Bein HaBetarim*, or a "covenant of the parts", meaning His promises were unconditional, and therefore not contingent on anything Abraham or his descendants did or failed to do (see also His covenant with Noah, Gen 9:8-17).

[33] Several years later God reiterated these promises, telling Abraham he would give him descendants as "numerous as the stars in the night sky" (Gen 15:5), and his descendants a land to inherit (Gen 15:7). Despite God reiterating His promise of children several times (Gen 15:1-21; 17:1-19), Abraham – in a moment of doubt as well as the encouragement by Sarah after waiting 11 years – had a child (Ishmael) with Sarah's servant Hagar (Gen 16:1-15). Note God reiterated His covenantal promise to Abraham's son Isaac (Gen 26:1-5), and Isaac's son Jacob (Gen 28:10-15).

---

many as 2.5 million people.[34] But as Israel grows in number, the Egyptians – viewing her as a threat – subject the Israelites to "hard bondage" and their lives were made "bitter" (Ex 1:7-14). The Israelites cry out to God, who "remembered His covenant with Abraham" (Ex 2:23-25). God calls Moses, a fugitive "Hebrew", to go and represent Him in calling Pharaoh to release the people of Israel.[35] When Pharaoh unsurprisingly refuses, God finds it necessary to bring ten plagues to "influence" Pharaoh to reconsider.[36]

Pharaoh finally relents, and the people of Israel joyfully begin their journey out of Egypt enriched with silver, gold, and clothing after "plundering the Egyptians" who couldn't rid themselves quickly enough of the Hebrews whose God had cursed them with the plagues (Ex 12:35-36).[37] But seeing the loss of the cheap labor Egypt is losing, Pharaoh sends his army out to bring the people of Israel back – only to see them walk through the Red Sea God has miraculously parted. Pharaoh impetuously sends his army after them only to see the parted waters collapse and his soldiers drowned (Ex 14:1-30). And it was on that day – after witnessing the miraculous ways God graciously and mercifully delivered them from bondage – the people of Israel, a people not special or more deserving in any way – "feared...and believed in the Lord and in his servant Moses" (Ex 14:31).[38]

Now God's intent was not only to deliver the people from bondage, but to bless them with the opportunity to experience abundance in the Promised Land – a land "flowing with milk and honey – God promised

---

[34] The 2.5 million population estimate is based on Exodus 12:37, which tells us the number of the people of Israel God freed from Egypt during the Exodus totaled about 600,000 men as well as their wives and children.

[35] In Gen 14:13 Abraham is referred to as "the Hebrew", which some (see Dennis Prager, The Rational Bible. Genesis: God, Creation and Destruction) propose stems from a Hebrew word meaning "pass, wanderer". It is also the name ascribed Abraham's descendants, the nation of Israel (see also Gen 39:14; Ex 1:19; Jonah 1:9).

[36] See Ex 7:14-12:41; cf Gen 15:13; Acts 7:6-7.

[37] Recall God had told Abraham his descendants would leave Egypt with "great possessions" (Gen 15:14).

[38] About 40 years later, Moses tells the people of Israel God's decision to "...set His love on you nor choose you because you were more in number than any other people, for you were the least of all peoples...but because the Lord loves you, and because He would keep the oath which He swore to your fathers..." (Deut 7:6-8).

Abraham 700 years earlier.[39] Before leading them there, however, God seemingly deemed it necessary to address two things.

Consider this is the "Exodus" generation's first encounter with the "God of their father Abraham". Their concept of "god" had been shaped through a lifetime immersed in the polytheism of the Egyptians. In addition, their concept of governance, justice, and goodness came through their experience as slaves. So, God leads them to Mount Sinai, where He gives Moses the "Mosaic Law": the Ten Commandments and 613 tenants providing civil and ceremonial instruction of how-to live-in relationship with God and each other.[40]

We've taken the time to explore Israel's history as God didn't randomly choose Israel to simply bless her with abundance, as He had a larger purpose in mind: Israel would be a "light onto the Gentiles" in by seeing how He was blessing Israel other nations would turn from their gods to the one true God.[41] But His promises came with a condition: living up to the standards of the Law – standards reflecting the goodness and righteousness of God Himself – and the immense challenge presented in trying to live up to them. Fortunately for the people of Israel, God wove into the Law a process for which the people could confess their shortcomings and experience His grace and mercy through the forgiveness He would extend to them. Sadly, the people of Israel largely failed, as we will see.

Trying to measure up to God's standards is like attempting to swim across the Pacific Ocean: some of us may swim farther than others, but we'll inevitably find ourselves a lot closer to the shores of our fallen nature than anything close to resembling the perfect goodness and righteousness seen in the person of Jesus. In fact, Paul tells us the purpose of the Law is to help us see our inadequacies and resultant need for His grace and mercy:

> *"Therefore, the law was our tutor to bring us to Christ,*
> *that we might be justified by faith." (Gal 3:24)*

---

[39] Note this promise was made repeatedly (Ex 3:8, 17; 13:5).

[40] The Ten Commandments and 613 tenants of the Mosaic Law are found in Ex 20:1-23:33 and the book of Leviticus. They are repeated in the book of Deuteronomy, the "Second Law", when given to the "Entrance" generation. More on this in *Chapter Six*.

[41] The Prophet Isaiah states this in describing both God's servant Israel and His Servant Jesus, the Messiah (Is 42:6-8; 49:6; 60:3).

From the ashes of Israel's failures arose His Servant Jesus, who lived the perfect life and freely offered Himself up as a sacrifice to take away the guilt of our sins and free us from the bondage of living up to the high standards of the Law![42] In fact, we propose – as we will see – that the abundance we all hope to experience is contingent on how deeply we come to realize the gift God has given us:

"Cheer Up! You're a worse sinner than you ever dare imagine.
But you're also more loved than you ever dare hope." [43]

But a warning to those who have <u>not</u>:

"For God did not send His Son into the world
to condemn the world, but that
the world through Him might be saved. He
who believes in Him is not condemned;
but he who does not believe is condemned
already, because he has not
believed in the name of the only begotten
Son of God." (John 3:17-18)

If you have accepted Jesus as your Savior, but are still struggling to experience the wholeness of the abundant life, read on, as we consider two important questions:

Can I trust God?
Do I want to trust God?

---

[42] John the Baptist proclaimed Jesus, "The Lamb of God who takes away the sin of the world!" (John 1:29-36). This is a clear reference to the tenth plague (see Exodus *Chapter Twelve*) God brought upon Egypt to deliver Israel from the bondage of captivity through striking down the firstborn of all of Egypt. Before striking the firstborn, God instructed the people of Israel to sacrifice an "unblemished lamb", then to put the blood of the lamb upon their doorposts. God then "passed over" the homes of those who believed and followed these instructions. This event spawned the "Passover" Jews have celebrated for 3,500 years. And just as God delivered Israel by virtue of an unblemished lamb, Jesus offered Himself as the sacrificial lamb to deliver the world from sin. The gift of salvation is available to anyone simply by believing in Jesus as one's Savior from sin (John 3:16).

[43] https://www.goodreads.com/quotes/740717-cheer-up-you-re-a-worse-sinner-than-you-ever-dared

CHAPTER 2

DO I REALLY KNOW YOU?

INTRODUCTION

Have you ever imagined what it would have been like to have walked in the sandals of the twelve disciples Jesus chose to be His apostles? Imagine three-plus years walking, talking – literally <u>living</u> – with Jesus hearing His teachings with your own ears, and watching Him perform miracles with your own eyes. Three-plus years in the presence of the Living God!

Now we certainly can get a good idea of what He is like by reading the Gospel accounts.

But the Bible tells us that through the indwelling of the Holy Spirit, we can know Jesus every bit as well as those disciples who lived with Him (John 14:16)![44] It is the same kind of relationship Adam and Eve enjoyed with God, living with Him as they went about their days. But that all changed that moment they ate the forbidden fruit.

Their sin changed everything: no longer innocent, they were cast out of God's presence (Gen 3:23-24) to a life of pain, toil and futility until the day they died (Gen 3:16-19). While God hadn't changed, they had. And with that the seeds of doubt of who God really is took root. Fast forward multiple millennia in a world corrupted by the sin virus (Rom 8:22), and those seeds Satan planted so long ago have brought forth the fruit of an increasingly distorted view of who God is. This is seen in the atrocities committed "in the name of God" including the Crusades, the Spanish

---

[44] See also John 14:26; 15:26; 16:7. See also 1 John, in the original Greek, "knowing" God goes beyond factual knowledge to knowing Him personally.

Inquisition, the Salem witch trials, and the mass slaughters perpetrated by ISIS and ISIL-affiliated terrorist groups. Given this, we address the first of two questions we posed at the end of Chapter One: *Can I trust God?*

WHO IS GOD?

Now for some this may seem obvious: you've long been a believer in Jesus, attended more than your share of church services and heard hundreds of sermons, and even read the Bible cover-to-cover at least once. You may feel you have a pretty good idea of who God is. But bear with me on this, because there is more than enough evidence to suggest most people see only part of, or have a distorted view, of who God really is.[45] To illustrate this, we'll borrow a parable from the Far Eastern religious traditions:

Once upon a time, there lived six blind men in a village. One day the villagers told them, "Hey, there is an elephant in the village today." They had no idea what an elephant was.

They decided, "Even though we would not be able to see it, let us go and feel it anyway."

All of them went where the elephant was. Every one of them touched the elephant.

"Hey, the elephant is a pillar," said the first man who touched his leg.

"Oh, no! it is like a rope," said the second man who touched the tail.

"Oh, no! it is like a thick branch of a tree," said the third man who touched the trunk of the elephant.

"It is like a big hand fan" said the fourth man who touched the ear of the elephant.

"It is like a huge wall," said the fifth man who touched the belly of the elephant.

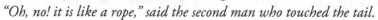

[45] Note, for example, 1 Cor 13:12 (see also Jam 1:23). Paul tells us that in this life we see God as if we're looking at Him through a "dim mirror". In Paul's day, mirrors were made of a polished metal such as brass or bronze rather than the glass we use today.

"It is like a solid pipe," Said the sixth man who touched the tusk of the elephant.

They began to argue about the elephant and every one of them insisted that he was right. It looked like they were getting agitated. A wise man was passing by and he saw this. He stopped and asked them, "What is the matter?" They said, "We cannot agree to what the elephant is like." Each one of them told what he thought the elephant was like. The wise man calmly explained to them, "All of you are right. The reason every one of you is telling it differently is because each one of you touched the different part of the elephant. So, actually the elephant has all those features what you all said."

"Oh!" everyone said. There was no more fight. They felt happy that they were all right.

Every known culture throughout human history has believed and had some concept of a divine being(s) we refer to as "God". This is due to the fact the universe itself provides undeniable evidence for His existence, as seen in the following passages:

"The heavens declare the glory of God; And the firmament shows His handiwork." (Ps 19:1)

"For since the creation of the world His invisible attributes are clearly seen, being understood by the things that are made, even His eternal power and Godhead..." (Rom 1:20)

Since we believe the Bible was inspired by God, and as a result is true in all it says, we propose Christians can have the most complete construct of the person of God. But research suggests we can be – and often are – "blind" to some aspects of who God truly is.

AMERICA'S FOUR GODS [46]

Drs. Paul Froese and Christopher Bader, professors at Baylor University, did a survey to determine Americans' understanding of who God is, and

[46] Drawn from and used by permission by Paul Froese & Christopher Bader. America's Four Gods" What We Say About God & What That Says About Us. New York: Oxford University Press, 2010.

how He interacts with the world today. What they found is while most people believe in God and believe He influences events that occur in the world, they also found areas of significant difference:

- While 47% believe God is a "He", 33% are undecided, 20% believe God is sexless;
- While 81% believe God performs miracles today, 19% don't; and,
- While 50% believe God rewards the faithful in small ways today, 50% don't.

So, Froese and Bader performed a research study of over 1,600 participants selected randomly to obtain unbiased conclusions and were able to reduce the questionnaire to 16 questions focused on two areas: God's "Judgment" and His "Engagement with the World Today". From this they found four general constructs of who God is:[47]

1. "Authoritative": God is both engaged and judgmental (31%)

God is "Authoritative", and both engaged and actively judging the world today. While a "loving" being, He also not only allows bad events to happen to those who displease Him but has actively exercised judgments through history including the destruction of Sodom and Gomorrah (Gen 19), and more recently Hurricane Katrina and the terrorist attack of 9/11 as demonstrations of His wrath upon a nation that has "turned from God".

2. "Benevolent": God is engaged, but not judgmental (24%).

God is "Benevolent", so we should neither fear Him nor feel inhibited in His presence. God cares for us and desires to have a personal relationship with us. He is a force for good focused on saving rather than condemning and punishing us and is the "all powerful and ever-present life coach" who won't inflict harm upon us. We can comfortably approach God since He forgives our shortcomings and is not only willing but <u>wants</u> to answer our prayers. He is the "encouraging" Father who takes pleasure in His children.

---

[47] While their initial questionnaire contained 400 questions, Froese and Bader were able to narrow them down to the 16 questions referenced while obtaining comparable results. See *Appendix* if you'd like to take the survey.

While tragedies are opportunities for God to "show up" and demonstrate His love for us, those who view God as Benevolent are vulnerable to becoming confused – and perhaps doubtful – when He allows "bad" things to happen or doesn't answer our prayers. Case in point is the person diagnosed with a serious illness that despite fervent prayer is not healed and has difficulty seeing God bringing "good" in allowing the illness to persist.

3. "Critical": God is judgmental but disengaged.

Froese and Bader cite the example of Pope Benedict XVI, who while visiting Brazil in 2007 said the following during a speech addressing those profiting from dealing drugs:

> *"I…urge the drug dealers to reflect on the grave harm they are inflicting on countless young people and on adults from every level of society… God will call you to account for your deeds."* [48]

The "Critical" God is highly judgmental but disengaged as He does not execute judgment upon evildoers until the afterlife. This view is most found in ethnic minorities, the exploited and the poor, whose prayers have seemingly gone unanswered as God hasn't punished their oppressors or alleviated the persecution they are suffering. They relate to the Psalmist who wondered, "How long will God be partial to the wicked?" (Ps 82:2), and "How long will the wicked prosper?" (Ps 94:3).

4. "Distant": God is both disengaged and nonjudgmental (24%)

While the all-powerful creator of the universe, God is also the "cosmic watchmaker" who has "wound up" the universe only to step back and let it run on its own. God neither wants or demands our worship and praise and doesn't answer prayer which is merely a fruitless exercise reflective of our inflated sense of self-importance. Case in point is American founding father Ben Franklin:

---

[48] Froese & Bader, citing Wade & Pullella, 2007.

*"I imagine it a great vanity in me to suppose
that the Supremely Perfect (God)
does in the least regard such an inconsiderable
nothing as Man…. I cannot
conceive otherwise than that He the
infinite Father expects o requires
no Worship or Praise from us, but that He
is even infinitely above it."* [49]

These widely diverse perspectives suggest Americans – many who shape their construct of God from the same Bible – are not unlike the six blind men "touching" only a part of the elephant but left with a distorted, or even completely inaccurate – perception of who God is. Noteworthy as well is the fact these constructs reflect the influence of individualism common in Western industrialized countries in which merit based on one's adherence – or failure to adhere – to the generally accepted moral standards of one's community result in guilt or innocence and receiving what he or she "deserves".[50]

But this begs the question, "How do we arrive at these differing views of who God is?"

FACTORS THAT INFLUENCE WHY
WE VIEW GOD DIFFERENTLY

Froes and Bader also identified factors that contribute to these diverse perspectives of God. First is how you view the Bible, as those most convinced it was inspired by God and is to be understood literally tend to

---

[49] Ibid, citing Franklin, 1728.

[50] Georges contrasts the "guilt-innocence" construct common in America and Western European countries with the "shame-honor" construct common in the more collectivistic mindset of Eastern Asian cultures in which "morality" is seen more through the perspective of how one's behavior reflects on his or her family or community, or the "fear-power" construct common in African and tribal communities in which appeasement is the means to obtaining favor and avoiding the wrath of the gods. Georges also proposes American youth are adopting more of the collectivistic, shame-honor construct and a resultant relativistic view of morality in which "right" and "wrong" is determined by the community rather than an authority such as the Church.

see God as Authoritative or Benevolent, while those who hold the Bible less literally or authoritatively tend to see Him as Critical or Distant.

A second factor is where you grew up and/or live today. Southerners tend to view God as Authoritative, with Midwesterners tending towards a more Benevolent God, those from the West Coast a more Distant God, and those from the East Coast a more Critical God.

A third factor is one's political affiliation, with conservatives tending to view God as Authoritative and liberals viewing Him as Distant. And finally, there is how you view laws and rules. While those who interpret laws or rules as "absolute" tend to view God as Authoritative, those who view rules as "relative" to the situation tend to view Him as Distant, and those more in the middle – seeing some rules as absolute but others relative to the situation – tend to view God as Benevolent or Critical. An example is how respondents viewed "homosexuality".[51]

But there is one more factor that research suggests influences the factors already considered, and as a result has perhaps the most powerful and lasting impact on how people view God – and that's the quality of our childhood relationship with our parents.

"ATTACHMENT THEORY" AND OUR VIEW OF GOD

Consider the fact Adam and Eve didn't experience childhood and "grow up" like the rest of us, as they were created fully-grown with the physical and cognitive capabilities of an adult. Given this, they didn't have the opportunity to hone the ability to control the impulses that too often lead to the regrettable mistake adolescents are prone to make.

That said their primary "childhood" influence was something no human being since has experienced, and that's the perfect "parent" in the

---

[51] As of 2004, 70% of Americans viewed "homosexuality" as "wrong", but numbers varied significantly relative to how one views God. For example, 85% those who view God as "Authoritative" viewed homosexuality as always wrong compared to 67% of those who view God as "Benevolent", and 58% of those who view God as "Critical". Those who view God as "Distant" tend to see homosexuality as a "minor" issue. One's view of God also influenced attitudes toward abortion, with those who view God as "Authoritative" being least tolerant of extenuating circumstances while those who view God as "Distant" were more open to consider extenuating circumstances. Also noteworthy is the view that homosexuality is wrong has declined from 89% since 1973.

person of God their heavenly Father: A Father consistently available, loved them perfectly and unconditionally, and provided all their needs, and the reason Jesus frequently referred to God as our "Father".[52]

You'd be hard-pressed to find anyone who doesn't think parenting matters because it does, as our child experiences with primary caregivers significantly influences all aspects of our being including our perception of God. When we come into this world, the first two faces we may see are our mother's and father's. And from that moment forward, we innately realize we are completely dependent upon them to provide safety, shelter, food, clothing, and guidance as to how to survive and thrive in life. Our parents are "all powerful" in that they provide things we can't provide for ourselves, consolation when troubled, and solve the problems we cannot solve by ourselves. Given this, children come to perceive God –who He is, what He is like, and if He even exists – through what our parents teach us through their words, and what they model to us through their actions.

In their research, for example, Froese and Bader found the following:

- Those who had authoritative parents who took them to church regularly are more likely to view God as authoritative in "demanding" religious participation,
- Those whose parents were less diligent about regularly attending church tend to see God as less judgmental, less engaged, and more likely to view God as Distant,
- Those who describe themselves as "non-religious" tend to view God as Distant, while the "very religious" view Him as Authoritative or Benevolent; and,
- Those who never attended church as children were more likely to describe themselves as "atheists".

As you read this you might find yourself reflecting on your experience growing up, and how the home environment you grew up in shaped your view of God, since these findings point to the profound influence our parents have in developing our perception of God. This also reflects the

[52] Note, for example, His frequent references to God as "Father" in the Sermon on the Mount (Matt 5-7; cf Luke 6:20-49) as well as referring to God as His Father in the Upper Room Discourse (John 13-17).

findings by researchers who have studied what is referred to as *Attachment Theory*. Tenants foundational to Attachment Theory include:

- A child's psychological, emotional, and even physical health is significantly influenced by how well they can "attach" to their parents,
- A child's innate sense of their own value and worth, as well as their perception of how much they can trust that others (including God) will help them in their time of need is shaped by their interactions with their parents or primary caregivers; and,
- The quality of a child's attachment is determined by two factors: 1) were parents consistently <u>available</u> when experiencing distress, and 2) were parents consistently <u>approachable</u> when distressed.[53]

The consistently available parent takes time and makes sacrifices for his or her child and is responsive when a child is distressed or needs help. The consistently approachable parent communicates both concern for and a desire to help his or her child when in need.

When both are present a child feels: 1) <u>secure</u> in his or her sense of value and worth; 2) <u>safe</u> in approaching his or her parents; and 3) is comfortable help is there when needed.

A child's experiences with his or her parents results in one of four patterns of attachment:

- ***"Secure" Attachment***

Your parents were consistently available and consistently approachable, and rarely expressed irritation if "interrupted" when you were upset or needed help. As an adult you find it relatively easy to become emotionally close to others, are comfortable asking for help, being alone, and rarely experience any doubt as to whether others will accept you.

---

[53] Material in this section drawn from <u>Safe Haven Marriage: Building a Relationship You Want to Come Home To,</u> by Drs. Archibald D. Hart and Sharon Hart Morris (Nashville, TN: Thomas Nelson Publishers, 2003), 57-66. Attachment Theory was originally developed by psychiatrist John Bowlby, and further developed by psychologists such as Mary Ainsworth.

- *"Insecure-Preoccupied" Attachment*

Your parents were inconsistent in being available and/or approachable when you were upset or needed help and felt anxious or angry when your parents weren't available for you. As an adult you are hesitant to ask for help or pursue close relationships, and uncertain if you can really trust others.

- *"Insecure-Fearful" Attachment*

Your parents tended to express irritation when you needed help or comfort, and you were generally cautious around them. As an adult, you tend not to ask others for help because you don't want to be a bother, are uncomfortable getting emotionally close to others, and avoid being transparent out of fear you will get hurt in some way.

- *Insecure-Dismissive" Attachment*

Your parents were both unavailable and emotionally unapproachable when you needed help. You were taught to "stand on your own two feet", and as an adult tend to be independent, driven, and at times prone to perfectionism. You are generally self-reliant and tend to avoid close relationships or asking others for help.[54]

There appears to be a link between one's attachment experience and their view of God:

- Secure Attachment leads to a "Benevolent" view of God,
- Insecure-Preoccupied Attachment leads to an "Authoritative" view of God,
- Insecure-Fearful Attachment leads to a "Critical" view of God; and,
- Insecure-Avoidant Attachment leads to a "Distant".

Research also suggests our early attachment experience profoundly affects our ability to "attach" to God. Those who report a secure attachment tend to be less anxious and uncertain in their relationship with God and

---

[54] There are numerous Attachment Styles tests and questionnaires available online. A questionnaire is provided in the *Appendix*.

are better able to ride out the ups and downs of life. But those who report insecure attachment are more likely to:

- Avoid intimacy in their relationship with God (Insecure-Avoidant),
- Feel God is distant, unresponsive, or absent (Insecure-Dismissive),
- Question whether God really loves and is working for them (Insecure-Fearful),
- Have difficulty experiencing intimacy and closeness with God (Insecure-Avoidant),
- Have a higher likelihood of atheism or agnosticism.[55]

God created us with an inherent need to live in healthy relationships with Him and others in which we feel valued and respected and can count on others when in need. But those who experienced unhealthy relationships with their parents doubt whether their needs – and as a result he or she – even matter to others. They learn they can't consistently trust others to be there when they need them. And those coming from a childhood marred by abuse grow up to become the adult with a deep distrust of authority, and who almost instinctively avoids vulnerability to protect against getting hurt again.[56]

Sadly, these same doubts and fears are projected into our construct of God. After all, it is almost logical that a child who learned he or she not only can't trust but should <u>fear</u> his or her earthly parents may wonder, "Why should I put my trust in a heavenly Father when I couldn't trust my earthly parents?", or subconsciously and instinctively avoid trusting or flat-out reject approaching God out of emotional self-protection.

Now some may dismiss this as nothing more than "blaming the parents" for the problems some experience as adults. But God Himself – on <u>five</u> occasions – addressed the impact of parents' actions on not only themselves, but their children, their grandchildren, and great-grandchildren as well:

---

[55] From Froese & Bader; A. McDonald, R. Beck, S. Allison, & L Norsworthy (2005) <u>Attachment to God and Parents: Testing the Correspondence vs. Compensation Hypotheses,</u> *Journal of Psychology and Christianity, 24,* (1), pp 21-28; D.F. Reinert, C.E. Edwards, & R.R. Hendrix (2009). *Counseling & Values, 53,* pp 112-125; http://www.mbird.com/2016/10/attachment-theory-and-your-relationship-with-god/

[56] We will address the issue of "abuse" in more detail in *Chapter Five.*

> *"...For I, the LORD your God, am a jealous*
> *God, visiting the iniquity of the fathers on*
> *the children to the third and fourth generations*
> *of those who hate Me..." (Ex 20:5b)* [57]

And while our perception of the God has become increasingly distorted since the fall of Adam and Eve, He is the same loving, gracious Heavenly Father who communicated the standards inherent in the Law that serve to uphold the nature of His character as when He brought Adam and Eve into existence. In the remainder of this chapter, I'll offer my perspective of a comprehensive view of the Person of God as presented in the Bible.

A COMPREHENSIVE VIEW OF OUR "HEAVENLY FATHER"

So far, we have considered four American constructs of the Person of God:

- "Authoritative": God is both engaged, and judgmental.
- "Benevolent": God is engaged, but nonjudgmental.
- "Critical": God is disengaged, but judgmental (not in this life).
- "Distant": God both disengaged, nonjudgmental.

And each, like the perspectives of the blind men perceiving an elephant, have some merit.

God is "Authoritative"

God is the "Alpha and Omega", the Creator of all that exists, and by His very nature the epitome of truth, righteousness, and goodness.[58] He has the right to claim authority over His creation, issue commandments, judge human actions, and to reward obedience and discipline disobedience. And as we saw, He demonstrated His "Authoritative" qualities in rendering an immediate and firm judgment after Adam and Eve's disobedience.

---

[57] See also Ex 34:7; Lev 26:40; Num 14:18; Deut 5:9.
[58] See Rev 1:8, 11; 21:6; 22:13.

Throughout the Old Testament, God consistently communicated His standards of right and wrong to His chosen people the nation of Israel, rewarding their obedience with blessings, and disciplining their disobedience with consequences. Through the Mosaic Law, God entered what is essentially a behavioral contract with the *Exodus* Generation He delivered from Egypt. And the Bible tells us:

"So Moses came and told the people all
the words of the LORD and all
the judgments. And all the people answered with one voice and said,
"All the words which the LORD has said we will do." (Ex 24:3)[59]

It is important to understand God's commandments are not simply rules He arbitrarily chooses to impose on His human subjects; rather, they reflect the standards of goodness and righteousness He intended us to live by to enjoy the privilege of residing His "garden". He gets angry when we fail to uphold His standards, as said violations inevitably harm or devalue Him or others (Ex 4:14; Deut 7:4; Matt 21:12; Mark 3:5); and He gets jealous when what is rightfully His is taken from Him (Ex 20:5; Deut 6:15; Josh 24:19). In addition, we're told His discipline is actually an act of His love for us:

"And you have forgotten the exhortation which
speaks to you as to sons: "My son, do
not despise the chastening of the LORD, nor
be discouraged when you are rebuked
by Him, For whom the LORD loves He
[disciplines], And scourges every son whom
He receives. If you endure discipline, God deals
with you as with sons; for what son
is there whom a father does not discipline? But
if you are without discipline, of which
all have become partakers, then you are
illegitimate and not sons." (Heb 12:5-8)

---

[59] See also Leviticus Chapter 26 and Deuteronomy Chapter 28.

Given this, our challenge is to "fear" God by respecting His authority and right to rule. Unfortunately, in our post-Fall world, we are prone to fear a God who will abuse His authoritative power in the same way human authorities are prone to abuse their power. We can see hints of this through the reaction of His disciples after Jesus calms a storm:

> *"And a great windstorm arose, and the waves beat*
> *into the boat, so that it was already filling.*
> *But He was in the stern, asleep on a pillow. And*
> *they awoke Him and said to Him, 'Teacher,*
> *do You not care that we are perishing?' Then He*
> *arose and rebuked the wind, and said to the*
> *sea, 'Peace, be still!' And the wind ceased and there*
> *was a great calm. He said to them, 'Why*
> *are you so fearful? How is it that you have no*
> *faith?' And they feared exceedingly, and said*
> *to one another, 'Who can this be, that even the wind*
> *and the sea obey Him!' (Mark 4:37-41)*[60]

This, along with the numerous miracles He performed, served to validate His claim to be God's anointed in fulfillment of Isaiah's prophecy over 700 years earlier anticipating the coming of their Savior and Messiah (Is 61:1-3; cf Luke 4:18-19). Yet despite seeing Jesus use His power exclusively for good, their gut reaction was to feel <u>fear</u> in seeing Jesus exert power over nature.

You can almost see them stepping back – not only awestruck but unnerved at being in the presence of this profound display of power. And like Jesus' disciples, those who view God as "Authoritative" are prone to be more fearful of His discipline than expectant of His blessings. While acknowledging the Bible says God rewards the faithful, they have difficulty personalizing this to themselves – praying with more conviction for the benefit of others than asking for themselves. God is the boss you respect and obey, but one you are fearful of asking for favor of, revealing a mistake, or sharing a personal problem with.

---

[60] See also Matt 8:23-27; Luke 8:22-25.

God is "Benevolent"

While God rightful claims authority over His creation, the Bible clearly proclaims God's "benevolence", which is reflected in the following definition:

> *"An inclination or tendency to perform kind, charitable acts; to help or do good to others; a gift given out of generosity."*[61]

God's benevolence is seen in three characteristics foundational to Christianity as well as knowing Him personally: His love, grace, and mercy towards us. His love is reflected in the Greek word *agape*, which means "love, generosity, kindly concern, devotedness." God's grace is reflected in the word *charis*, which means, "kindly bearing, to benefit, a generous or charitable act, free favor." And God's mercy is reflected in the word *eleeo*, which means, "to pity, have compassion, to be gracious towards another."[62]

The Bible is clear that as fallen human beings, we are dead in our sins (Eph 2:1-3), enemies of God (Rom 5:10), and deserving of nothing other than death (Rom 6:23). BUT GOD – rich in mercy out of His great love for us – demonstrated His benevolence towards us through offering up His one and only Son Jesus to die on our behalf (John 3:16).

While God gets angry or jealous when we fall short of His perfect standards, He also feels compassion and pain when we are suffering. We see this in the fact Jesus was frequently moved with compassion as He observed the suffering of the people of Israel:

> *"And when Jesus went out He saw a great multitude; and He was moved with compassion for them and healed their sick." (Matt 14:14)*

> *"Now Jesus called His disciples to Himself and said, "I have compassion on the multitude, because they have now continued*

---

[61] https://www.thefreedictionary.com/benevolence
[62] William D. Mounce. The Analytical Lexicon to the Greek New Testament. Grand Rapids, MI: Zondervan Publishing House, 1993.

with Me three days and have nothing to eat. And I do not want to send them away hungry, lest they faint on the way." (Matt 15:32)

"So Jesus had compassion and touched their eyes. And immediately their eyes received sight, and they followed Him." (Matt 20:34)

And people took notice of depths of the compassion Jesus felt for the family and friends of Lazarus as they grieved his death:

"Jesus wept. Then the Jews said, 'See how He loved him'!" (John 11:35-36)

While the depths of God's love and compassion are beyond our capacity to both comprehend and to extend others, His grace and mercy are as well. Christianity is unique in the premise we do not have to earn God's favor because Jesus did it for us – a necessary step He took on our behalf because we are incapable of earning His favor. This premise rests upon God's grace and mercy, which can be understood simply as:

Grace is getting what you _don't_ deserve.

Mercy is _not_ getting what you _do_ deserve.

God's benevolence flows freely from Him as it is literally the essence of who He is:

"And we have known and believed the love that God has for us. God is love, and he who abides in love abides in God, and God in him." (1 John 4:16)

This is evident in the favor Jesus extended to the "undesirables" of His day:

- Inviting a tax collector named Levi (more frequently referred to as Matthew in the Gospels) to be one of His core group of disciples (Matt 9:9; Mark 2:14; Luke 5:29);

- Appointing Peter to be the leader of the core group He would build His church upon while knowing Peter would repeatedly deny being with – and even <u>knowing</u> – Him (Matt 26:70-74; Mark 14:68-71; Luke 22:57-60; John 18:17, 25); and,
- Not only forgiving Paul for persecuting earlier believers prior to his conversion, but appointing him to be the first, and arguably most influential, evangelist in Christian history (Acts 7:57-8:3; 1 Tim 1:12-14; cf Eph 3:8).

God's love for people – including YOU – has nothing to do with what you've done, or what you will do. God's love is simply a reflection of Who He is as well as the care He took in uniquely created you. This truth is expressed well by David in the following Psalm:

"For You formed my inward parts; You
covered me in my mother's womb.
I will praise You, for I am fearfully and
wonderfully made; Marvelous
are Your works, and that my soul knows very well." (Ps 139:13-14)

God determined to redeem us very imperfect and underserving human beings because He values us and CARES about us – faults, flaws, and all. The question is if we see how He uniquely created each one of us as a blessing or a cursing.

God is "Critical"

While God is authoritative and benevolent, it appears God at times deals quite "critically" with the world as well. Recall, those who view God as "Critical" tend to view Him as judgmental, but seemingly standing back, keeping score, and withholding judgment until the afterlife. Case in point is the experience of His chosen people, the nation of Israel.

As we saw in *Chapter One*, God's benevolence was evident in how Jacob's family of 70 prospered and grew into a virtual nation while living in Goshen. But His benevolence likely felt absent for those who endured the 400-plus years of bondage, during which countless Israelites cried out in futility to the God of their father Abraham:

*Now it happened in the process of time that
the king of Egypt died. Then the
children of Israel groaned because of the
bondage, and they cried out,
and their cry came up to God because of the bondage." (Ex 2:23)*

As many 20 generations of Israelites left to live out their entire lives as slaves, and to never see God vindicating their suffering by rendering justice upon their Egyptian oppressors. Given this, we can understand how an aging Israelite – having spent his or her whole life in slavery desperately appealing for God to act and waiting futilely only to see the sands of mortality in the hourglass of his or her life running out – come to perceive God as "critical". You can almost hear the suffering Israelites crying out like the Psalmist:

*"LORD, how long will the wicked, how long
will the wicked triumph?" (Ps 94:3)*

*"How long will you judge unjustly, and show
partiality to the wicked?" (Ps 82:2)*

The Bible does tell us that there will be a final judgment (The "Great White Throne") of unbelievers, which certainly will occur – but not until well after they have died (Rev 20:11-12). And Jesus Himself warned of this judgment:

*"And do not fear those who kill the body but
cannot kill the soul. But rather
fear Him who is able to destroy both soul
and body in hell." (Matt 10:28)*

The tendency of those who grew up with emotionally distant parents who tended to be more critical of their failures than affirming of their successes will be to view God as more "critical". You may appeal to Him in times of need, but deep down won't expect Him to act – and in fact, may be more surprised than anything when He does.

God is "Distant"

The Bible, particularly the Old Testament, presents God as distant in that while we toil away here on earth, He is seated on His throne so "high and exalted" in the heavens that He must "stoop down" to behold us (Is 6:1-5; cf Ps 113:5-6). Given this, Moses had to climb some 7,500 feet to the top of Mount Sinai to meet with God (Ex 19:3).[63]

As physical beings, we are limited by time and space and engage with others through our five senses. But God is "spirit" (John 4:24), and not bound by either time or space since He is the Creator of both (Acts 17:24-25). While we think of God residing in the heavens, the Bible also tells us the "heavens cannot contain" Him (2 Chron 2:6, 18; Ezek 9:5). Even His thoughts and ways are "higher" than ours" (Is 55:9).

Just thinking about this makes God seem quite "distant", doesn't it? What really makes Him seem distant, however, are the trials we experience that leave us wondering if He has simply forgotten about us. In His humanness, even Jesus experienced this:

> *"And at the ninth hour Jesus cried out with a loud voice, saying, 'Eloi, Eloi, lama sabachthani?' which is translated, 'My God, My God, why have You forsaken Me'?" (Mark 15:34; cf Matt 27:46)*

As time passes and our suffering persists, we may look in vain for any evidence God is engaged in our life in any way. We may become cynical, and more than a little disillusioned. And if we grew up with parents who were neither available nor approachable, we are prone to almost expect God to be every bit as "distant" and unavailable to us as they were.

This seemed to be the experience of the early Jewish believers suffering under both the oppression of the Romans, and the ostracism of their unbelieving Jewish brethren. While initially expecting God to act, they apparently became doubtful, and even disillusioned, as the days and years rolled by without His intervention. To which Peter wrote:

> *"But, beloved, do not forget this one thing, that*
> *with the Lord one day is as a thousand*

---

[63] https://www.britannica.com/place/Mount-Sinai-mountain-Egypt

years, and a thousand years as one day. The Lord
is not slack concerning His promise, as
some count slackness, but is longsuffering toward
us, not willing that any should perish but
that all should come to repentance. But the day of
the Lord will come as a thief in the night,
in which the heavens will pass away with a great
noise, and the elements will melt with
fervent heat; both the earth and the works that are
in it will be burned up." (2 Pet 3:8-10)

Consider every decision we make is limited to the information we have available to us in that given moment. This is seen in the decision you later came to regret: a decision you made based upon the best information you had available to you at the time, but without the perfect foresight of knowing how it would work out. And whether lacking a critical bit of information that may have changed the decision you made – or simply not "thinking it through" sufficiently – you later come to a point where you metaphorically "kicked yourself", and perhaps wondered aloud, "How could I have missed that?"

This doesn't happen with God. He is the self-existent "Alpha and Omega" – the Creator of all things who has existed eternally – and while "above" all things on earth, is also "ever-present".[64] He knows <u>everything</u> – whether past, present, and future – as He is not bound by time, and perfectly knows how things will ultimately work out. But understanding this – and particularly being reminded of this by someone who is simply trying to encourage you – can seem rather trivial, and even insulting, amid your suffering.

KNOWING GOD IN THE MIDST OF SUFFERING

In the movie *Bruce Almighty*, Jim Carrey plays Bruce Nolan, a reporter frustrated in being stuck in a role that doesn't maximize the use of his

---

[64] Ex 3:14; Job 38:4; Ps 139:7-10; Is 46:10; 66:1; John 5:26; 10:17-18; Acts 17:27-28; Rev 1:8, 11; 21:6; 22:13.

abilities, and in his "humble" opinion is beneath him. Then after an unusually bad day and a Job-like rant about how unfair God is being to him, something strange happens: Bruce gets a text message with an unfamiliar phone number. So, he calls the number, which has a recorded message offering him the job of a lifetime. But upon arriving for his interview at what appears to be an empty building, he meets none other than God (played by Morgan Freeman) Himself!

Bruce is not a character who will generate empathy for his "sufferings". He is clearly a self-centered man who fails to see the blessings he enjoys (including a loving girlfriend), and prone to tantrums when he doesn't get what he wants. But Hollywood does offer a character in which the viewer can't help but empathize with the seemingly cold (cruel?) way in which fate (God?) randomly lands with both feet on a more deserving person.

In the movie, *The Shawshank Redemption*, Tim Robbins plays Andy Dufresne, a young man seemingly living the dream life. He is a successful young banker married to the woman of his dreams when his life comes crashing down on him. Andy suspects his wife is having an affair and finds her with her lover in a motel room. Sitting in his car drinking from a bottle of whiskey, Andy fumes and plots his revenge. In the last minute, however, he has a change of heart and leaves. But as "fate" would have it, a known thief and serial killer just "happens" to come upon his wife and her lover, then robs and kills them both.

But Andy is accused of the murder, after which he is convicted and sentenced to two life terms at Shawshank – a maximum-security prison known for its cruelty. Convinced that somehow, some way "justice" will prevail, Andy settles into prison life. A shrewd man, he soon learns how things work at Shawshank, makes friends, and uses his financial skills to earn the warden's favor by managing his under-the-table financial schemes. And for the next 19 years he bides his time: his spirits sustained with the hope one day truth will prevail, the injustice he has suffered will be vindicated, and he will regain his freedom.

And then comes the day Andy has patiently waited all those years for. A new convict named Tommy arrives at Shawshank. Tommy recounts how a former cellmate bragged about killing a woman and her lover, and how her husband – a banker – took the fall for it! Andy goes to the warden to plead his case, but the warden – not wanting his schemes discovered – has Tommy killed. And with that, Andy's hopes of redemption are dashed.

This leads to a powerful scene in which a distraught Andy reflects on the nightmare his life has become. He has already humbly acknowledged his inability to be emotionally available contributed to his wife's waywardness. While not deserving her unfaithfulness, he has come to accept his part in the cruel turn of events he has suffered. But he can't reconcile the severity of it: he can't accept that he <u>deserved</u> to be punished in this way:

> *"Bad luck, I guess. It floats around. It's got to land*
> *on somebody. It was my turn, that's all.*
> *I was in the path of the tornado. I just didn't expect*
> *the storm would last as long as it has."*

The Shawshank Redemption would go on to be nominated for seven Academy Awards, including best adapted screenplay. It is one of those movies in which you can't help but empathize with Andy, and only try to imagine how you would cope with the injustice he has suffered. Now *The Shawshank Redemption* is only a fictional story, but at some point, you will hear real-life accounts of human suffering that certainly equal, if not surpass, the depths of the pain, suffering, and confusion Andy Dufresne experiences.[65]

In the fall of 1991, Jerry Sittser was living the life he had hoped and worked for: happily married with three children, working as a professor of religion, and actively engaged in his church. Then one day he found himself – like Andy Dufresne – in the "path of the tornado" when "bad luck" landed on him. While returning from a Native American reservation on a mission trip, a drunk driver plowed into their van – killing his wife Lynda, their four-year-old daughter Diana Jane, and Sittser's mother.

As a Christian and professor with a doctorate degree in religious studies, Sittser certainly knew what the Bible has to say about evil and suffering. But all this head knowledge did little to prepare him for the nightmare he found himself experiencing. In his book, *A Grace Disguised*,

---

[65] See also the cruel turn of events suffered by Edmond Dantes in, *The Count of Monte Crisco*. By Alexandre Dumas.

Sittser describes with raw emotion his season of wrestling with questions like, "Why is this happening? and, "What did I do to deserve this?"[66]

By God's design, human beings are planners. We learn the "rules", set goals, and execute plans to realize those goals. We may pray that God will bless us by seeing our plans to fruition, and express gratitude when they do. The challenge, however, is when our plans don't work out – particularly when things go horribly wrong. When words like "trial" or "testing" don't even begin to describe the pain and confusion we are experiencing. When life smacks us right in the face with something so unfair and inconceivable, we can't begin to comprehend why God is allowing it to happen to us as we drown in despair.

Jewish writer, political activist and Holocaust survivor Elie Wiesel also experienced this. In his book, *Night*, Wiesel describes his experience as a teenager when Germany occupied Hungary, and Wiesel and his family were ripped from their comfortable middle-class lives and deported to Auschwitz. During the next year, Wiesel saw atrocities he couldn't comprehend. He and his fellow Jews prayed to God for deliverance, but as the days passed and the death toll mounted, their hope – and faith – began to wane. Wiesel recalls the words of the rabbi he turned to for strength and inspiration as his own faith waned:

> *"'It's over. God is no longer with us.' And as though*
> *he regretted having uttered such words so*
> *coldly, so dryly, he added in his broken voice, 'I know.*
> *No one has the right to say things like that.*
> *I know that very well. Man is too insignificant, too limited, to*
> *even try to comprehend God's mysterious ways. But what can*
> *someone like myself do? I'm neither a sage nor a just man. I*
> *am not a saint. I'm a simple creature of flesh and*
> *bone. I suffer hell in my soul and my flesh.*
> *I also have eyes and I see what is being done here.*
> *Where is God's mercy? Where's God?*
> *How can I believe, how can anyone believe*
> *in this God of Mercy?'"* [67]

---

[66] Jerry Sittser, A Grace Disguised: How the Soul Grows Through Loss. Grand Rapids, MI: Zondervan Publishing House, 1995.

[67] Elie Wiesel. Night. https://www.goodreads.com/work/quotes/265616-la-nuit?page=2

And Wiesel recalls the following as he observes two adults hanging dead on the gallows, and a young boy – being hung for stealing food – who is "struggling between life and death, dying in slow agony under our eyes" on those same gallows:

> *"Behind me, I heard the same man asking: 'Where*
> *is God now?' And I heard a voice within*
> *me answer him: 'Where is He? Here He is – He*
> *is hanging here on this gallows'."* [68]

Like Wiesel, Edith Eger suffered the horrors of the Holocaust. In 1944, at the age of 16, Eger and her family were sent to Auschwitz – a place she had never even heard of. Upon arriving, she was first separated from her father, then her mother on orders from the infamous Dr. Josef Mengele, who told her and her sister, "You're going to see your mother very soon. She's just going to take a shower." In fact, her mother was sent to a gas chamber. Shortly after, Eger was forced to dance for her mother's executioner's entertainment.

As the war waged on, Edith was moved by her captures to Austria. In May 1945 an American soldier noticed her hand moving amongst numerous dead bodies. Near death and suffering from a broken back, typhoid fever, pleurisy, and pneumonia, she weighed 70 pounds. In reflecting on her experience in 2018 at 90 years of age, Eger said:

> *"I give lectures all over the world about PTSD, yet I still*
> *have it myself – I still have nightmares about that time."* [69]

Throughout history, the wisest religious and philosophical sages have tried to reconcile the existence of an all-powerful, all-knowing, and all-loving God with the all-too frequent experiences of evil and suffering. Scottish philosopher David Hume posited it this way:

---

[68] Elie Wiesel, *Night*, Bantam, 1982, pp. 75-6, quoted in *When God Was Taken Captive*, W. Aldrich, Multnomah, 1989, pp. 39-41.
[69] https://dreditheger.com/about/; https://www.dailymail.co.uk/home/you/article-6020105/Holocaust-survivor-Edith-Eger-spirit-kept-alive.html. See also Edit Eger's book, The Choice: Embrace the Possible, published by Scribner, 2017.

*"Epicurus's old questions are still unanswered:
Is He willing to prevent evil, but not
able? If so, He is impotent. Is He able, but not
willing? Then He is malevolent."*[70]

Some of the smartest thinkers further debate the definition, and even the very <u>existence</u>, of evil and suffering with questions such as, "If suffering leads to good, is it really evil"? And they present examples such as the pain and discomfort (i.e., "suffering") experienced in the dental chair as your dentist removes the abscessed tooth causing you pain, and pose the question, "If it leads to good is it really suffering?", or, "Would you consider the dentist inflicting the pain you are suffering therefore 'evil'?"[71]

And then there's "free will", and the contrast between the suffering we choose, and the suffering we experience from circumstances we don't choose but are inflicted upon us by others, nature, or a random accident. We may choose, for example, to push ourselves to the point of physical discomfort exhaustion at the gym but don't consider it "suffering" since we have willfully chosen it for the benefits exercise provides. In contrast, you'd be hard-pressed to find someone who wouldn't consider the experience of the slave bull-whipped to maximize a plantation owner's profits, anything less than "suffering".

Our first impulse amid trials is to try to make sense of it, and to assess whether we "deserve" what's happening to us. We are prone to justify the conclusion that in fact we don't, someone (God?) isn't being fair to us, and we are being wronged in some way. We struggle to accept the fact we no longer live in the perfect harmony and goodness that reigned in the Garden before Adam and Eve brought sin into the world.

Certainly, the experience of those like the victims of the Holocaust is the extreme, but our reality is the world is no longer perfect, and suffering is a part of life. Whether health problems, job losses and financial stresses, or the loss of a loved one, we will inevitably suffer at one time or another.

---

[70] https://www.goodreads.com/quotes/21890-epicurus-s-old-questions-are-still-unanswered-is-he-god-willing
[71] Theologian Millard Erickson devotes 21 pages to presenting the various views offered by philosophers and theologians to address the topic of evil and suffering in <u>Christian Theology, 2nd ed.</u> Grand Rapids, MI: Baker Books, 1999, pp 536-556.

And amid our suffering, we are prone to look up to God and ask, "Why are You doing this to me?" or "What did I do to deserve this?"

The Bible is full of accounts of human suffering – the Book of Job being an example, and seemingly written for the express purpose of addressing these questions. Job, who lived about 4,200 years ago, is described as a "blameless and upright" man (Job 1:1) who "feared God and shunned evil", and whom God had blessed abundantly. Satan – always looking for ways to undermine God – approaches Him, seemingly to ask permission for someone he could torment as a means of testing the person's devotion to God. God, confident in Job's faith and resilience, allows Satan to afflict Job with any kind of pain and suffering he wants short of taking Job's life (Job 1:6-12). And Satan certainly does.

Soon Job lost his children, his wealth, and his health. He is in extreme physical and emotional pain and would just as soon die. Yet, despite the seemingly unfair events that have befallen him, Job refuses to "curse" God (2:11). Through the next 36 chapters, Job tries to make sense of his suffering, and debates four friends who repeatedly come to God's defense. And as his suffering persists, Job suggests God has been unfair to him:

"As God lives, who has taken away my justice, And the Almighty, who has made my soul bitter…" (Job 27:2) [72]

Eventually Job – unable to comprehend what he has done to deserve this – begins to question God's justness. To which God essentially responds, "I'm God and you're not – who are you to question Me?"[73] But then something interesting and insightful happens. First, God chastises Job's friends for their feeble and uninformed attempts to explain Job's suffering. Then God tells Job – who has called out God's very character – to pray for his friends! Now God eventually blesses Job with double the material provisions he enjoyed before Satan's attack. But He never tells Job why He allowed all his suffering to occur.

At times, understanding why things are happening to us is difficult, if not impossible, to comprehend. We wonder if His lack of action is because

---

[72] Another example is the prophet Habakkuk (1:2-23), who while seeing the need for God to discipline the rebellious children of Israel, struggles to comprehend how God could use the wicked Babylonians as His instruments of discipline.

[73] See the book of Job, *Chapters 38-39.*

He can't do anything about it or <u>won't</u> do anything about it. And as we suffer, we are left to trust in God's "higher" ways and the "depths of the riches of His wisdom and knowledge":

"For as the heavens are higher than the earth, so are My ways higher than your ways, And My thoughts than your thoughts." (Is 55:9)

"Oh, the depth of the riches both of the wisdom and knowledge of God! How unsearchable are His judgments and His ways past finding out!" (Rom 11:33)

One who came to realize this despite years of unjust suffering is Joseph. A great-grandson of Abraham and the favorite of his father Jacob, Joseph is sold into slavery by his jealous brothers (Gen 37), and falsely accused of sexual assault and sent to prison (Gen 39:7-20). But God is clearly with Joseph, who is not only freed from prison, but repeatedly finds "favor" with the Pharaoh until given virtually complete authority over all of Egypt.[74]

It is during this time the great famine that would bring Jacob and his family to Egypt afflicts the Near East. Jacob sends his sons to Egypt for food, where they encounter the brother, they had sold into slavery decades earlier. Joseph extends them mercy, and through the favor he has with the Pharaoh is permitted to invite Jacob and his family to resettle in Goshen. But it is literally <u>decades</u> later before Joseph can see that while "unfair", God had a greater purpose for the unfairness of the injustice he had suffered:

"Joseph said to them, 'Do not be afraid, for am I in the place of God? But as for you, you meant evil against me; but God meant it for good, in order to bring it about as it is this day, to save many people alive'." (Gen 50:19-20)

---

[74] See Gen 39:4, 21; 41:41-45.

Joseph was blessed with the privilege of seeing his suffering redeemed during his lifetime through the "good" God brought out of it. Likewise, the *Exodus* Generation of Israel experienced the privilege of seeing with their own eyes how God snatched victory from the jaws of defeat by miraculously delivering them from Egyptian bondage. But there were many who didn't – case in point the 20 generations of the descendants of Joseph's brothers, who spent their whole lives suffering in bondage.

As believers, we are reminded that Jesus Himself understands suffering, because He has suffered everything we will ever suffer:

> *"Therefore, in all things He had to be made*
> *like His brethren, that He might*
> *be a merciful and faithful High Priest in*
> *things pertaining to God, to make*
> *propitiation for the sins of the people. For*
> *in that He Himself has suffered,*
> *being tempted, He is able to aid those who*
> *are tempted." (Heb 2:17-18)*

In fact, it seems God intended Jesus to suffer as a means of proving His worthiness to rule:

> *"As He also says in another place: 'You are*
> *a priest forever According to the*
> *order of Melchizedek'; who, in the days of*
> *His flesh, when He had offered up*
> *prayers and supplications, with vehement cries*
> *and tears to Him who was able to*
> *save Him from death, and was heard because*
> *of His godly fear, though He was a*
> *Son, yet He learned obedience by the things*
> *which He suffered. And having been*
> *perfected, He became the author of eternal*
> *salvation to all who obey Him, called*
> *by God as High Priest "according to the order*
> *of Melchizedek…" (Heb 5:6-10)*

God the Father understands the suffering of the parent who has lost a child because He, too, lost His "only begotten Son". In fact, God the Father willingly offered up His only Son so we can experience eternal life and a relationship with Him (John 3:16). [75] And God the Holy Spirit understands the soul-crushing suffering when rejected, ridiculed, taunted, insulted, and falsely accused. Nicholas Wolterstorff offers this profound perspective:

> *"It is said of God that no one can behold his face*
> *and life. I always thought this meant*
> *that no one could see His splendor and live. A*
> *friend said perhaps it means that no*
> *one could see His sorrow and live. Or perhaps*
> *His sorrow is His splendor."[76]*

Perhaps it is God's <u>suffering</u> – and not His sovereignty – that should render us awestruck.

Perhaps it is only amid our suffering we can come to really know and appreciate Jesus the "Suffering Servant" (Is 52:13-53:12) Who gave His life so we, too, can have life. And perhaps it is only by persevering faithfully through the trials that confront us that we can truly comprehend it isn't that God isn't good or doesn't love us. In fact, we may come to realize just how good God is, and much He loves us <u>through</u> our suffering.

Pastor "William" came to understand this.[77] William is the founding pastor of a large Evangelical Church that has planted several churches throughout the world. At a Trauma-Informed conference for pastors and therapists, Pastor William shared how as he experienced physical, verbal, and sexual abuse as a child, and like most abuse victims the abuse left him feeling inadequate and full of shame. But he will tell you his suffering was instrumental in preparing him for the work God would call him to as a pastor.

---

[75] This is beautifully illustrated in the example of a father who gives up his only child when it is determined his son is the only living person whose blood can be used to cure a disease that is wiping out humanity. See http://www.inspire21.com/stories/christianstories/cleanblood

[76] Sitter quoting Wolterstorff, p. 133.

[77] While "William" is not his real name, a pseudonym has been used to protect his confidentiality as while he shared this in a public forum express permission was not obtained for purposes of this book.

William experienced the healing only God can provide. He came to realize that he had value, dignity, and worth in being "fearfully and wonderfully made" in God's image (Ps 139:13-14; Jam 3:9), and that no amount of abuse could take that away from him. And Pastor William came to realize that God had called him to be a suffering servant to help build His kingdom. Through the pain he had suffered, William could relate on a personal and emotional level to the suffering of many of his congregants that most other pastors and therapists can't. Like Joseph, Pastor William – through doggedly trusting God – came to realize that what his abusers meant for evil, God would redeem by using it in one those "higher ways" for good.

The Bible tells us we will face circumstances we cannot fully understand. And we may not – in this life – fully comprehend the plans, purposes, and even the very <u>person</u> of God:

> *"When I was a child, I spoke as a child, I understood*
> *as a child, I thought as a child; but when I*
> *became a man, I put away childish things. For now*
> *we see in a mirror, dimly, but then face to*
> *face. Now I know in part, but then I shall know*
> *just as I also am known." (1 Cor 13:11-12)*

But as we contemplate the suffering we have experienced – perhaps in those moments when we share Communion with other believers – we might remember just how much Jesus suffered on our behalf. And we might remember that even though God may have permitted it to happen for reasons we can't comprehend, He isn't just coldly sitting back and observing. Instead, He is feeling the same compassion Jesus felt for the lost, and the same anger Jesus felt towards the insensitivity and mercilessness of the Pharisees:

> *"Then He said to them (the Pharisees), 'Is it lawful*
> *on the Sabbath to do good or to do evil, to save*
> *life or to kill?' But they kept silent. And when He*
> *had looked around at them with anger, being*
> *grieved by the hardness of their hearts, He said to*
> *the man, 'Stretch out your hand." And*
> *he stretched it out, and his hand was restored*
> *as whole as the other'." (Mark 3:4-5)*

In their zeal to uphold the standards of the Mosaic Law, the Pharisees failed to realize the suffering Jesus intended to alleviate through healing the man's affliction, and in doing so failed to comprehend where compassion and mercy fit in applying the standards of the Law in everyday life.[78] In contrast, Jesus demonstrated a profound understanding of suffering in anticipation of the suffering He knew He would soon experience.

While as adults we may have difficulty comprehending the suffering we are experiencing, it is even more difficult for children suffering abuse and neglect. Children are incapable of processing and reconciling the shame-inducing messages that "you're no good", "you're worthless" or "you're not worth my time" abuse and neglect inflict. And these messages become engrained in a child's psyche at such a deep level a child isn't even aware of it.[79]

Rather than burdens or irritants, Jesus saw children as precious beings. Despite the pressing demands of the adults wanting His attention, Jesus always made time for children as He knew better than we can comprehend how impressionable they are:

"Then they brought little children to Him,
that He might touch them; but the
disciples rebuked those who brought them.
But when Jesus saw it, He was
greatly displeased and said to them, "Let the
little children come to Me, and
do not forbid them; for of such is the kingdom
of God." (Mark 10:13-14)

The Bible describes children as a blessing from God (Ps 127:4-5). But in entrusting a parent with a child, God is also placing a tremendous responsibility upon parents to not only <u>teach</u> them His ways, but to model the love God has for them, and the inherent value and dignity He has created them with (Deut 6:7; Eph 6:4; Col 3:21 cf Prov 22:6).

As a child, Elie Wiesel and Edith Eger didn't have the maturity to

---

[78] For an overview of who the Pharisees were in Jesus' day, see <u>https://overviewbible.com/pharisees/</u>; https://www.biblestudytools.com/dictionary/pharisees/

[79] We will explore abuse and neglect and how it impacts us in more detail in *Chapter Five*.

reconcile what was happening to them and their fellow Jews. And even Jerry Sittser – a mature adult and well-schooled theologian – struggled to make sense of why God was allowing him to experience the losses he had suffered. God had become "terrifying and inscrutable" to him, as in the absence of answers he found himself wondering if in fact, "God does not seem to hear or want to answer, as if we were too insignificant for reply."[80] Yet, in time as he reflected further upon the Easter story, Sittser came to realize just how much God <u>does</u> love him in realizing God was there grieving with him all along – just as He grieved while watching the Son He had given up suffer on our behalves. And during his season of suffering, perhaps Sittser came to realize something articulated so well by N.T. Wright:

> *"Jesus doesn't give an explanation for the pain
> and sorrow of the world. He comes where
> the pain is most acute and takes it upon himself.
> Jesus doesn't explain why there is
> suffering, illness, and death in the world. He
> brings healing and hope. He doesn't
> allow the problem of evil to be the subject of
> a seminar. He allows evil to do its
> worst to him. He exhausts it, drains its power,
> and emerges with new life."[81]*

For Sittser, his suffering eventually brought him from a place of questioning God's love to one of experiencing it more deeply. He came to appreciate the Resurrection – the new life that came after Jesus' suffering – more deeply. And he came to know God as more than a supreme and powerful being, but as his Heavenly "Father":

> *"But when the fullness of the time had come, God
> sent forth His Son, born of a woman,
> born under the law, to redeem those who were
> under the law, that we might receive*

[80] Ibid, p. 135-136
[81] N.T. Wright. <u>Simply Good News.</u> San Francisco, CA: HarperOne Publishers, 2015.

the adoption as sons. And because you are
sons, God has sent forth the Spirit of
His Son into your hearts, crying out, "Abba,
Father!" Therefore you are no longer
a slave but a son, and if a son, then an heir
of God through Christ." (Gal 4:4-7)

Sittser realized the depths of his suffering were the product of the deep love he had for his mother, his wife, and his daughter. While comforted by his Heavenly Father, Sittser also experienced the comfort of friends who mourned with him, walked with him, and loved him through his season of healing. And in this he realized something else:

"The risk of further loss, therefore, poses a
dilemma. The problem of choosing to love
again is that the choice to love means living
under the constant threat of further loss.
But the problem of choosing not to love is that
the choice to turn from love means
imperiling the life of the soul, for the soul
thrives in an environment of love.... If
people want their souls to grow through loss,
whatever the loss is, they must
eventually decide to love even more deeply
than they did before. They must
respond to the loss by embracing love with
renewed energy and commitment."[82]

For you, this may mean seeking counseling, or participating in a support group to grieve and heal from the abuse or losses you have suffered.[83] But first and foremost, it will mean taking the risk of turning to and trusting in God your Abba Father for the love and comfort He desires to share with you3

---

[82] Sittser, p. 165
[83] Again, this will be addressed in more detail in *Chapter Five.*

CHAPTER THREE

THE PRODIGAL ME

INTRODUCTION

In the fourth year of His ministry as "the time approached for Him to be taken up to heaven", Jesus "steadfastly set His face to go to Jerusalem" and the suffering He would soon undergo (Luke 9:51-52).[84] His time short, Jesus became very deliberate in teaching His disciples about true discipleship. One example is, *The Parable of the Prodigal Son:*

> *"Then He (Jesus) said: 'A certain man had two sons. And the younger of them said to his father, 'Father, give me the portion of goods that falls to me.' So, he divided to them his livelihood. And not many days after, the younger son gathered all together, journeyed to a far country, and there wasted his possessions with prodigal living. But when he had spent all, there arose a severe famine in that land, and he began to be in want. Then he went and joined himself to a citizen of that country, and he sent him into his fields to feed swine. And he would gladly have filled his stomach with the pods that the swine ate, and no one gave him anything. (Luke 15:11-16)[85]*

---

[84] In Jesus' "Journey to Jerusalem" (Luke 9:51-19:27), which covers a period of approximately nine months, reveals Jesus focusing His attention on His disciples to prepare them for the work He would leave to them upon His death and resurrection.

[85] A parable is a simple story to illustrate a deeper moral lesson. See https://www. biblestudytools.com/topical-verses/parables-of-jesus/ for a list of the parables Jesus used to teach His hearers.

Here Jesus presents a successful man with two sons living a blessed life simply for being his sons: they will never have to worry financially as they live off the fruits of his labor, while privileged with the opportunity of learning from their father. But the younger son isn't satisfied: instead, he mistakenly believes the abundant life is found in enjoying the fruits of his father's labor rather than the principles that have produced that fruit.

Sounds like the story of Adam and Eve, doesn't it? They, too, had the perfect Father who had given them all needed for a blessed life: just work the "family business", learn from their "father", and be thankful for all that He had provided them. But they, too, wanted more, rejected their father's counsel, and threw it all away for "prodigal" living.

This is evident in examining the meaning of the Greek word translated "prodigal", which despite having two Master's degrees I needed to look up to know what the English word meant.[86] It comes from the Greek *asotos*, which means "to excess, and without wisdom".[87] It appears the "prodigal" son had blown through all his inheritance in a relatively short period of time by living it up on booze and women (v 30).

Noteworthy as well is the fact *asotos* stems from the negative of the Greek word *sozo*, which means, "life, or to save", the Greek word translated "save" or "salvation"! By rejecting his father's ways, the Prodigal (like Adam and Eve) had chosen the road of death and destruction over that of abundant life.[88] But something else to consider is the fact this is also the story of us. This is the story of every human being who has ever lived, because as descendants of Adam and Eve, we, too are prone to "prodigal" tendencies.[89]

We concluded *Chapter One* with the ramifications of inheriting the sin nature, and two questions that hinder our ability to experience the abundant life and the fruit of the Spirit: 1) Can I trust God? and, 2) Do I really want to trust God? Having addressed factors that hinder our ability to trust God, we now turn to the sobering reality that by virtue of our sin nature, there is a part of us that questions whether we really want to trust

---

[86] New King James Version translation.
[87] Mounce. The Analytical Lexicon to the Greek New Testament. Other translations include "riotous, loose, dissolute, debauchery".
[88] Ibid. Note in Rom 6:23, Paul tells us, "The wages of sin is death".
[89] See Psalm 51:5; Rom 5:12-14.

Him. To do this we begin by addressing how our sinful nature affects all aspects of our being.

"MAN": A TRINITY IN BEING

We've considered the painstaking care in which God created all that exists, and even in the post-Fall world we live in today, the splendor of His handiwork remains evident. Whether the beauty of a sunrise or sunset, the awe-inspiring sight of snow-covered mountains, the calming rhythms of the waves of the ocean breaking over a beach, or the countless stars we can see on a clear night, human beings throughout history have recognized our collective smallness relative to the vastness of the universe we live in.

And then there's the care God took to ensure life on earth is even possible. Scientists have calculated the odds of life randomly evolving through the presence of the right chemicals (oxygen, hydrogen, etc.) as well as the conditions necessary to sustain life (temperatures, water, etc.) at 1 in 10 to the 40th power![90] Even without this knowledge, the writers of the Bible proposed the complexity of our universe points to the handiwork of a Creator.[91]

But as we've seen, God didn't declare His creation to be "very good" until after He had created humankind (Gen 1:31). In declaring "let us make [humanity] in our image according to our likeness" (Gen 1:26), God states He exists in the form of a "Trinity" (the Father, the Son, and the Holy Spirit).[92] In the same way, we as human beings are arguably best understood as triune beings comprised of a "body", "soul", and "spirit":

"Now may the God of peace Himself sanctify you completely; and May Your whole spirit, soul, and body be preserved blameless at the coming of our Lord Jesus Christ." (1 Thess 5:23)

---

[90] https://www.scienceforums.net/topic/67884-what-are-the-odds-of-life-evolving-by-chance-alone/

[91] Again, see Ps 19:1-2; Rom 1:20a

[92] While most traditional English translations of the Bible use the word "man" in Gen 1:26, the best rendering of the original Hebrew is "humanity" or "humankind" to reflect both genders.

*"For the word of God is living and powerful,
and sharper than any two-edged
sword, piercing even to the division of soul
and spirit, and of joints and marrow,
and is a discerner of the thoughts and
intents of the heart." (Heb 4:12)*[93]

It is important to realize these three aspects of our being are intricately woven together: impairment to one affect all our being.[94] Given this, we will address each aspect, as well as how the effects of the Fall on each hinders our ability to trust God and to experience the life of abundance, we all desire.

The "Body"

Despite the compelling evidence of a Creator God who carefully brought everything into existence, some refuse to acknowledge God's handiwork – and His very existence – by pointing to evidence they propose supports the theory that all life forms evolved naturally and randomly over a long period of time without the help of a divine being.[95] And they point to evidence obtained through observing God's creation to support this.

First there is increasing genetic similarity between human beings and other species as you move up the hierarchy of the animal kingdom. While 60% genetically like chickens, we are 75% like mice, 80% like cows, 90% like cats, and 96-98% like chimpanzees.[96] While helpful in the advancements in medical science we benefit from today, this doesn't

---

[93] Theologian Millard Erickson argues effectively through his analysis of Scripture that human beings are to be understood as a "conditional unity" of body, soul, and spirit. See Christian Theology, 2nd ed. Grand Rapids, MI: Baker Books, 1999, pp 554-7.

[94] The Bible tells us that our sins and those done against us affects us physically and psychologically as well as spiritually (Ps 6; 32:1-5; 38:5; Prov 18:14); and physical ailments affect us psychologically and spiritually as well (John 5:1-9).

[95] https://www.americanthinker.com/articles/2011/09/what_darwin_said_about_god.html; http://www.historyandapologetics.com/2015/02/st-augustine-on-evolutio.html. Charles Darwin, author of *Origin of the Species*, was raised in the church, believed in God, and at one point during his studies at Cambridge considering ministry. Darwin came to the same conclusion as St. Augustine in proposing life developed through a "God-guided" evolutionary process.

[96] Human beings are 99.5% like one another.

disprove a Creator God, and in fact affirms the order of creation presented in Genesis.[97]

To create the various life forms that exist, God seemingly used elements He had already created. Roughly 96% of the mass of the human body is comprised of just four elements: oxygen, carbon, hydrogen, and nitrogen.[98] And the mechanisms He built into the physical prototypes of each species to survive, thrive, and reproduce – starting with the structure of the cells upon which each body part is constructed – is remarkably similar.

The psalmist's proclamation, "…I am fearfully and wonderfully made; your works are wonderful" (Ps 139:14) reflects how God intricately knitted together 30 trillion cells to form the human body: the perfect engine designed to run indefinitely at peak efficiency, needing only to be refueled through the food He abundantly provided in the Garden. [99]

Woven into this complex piece of organic machinery are the drives and hormones God intended to sustain and perpetuate life. We don't have to learn or remember to breathe, eat, or for our heart to pump blood. And we don't have to take a class to develop the sex drive is the catalyst to "be fruitful and multiply" (Gen 1:28; cf 9:1, 7) as well as facilitating the pleasure a husband and wife are to experience when they "become one flesh" (2:24).

Sadly, the Fall changed all this, as the effects of sin ravaged the once perfectly designed machine represented in the human body through crippling, debilitating, and ultimately fatal diseases such as cancer, muscular dystrophy and muscular sclerosis, cystic fibrosis, COPD, ALS, diabetes, and various types of heart disease.[100] We live with the sobering reality that "life is but a vapor" that is too quickly gone (Jam 4:14; cf Ps 39:5).

---

[97] My father-in-law benefited from this when doctors replaced his mitral valve with one taken from a pig.

[98] https://www.livescience.com/3505-chemistry-life-human-body.html. In Gen 1, Moses uses various Hebrew words to describe God's creative process. In verses 3, 6, 9, 14, 15 the word describes *ex nihilio* (from nothing). He then uses words meaning "bring forth" (from something already existing) in verse 11 to describe creating plants; "created" (something new) of moving creatures (fish, birds); "bringing forth" (verses 24, 25) suggesting mammals were adapted from fish and birds; and "made", "created", and "formed" in verses 26-27 and 2:7, suggesting humans were adapted from something already existing yet new and unique.

[99] Note 1 Cor 12:14-26; Eph 4:11-16. The human body is described as the "temple" that houses our soul and spirit (1 Cor 6:19).

[100] From http://www.healthcarebusinesstech.com/the-12-most-debilitating-diseases/3/.

The "Soul"

The human soul is comprised of the mind, heart, emotions, and will. To understand the biblical concept of the "mind" we contrast it with the physical organ called the "brain".

The "Brain" vs the Human "Mind"

Observe God's creatures, and you will see their capability to survive in even the harshest environment through their ability to learn and adapt. Each spring, at about 8:45pm geckos will venture onto the screen covering our living room window as they search for the bugs drawn to the light. And I'm not the only one who has observed this, as our cat Archie will camp out – sitting motionless on his haunches staring at the same window – in anticipation of their arrival.

You may have observed something similar in the behavior of birds. While they generally fly away if we get too near them, they will boldly approach us at an outdoor café in search of any crumbs that may have fallen from our table. And seagulls literally fill the sky above Oracle Park on a typical San Francisco evening towards the end of a Giants baseball game in anticipation of the scraps of food left behind when the game concludes.

As you work your way up the Animal Kingdom, you will see the increasingly complex ability of God's creatures to make associations, learn cause and affect relationships, and to adapt in ways necessary to enable them to survive. But even chimpanzees – equipped with a brain that enables them to also form social groups, communicate, and use tools to forage for food – pale in comparison to what God has equipped human beings to achieve.

The capabilities God has endowed us with is seen in our advancements in the fields of agriculture and technology. We transitioned from nomadic hunter-gatherers to domestic farmers by learning how to maximize crop production in even the harshest environment. We can live in both frigid and brutally hot environments with the development of heating and air conditioning, communicate with others regardless of their location via phone, and travel worldwide in a 24-hour day. And with the advent of computers and the complex algorithms they operate upon, machines increasingly do the "thinking" humans once did.

With all our "genius", however, there remains the mystery of life itself that arguably will remain hidden behind the curtain God has reserved for Himself. While able to maximize the crops a field will yield, we have yet to figure out how a seed planted in soil, watered, and exposed to sunlight becomes the robust plants or trees that produce the vegetables and fruits we depend upon for food. And while we have developed machines that duplicate work previously reserved for human beings, even the most complex computer or robot does not "feel", "desire", or is "self-aware" in the way that even an infant child is.

God created all His creatures with a brain that serves to guide and direct its behaviors, and to facilitate its survival. And the brain of every living creature is comprised of cells called "neurons", which are like the "byte" – or single unit of data – upon which technological devices such as computers and cellphones are constructed.[101] And as these neurons naturally connect, they become the facts, images, and narratives that in turn become memories that enable us to learn, anticipate, adapt, and survive.

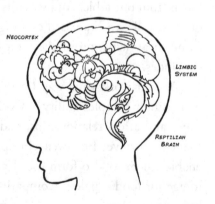

But neuroscience tells us God did not create all brains equally. There is a vast difference in the number of neurons between the brain of a frog and that of even a human infant.[102] And this is evident in considering the uniqueness of the human brain as presented in "Triune Brain" theory.

Proponents of Triune Brain Theory propose the human brain is

---

[101] https://searchstorage.techtarget.com/definition/byte

[102] https://ipfs.io/ipfs/QmXoypizjW3WknFiJnKLwHCnL72vedxjQkDDP1mXWo6uco/wiki/List_of_animals_by_number_of_neurons.html. A frog's brain has 16 million neurons, higher primates' range from 1-6 billion, but the human brain has 86 billion at birth.

comprised of three general regions that serve distinct functions.[103] First, there is the Reptilian or "lizard" brain. Functioning much like the brains of reptiles and birds, it must be fully developed at birth to ensure the child's physical survival, and it functions mechanically and unconsciously. It represents about 30% of the human brain, and includes the brainstem (medulla), the cerebellum, and the thalamus which regulate our heart rate, breathing, and body temperature, facilitates gross motor skills (balance, etc.), and regulates primitive survival instincts such as fear, aggression, and the need to bond with its caregivers. The reptilian brain at work is seen in the instinctive reflex to pull your hand away from a hot stove to duck from a baseball coming at your head, or the flailing of your arms when falling to regain your balance. But even the primitive brain and the survival instincts it generates are learned to a degree.

An example is seen in watching 8–10-month-old infants learning to walk. Early on they need to focus on keeping their balance and will fall if distracted by a toy on the floor. Soon, however, muscle memory takes over and balance becomes automatic, enabling them to "multi-task" and walk while focusing their attention on something else. And as the child grows, the ability to multi-task becomes more complex, facilitating the ability for a basketball player to dribble a ball while deciding which teammate to pass to, a musician to play a guitar while singing, or the office worker to type 60+ words a minute while crafting a word document. And this is possible because unlike the machine designed constructed by an engineer intentionally putting parts together to accomplish the function it is designed to perform – neurons that comprise the brains of all of God's creatures naturally bond together in "synaptic connections".

While the Reptilian portion of our brain utilizes a form of learning and memory in ensuring our survival, the Mammalian or "dog" portion of our brain takes it to a more complex, conscious, and emotional level. This region – also known as the "limbic" system – is the "feeling" center of the brain and includes the amygdala (the "security system" where "fight or flight" reactions originate), the hippocampus (where explicit memories such as facts and events are formed), the hypothalamus (where hormones are

---

[103] Drawn from: David Ziegler, Ph.D., Traumatic Experience and the Brain (Jasper, OR: Ziegler, 2002); Andrew Newberg, M.D., Eugene D'Aquili, M.D., Ph.D. and Vince Rause, Why God Won't Go Away (New York: Ballantine Books, 2002.

produced and activated), the "reward center" (where we learn the behaviors rewarded with pleasant sensations and those with unpleasant sensations), and the cingulate gyrus (the "decision-maker" and link between the limbic system and higher parts of the brain).

The limbic system is where feelings of love, affection, friendship, and trust – as well as feelings of "hate" and distrust – are learned in direct relation to one's experiences with others from the moment a newborn comes out of his or her mother's womb. While the reptilian brain enables us to discern whether things within our physical environment are safe or represent a threat to our physical well-being, the limbic system discerns at an emotional level what is safe, and what is psychologically threatening. It is the part of the brain that enables us to form the "attachments" necessary to ensure not only our physical survival, but our psychological well-being as well.[104] It is where emotional sensations such as anticipation and the pleasure of eating something tasty, doing things we enjoy, or socializing with someone we like and feel safe with originate. But it also generates feelings of apprehension of a surgical procedure or being with people we don't like or distrust, or repulsion at the sight or smell of a food item that once gave us food poisoning.

This is possible through what is referred to as the "reward center". In puberty our bodies begin to produce the hormones that generate sexual urges, it is the reward center that "reminds" us through the urges it generates to repeat the behaviors we have found to be pleasurable. Unfortunately, it is also the reward center that reminds us of and generates the same urges that can lead to the development of destructive habits such as alcohol, drug, and other types of addiction. And it also generates strong feelings of aversion – and even repulsion – to sexual intimacy for those who have been victimized by sexual abuse.

Finally, there is the "Primate", or "Neo-Mammalian" brain. Unique to higher primates and located in the neocortex, it is the last region of the brain to mature and continues to develop and change throughout life. It is the part of the brain that facilitates abstract and concrete thought, inductive and deductive reasoning, where cognitive memory, cause and

---

[104] Ziegler, in referencing John Bowlby (Attachment and Loss: Volume 3, Loss: Sadness and Depression (New York: Basic Books, 1980), states that successful bonding and developing a secure attachment is critical for a child to thrive psychologically.

effect relationships and associations are formed, and enable us to plan and develop goals.

The neocortex is essentially the brain's "CEO" in that its function is to discern and make the decisions the rest of our body puts into action. It enables us to make decisions and determine goals, to plan and organize, to monitor our thoughts and actions, and to be self-aware. It is the part of the brain that allows us to calculate the ramifications of the decisions we make (i.e., the "pros and cons" of options being considered), and as a result to control (or more specifically to inhibit) our emotions. It is the part of the brain that facilitates the capacity for human beings to have "free will", or what some propose is better termed "free won't": the ability to choose not to act upon the urges or impulses that may feel good in the moment but produce the negative outcomes we wish to avoid.

Human beings are uniquely capable of developing "delayed gratification", or the ability to anticipate the positive rewards of resisting what is immediately rewarding by choosing to do something that will provide greater long-term benefits. The importance of parents encouraging the development of delayed gratification beginning in early childhood was demonstrated in the "Marshmallow Experiment" conducted by Stanford psychologist Walter Mischel in 1972. Dr. Mischel tested over 600 children aged 4-6 to see if they could delay eating one marshmallow for 15-20 minutes with the reward of receiving a second marshmallow at the end of the testing period. About 30% of the children tested were successful in abstaining from eating the one marshmallow. But the rewards of waiting 15-20 minutes turned out to be much more than getting an additional marshmallow.

In following up with the test subjects 18 years later, Mischel found those able to delay eating the first marshmallow had average SAT scores 210 points higher than the non-delayers. In addition, the non-delayers were found to have more difficulty managing negative emotions, more behavioral problems at both home and school, more difficulty in maintaining friendships, and more likely to have alcohol, drug, and obesity problems.[105]

---

[105] http://www.newyorker.com/reporting/2009/05/18/090518fa_fact_lehrer#ixzz1hwprJodA. See also http://www.whatispsychology.biz/deferred-gratification-stanford-marshmallow-experiment.

Now you might be wondering, "What does all this brain science stuff have to do with experiencing more joy in life?" Well, the answer begins with realizing the neocortex is the part of the brain that houses what the Bible refers to as the human "mind".

Spiritual growth requires being "...transformed by the renewing of [our] minds" (Rom 12:2), which occurs as we learn the truths and principles God has communicated to us through the words in the Bible and begin applying them in our lives. The problem is when information doesn't lead to application. And there are two reasons for this.

The amazing thing about the human brain is how these three areas of the brain were designed to work in perfect complement with each other: the Reptilian brain enabling us to develop gross motor skills, the Mammalian brain to develop relationships, and the Neo-Mammalian brain to think, calculate and adapt in complex ways. But in the fallen world we live in today, these different parts of the brain often compete with one another.

God didn't intend for us to experience neglect, abuse, or rejection; the tragic accidents or other threats to our well-being, and traumatic stress these experiences generate. Research has found our limbic systems – particularly the hippocampus – are vulnerable to the effects of traumatic stress. [106] If we grow up in an abusive home, we quickly learn it isn't safe to approach others when in need. We learn our needs don't matter, anticipate people will hurt us rather than help us, and we are on our own in an uncertain and threatening world. These perceptions are generated at a subconscious level and generate powerful self-protective tendencies that make applying passages such as, "love one another" (John 13:34-35), "keep the unity of ... in the bond of peace" (Eph 4:3), or "be quick to listen, slow to speak, and slow to anger (Jam 1:19) difficult to apply.[107]

Consider the child conditioned to learn those who should provide care will inevitably hurt him- or her in some way. This child will grow up to become an adult conditioned to be on alert ("hyper-aroused" or "hyper-vigilant") to the potential threat anyone with power or position poses to him- or her. Or those who throughout childhood were told they are failures

[106] Ziegler, quoting B.S. McEwen, Brain Research, 886, 172-189.
[107] This will be addressed in more detail in *Chapter Five*

or will never amount to anything, and then grow up to become adults and are taught the Bible tells them they need not worry or be anxious, but merely think "good" or "pure" thoughts (Matt 6:25-34; Phil 4:6-7). While attempting to process these passages for application in the neocortex, the limbic system is screaming, "danger".

This helps us understand how reactive behaviors intended to protect us from harm become counter-productive. When we sense impending danger, our bodies naturally release hormones such as cortisol to enable us to protect ourselves from threats to our well-being.

Whether physical or psychological, threats generate feelings of anxiety, anger, pain, and frustration. The problem is we are prone to react impulsively to release the built-up tension and calm ourselves, only to regret the consequences of our actions. This alone can hinder us from walking in the joy and peace God desires for us.

Which leads to the second reason – one common to all human beings – and that is the fact that at the core of our very being is the same tendency toward rebellion that turned Adam and Eve away from God and toward self-satisfaction and self-sufficiency. The Bible tells us the fallen mind is darkened and ignorant (Eph 4:18), blind (2 Cor 4:4), corrupted (Titus 1:15), depraved (Rom 1:28), hostile to God (Col 1:21), and unable to perceive God's truth (1 Cor 2:14-15). Our fallen human minds innately seek to serve ME instead of GOD, rendering us vulnerable to Satan's lies and distortions (Gen 3:1-5; John 8:44-46). And this stems from the fact our minds tend to follow what the heart desires.

The "Heart"

The writers of the Bible present the "heart" as where life is experienced, where motives and passions originate, and where "wisdom" resides (Prov 2:10). But like the mind, the heart will either direct us towards, or away from, God. While the heart is the source of love and forgiveness (Matt 6:14; 22:37-38), it is also where sin originates (Matt 5:28; 15:19). And while our heart provides us the capacity to gain understanding and experience joy (Prov 8:5; 15:30), it is also the source of wicked plans (Prov 6:18), deceit (Prov 12:20), folly (Prov 12:23), bitterness (Prov 14:10), and pride (Prov 16:5).

While our mind equips us to learn both what makes us feel good as well as what causes pain and discomfort, it is our heart that generates the passions that motivate the actions we choose. An example is how an addiction to alcohol or drugs develops. Our mind forms the connection between the alcohol one drinks or drugs one uses, and the relief or pleasure they produce. Then our heart starts to desire drinking or using drugs, and that "passion" can become so powerful that even decent, well-intentioned people find themselves in bondage to the very chemical or activity they once found rewarding. This is why the Bible warns us of the importance of protecting our hearts:

> *"Above all else, guard your heart, for everything*
> *flows from it." (Prov 4:23)*

The things we allow to flow through our senses into our hearts have a huge bearing on our thoughts and beliefs. The question is, "What are you allowing to enter into your heart?"[108] Just as what you input into your computer will determine what it produces, whatever you allow into your heart will inevitably influence your words and actions:

> *"For a good tree does not bear bad fruit, nor*
> *does a bad tree bear good fruit.*
> *A good man out of the good treasure of his*
> *heart brings forth good; and an*
> *evil man out of the evil treasure of his heart*
> *brings forth evil. For out of*
> *the abundance of the heart his mouth speaks." (Luke 6:43-45)[109]*

Our heart is revealed through what we say whether words of faith and hope reflecting our trust in God, or of doubt and unbelief that minimize the power of God and His Word.

---

[108] An example is the profound impact of social media messages, as seen in the following quote by Dr. Edward Tufte from the documentary, *The Social Dilemma:* "There are only two industries who call their customers 'users': illegal drugs and software."

[109] See also Matt 12:34-35; 15:19; 24:48; Mark 7:21; Heb 3:12; 10:22.

The "Will"

The human will is the active expression of our minds and hearts. You might, for example, "will" yourself to get up early and go to the gym even if you don't want to because you've <u>learned</u> it is good for you and you have experienced some form of reward (feeling better physically and psychologically) because of it. Like exercise, the benefit of applying God's Word is an "acquired taste" that often begins with willing yourself to follow His guidance through a step of faith even if you aren't convinced it is in your best interest.

"Emotions"

The emotions we feel are influenced by how we interpret the events we experience. The grade on a paper or exam may generate emotions ranging from pure joy to despair. And simple words like, "promotion", "pay raise" or "cancer" will generate a strong emotional reaction based on how the ramifications of said turn of events will impact our well-being.

The Bible tells us we have the capacity to change how we feel simply through how we perceive and interpret the events generating them. Consider the following passage:

> *"Be anxious for nothing, but in everything by*
> *prayer and supplication, with thanksgiving,*
> *let your requests be made known to God; 7 and*
> *the peace of God, which surpasses all*
> *understanding, will guard your hearts and minds*
> *through Christ Jesus." (Phil 4:6-7)*

The moods we experience, however, are also a product of the neurochemistry of our brains. There is compelling evidence we all have a general "baseline" of the emotional range we will experience on any given day based on the levels of the neurotransmitters that affect our moods, and our capacity to enjoy recreational activities or to be motivated to work is dependent upon a proper balance of these neurotransmitters.[110] And while

---

[110] Lewis, Judith A., Dana, Robert Q., & Blevins, Gregory A. <u>Substance Abuse Counseling</u>, 4th <u>Ed.</u> (2011), Brooks/Cole, Cengage Learning, Belmont, CA, 44-46. These neurotransmitters are dopamine, serotonin, norepinephrine, GABA, opiate, and glutamate.

---

our thought processes do affect our moods, these discoveries have led to the development of psychiatric medications designed to help those prone to abnormally high rates of anxiety or depression due to an imbalance of one or more of these neurotransmitters.

God's desire is for us to experience joy in our lives (Gal 5:22). Now it is natural to feel at least some anxiety when facing difficult challenges, sadness when you've lost a loved one, anger when you've been wronged, or fear when feeling threatened. But feelings of prolonged anger, anxiousness, hopelessness, or despair suggest you may be well-served to explore the underlying issues causing them.

The "Spirit"

While we may see ourselves as physical beings who at times have spiritual experiences, Paul describes believers as spiritual beings living in temporary bodies awaiting the day we put on our immortal bodies (1 Cor 15:53-54). And while there are instances where "soul" and "spirit" are used interchangeably in the Bible, we'll contrast the two to explain how human beings are unique in our capacity to relate with God as spiritual beings.[111]

We've considered how the cognitive abilities God created us with sets us apart from every living creature that swims, crawls, walks across, or flies above the face of the earth. But in Genesis 2:7, we're also told God uniquely breathed the "breath of life", or a "spirit", into human beings. In the book of Job, we see the distinction between being "alive" and possessing a human spirit:

"As long as my breath is in me, And the breath of God in my nostrils..." (Job 27:3)

---

[111] The Greek word translated "soul" is *psuche* and can refer to one's physical life (Matt 2:20; Mark 3:4; John 10:11), the reflexive self (Luke 11:29; 12:19; John 12:24), inner emotions (Matt 6:25; 12:18; Mark 14;34; Luke 1:46); or the substance of life (Acts 20:10). Essentially the "soul" refers to the immaterial entity created by God, which is united to a body, gives it life, and exists after a human being dies. From Dr. Fred Chay, "A Diachronic Lexical Study of *Psuche*", Theology 502 Class Notes (Phoenix Seminary, Fall, 2000); and, Dr. Steve Tracy, "Human Constitution", Theology 502 class Notes (Phoenix Seminary, Fall, 2000).

Our spirit enables us to relate with God on a personal level. It is the human spirit that completes what we comprehensively refer to as the human "soul": the self-awareness that we are a human "being" that exists uniquely and distinctly as a part of God's creation. It is our sense of "consciousness" that sets us apart from all other life forms, and to this day stumps even the most brilliant thinkers in their efforts to explain the evolution of the species referred to as *homo sapiens* apart from the intelligent design of a divine Creator:

> *"Neither (psychologist) Steve Pinker nor I can*
> *explain human consciousness ...*
> *We don't understand it."*
> – Richard Dawkins, Evolutionary biologist

> *"Even the best computer in the world has no idea that it exists.*
> *You do. No one knows what creates that ineffable awareness that*
> *we're here, but there are plenty of theories."*
> – Steven Pinker

> *"So, how does the mind work? I don't know.*
> *You don't know. Pinker doesn't know.*
> *And I suspect, such is the current state of the art, that*
> *if God were to tell us, we wouldn't understand."*
> – Jerry Forder, "Reply to Steven Pinker, 2005 [112]

Human beings alone have an innate need to not only feel loved and accepted but valued and treated with dignity as God's "highest of creation". We alone have the innate need to determine our unique role and place in "tending and keeping the Garden" (Gen 2:15), and to experience a sense of accomplishment and achievement in doing so. But the advent of sin changed all that. Instead of serving God by tending to His garden, our innate tendency is to see it as <u>my</u> garden with a preoccupation of how much of it I can get for myself. Sin has rendered us spiritually dead and separated from God:

---

[112] Steven Pinker, "Consciousness", in <u>Your Brain: A User's Guide</u>, Jeffrey Kluger, gen ed (New York: Time Inc. Home Entertainment, 2009), 11.

"And you He made alive, who were dead
in trespasses and sins..." (Eph 2:1)

Spiritual deadness renders us unable to comprehend the truths of God – in fact, it renders God and His ways "foolishness" (1 Cor 2:14). The only thing that can make us spiritually alive is being "born again" through believing in Jesus as our Savior from sin (John 3:1-21).

There are two premises that set Christianity apart from every other religious system I am aware of. First, there is no system of works or deeds we can practice to be "right" with God or to earn His favor, as the Bible clearly states we are constitutionally incapable. And second, we don't <u>have</u> to, because Jesus did it for us (Rom 3:10-26). All we must do is believe this and accept Him as our Savior, and we are deemed "justified" and declared "righteous" through faith alone (Rom 3:24; cf Eph 2:8-9; John 3:16).

In the moment we are "born again", we are "made alive" and revived in our spirits (Titus 3:5). The Spirit of God becomes present within us, equipping us with the capacity to hear Him, comprehend the wisdom in His truths (1 Col 2:6-16), and through which we can be conformed to the image of Jesus (Gal 5:16, 25; 2 Cor 3:18) and experience *WHOLENESS*.

The challenge of realizing this transformation by living a life of faithfully trusting and willingly surrendering our lives to His will for us begins with addressing the effects of the sin virus on our souls. And this is summed up in what the Bible refers to as the "flesh."

The "Flesh"

In the New Testament the English "flesh" comes from the Greek *sarx*, which can refer to either our physical bodies or, "the human nature (and its passions), carnal". Insightful is *sarx* stems from a root word that means to "brush off, or sweep".[113]

While sin renders our body vulnerable to disease and disability, it still reflects God's design and can be used for good. [114] But this depends on

---

[113] Strong's Exhaustive Concordance.
[114] An example is the powerful healing effects of a simple hug.

the desires driving how we use it – case in point the devastating effects of physical or sexual abuse, which are products of our fallen or "fleshly" nature. The latter is described in Paul's letter to the Galatians:

"For what the flesh desires is opposed to the Spirit, and what the
Spirit desires is opposed to the flesh; for
these are opposed to each other
other, to prevent you from doing what you wish." (Gal 5:17)

Let alone questioning whether we can trust God, deep down we question if we even <u>want</u> to trust Him, as our nature is to "brush off" or "sweep aside" His plans and purposes for us in serving ourselves through what <u>we</u> think is good and what <u>we</u> want to do. The Bible tells us this inclination is something we are actually <u>born</u> with:

"Behold, I was brought forth in iniquity, and in
sin my mother conceived me." (Ps 51:5)

You probably wouldn't consider a beautiful new-born baby – that gift from God – as a "sinner". But we've all heard the two words that naturally seem to emanate from children as they begin to walk and talk and assert themselves: "no", and "mine"!

Children must be taught right and wrong: rewarding them when they do something good and disciplining them when they do something bad. Early on this includes teaching them to learn to "share" and to "get along" with other kids. But even the adult believer in Jesus remains afflicted with the sin nature and will battle the desires of the flesh. In fact, we may still live like the "natural man" through engaging in the "works of the flesh":

Now the works of the flesh are evident, which
are: adultery, fornication, uncleanness,
lewdness, idolatry, sorcery, hatred, contentions,
jealousies, outbursts of wrath, selfish
ambitions, dissensions, heresies, envy, murders,
drunkenness, revelries, and the like; of

> *which I tell you beforehand, just as I also told*
> *you in time past, that those who practice*
> *such things will not inherit the kingdom of*
> *God. (Gal 5:19-21; cf 1 Cor 2:14-3:4)*

Paul himself acknowledged the inner struggle he found himself engaged in:

> *For we know that the law is spiritual, but I am*
> *carnal, sold under sin. For what I am doing, I do not*
> *understand. For what I will to do, that I do not practice;*
> *but what I hate, that I do…For I know that*
> *in me (that is, in my flesh) nothing good dwells; for to will is present*
> *with me, but how to perform what is good I do not find…. For I*
> *delight in the law of God according to the inward man. But I*
> *see another law in my members, warring against*
> *the law of my mind, and bringing me into*
> *captivity to the law of sin which is in my*
> *members. (Rom 7:14-15, 18, 22-23)*

To be clear: Paul is <u>not</u> saying any hope of overcoming the flesh is an exercise in futility. Instead, he is calling it what it is: a spiritual battle we inherently will all have to fight. But to have victory we first must identify our enemy, to which we now look at works of the flesh that may be hindering your ability to experience the fruits of the Spirit. And we will do this by looking at eight vices that encapsulate the sin nature: The "Eight Deadly Sins".

THE EIGHT DEADLY SINS [115]

While you may be familiar with the *Seven Deadly Sins,* early Church Fathers such as St. John Cassian and Pope Gregory I included an eighth, referred to as *acedia.* These include:

---

[115] http://www.deadlysins.com/; http://www.bibleinfo.com/en/questions/what-are-seven-deadly-sins. https://www.atlasobscura.com/articles/desert-fathers-sins-acedia-sloth https://stjohntheforerunnerblog.blogspot.com/2017/04/the-eight-deadly-sins-st-john-cassian.html.

"Pride"

The Bible tells us that despite our fallen nature, we still have value and worth in God's eyes by virtue of being created in "His image" (Jam 3:9). Every human being is "fearfully and wonderfully made" (Ps 139:14) with unique characteristics, abilities, and areas of giftedness God desires to utilize to build His kingdom.[116]

As humble recipients of God's grace and mercy, it is God's intent for us to find our value, worth, and life's purpose through the gifts and abilities He has bestowed upon us. And as we employ these gifts and abilities in humble service to Him, we will have good reason to celebrate the work he accomplishes through us, while joining in and celebrating what He accomplishes through others as well. But pridefulness too often undermines all this.

Pride, also referred to as "Vanity", is an excessive preoccupation with one's own abilities and accomplishments and may also be revealed when negating or minimizing the abilities and accomplishments of others. Pride is evidenced by boastfulness and/or a persistent need for recognition. Instead of humbly thanking God for the abilities we have and the things we can accomplish, we are prone to proclaim, "Look what I did!" [117]

Foundationally, pride is a proclamation of independence from God. It is seen in the glorification of ME rather than acknowledging our abilities come from God and our accomplishments should be used to glorify Him. This is clearly seen in the Greek word *huperathanos* commonly translated "proud", which is a compound of two words that mean "above", and "light, lantern". In God's design, everything we do should point to the glory and goodness of God. But pride demands the light shine upon us instead of Him.

The Bible says a lot about God's perspective on pride.[118] Noteworthy is while exalting and giving grace to the humble, God resists (or "opposes") the proud (Jam 4:6; 1 Pet 5:5). Adam and Eve's pride is seen in their unwillingness to accept their role and place in God's creation, as well as

---

[116] Rom 12:6-9; 1 Cor 12:1-10; Eph 4:11-13; 1 Pet 4:10; cf Eph 2:10, 19-22.

[117] In his book, *Outliers: The Story of Success*, Malcolm Gladwell argues factors such as when and where we were born, and the material and educational resources available to us have more influence than our abilities and efforts in the success we achieve.

[118] See, for example, Jer 9:23-24; Prov 8:13; 13:10; 16:18; Gal 6:3; Rom 12:16.

their desire to "be like" Him through eating the fruit. They refused to accept what He determined was enough for them and rejected Him and His instruction through serving themselves. Instead of satisfying God, they chose to satisfy themselves.

Another example is seen in the Pharaoh of Egypt's pride-driven – and ultimately futile – efforts to thwart God's plans to deliver Israel from Egyptian bondage. Instead of accepting God had a plan and purpose for His chosen people, Pharaoh stubbornly resisted God's commands – only to see his country afflicted by plagues and his army destroyed.[119]

The epitome of pridefulness is seen in Satan – also known as Lucifer, the "son of the morning" and most beautiful of all the angels – and his obsession to "exalt his throne above the stars of God", but in the end will be brought down and cast into the lake of fire to suffer an eternity of torment (Is 14:12-15; Rev 20:10).

"Envy"

Envy is the desire for the status, traits, abilities, and/or giftedness that someone else has. Envy is a by-product of pride, as it reflects a general dissatisfaction with what I have, and wanting what God has given or allowed others to have. But envy will inevitably "rot the bones" (Prov 14:30) and destroy one's soul (Job 5:2), as it robs one of any sense of blessing and gratitude. And envy not only alienates us from God, but from others as well.

Despite having "everything they needed", Adam and Eve were dissatisfied. They lost sight of all God had given them and set their hearts on what God had but in their mind was keeping for Himself. So instead of asking and trying to understand why God instructed them not to eat the fruit of just ONE tree, they simply took it. And this quickly led to the blame-shifting and finger-pointing evident in the first conflict in human history.

"Anger"

Anger is manifested in negative feelings – and even ill will – towards another for something they've done or failed to do. And unresolved anger

---

[119] See *Chapter One*, Ex 5:1-13:30 (cf Gen 15:13-14).

will inevitably escalate to feelings of "wrath" or "malice", and a desire the target of our anger suffers in some way.

Anger is clearly seen in the person who is "venting", or "out of control". But sometimes anger is more subtly expressed in passive-aggressive behaviors such as the use of sarcasm, defensiveness, or using the "silent treatment" to punish another. And in some cases, "stuffed" anger – or anger turned inward – may manifest itself in depression.

A good example is the reaction of Cain when God rejected his offering in favor of Abel's:

> *"Abel also brought of the firstborn of his flock*
> *and of their fat. And the LORD*
> *respected Abel and his offering, but He did*
> *not respect Cain and his offering.*
> *And Cain was very angry, and his countenance*
> *fell. So, the LORD said to Cain,*
> *'Why are you angry? And why has your*
> *countenance fallen?'" (Gen 4:4-6)*

Here Cain appears defeated, even depressed, as his "countenance has fallen" (his head is hung low). But God sees what is really going on, as Cain is <u>angry</u>! And instead of humbly accepting God's correction, Cain lets his anger escalate into wrath, and then malice. And unable to vent his anger towards God, Cain turns and kills his brother (Gen 4:8).

Unresolved anger becomes resentment, which Nelson Mandela once so aptly described:

> *"Resentment is like drinking poison and*
> *hoping it will kill your enemies."*[120]

It is natural – and healthy – to feel anger when someone hurts or wrongs us in some way. God Himself, for example, is angered by the sins people commit – particularly when it hurts another person. The problem, however, is that our anger too often is the product of not getting something we want. And as Mandela once said it will eventually destroy us.

---

[120] http://www.quotemirror.com/nelson-mandela-collection-1/resentment/

"Greed"

Greed is the excessive desire for, and pursuit of, material wealth or gain. It is also referred to as "avarice" or "covetousness".[121] Greed is the kissing cousin of envy, in that while envy reflects the periodic assessment of what I have and don't have relative to others, greed is the insatiable drive to relieve the dissatisfaction reflected in envying what others have. It is seen in the response of early 20th century oilman John Rockefeller, who when asked, "How much is enough?" responded, "Just one dollar more".[122]

Greed is seen in the mindset of the two-year-old whose tendency is to say, "Mine!" But greed inevitably comes at the expense of others – whether through overtly taking more than one needs, or covertly resentment others for having what we don't have. And greed inevitably leads to poverty, brokenness, and emptiness, whether materially (Prov 11:24) or spiritually (Eccl 5:10). It is seen in the experience of Adam and Eve, who suffered guilt, shame, separation from God and each other, and were cast out of the Garden and relegated to a life of futility toiling the soil for taking what wasn't there's to have.

"Gluttony"

Gluttony is the excessive consumption of food or alcohol and other mood-altering substances. An important clarification here is it is not inherently wrong to indulge ourselves a bit – like most of us do – during the holidays or other days of celebration such as Easter, Thanksgiving, Christmas, or a wedding. And neither is it wrong to enjoy an occasional beer or glass of wine: in fact, God Himself told Israel it was an acceptable way to "rejoice" in the abundance God would bless them with if the people were obedient:

> *"And you shall spend that money for whatever*
> *your heart desires: for oxen or sheep,*
> *for wine or similar drink, for whatever your*
> *heart desires; you shall eat there before*
> *the LORD your God, and you shall rejoice, you*
> *and your household." (Deut 14:26)*

---

[121] See Ex 20:17; 34:24; Deut 5:21; 7:25; Rom 13:9

[122] https://starwinar.wordpress.com/daily-short-story/just-a-little-bit-more/

But noteworthy is when we do indulge ourselves a bit, it should be done "before (i.e., in submission to, and celebration of) the Lord" for what He has provided. As we've seen, this passage is one of the 613 laws of the Mosaic Covenant reflecting the terms and conditions required of Israel to enjoy the privilege of living in the Land God had promised her upon delivering her from Egyptian bondage. The point here is if Israel surrendered herself to His ways, she would experience His blessings and in turn be cause for celebration.

We become gluttonous when the provisions God created for us to enjoy and to sustain us become a "god" in and of themselves. Noteworthy is alcoholic beverages are referred to as 'spirits", which comes from the Latin *spiritus*, meaning "breath, breathing, air, soul, life."[123] Gluttony is turning to food, alcohol, and other mood-altering substances to calm anxiety, lift us out of depression, numb emotional pain, or to fill emptiness in one's soul.[124]

Gluttony essentially is the futile – and inevitably destructive – attempt to find life in God's provisions rather than His presence. As psychiatrist Gerald May so aptly states, gluttony not only hinders our ability to experience God, but is a form of bondage that robs us of our freedom, and ultimately binds us to the object of our desire:

> *"I have now come to believe that addiction is a separate and even more self-defeating force that abuses our freedom and makes us do things we really do not want to do. While repression stifles desire, addiction attaches desire, bonds and enslaves the energy of desire to certain specific behaviors, things, or people. These objects of attachment then become preoccupations and obsessions; they come to rule our lives.*
>
> *The word attachment has long been used by spiritual traditions to describe this process. It comes from the old French atache, meaning 'nailed to.' Attachment 'nails' our desire to specific objects and creates addiction…. [Addictions] enslave*

---

[123] http://www.atrlatin-dictionary.net/definition/35530/spiritus-spiritus

[124] We will see in more detail in *Chapter Five* how some due to trauma and abuse are more vulnerable to addictive tendencies.

us with chains that are of our own making and yet that, paradoxically, are virtually beyond our control. Addiction also makes idolators of us all, because it forces us to worship these objects of attachment, thereby preventing us from truly, freely loving God and one another."[125]

Gluttony inevitably leads to material, psychological, and spiritual poverty (Prov 23:20-21; cf Eph 5:18; Phil 3:18-19), as it reflects a growing compulsion and increasing difficulty in controlling how much we eat, drink, or ingest. A simple way to determine if you are struggling with gluttony is to ask yourself – and perhaps even more importantly those closest to you – the following:

- *Do I even occasionally eat, drink, and/or use more drugs than I intended or was prescribed (difficulty controlling how much I consume)?*
- *Do I find myself looking forward to eating, drinking, and/or using drugs as a way to feel better or escape some form of emotional discomfort?*
- *Is my eating, drinking, and/or drug use causing problems at home, at work, and/or is it negatively affecting my physical well-being?*
- *Do I need to drink and/or use more drugs to get the same effect ("tolerance")?*
- *Do I feel discomfort when I don't drink and/or use drugs ("withdrawal")?*[126]

If you or those you know you the best suspect you may be battling some form of addiction, we encourage you to seek the counsel of your pastor or a mental health professional.[127] We recognize it is difficult – and humbling – to admit you may have a "problem", something I know all too

---

[125] Gerald G. May, Addiction and Grace: Love and Spirituality in the Healing of Addiction. Harper Collins Publishers, New York, 1988.

[126] These same questions might be adapted to assess whether greed is an issue as evidenced in a preoccupation with shopping.

[127] The link below provides the diagnostic criteria used by mental health professionals to assess whether a person is exhibiting symptoms of substance use disorder: https://www.verywellmind.com/dsm-5-criteria-for-substance-use-disorders-21926.

well (more in *Chapters Four and Five*). But it may be the first step towards experiencing the life you want, and the life God wants for you.

"Lust"

Lust is the passion or longing for sexual fulfillment, but in a self-indulgent disregard for God's original design for sexual intimacy. While the Sixth Commandment tells us we are not to commit "adultery" (Ex 20:14; cf Deut 5:18), Jesus tells us that when we "lust" after (covet, want to have) someone other than our husband or wife, we are guilty of committing adultery (Matt 5:28). Given this, viewing pornographic material would be one expression of lust.

Just as gluttony is seeking life through God's provision rather than His person, lust is seeking life through God's <u>people</u> rather than His Person. God created sexual intimacy exclusively for a husband and wife to share their love by sharing their bodies with one another (1 Cor 7:1-6). In God's design, sex should be mutually fulfilling. But when sexual fulfillment is pursued lustfully, it reflects taking, not sharing. Lust is like a leech that attaches to and sucks the life-giving blood out of its host. While God has an infinite supply of love to give, human beings do not, and the result is the person used to satisfy one's lustful desires will inevitably feel used and discarded.

We inevitably act on what we allow to rule in our hearts, and lust – like the other deadly sins – is a clear example of this. But the destructiveness of lust is evident in the Bible, as lust "wars against the soul" and leads to death:

> *"But each one is tempted when he is <u>carried away and enticed</u> by his own lust. Then when lust has conceived, it gives birth to sin; and when sin is accomplished, it brings forth death." (Jam 1:14-15, cf 2 Sam 11:1-4)*

And like greed and gluttony, the lure of lust is powerful, and once acted upon can lead to a free-fall into addictive compulsion. This is described well in the following illustration:

*"Being carried away and enticed comes from
the language of fishing. The first
word describes the act of luring fish from
their hiding places. The second
word describes the enticing of fish as with
a juicy worm on a hook."*[128]

And while in the strictest sense lust specifically addresses an unhealthy and destructive desire for sexual satisfaction, we propose "lust" can be extended to include an unhealthy, need-driven emotional attachment to others. This might include an unusually strong need for attention, affection, and/or the affirmation and admiration of others, and feelings of hurt, anger, resentment, and ill-will towards those who fail to meet one's demands.

In extreme cases, a person prone to excessive dependence on others may meet the criteria of one of the "Cluster B" Personality Disorders including narcissistic (need for affirmation and admiration of others), histrionic (attention of others) or borderline (affection of others). Sadly, common in each of these disorders is having had experienced the devastating effects of abuse or another form of trauma during childhood.[129]

"Sloth"

Sloth is the avoidance of work and the failure to utilize one's God-given talents and abilities in a productive way. Sloth may also include feelings of resentment for "having" to fulfill one's responsibilities – whether at home, work, or while serving in the church.

While gluttony is seeking life through God's provisions and lust through God's people, sloth is the failure to identify, embrace, and live out God's purposes for you. Sloth may reveal a general dissatisfaction with the skills and abilities God has given you; rejecting God's proposition you are "fearfully and wonderfully made" (Ps 139:13-14); and as a result, the admonition we should work as if Jesus Himself was our boss, regardless of whether we enjoy and find our work responsibilities or conditions fulfilling (Col 3:23).

---

[128] Holman Commentary.
[129] https://www.medicalnewstoday.com/articles/320508.php

The Bible is quite clear in warning us of the destructiveness of sloth as it leads to both material and spiritual poverty (Prov 13:3-4; 24:33-34). And sloth is not only a sin against God, but against others as well. The person who will not work is essentially demanding others provide what one should provide for his- or herself and is disrespectful of those who are doing their fair share (Rom 12:10-13). The seriousness of sloth is seen in Paul instructing the Thessalonians to refuse even food to those who wouldn't work for it:

> *"For even when we were with you, we commanded you this: If anyone will not work, neither shall he eat...Now those who are such we command and exhort through our Lord Jesus Christ that they work in quietness and eat their own bread." (Thess 3:10, 12)*

One caveat we offer is the fact a period of "sloth" – a general lack of motivation and having to "push" oneself harder to perform tasks one usually completes without much effort – may reflect fatigue and the need for a healthy period of rest or recreation.

"Apathy"

While sloth is seen in a lack of effort, *acedia* – which we'll refer to as "apathy" – is seen in a lack of interest, enthusiasm, or enjoyment. While sloth refers to the unwillingness to put forth effort, *acedia* is seen in lacking the energy or motivation to put forth said effort.

Acedia seemingly begins with a sense of discouragement or disillusionment due to the lack of a sense of purpose or feelings of inadequacy and leads to a sense of listlessness. It is seen in those who exhibit symptoms of what today might be diagnosed as clinical depression. If you sense you are experiencing apathy, we encourage you to seek the counsel of a pastor, trusted friend, or mental health professional (Prov 20:5).

Searching Where it Cannot be Found.

In his book, *The Return of the Prodigal Son*, renowned theologian, professor, and Catholic priest Henri Nouwen reflected on his journey and struggles in experiencing God more intimately as he pondered Jesus' words in the Parable of the Prodigal Son, as well as Rembrandt's rendering in his painting of the same title. Nouwen wrote:

> *"To whom do I belong: To God or to the world?*
> *Many of my daily preoccupations suggest*
> *that I may belong more to the world than to God.*
> *A little criticism makes me anger, and a*
> *little rejection makes me depressed. A little praise*
> *raises my spirits, and a little success excites*
> *me…. I give all power to the voices of the world*
> *and put myself in bondage because the world*
> *is filled with 'ifs'. The world says, 'Yes I love you*
> *if you are good-looking, intelligent, and*
> *wealthy. I love you if you have a good education,*
> *a good job, and good connections. I love*
> *you if you produce much, sell much, and buy*
> *much.' There are endless 'ifs' hidden in the*
> *world's love. These 'ifs' enslave me, since it is*
> *impossible to respond adequately to all of*
> *them. The world's love will always be conditional."[130]*

Nouwen goes on to write:

> *"Addiction might be the best word to explain the lost-ness*
> *that so deeply permeates contemporary society. Our addictions*
> *(obsessions or compulsions?) make us cling to what the world*
> *proclaims as the keys to self-fulfillment: accumulation of*
> *wealth and power; attainment of status and admiration;*
> *lavish consumption of food and drink, and sexual gratification*
> *without distinguishing between lust and love. [They] create*
> *expectations that cannot but fail to satisfy our deepest needs.*
> *As long as we live within the world's delusions, our addictions*
> *condemn us to futile quests in the 'distant country', leaving*

---

[130] Henri J.M. Nouwen. The Return of the Prodigal Son: A Story of Homecoming. New York: Bantam Doubleday Dell Publishing Group, Inc., 1994, pp 42-43.

us to face an endless series of disillusionments while
our sense of self remains unfulfilled."[131]

Nouwen is describing the futility of allowing the desires of the flesh usurp the promptings of the Holy Spirit, and seeking fulfillment through position, power, praise, and pleasure apart from the presence of our Heavenly Father and the privilege of serving Him. And while words like "greed", "lust", or "addiction" may seem a bit harsh, if you've humbly examined your heart, you've likely identified at least one you are prone to.

WHAT NOW?

To which we say, take heart – because you are not alone! By virtue of being fallen human beings, we all will struggle with one or more of these issues at some point in our lives as while the Spirit of God is fighting for us, our flesh is fighting against us.

We make decisions daily that may profoundly influence the trajectory of our lives. After reciting the terms of the Mosaic Covenant to the *Entrance* Generation as they prepared to enter the Promised Land, Moses concluded with this exhortation: "*...This day I set before you life and death, blessing and cursing. Choose life that you and your descendants may live*" (Deut 30:19).

You would think their choice would have been obvious, yet they – like all of us "prodigal" sons and daughters – have moments when we allow our flesh to rule our thoughts, desires, and the choices we make. Case in point we return to Parable of the Prodigal Son.

In choosing the "prodigal" way, he finds himself down and out, destitute, with nowhere to turn. To which we pick up where we left off in the parable:

> "*But when he came to himself he said, 'How many of my father's hired servants have bread enough to spare, and I perish with hunger! I will arise and go to my father...'" (Luke 15:17-18a)*

---

[131] Nouwen, Ibid.

The Prodigal has not only dismissed his father, but disrespected him and everything he stood for, yet something in the Prodigal tells him his father may actually take him back! But will he? And if his father is in fact willing to take him back, on what conditions? Which brings us back to the questions we've addressed these past two chapters:

Can I trust God?
Do I really <u>want</u> to trust God?

And with that we will now consider the answer to both questions is a resounding, "YES!"

CHAPTER 4

RETURNING TO THE FATHER, PART I

INTRODUCTION

To fully grasp the significance of the Parable of the Prodigal Son, put yourself in the sandals of Jesus' disciples: all descendants of Jacob who were born and raised in Israel, a 1,500-year-old nation steeped in the heritage of the 613 tenants of the Mosaic Law. Again, these tenants were the guidelines under which the people of Israel would prosper in the Promised Land. The Hebrew word used to describe the blessings they would experience through following these tenants is *shalom*: the sense of peace, fullness, and wholeness available to those who choose to live in God's presence and according to His principles.[132]

In some ways, the people of Israel took these tenants very seriously, as each Israelites' actions affected the fate of the nation.[133] Judgment was swift and severe, and violations called for discipline as severe as death.[134] Yet, too often the people of Israel – like Adam and Eve and the Prodigal Son – set aside

---

[132] Strong's Exhaustive Concordance

[133] Note, for example, the nation would experience "blessings" or "cursings" subject to the collective actions of each Israelite (see Lev 26:1-45; Deut 28:1-30:20). An example is seen in Israel suffering a stunning defeat at Ai after God determined "Israel had sinned" when one man (Achan) kept some of the "devoted" things of Jericho that should have all been destroyed (Josh 7:1-26).

[134] Some, like murder (Ex 21:12; Lev 24:17, 21) are understandable. But consider death is also the consequence for adultery (Lev 19:20); kidnapping (Ex 21:16); worshipping false gods (Ex 20:2; Deut 13:6-9); blasphemy (Lev 24:16); false prophecy (Deut 13:5); working on (i.e., "profaning") the Sabbath (Ex 31;14-15; 35:2); and even for striking, cursing one's parents (Ex 21:15, 17; Lev 20:9-13), or being a "stubborn" or "rebellious" son (Deut 21:18-21).

some of these tenants in pursuit of the "desires of the flesh. Case in point is the 325-year period after conquering the Promised Land, as well as the moral decline that occurred after the death of King Solomon in 931 BC.[135]

Like Adam and Eve, God's patience finally wore out, and the people of Israel were banished from their "Garden of Eden" and subjected to the futility of "eating peapods" under foreign rule. Since 586 B.C., the people of Israel anxiously awaited their Messiah: The Anointed One who would deliver them from captivity.[136] Yet generations of Jews lived out their lives only to die in captivity. And many – like the disciples listening to Jesus teach this parable that day – wondered if God would ever deliver them.

But through this parable, Jesus wanted His disciples to understand that the story of their lives had the potential to end on a happy and hopeful note. Jesus wanted them – and us today – to understand two things: first, they could in fact trust that their heavenly Father wanted to take them back. And second, they needed to understand that *shalom* – the abundant life they desired – comes through the privilege of experiencing His <u>presence</u>, not His provisions. So, the two questions we now consider are:

Can I trust God to take me back?
Am I willing to trust God on <u>His</u> terms?

And with that we return to the Parable of the Prodigal Son.

THE ROAD OF RETURN TO THE FATHER

We left off with the Prodigal requesting his inheritance, traveling to a "far country", and blowing it all through reckless living. He is broke and all alone, with nowhere to turn and no one to help him. In his desperation, the Prodigal determines to return to his father:

---

[135] The 325-year period after Israel's conquest of the Promised Land is recorded in the book of Judges. The period after King Solomon's death is recorded in 1 Kings 11:1-2 Kings 25:30; 2 Chron 10:1-36:21. The prophetic books beginning with Isaiah describe the violations of the Law that eventually rendered God's judgment through banishment of Israel from the Promised Land necessary. Again, a timeline of these events is provided in the *Biblical History* chart found in the *Appendix*.
[136] See Is 7:14; 9:6; Dan 7:25-26.

"But when he came to himself, he said, 'How
many of my father's hired servants
have bread enough and to spare, and I perish
with hunger! I will arise and go to
my father, and will say to him, Father, I have
sinned against heaven and before
you, and I am no longer worthy to be called
your son. Make me like one of
your hired servants.' And he arose and came
to his father." (Luke 15:17-19)

In these three short verses, we see Jesus laying the foundation for what it takes to experience *shalom*, the abundant life, and the fruit of the Spirit we all desire.

1. Reflection: He "came to himself".

First, he "came to himself". In verse 17, the Greek word translated "came" is *eltho*, which means, "to appear, accompany, to go, grow". Essentially this means his circumstances provided him the painful but much needed "reality check", or "wake-up call", prompting him to take the proverbial "look in the mirror".[137] And he didn't like what he saw.

The value of a clean mirror is it provides a perfect reflection of what we can't see, and perhaps things we don't <u>want</u> to see. On a surface level it will reveal the blemishes we might cover up, the facial hair we missed while shaving, or any flaws in the hair cut we just got. But at a deeper level, reflection exposes the flaws or shortcomings we don't want to look at – nor have others see – as they leave us feeling embarrassed or ashamed.

We become willing to take that that proverbial look in the mirror when realize we've headed down a bad road and our lives are a mess. For the Prodigal, it was the realization he was broke, all alone with no one to turn to, and left eating anything he could find.

But any feelings of dissatisfaction we are experiencing are merely the tip of the iceberg – the cursory fly-by glance suggesting something isn't as

---

[137] This and subsequent Hebrew or Greek word translations in this chapter derived from Strong's Exhaustive Concordance.

it should be – and likely are symptomatic of issues that lie in the deeper recesses of our souls. To get at these root issues, we can take a cue from a few passages in the Bible. First:

> *"Be <u>still</u> and know that I am God I will be exalted among the nations, I will be exalted in the earth!" (Ps 46:10a)* [138]

There are three Hebrew words in this passage that warrant a closer look, as they reveal the intended meaning here. First the word translated "be still" is *raphah*, which means, "to cease, be still, weaken, to let go". It is not the casual, passing glance at the mirror – instead it reflects stopping and looking <u>closely</u>. But therein lay the challenge. Despite all the modern conveniences that allow us to take care of the tasks and household chores that used to consume a significant portion of one's day, present-day Americans have become increasingly busy and preoccupied. And for many of us, this busyness may be more about ignoring God's subtle calling for our attention than being productive.

Second, the Hebrew word translated "know" is *yada*. You may have heard the expression, "yada, yada, yada", which in the English is the "I know, I know" we may blurt out in frustration when life or a loved one is telling us, "I told you so". But this goes beyond knowing basic facts or principles, and to really understanding and comprehending the significance of that fact or principle. Which brings us to the third, and arguably most important word found in this passage.

Our English translations of the Old Testament fail to capture the number of Hebrew words translated "God" and the depth of meanings they provide. As we've seen there are over a dozen different Hebrew words used to reflect various attributes of His person and character. In this passage, the Hebrew word translated "God" is *Elohim*. And noteworthy is that in the New King James Version of Genesis alone, of the 196 occurrences in which we see the English "God", 179 – or 91% of the time – it is the translation of *Elohim*.

We presume this is because the book of Genesis is the "beginning": the story of how all things that exist came into being. And through using the Hebrew *Elohim*, Moses appears to be emphasizing the fact God alone is the

---

[138] See also Psalm 139:23.

self-existent Creator, and as a result He alone has the right to rule over all He has created. The problem, however, is that it didn't take long for some of God's created beings to begin to challenge that authority beginning with Satan, followed by Adam and Eve and every human being who has come after them.

If we really want to get at the underlying issues generating that gnawing sense of dissatisfaction, apathy, and lack of abundance in our lives, it begins with "being still". It requires putting aside the problems of the past and concerns about the future that preoccupy our attention in the here and now, for if we want to experience His presence we must stop moving and be PRESENT. It is only when we are still and quiet that we will realize – like Adam and Eve – that at least part of the problem is usually our desire to "be like God", and like the Prodigal to have things OUR way and in OUR time.

We may realize, for example, that our dissatisfaction with our relationships stems from the expectation others please US and see things OUR way rather than being willing to compromise and be at peace with them. Or it may be envying the positions or possessions others have that we want. Or it may be dissatisfaction with our physical appearance, our skills and abilities, or the opportunities He has provided us to utilize those skills.

And it may be revealed in a lack of close relationships; behavioral issues (substance abuse, gambling, over-spending, unhealthy eating habits) that have compromised your physical or psychological health, your financial condition and/or relationships with those closest to you; a lack of a sense of purpose or meaning in life; and an overall sense God seems very distant to you. And in these moments, we might consider:

> *"As water reflects a face, so a man's heart*
> *reflects the man." (Prov 27:19)*

TerKeurst describes this as follows:

> *"I can't always see what's inside my heart, but*
> *I can listen to what spills out."*[139]

---

[139] TerKeurst, p 101.

Dissatisfaction will usually reveal something about our relationship with God. We may be resisting His promptings, or unwilling to accept what He is allowing to happen in our lives. To this, we offer the following action steps. First, take the time to allow God's Word to reveal those areas of disconnect between you and God. As the writer of Hebrews tells us, the "word of God…is a discerner of the thoughts and intents of the heart" (Heb 4:12).

Second, invite the Holy Spirit to reveal those "inner secrets" hindering your ability to experience Him more deeply in your life:

*"Would not God search this out? For He knows
the secrets of the heart." (Ps 44:21)*

*"Likewise, the Spirit also helps in our weaknesses. For we
do not know what we should pray for as we ought, but the
Spirit Himself makes intercession for us with groanings which
cannot be uttered. Now He who searches the hearts knows
what the mind of the Spirit is, because He makes intercession
for the saints according to the will of God." (Rom 8:26-27)*

In his book, *Spiritual Formation*, Henri Nouwen proposed spiritual growth is a journey that occurs in a series of "movements" that begins with an inward journey to our hearts through periods of reflection. Nouwen termed this initial season as the transition, "From Opaqueness to Transparency" in which we begin to at once begin to gain greater clarity of Who God is and what He is doing as revealed in the Scriptures as well as what we are experiencing in our lives. [140] Our willingness to begin this movement is usually prompted through feelings of dissatisfaction and discomfort but is the road to discovery.

Through this process you may find the areas in your life in which dissatisfaction has crept into your soul. You may find you have been questioning His plans and purposes – perhaps even to question if He really cares about you. This is what the Prodigal came to realize.

---

[140] Henri Nouwen. Spiritual Formation: Following the Movements of the Spirit. New York: HarperCollins Publishers, 2010.

2. Regret: Realizing the price he is paying for his poor choices.

Through the discomfort of his dire circumstances, the Prodigal has come to realize his dissatisfaction and resultant demand to get his inheritance early so he could live it up turned out to be one huge mistake. It is seen in this sobering realization:

> *"But when he came to himself, he said, 'How*
> *many of my father's hired servants*
> *have bread enough and to spare, and I*
> *perish with hunger!" (Luke 15:17)*

Reflection begins with an assessment of our present situation, and concluding things aren't good and could be a whole lot better: for the Prodigal it was the realization even his father's hired servants are better off than him, as while they had "enough and to spare", he was "perishing with hunger". And in this process the Prodigal comes to realize not only what has gone wrong, but <u>why</u> it has gone wrong as well.

As the younger of two sons of a seemingly well-to-do business owner, the Prodigal not only had "enough and to spare", but an inheritance awaiting him that assured him he would never have to worry about his next meal. Barring some unforeseen disaster, the Prodigal was in the enviable position of being "set for life". But like Adam and Eve, he was dissatisfied. Instead of seeing all he had, he became obsessed with what he <u>didn't</u> have.

This may have begun with falling prey to playing the "comparison" game. In the ancient Near East, the first son to usually received double the inheritance of any younger sons (note Deut 21:17). Case in point is Jacob's scheme to prey upon his older brother Esau's vulnerability to swindle him out of his "birthright" (Gen 25:29-34). Perhaps the Prodigal compared his future with those of his elder brother, and resented the fact his brother would receive twice the inheritance he would receive.

But something else is implied in this parable. We can assume the father didn't just come into all his wealth – rather, he had prospered through hard work, developing the skills necessary to build a business, and the ability to manage his hired hands so his business would thrive and grow. The father had learned the wisdom of living a disciplined life:

"The soul of a lazy man desires, and has nothing; But the soul of the diligent shall be made rich." (Prov 13:4)

"The hand of the diligent will rule, But the lazy man will be put to forced labor." (Prov 12:24)

"The plans of the diligent lead surely to plenty, But those of everyone who is hasty, surely to poverty." (Prov 21:5) [141]

In his desire to live life to the fullest, the Prodigal learned hastiness leads to poverty. The Prodigal, humbled by the choices he has made, is willing to accept whatever he can get. But in his decision to return to his father, we see something else he has come to realize.

Nouwen insightfully observes the Prodigal's return to his father implies a "leaving". In the case of the Prodigal, he "journeyed to a far country" (Luke 15:13). Noteworthy is the English "journeyed" comes from the Greek *apodemos*, which is a compound word that means, "absent or away from one's people". This implies he not only left his father's physical presence, but the wisdom, values, principles, and discipline of his father that served to curb his youthful desires and impulses as well. As Nouwen writes:

"The farther I run away from the place where
God dwells, the less I am able to
hear the voice that calls me the Beloved, and
the less I hear that voice, the more
entangled I become in the manipulations
and power games of the world." [142]

No longer restrained by the guiding influence of his father, the Prodigal desires have "given birth to sin" and the "death" it brings forth" (Jam 1:14-15). He has come to realize the "grass isn't always greener on the other side of the hill". And you can almost hear him saying to himself, "If I had only known...", or, "I wish I knew then what I know now".

---

[141] See also Prov 4:23; 10:4; 12:24; 12:27; 27:3-4.
[142] Nouwen, The Return of the Prodigal Son, pp 34, 47.

Perhaps you've made choices or decisions you have come to regret:

- You left a comfortable job for the "dream" job that turned out to be a nightmare,
- You stretched financially to buy that "dream" car or house only to find yourself struggling to keep up with the payments,
- You've allowed yourself to get caught up in the snare of alcohol or drug addiction, or some other form of obsessive-compulsive behavior; or,
- You've gotten involved in an affair or business relationship with someone who turned out to be untrustworthy.

When this happens, we experience "regret" – that nagging feeling that accompanies the assessment we've made a huge mistake – and we're <u>paying</u> for it through the negative consequences we are now experiencing. And the Prodigal certainly has his regrets. But he is also experiencing something else: a profound sense of <u>remorse</u>.

3. Remorse: Realizing the pain his choices have caused others.

We feel regret when we make decisions that negatively affect <u>us</u>. But remorse is something different, as reflected in this definition:

> *"A gnawing distress arising from a sense of*
> *guilt for past wrongs, self-reproach"* [143]

Remorse involves regret as we begin to count the costs of the bad decisions or poor choices we make. But regret becomes remorse when we consider how our actions have hurt <u>others</u> as well. And for all his faults, the Prodigal has humbly come to realize this:

> *"I will arise and go to my father, and will say to him,*
> *"Father, I have sinned against heaven and before*
> *you, and I am no longer worthy to be called*
> *your son. Make me like one of your hired servants." (Luke 15:18-19)*

---

[143] https://www.merriam-webster.com/dictionary/remorse

For all his regrets, the Prodigal is also experiencing <u>remorse</u> in realizing that not only is <u>he</u> suffering for his poor choices, but his choices have hurt his father as well. He has disregarded the wisdom and counsel his father has painstakingly invested in him so he would thrive in life. He has disrespected his father by not only rejecting his counsel, but essentially wishing his father was dead so he could get his inheritance. And we can only imagine the distress and despair his father experienced during the Prodigal's absence,

In telling this parable, Jesus doesn't tell us how many times the Prodigal grumbled or nagged his father before being granted his wish. But we can assume they had numerous conversations in which the father encouraged his impetuous son to stay the course and follow in his footsteps and warned him about the dangers of the lifestyle he wanted. But the Prodigal persisted, and his father finally relented. And likely having seen too many lives go completely off the rails in living the "prodigal" life his son left to pursue, we can imagine how many nights the father worried about his son's well-being. And in his remorse, the Prodigal is only now realizing how his actions have hurt his father.

I came to learn and understand this all too well. Through my childhood and adolescence, I generally felt a nagging sense of insecurity and anxiousness. And I can still remember at age 16 the night when my buddies and I went to our first beer kegger party. Oh, we had our share of laughs, and we certainly had many good times. But I experienced something more: almost a sense of "nirvana" in which the anxiety and inhibitions that frequently haunted me disappeared after having a few beers. By the time I graduated from high school, I was the proverbial "weekend warrior" and poster child of *Loverboy's* song, "Working for the Weekend". But in college, "weekends" soon became 5-6 nights of the week, and my dorm room became firmly established as party central in our dorm.

While in college, I met and married my wife, Mary. But I – as they say in the AA world – became adept at rationalizing, justifying, and minimizing my drinking: I never missed classes, graduated in three years, and by age 21 had a job as loan officer at a bank. In my mind, a "few beers" was my reward for working hard and being responsible. But the drinking didn't stop despite the problems it began to cause in my marriage. A DUI and our third separation finally brought negative consequences and the regret I began to feel. And after a period of reflection and taking ownership for my actions, I also experienced a deep sense of remorse for how I had hurt the most important people in my life.

4. Repentance: "I was wrong, and I want to make things right".

While the Prodigal is certainly "getting what he deserves" through the consequences he is suffering, he has come to realize something else: his father <u>was</u> right. His father wasn't "lording it over" in demanding the Prodigal do things his way, but simply wanted the best for his son.[144] Like Adam and Eve after disregarding God's warnings about eating the fruit of that one tree, we can almost hear the Prodigal saying to himself, "I should have listened to him." And like Adam and Eve, the Prodigal has demeaned his father and is bound and determined to travel the long distance back home to make things right with his father.

In this the Prodigal is demonstrating what is referred to in the Bible as "repentance", which comes from the Greek *metanoew* meaning, "a change of mind". And with this change of mind is implied a resultant change in actions. The Prodigal is not only sorry for what he has suffered, but he also realizes that his poor choices have hurt his father, he no longer deserves the honor and privileges that come with being his father's son, is ready to change his ways, and is willing to accept being "like one of your hired servants" (v 19).

Due to our fallen nature, we are <u>all</u> apt to dismiss God and do things our way. As a result, it is only with at least some emotional distress we truly experience the repentance that leads to the changes God desires in us. Paul sums this up in these words to Corinthians:

> *"Now I rejoice, not that you were made sorry,*
> *but that your <u>sorrow</u> led to <u>repentance</u>.*
> *For you were made sorry in a godly manner,*
> *that you might suffer loss from us in*

---

[144] Note Jesus contrasts Himself with rulers who "lord it over" their subordinates (Matt 20:25; Mark 10:42).

nothing. For godly sorrow produces repentance
leading to salvation, not to be
regretted; but the sorrow of the world
produces death." (2 Cor 7:9-10)

As he wrote this Paul wasn't revealing himself to be a masochist who enjoyed inflicting pain upon the Corinthians. Rather, he is rejoicing in learning that by "speaking the truth in love" (Eph 4:15) through his first letter to them, the pain of remorse it generated within the Corinthians was sufficient to move them to "return" to God.

Noteworthy in this passage is the "salvation" Paul refers to. It comes from the Greek word *soteria*, which describes being rescued or delivered from danger, and includes being restored to a state of safety, soundness, health, and well-being (i.e., *shalom*).[145] The Prodigal has painfully come to realize his perception the "good" life is one of prodigal living was not only misguided, but in fact destructive and self-sabotaging as well. He has no expectation he will return to his place of privilege as one of his father's sons; instead, he is only hoping to be delivered from his present state of suffering.

5. Recognition: God is God, and I'm Not.

The Prodigal has come to realize that his rebellion against his father has left him alone, broke and with nothing to eat. He has – as they say in the AA world – "hit bottom". Having received "the gift of desperation", He is willing to return to his father, and has become open to doing things his father's way.

We may all find ourselves feeling "lost" at times and struggling to find our way back to a sense of *WHOLENESS*. We can glean some wisdom, however, from what the writers of the *Twelve Steps of Alcoholics Anonymous* found in their search for answers in the Bible:

> *Step 1: We admitted we're powerless over alcohol (or whatever your struggle is) – our lives had become unmanageable.*

---

[145] As seen in the Introduction to *Chapter Three*, it is the opposite of "prodigal" living.

Step 2: Came to believe that a Power greater than
ourselves (for us, that power comes through a relationship
with Jesus Christ) could restore us to sanity.

Step 3: Made a decision to turn our will/lives over
to the care of God as we understood Him.

Notice the Prodigal was willing to accept life on his father's terms –
even if it meant giving up the prestigious position of being "the owner's
son" and being reduced to the standing of "a hired servant". Like the
Prodigal, the founders of Alcoholics Anonymous recognized that to
overcome addiction, one must not only regret the consequences one has
suffered but repent of how one has "sinned" against God and others, and
to <u>confess</u> this to God and another human being.[146] This is accomplished
through the completion of *Steps 4–9:*[147]

Step 4: Made a searching and fearless
moral inventory of ourselves.

"Let us examine our ways and test them and
let us return to the Lord." (Lam 3:40)

Step 5: Admitted to God, to ourselves, and to another
human being the exact nature of our wrongs.

"If we say that we have no sin, we deceive
ourselves, and the truth is not in us.
If we confess our sins, He is faithful and just to forgive us our sins
and to cleanse us from all unrighteousness." (1 John 1:8-9)

---

[146] Note when confronted by Nathan, David readily acknowledged and confessed his sins
against Bathsheba and Uriah to God (2 Sam 11:1-12:13; Ps 51:4). While we are not required
to confess our sins to another human being to receive God's forgiveness, the Bible encourages
us to confess our sins to others as "the effective, fervent prayer of a righteous man avails
much" (Jam 5:16).
[147] Bible passages added for our purposes. Note the *Twelve Steps* were inspired by the principles
of the Oxford Bible Study Group.

*"Confess your trespasses to one another, and
pray for one another, that you may be
healed. The effective, fervent prayer of a
righteous man avails much." (Jam 5:16)*

*Step 6: Were entirely ready to have God
remove all these defects of character.*

*"Search me, O God, and know my heart; Try me, and know
my anxieties, and see if there is any wicked way in me,
And lead me in the way everlasting." (Ps 139:23-24)*

*"Trust in the LORD with all your heart, and
lean not on your own understanding;
In all your ways acknowledge Him, And He
shall direct your paths." (Prov 3:5-6)*

Step 7: Humbly asked Him to remove our shortcomings.

*"Therefore, humble yourselves under the mighty hand of God,
that He may exalt you in due time…" (1 Pet 5:6)*

*Step 8: Made a list of all persons we had harmed and
became willing to make amends to them all.*

*"If it is possible, as much as depends on you,
live peaceably with all men." (Rom 12:18)*

*Step 9: Made direct amends to such people wherever possible,
except when to do so would injure them or others.*

*"Therefore, if you bring your gift to the altar,
and there remember that your brother
has something against you, leave your gift there
before the altar, and go your way.
First be reconciled to your brother, and then come
and offer your gift." (Matt 5:23-24)*

The Prodigal owns up to the fact that his actions have not only hurt him, but his father as well. Yet despite his "selfish" choices, the Prodigal reveals something good about him: he has a conscience. He realizes he has no one to blame but himself and has accepted the consequences of his actions. And he realizes he has violated God's standards of right and wrong and is troubled by his violation of those standards. His conscience has been sharpened and brought more in line with God's, and the immediate gratification he enjoyed through his prodigal living now pales in comparison to the guilt he feels for he "sinning against heaven".

He has renounced his "right" to live life on his terms and is humbly willing to accept life on whatever terms his father is willing to have him back – even if it means being reduced to a "hired servant". He is willing to recognize God as *Elohim* – the Supreme One – and to surrender his life to the will and care of his father.

For me personally, it required some serious self-reflection. It meant becoming willing to return to the "father" (God) I'd dismissed years before. It meant completing *Steps 4-9* of AA, and making amends to people like my wife, my daughters, and other family members. And it meant then, and continues to mean today, that I accept His will as best as I can, trusting He will complete the good work He has begun in me (Phil 1:6).

6. Return: Turning Back to God.

Having recognized the error of his ways, the Prodigal is repentant: he is resolved to not only turn away from his destructive choices, but to return to his father and his father's ways as well. He has come to realize that life change involves not only turning <u>from</u> what isn't working, but <u>towards</u> something we are willing to trust will work as well. But notice the Prodigal's decision is demonstrated through a firm and formal action step as well:

"I will <u>arise</u> and go to my father…" (Luke 15:18a)

The Greek word translated "arise" is *anastas*, which means to "rise, stand up, to appear". You get a sense the Prodigal is saying to himself, "Today everything changes". There is a determination in this statement reflecting both intentionality and commitment. The challenge, however, is living out this decision would not be easy.

Upon receiving his inheritance, the Prodigal traveled to a "far" country. This suggests his journey back to his father was going to take time and would be difficult given it likely was fraught with numerous obstacles – one being the Prodigal was flat broke and had no money for food or travel. Bottom line: returning to his father would take some resolve.

Now it is easy to look at the Prodigal's decision and conclude, "Of course he went home – he's expecting daddy will bail him out". But he has humbly realized he deserves to be disowned and expects nothing. He has become <u>teachable</u> in his willingness to <u>surrender</u> his life to the will of his father. Whatever his father decides, the Prodigal will accept. He will trust his father's judgment and embrace whatever happens – whether good or bad.

So, the Prodigal sets off to make things right with his father. He is ready to confess to his father how he has wronged him. He is willing to submit himself to the will of his father with no reservations, and no expectations – even if means accepting the lowest level position in his father's business. For all his moral failings, the Prodigal appears to have become a new man – he has been "purified by the fire" of his sufferings (Num 31:23; cf 1 Pet 1:22). He is now more motivated by the desire to serve his father than the desires of his eyes, flesh, and ego. But, as he is traveling on the long road back from that "far country", it is reasonable to assume he can't help but wonder, "What will dad say?"

A WARM WELCOME HOME

To which Jesus continues with one of the most beautiful and heart-warming pictures of the love, grace, and mercy of our Heavenly Father you'll see in the Bible:

> *"And he arose and came to his father. But when*
> *he was still a great way off, his father*
> *saw him and had compassion and ran and fell*
> *on his neck and kissed him. And the son*

said to him, 'Father, I have sinned against heaven
and in your sight, and am no longer
worthy to be called your son.' But the father said
to his servants, 'Bring out the best robe and
put it on him and put a ring on his hand and
sandals on his feet. And bring the fatted calf
here and kill it, and let us eat and be merry; for
this my son was dead and is alive again,
he was lost and is found.' And they began
to be merry." (Luke 15:20-24)

Wow! The son has disrespected his father by rejecting his advice: the Prodigal has essentially wished his father would hurry up and die through demanding he receive his inheritance early. He went out and blew it all, and with nothing left has come home with his tail between his legs. But instead of a cold reception or flat-out rejection, here is how his father responds:

1. He "had compassion".

Rather than a cold reception or contempt, the father feels compassion for his son's wretched condition. The Greek word translated "compassion" is *splagchnizomai* (a tongue-twister), which means, "to feel pity or sympathy, to have the bowels yearn", and comes from a root word that means, "intestine". It implies the gut-wrenching, deeply moving sense of pity for someone who is suffering.

Since the Prodigal is flat-broke and starving, he is probably gaunt from a lack of food, and dirty and shabby from the long journey home. And being a wise and intuitive man, his father knew he had to let his son go and learn the lessons he had taught him the hard way and knows what his son has put himself through. He sees no need to punish him as the son has already punished himself through "reaping what he sowed" (Gal 6:7-8).

Can you imagine your parents – or anyone you've offended so deeply – responding like this? Most of us would likely understand if the father wasn't so moved. A reaction more like, "Maybe you learned your lesson", or "Next time maybe you'll listen to me" would seem more realistic, wouldn't it? But instead of being offended and telling his son, "I told you so" or simply blowing him off altogether, the father feels the pain the Prodigal has brought upon himself through his own destructive choices.

And rather than just standing there, waiting for the Prodigal to come to him, the father literally <u>runs</u> out to receive him! In this we see a powerful display of the unconditional love and desire to forgive the father holds for son, and God holds towards us – no matter how far away we "travel" from Him in our lives today. And then....

2. He throws his son a party!

The father is not only moved with compassion but throws the Prodigal a party as well! In Jesus' day, meat wasn't a staple in the diet of the common Jew: instead, it was reserved for only the wealthiest, or those rare occasions like a wedding celebration. But the father rolls out the proverbial red carpet – only the best for my son![148] And he isn't finished...

3. He restores his son to a position of prominence.

His joyful reception of his son absent a lecture, consequences, or a myriad of conditions is a powerful testament to his father's grace and mercy in and of itself. While the Prodigal's physical appearance is evidence enough of the shame he has brought upon himself, his father refuses to let him suffer any further. But the father goes beyond this. First, he commands his servants to "bring out the best robe" for his son. In Jesus' day, it was common for hosts to present a guest of honor with a ceremonial robe. His father is actually "honoring" him![149]

Then the father has his servants "put a ring on his hand". This would

---

[148] While providing His disciples a powerful illustration of the grace and warm reception will God joyfully extend to even worst of the worst, it is consistent with the imagery of a banquet He will use to provide them a picture of what the inauguration of His Millennial Kingdom will look like. See also Matt 22:1-14. Here, Jesus uses the imagery of a wedding banquet to communicate His union with His Church. Note all are invited and welcomed, whether "good or bad" (v 10). Note just days before also He utilized the imagery of a wedding feast to teach His disciples the example of humbly welcoming all guests (Luke 14:8-11).

[149] See Zechariah 3:1-10 in which the prophet Zechariah sees a vision in which God commands the "filthy" garments the High Priest Joshua is wearing be replaced with "rich robes" signifying his sins have been forgiven.

have been one of the family's "signet" rings, or rings used to seal formal documents. Given the Prodigal would have had a signet ring before setting out on his fateful journey, we can only assume he had either sold it for food or lost it blowing his inheritance during one of his "memorable" evenings out on the town. Yet he is not only accepted back and honored, but now fully restored to the position of prominence in the family business he once held as well.

Finally, the father instructs his servants to put sandals on his feet. The Prodigal had either worn out his sandals on his journey home or sold them for food as well. And while replacing worn-out sandals may not seem like a big deal, this, too, spoke volumes. In Jesus' day, servants and slaves typically didn't wear sandals or other forms of footwear. By replacing his sandals, the father is restoring him to the position of a free man, and through this essentially saying, "Any debt or obligation you owe me has been forgiven".[150]

The symbolism in these three actions is powerful: the father has graciously extended his undeserving son the robe of honor, the ring of inheritance, and the footwear of prestige.[151] The Prodigal son has been fully restored!

Through the Parable of the Prodigal Son, as well as the two parables that precede it, Jesus clearly wanted His disciples – and us today – to understand this is how God responds when we "return" to Him, no matter how lost we are, or how far we have "journeyed" from Him. [152] He is the compassionate father who understands His children will fall short and make mistakes, anxiously awaits our return, and celebrates when we do. He doesn't demand we first get our life right or prove our worthiness: rather, He joyfully accepts us back. He is the Benevolent Father who simply wants the best for us. He lets the painful consequences of our mistakes be our teacher and sees no need to punish us further.

Now, perhaps you have had a hard time relating to the Prodigal Son: you've never indulged in "prodigal" living and found yourself destitute

[150] Walter L. Liefeld. The Expositor's Bible Commentary: Luke, Frank E. Gaebelein, gen ed. Grand Rapids, MI: Zondervan, 1984; https://www.studylight.org/commentary/luke/15-22.html
[151] Nouwen, The Return of the Prodigal Son, p 112.
[152] See the Parables of the Lost Sheep and the Lost Coin (Luke 15:1-10) that immediately precede the Parable of the Prodigal Son.

and "eating pea pods". Perhaps you would say, "I'm a good person: I obey the Ten Commandments, I haven't killed anyone, stolen anything, or cheated on my spouse". Perhaps you can't think of anything you need to "repent" of, and in fact have had a hard time comprehending this is how God responds to the "sinners and tax collectors" who should "get what they deserve".

At the same time, you may not be experiencing *shalom* and the sense of *WHOLENESS* you want to experience in life. You may be experiencing feelings of discontentment, or disillusionment in your relationship with God. You sense "something's missing", but you haven't been able to put your finger on exactly what it is. You may be thinking life would be a whole lot better if you only had…. You may find yourself envious or resentful of the blessings God has granted others but seems to have withheld from you.

Well, as Jesus continues the parable, He may have provided some insight as to why.

A NOT-SO-WARM WELCOME

Up until this point, Jesus has told us nothing about the Prodigal's brother other than he is the older of the two (Luke 15:11-12). But now, Jesus introduces the elder brother and his reaction upon hearing of his father's gracious reception of the Prodigal:

> "Now his older son was in the field. And as he came and drew near to the house, he heard music and dancing. So, he called one of the servants and asked what these things meant. And he said to him, 'Your brother has come, and because he has received him safe and sound, your father has killed the fatted calf.' But he was angry and would not go in.
>
> Therefore, his father came out and pleaded with him. So, he answered and said to his father, 'Lo, these many years I have been serving you; I never transgressed your commandment at any time; and yet you never gave me a young goat, that I might make merry with my friends. But as soon as this son of

*yours came, who has devoured your livelihood with harlots,
you killed the fatted calf for him.'*

*And he said to him, 'Son, you are always with me, and all
that I have is yours. It was right that we should make merry
and be glad, for your brother was dead and is alive again and
was lost and is found.'" (Luke 15:25-32)*

Unlike his father, the older son is less than over-joyed to see his younger
brother has come home – in fact, he is "angry" and resents the fact his
father is celebrating the Prodigal's return, so he refuses to join the party.
And we are provided insights into why.

In contrast to his Prodigal brother, he has been the "Perfect" son, and
is not shy in saying so. He adamantly proclaims, "I never transgressed
your commandment", i.e., he has always done what his father has asked.
While the Prodigal rebelled against their father's instructions, the Perfect
religiously obeyed them. But then the Perfect reveals his true heart: he not
only resents "this son of yours", but he seemingly resents his <u>father</u> as well.

The Perfect feels his father has dissed him in not rewarding him for his
obedience.[153] But in this, he reveals his true motives: he's more interested
in his father's provisions than his presence. Like the Prodigal, he too would
much rather be out "making merry with his friends" than following in
his father's footsteps. And like the Prodigal, he too is dissatisfied – he just
hasn't been as honest and straightforward about it as his brother.

Perhaps your experience is more like that of the elder son. Perhaps
you have "never transgressed [His] commandments", and faithfully done
what you thought you were "supposed" to do. Perhaps you have a hard
time feeling compassion and extending grace to the "Prodigals" you've
encountered. And perhaps you, too, have had difficulty experiencing joy
in simply having the privilege of enjoying your God's presence.

The Perfect son seemingly represents many Christians in that while
he remained in his father's house, he was not experiencing the abundance
that was available to him. This is the case for those who go through life

---

[153] A short time later Jesus would address this mindset through the Parable of the Day
Laborers in which those who were hired first and worked a full day complained when paid
the same as those hired later and put in only part of a day.

waiting for something more while missing out on the full life that is already there for them to experience.

Vital to experiencing God's grace is realizing that sin is much more than simply "doing something bad" – and how much every one of us needs it. The Greek word most often translated "sin" in the New Testament is *hamartia*, which means, "to miss the mark". The imagery here is of a marksman shooting at a target. In a shooting competition, for example, you may win a competition because your shots hit closer to the bullseye than those of your competitors, even if you never actually hit it or came close to it.

The English word "sin" comes from a Latin word that means, "without". Obedience, therefore, is more than just not doing the "bad" things, but the absence of or failing to do something good. In the Sermon on the Mount (Matt 5-7; Luke 6:20-49), Jesus squarely confronts the human tendency to grade ourselves against the Law of God by comparing ourselves to others. Clearly, this is nothing more than an exercise in futility:

> *"As it is written: 'There is none righteous, no,*
> *not one; There is none who understands;*
> *There is none who seeks after God. They have*
> *all turned aside; They have together*
> *become unprofitable; There is none who does*
> *good, no, not one." (Rom 3:10)*

> *"For by grace you have been saved through*
> *faith, and that not of yourselves;*
> *it is the gift of God, not of works, lest*
> *anyone should boast." (Eph 2:8-9)*

What these verses tell us is: 1) we are <u>all</u> sinners who not only fall short of the perfect goodness of God, but have "turned aside" (i.e., avoided or rejected altogether) at least some of His standards; and 2) we are saved by God's grace alone rather than anything we have done – something the Prodigal has come to realize this all too well (Luke 15:19),

Perhaps one reason you are not experiencing joy and the abundant life is because you have yet to fully experience God's grace in your life.

While intellectually recognizing you are not "perfect", you haven't had that honest soul-searching moment of reflection, identified your shortcomings, and humbly sought God's forgiveness. And as a result, you have yet to experience the warm welcome home the father extended to the Prodigal.[154]

A LESSON FOR THE HEART

So far, we have proposed there are two issues reflected in the following questions that hinder our ability to experience the abundant life and the fruits of the Spirit: *Can I trust God?* and, *Do I really want to trust God?*

In *Chapters Two* and *Three,* we addressed factors that contribute to this inner struggle.

But there is more to each, which we will address beginning with the question, "Do I really want to trust God?"

By the time Jesus was teaching this Parable, His disciples had spent the better part of three years living with Him, listening to Him, and learning from Him. They had "left everything" to follow Him, as they had come to realize He wasn't just another wise teacher, but something much more: He was nothing less than the Son of God.[155]

Yet, despite all His diligent patience and efforts, His disciples generally failed to grasp the true meaning of the Mosaic Law, and how any favor we receive from God is solely a product of the mercy He has graciously given us. And this is seen in the following:

1. Resting on our Works of the Law

First, we – like the Perfect son – are prone to rest on our merits rather than rely upon His mercy by appealing to how well we are performing through adherence to His perfect standards. This is clearly illustrated in a parable Jesus taught a short time later:

---

[154] Nouwen, The Return of the Prodigal Son, p. 79. Nouwen insightfully observes the father "came" to the Perfect son in the same way he ran out to the elder son.

[155] See Luke 5:11; cf Matt 16:24; Mark 8:34; Luke 9:23. Cheney and Ellisen propose Peter's response of "You are the Messiah, the Son of the Living God" (Matt 16:16) occurred nearly a year before Jesus taught His disciples this parable.

> *"Two men went up to the temple to pray, one a Pharisee*
> *and the other a tax collector. The Pharisee stood and*
> *prayed thus with himself, 'God, I thank You that I am not*
> *like other men -- extortioners, unjust, adulterers, or even*
> *as this tax collector. I fast twice a week; I give tithes of*
> *all that I possess.' And the tax collector, standing afar off,*
> *would not so much as raise his eyes to heaven, but beat*
> *his breast, saying, 'God, be merciful to me a sinner!'*
> *I tell you, this man went down to his*
> *house justified rather than the other; for everyone*
> *who exalts himself will be humbled, and*
> *he who humbles himself will be exalted." (Luke 18:10-14)*

Notice the difference in the two men's prayers. First there's the Pharisee, proclaiming religious perfection: he doesn't break the rules, he fasts, and he tithes. The tax collector, however, can't even look upon God: he has reflected, and seen his imperfections. He is remorseful and repentant, realizes he is completely undeserving of God's favor, and that all he can hope for is God's willingness to extend him mercy. And this leads to the second way we are prone to resist trusting God through accepting upon His grace.

2. Rewriting the Words of the Law

Notice while both the Perfect son and the Pharisee rest on their merits rather than God's mercy, they also find the need point to the failures of the Prodigal and tax-collector, respectively, to bolster their case. Through this, they fail to heed a warning Jesus had taught His disciples early on in His ministry:

> *"And why do you look at the speck in your*
> *brother's eye, but do not consider*
> *the plank in your own eye? Or how can you*
> *say to your brother, 'Let me remove*
> *the speck from your eye'; and look, a plank is*
> *in your own eye? Hypocrite! First*

remove the plank from your own eye, and
then you will see clearly to remove
the speck from your brother's eye." (Matt 7:3-5; cf Luke 6:41-42)

In proudly proclaiming their deservedness, they are essentially "being like God" in grading themselves on a self-determined curve – something Jesus confronted a few months earlier when the Jewish scribes and Pharisees brought a woman "caught" in adultery to Him to see how He would discipline her:

"Then the scribes and Pharisees brought to Him a
woman caught in adultery. And when they
had set her in the midst, they said to Him, 'Teacher,
this woman was caught in adultery, in
the very act. Now Moses, in the law, commanded
us that such should be stoned. But what do
You say?' This they said, testing Him, that they
might have something of which to accuse Him.
But Jesus stooped down and wrote on the ground
with His finger, as though He did not hear. So,
when they continued asking Him, He raised Himself up and
said to them, 'He who is without sin among you, let him throw
a stone at her first.' And again He stooped down and wrote
on the ground. Then those who heard it, being convicted by
their conscience, went out one by one, beginning with
the oldest even to the last. And Jesus was left alone,
and the woman standing in the midst. When
Jesus had raised Himself up and saw no one but the
woman, He said to her, 'Woman, where are
those accusers of yours? Has no one condemned you?'
She said, 'No one, Lord.' And Jesus said
to her, 'Neither do I condemn you; go and
sin no more'." (John 8:3-11)

Like the father in the Parable of the Prodigal Son, Jesus sees no need to condemn the woman because she has repented, and like the Prodigal has learned her lesson. But like the father with his "perfect" son, Jesus finds it necessary to instruct these religious leaders and spiritual authorities what God's standards of righteousness really are.

3. Restricting the Width of the Law

This encounter reveals our tendency to narrow the scope of God's standards, and cherry-pick those we feel are most important – and ones we are more consistent in measuring up to – while conveniently avoiding, or outright rejecting – the more difficult ones:

- Offering God our "sacrifices", but failing to extend mercy and compassion to others (Matt 9:13; 12:7; cf Hos 6:6; Matt 12:9-15; Mark 3:1-8; Luke 6:6-11),
- Loving your friends, but hating your "enemies" (Matt 5:38-48; Luke 6:27-36),
- Praying or helping others to be thought of favorably by others (Matt 6:1-18),
- Obeying some laws but failing to help those in need (Matt 15:3-11; Mark 7:9-16),
- Regularly tithing but failing to practice the "weightier" (i.e., the more important) matters of the law, which Jesus said are justice, mercy, and faith (Matt 23:23).

The targets of Jesus' teaching were those who "justified themselves" by selectively adhering to some laws while failing to uphold what He considered the most important Laws. And Jesus called them out for it, going so far as to calling them "hypocrites".[156] But He also taught those willing to accept His teaching that the highest form of obedience – what God will "grade" us upon the most – is our response to those in need, whether materially, spiritually, emotionally, or legally (Matt 25:31-46).[157]

And Jesus summed up all of God's laws and rules in these few words:

---

[156] In Matt 23:1-39, Jesus used the word "hypocrites" <u>seven</u> times to describe the self-righteous of these same Pharisees.

[157] See also the Parable of the Good Samaritan (Luke 10:25-37). More on this later.

"This is the first and great commandment. And the second is like it:
'You shall love your neighbor as yourself.'
On these two commandments
hang all the Law and the Prophets." (Matt 22:38-40)[158]

Jesus wanted His disciples to understand "goodness" is being gracious and merciful. He tells the Perfect it was "right" to celebrate the Prodigal's return, because while once "lost" he is now "found".[159] This "favor" had nothing to do with what the Prodigal deserves, but everything to do with the heart of a loving father choosing to extend grace and mercy.

Equally important is realizing the same applies to the Perfect: the favor <u>he</u> has received has nothing to do with how good he has been, but how good the father is.

In fact, Jesus tells us that through his reflection, remorse, and repentance, the Prodigal – like the "sinful" woman caught in adultery – has become more understanding of God's grace and favor than the religiously-obedient Perfect. Through the painful consequences he has suffered, the Prodigal has come face-to-face with the goodness of his father. But the Prodigal has also come to understand something else.

While challenged to strive for "perfection" in modeling Jesus in our lives (Phil 3:12) we will struggle to come even close to reaching His standards of goodness.[160] Our measuring stick will inevitably be skewed somewhere on the spectrum from being too "gracious" (i.e., "forgiving", allowing even subtly encouraging disobedience) to being too "truthful" (judgmental, condescending, or critical without taking the time to offer help or direction).

Cherry-picking God's laws and resting on our own efforts enables us to avoid the humbling experiences of the Prodigal Son and the tax collector in the Parable of Two Prayers. But in doing so, we fail to truly encounter the "Great Physician":

---

[158] See also Mark 12:28-31; Luke 22:24-27; cf Rom 13:9-10; Gal 5:13-14; Jam 2:8-10.
[159] See the Parables of the Lost Sheep and Lost Coin (Luke 15:1-10) that immediately precede this parable.
[160] See Matt 5:1-48. The standards of God's Laws culminate with loving your enemies in the same way you love your neighbors.

"When Jesus heard that, He said to them, 'Those
who are well have no need of a physician, but
those who are sick. But go and learn what this
means: 'I desire mercy and not sacrifice.' For
I did not come to call the righteous, but sinners,
to repentance'." (Matt 9:12-13)

Refusing to reflect and humbly assess the condition of our hearts and the shortcoming this inevitably reveals is essentially "hiding" from God. But in the end, we end up cheating ourselves out of fully experiencing the joy that comes from encountering the depths of the grace and goodness of a Father who loves us so much He would send His Son to die for us. And it also prohibits us from experiencing the "inheritance" of abundance Jesus offers those who follow His example:

"Blessed are the meek, for they shall inherit the earth." (Matt 5:5)

The English "meek" comes from the Greek *praus*, which means, "humble, kind, forgiving, benevolent". Important to realize is meekness isn't "weakness", nor is it "inferiority" or "inadequacy", as it is a character trait Jesus ascribed to Himself (Matt 11:29) as evidenced through his sacrificial life and death for us.[161] Meekness is the biblical equivalent of "humility", which is:

"A lack of false pride, arrogance, pretentiousness,
or superiority; a disposition
of patience and long-suffering, a feeling of
self-respect and personal worth."

Since humility requires setting aside one's pride and ego, it is <u>not</u> something we inherently have, but something we must cultivate. We practice humility by regularly acknowledging our shortcomings and falling upon the grace of God. Instead of grading ourselves on a curve like the Perfect and the Pharisee comparing themselves favorably to the real "sinners" like the Prodigal and the tax collector, it is seen in acknowledging

---

[161] See Phil 2:5-10

we fall short of God's goodness, and any favor we receive from Him is solely a product of His love, grace, and mercy towards us.

In a way, the Perfect Son was every bit as lost as the Prodigal. While he hadn't "journeyed to a far country" physically like the Prodigal, his rejection of his father and rebellion against his father's ways rendered him every bit as morally and spiritually lost as his wayward younger brother was. But while the Perfect remains lost, the Prodigal – in realizing just how lost he was – has allowed himself to be "found".

The Prodigal has returned home, fallen at the feet of his father, and unconditionally surrendered Himself to the grace and will of his father – and whatever that means for his life going forward. And like the tax collector in the Parable of Two Prayers, he is now "justified rather than the other" (Luke 18:14).

In reflecting on his own spiritual journey, Nouwen writes:

> *"For most of my life I have struggled to find God, to*
> *know God, to love God. I have tried hard to*
> *follow the guidelines of the spiritual life – pray always,*
> *work for others, read the Scriptures – and*
> *to avoid the many temptations to dissipate myself. I have failed*
> *many times but always tried again, even when I was close to despair.*
> *Now I wonder whether I have sufficiently realized that during*
> *all this time God has been trying to find me, to*
> *know me, and to love me. The question is not,*
> *'How am I to find God?' but 'How am I to*
> *let myself be found by Him?'"*[162]

The answer is seen in the contrasting examples of these two sons. Like the Prodigal, it begins with the sober self-assessment of the condition of our heart, and humbly returning to our Heavenly Father. And unlike the Perfect, it is casting aside any sense of superiority and self-sufficiency and accepting the grace and mercy we each so desperately need if we really want to know Him. Which begs the question: "Are you ready to do the same?"

---

[162] Nouwen, The Return of the Prodigal Son, p. 106.

With that, we'll address some obstacles – some you may not be fully aware of – that may still be hindering your ability to experience *shalom* and the abundant life you desire. Which brings us back to the second question:

Do I really <u>want</u> to trust God?

CHAPTER 5

RETURNING TO THE FATHER, PART II

INTRODUCTION

There is a profound paradox in the Christian life. From the moment we begin walking we are taking the first steps towards independence, and by adulthood hopefully realized self-sufficiency: we have acquired the education and skills to be gainfully employed, we've learned how to manage our money, and have learned the social skills needed to develop meaningful relationships. But then Jesus tells us for us to have a meaningful relationship with God, we must become like "little children", or fully dependent upon Him:

> *"Then Jesus called a little child to Him, set*
> *him in the midst of them, and*
> *said, 'Assuredly, I say to you, unless you are*
> *converted and become as little*
> *children, you will by no means enter the*
> *kingdom of heaven'." (Matt 18:2-3)[163]*

Experiencing a sense of "heaven" in our lives today begins with regressing to a state of complete reliance upon our Heavenly "Parent". This requires a willingness to trust God will be consistently available and approachable in our time of need. For some, this can be a daunting

---

[163] See Matt 19:13-14; Mark 9:33; 10:13-15; and Luke 18:16-17. See also 1 John, in which the Apostle John refers to his audience as "little children" nine times.

proposition, and one you may find yourself almost instinctively resisting.

As we saw in *Chapter Two*, our childhood experience with our parents has a profound impact on our sense of safety and security in our relationships, and the prospect of diving head-long into childlike dependence again may generate more than a bit of apprehension. And His disciples' difficulty in grasping this is understandable given the fact God had expelled His "children" from the Promised Land 600 years earlier. This may have been a factor in Jesus using parables to help them come to know God as their Heavenly Father.

What the disciples and other Jews had yet to grasp was the meaning and significance of the New Covenant foretold through the prophets Jeremiah and Ezekiel.[164] Under the New Covenant, God's grace and favor is offered solely on Jesus' sacrifice on our behalf rather than our ability to live up to the standards of the Law. As a result, we can approach God with complete confidence, as there is "no condemnation for those in Christ Jesus".[165]

Through these Parables – as well as His gracious acceptance of the "worst of the worst" of His day – Jesus modeled the example of our Heavenly Father, who warmly welcomes us home just as the Prodigal's father welcomed his remorseful and repentant son's return. Now Jesus didn't provide explicit insight into the Prodigal's assumptions about how his father would receive him after his blatant acts of disrespect. But our hunch: the disciples assumed the best the Prodigal could hope for was maybe his father would take him back as a servant (Luke 15:18-19), and any favor he would receive would have to be earned.

Perhaps this is how you anticipate God will respond to YOU if you dare return to Him. Instead of a party complete with fatted calf, ceremonial robe, a new ring, and restoration to a place of honor, He will turn His back on you and condemn you. Despite everything the Bible says about His unconditional love, grace, and mercy, you are more than a bit skeptical of becoming like a "little child" and trusting God will welcome YOU home.

[164] See Jer 31:31-40; 32:40-44; Ezek 34:24-31; 37:21-28. See also Matt 26:28; Mark 14:24; Luke 22:20; 1 Cor 11:25; Heb 8:8-13; 9:15; 12:24. Both Jeremiah and Ezekiel prophesied to the "Exile" generation, or those Jews who experienced the fall of Jerusalem and the loss of Israel's freedom to the Babylonians.
[165] See, for example, Rom 8:1.

With that we will further explore how you – like the six blind men – may still be seeing God through the distorted lens shaped by your past experiences, and if this is the case how you can take a step of faith to see you can in fact trust what God says. With that we address the second obstacle some of us must overcome: *"Can I really trust God?"*

THE GARDEN, CATARACTS AND OUR DISTORTED VIEW OF GOD

You may be familiar with cataracts: a condition common in older adults in which a build-up of protein in the lens of your eyes causes your vision to become blurred or cloudy. Cataracts can be congenital in being born with a predisposition through infection, injury, or poor development while in your mother's womb; or contracted through secondary factors such as diabetes, the effects of toxic substances, or medications such as diuretics or corticosteroids. Cataracts can also develop through traumatic injury to the eye.[166]

We use the analogy of cataracts as an example how sin blurs or clouds our vision of who God really is. Recall Satan sowed seeds of doubt in Adam and Eve by questioning God's words and intentions, and through acting upon their desire introduced a form of spiritual "cataracts" into the world. And this condition is "congenital" in that we are all born with the sin nature and resultant blurred vision (Ps 51:5; Rom 5:12-14). Yet it is exacerbated through "secondary" factors such as our childhood experiences with imperfect parents, and if left untreated will worsen to the point we may lose "sight" of who God is altogether.

As you reflect on the father's reception of the Prodigal, consider: "Is this how your parents would have responded upon your "return"? Is this how your parents responded in your time of need, or when you simply wanted some attention, affection, or affirmation? And is this how they would have responded if you'd dismissed everything they had taught you, and disrespected them by bringing shame upon your family?

Would your father and/or mother have felt the same gut-wrenching compassion the Prodigal's father felt when seeing you hurting, then "come

---

[166] From https://www.webmd.com/eye-health/cataracts/what-are-cataracts#1

running" and "fell on your neck and kissed" you? Or would their response have been something quite different: something much less affirming, perhaps more condemning, and more like the following:

- If more "Authoritative", your parents might have been quick to point out your profound lack of judgment. Instead of a warm welcome, you more than likely heard, "We're glad you're home, but this better not happen again."
- If more "Critical", your parents might have chewed you out for not heeding their advice, pointed out all your mistakes, and perhaps called you a "mistake".
- If more "Distant", your parents might have given you the cold shoulder or the silent treatment, and not taken the time to even acknowledge your return. All you may have heard was, "You made your bed, now go lie in it."

You might be thinking, "My parents weren't perfect, but they did the best they could", or "That's all in the past". You're not into "blaming my parents for my problems", and just want to learn what it takes to experience the abundant life. Yet if you're honest, you may admit you are a bit ambivalent about God: a part of you really <u>wants</u> to trust Him, but you find yourself flinching and pulling away at the thought of it. Or perhaps the whole idea of God being a loving and caring "Father" just generates feelings of anger and disdain within you. And this may be symptomatic of more "traumatic" form of cataracts, i.e., <u>abuse</u>.

UNDERSTANDING "ABUSE"

Abuse is a strong word – one we don't throw around casually, and one you might be hesitant to use to describe your childhood.[167] While the concept of "abuse" is often limited to "beatings" or "sexual molestation", it extends far beyond this. In his book, *Mending the Soul*, pastor, and seminary

---

[167] The English "abuse" comes from either the Old French *abus* or the Latin *abusus*, which mean, "improper use, misuse, using up"
https://en.wiktionary.org/wiki/abuse

Professor Dr. Steve Tracy defines abuse as "the abuse of power over another individual that perverts the divinely ordained image of God".[168] This "perversion" includes the actions – or <u>lack</u> of actions – that disaffirm the value, dignity and worth God intended all human beings to experience. Abuse includes:

Sexual Abuse: Perversion of "One Flesh"

God intended sexual intimacy to be the culmination of a man and woman coming together in the union of marriage (Gen 2:24). It is a powerful bond when shared openly and willingly, but when exploited for another's sexual gratification the effects are devastating. Sexual abuse implies, "You are here solely for my sexual satisfaction." Also, important to realize is sexual abuse extends beyond penetration and groping to unwanted touching, or exposing a minor to pornography, sexual activity, or exhibitionism.

Physical Abuse: Perversion of "Let Them Rule"

Upon creating Adam and Eve, God placed them in a position of prominence in making them stewards over all His creation (Gen 1:26-28). He intended for them to tend to and care for His creation so it would thrive. Physical abuse is any show of force including punching, kicking, slaps or shaking – whether committed or merely threatened – and is a means of asserting control and venting anger rather than teaching, correcting, and promoting growth. Rather than building up, physical abuse tears down and hinders a child's development.

Verbal Abuse: Perversion of "Be Fruitful"

God empowered Adam and Eve with the words, "be fruitful and multiply, fill the earth and subdue it, have dominion over... every living thing" (Gen 1:28). Verbal abuse is the antithesis of this as rather than empowering and building another up, words are used to tear down and devalue. It might

[168] From Steven R. Tracy, Th.D. <u>Mending the Soul: Understanding and Healing Abuse.</u> Grand Rapids, MI: Zondervan, 2005, pp 27ff.

include statements like, "Can't you get anything right?", "You'll never amount to anything", or "You're worthless."

You may have heard the adage, "Sticks and stones may break my bones, but words will never hurt me", but this couldn't be further from the truth. "Death and life and are in the power of the tongue..." (Prov 18:21), and words have the power to penetrate, corrupt, and destroy the inner-most parts of our being (Prov 18:8). While empowering words are like the medicine that yields the "merry heart [that] does good", a preponderance of negative words yields the "broken spirit [that] dries the bones", produces "wrath", and generates "discouragement" (Prov 17:22; cf Eph 6:4; Col 3:21).

God intended words to be instructive – and when necessary, corrective – in "train[ing] up a child in the way he should go" (Prov 22:6). But words that highlight a child's faults and shortcomings absent anything positive generate a sense of inadequacy, inferiority, and unworthiness of the dignity and worth inherent in being God's image-bearer.[169]

Neglect: Perversion of "Cultivate the Ground"

While the above represent abusive actions, neglect is abuse perpetrated through the <u>lack</u> of action, and includes failing to provide adequate food, clothing, medical care, protection, supervision, and emotional support. While more subtle, neglect is equally destructive in communicating, "Your needs don't matter", or "you're not worth my time or effort."

Spiritual Abuse: Perversion of "Image of God"

Spiritual abuse is the use of one's spiritual authority to serve one's need for success or affirmation at the expense of others. It may include imposing one's authority to compel another to do something unhealthy or detrimental to that person's wellbeing, arbitrarily imposing unspoken rules upon others that are not applied to those in leadership or using Scripture or God Himself ("God said...", or "God told me...") to coerce compliance.

Spiritual abuse inevitably distorts the recipient's perception of the Person of God, as we innately need to be able to trust that our spiritual leaders reflect Him in some way. When spiritual leaders (pastors, elders)

---

[169] Ps 139:13-14; cf Matt 15:18; Jam 3:3-9.

abuse their authority at our expense, we will conclude perhaps God will as well. This renders us vulnerable to questioning His intentions and perhaps His very goodness as well.

THE SYMPTOMS OF ABUSE

The symptoms of abuse are extensive and include:

Shame:

Shame is a powerful emotion – one Tracy describes as, "the most powerful human emotion. It often overwhelms, directs, and transforms all other emotions, thoughts, and experiences." Dr. Tracy offers these definitions of shame:

> *"Shame is a deep, painful sense of inadequacy*
> *and personal failure based on the*
> *ability to live up to a standard of conduct –*
> *one's own or one imposed by others."*[170]

> *"Shame is a very heavy feeling. It is a feeling*
> *that we do not measure up and*
> *maybe never will measure up to the sorts of*
> *persons we are meant to be. The*
> *feeling, when we are conscious of it, gives us a*
> *vague disgust with ourselves, which*
> *in turn feels like a hunk of lead on our hearts...*
> *[Shame] is like an invisible load that*
> *weighs our spirits down and crushes out our*
> *joy. It is a lingering sorrow."* [171]

While painful, our capacity to feel shame is God-given, and therefore beneficial as it serves as a form of emotional cattle prod to steer us away

---

[170] Tracy, p. 74.
[171] Lewis B. Smedes, <u>Shame and Grace: Healing the Shame We Don't Deserve.</u> San Francisco, CA: Harper San Francisco, 1993, 5; quoted by Tracy, p. 75.

from wrongful thoughts and behaviors, and towards those in line with His moral standards.[172] The problem, however, is not all shame is legitimate, and as a result can be downright destructive.

To contrast legitimate and illegitimate shame, we'll first consider the relationship between shame and guilt. Guilt is the awareness of having violated a law or standard of conduct, rendering one liable to some form of disciplinary action. Given this, guilt is a healthy consequence for doing something wrong. Legitimate shame accompanies guilt in _feeling_ bad about doing something that violates said value or standard, generates the fear of rejection or reprisal, and moves us towards repentance and redemption.

But illegitimate, or "toxic", shame is a gross corruption and distortion of what God intended it to be. It is "illegitimate" if: 1) it is the result of an illegitimate or grossly distorted charge, or, 2) excessive in relation to the severity of the violation.

Victims of sexual abuse may take on the guilt and shame of doing something the abuser should rightfully suffer. And victims of physical abuse may feel shame for failing to live up to the standards of one's parents – whether said standards are legitimate or not.

Illegitimate shame is the weapon Satan used to convince Adam and Eve they were irredeemable and became the catalyst of their futile efforts to hide from God and each other. Illegitimate shame destroys the dignity and worth inherent in every human being simply by virtue of being an image-bearer of God. It generates a sense of inferiority and inadequacy, and tells us we are defective, irredeemable, and unlovable.[173] Rather than feeling bad for _doing_ something wrong, we feel bad for _being_ "wrong" or flawed. And it renders victims living in a perpetual state of fear.

Symptoms of illegitimate shame are seen in the form of:

- Chronic low self-esteem including feelings of inferiority relative to others, and difficulty believing God loves you and will unconditionally forgive your sins,

---

[172] Tracy refers to appropriately experienced shame as "legitimate" shame.
[173] Ibid, p. 76.

- Chronic feelings of anger, anxiety, or depression generated by a nagging sense of feeling flawed, inadequate, inferior, and uncomfortable in social settings,
- Frequent feelings of insecurity, or jealousy of the successes of others,
- A tendency toward over-work or perfectionism, or competing with others as a means of striving to earn a sense of self-acceptance,
- Heightened sensitivity to criticism, a deep-seated fear of rejection or dismissal, or a tendency to be hyper-critical of others,
- A tendency to shift blame (note Gen 3:12-13) or to accept too much blame,
- A heightened need to be in control of your environment, unease when forced out of your comfort zone, and impatience and/or difficulty in dealing with problems,
- Avoidance of introspection and transparency necessary for personal growth and developing close and supportive relationships with others,
- A tendency towards passivity or over-dependence in relationships; and,
- A tendency towards risky behaviors including substance abuse, sexual promiscuity, or other compulsive behaviors.[174]

Powerlessness and Deadness:

Secure attachment instills a sense of value and worth, and the sense of security stemming from the innate assurance others can reasonably be relied upon when needed. But insecure attachment – particularly when it involves abuse – instills a sense others can't be trusted, I'm "on my own", and the world is an unsafe place in which a person has little control over what happens to or around him or her. This leads to a deep-seated sense of powerlessness, resignation to the fact he or she will inevitably be hurt again, and ultimately a sense of "deadness". Symptoms of powerlessness and deadness include:

---

[174] See also Lynn Heitritter & Jeanette Vought. Helping Victims of Sexual Abuse: A Sensitive, Biblical Guide for Counselors, Victims and Families. Minneapolis, MN: Bethany House Publishers, 1989; pp. 45-46.

- *Hyper-arousal:*

Hyper-arousal is a condition in which we remain in a state of arousal long after a traumatic event has passed, and is experienced through increased anxiousness, being easily startled, sleeplessness, irritability, and for some nausea.[175] Examples are those who after repeated experiences of physical, sexual, or verbal abuse are on alert for cues signifying the trauma or abuse may happen again. Victims of abuse can be triggered by words or facial expressions reminiscent of those of his or her abuser – even if they occur years after the abuse and come from others who merely <u>remind</u> the victim of the abuser.

- *Intrusion:*

Intrusion is reliving traumatic events through flashbacks – whether awake or through nightmares experienced when asleep – and can involve intense emotional reactions such as panic or rage. The term "intrusion" is apropos in describing the experience of the victim who has limited if any ability to stop the memories from coming back to mind.[176]

- *Numbing:*

Hyper-arousal and/or intrusive memories render a person living in a perpetual state of agitation. Some cope with intense emotional pain through detaching or dissociating from their emotions altogether. This may occur through a sub-conscious shutting down of all emotions, or by using alcohol, drugs, or other distracting behaviors to numb them out.[177]

Isolation:

Victims of abuse, particularly childhood abuse, internalize the message that people will inevitably let them down or hurt them. They avoid close and vulnerable relationships and are prone to "mask" their true feelings since revealing emotions such as anger or sadness will only lead to chastisement

---

[175] Tracy, p. 97.
[176] Ibid, p. 98.
[177] Ibid, p. 100

or rejection. As a result, victims of abuse often feel a profound sense of being alone even when they are in the company of others.

Am I suffering the effects of abuse, trauma, or neglect?

A resource used to assess one's exposure to abuse, trauma, or neglect is the *Adverse Childhood Experience (ACE) Questionnaire.*[178] Research has found if you scored "2" or more on the *ACE Questionnaire*, you are at greater risk for numerous physical health issues, psychological disorders (anxiety, depression, substance abuse), and relational difficulties. A copy of the *ACE Questionnaire* can be found in the *Appendix*.

THE DEVASTATING EFFECTS OF ABUSE

A biblical example of the devastating and cascading effects of abuse is seen in King David's family when his son Amnon rapes David's daughter Tamar.

Abuse is an Attack on Our Value and Worth as Image Bearers of God

Tamar begs her brother to "not do this disgraceful thing" as it will bring shame upon her, and afterwards is clearly devastated as she "put ashes on her head", "tore her robe" and "went away crying bitterly" (2 Sam 13:1-19).[179] In the original Hebrew, Tamar – her virginity forever stolen from her – is literally shrieking in anguish. But every bit as devastating is the effects generated in the responses of Absalom and David:

> *And Absalom her brother said to her, 'Has*
> *Amnon your brother been with you?*
> *But now hold your peace, my sister. He is your*
> *brother; do not take this thing to*

---

[178] Its validity strongly supported by research, the *ACE Questionnaire* is one of the most widely used assessment tools in the fields of psychology and social work. The questionnaire can be found in the *Appendix*.

[179] These actions were ancient rituals of grieving common in the Near East. While

heart'. So, Tamar remained desolate in her
brother Absalom's house. But when
King David heard of all these things; he was
very angry." (2 Sam 13:20-21)

Absalom tells her, "Do not take this thing to heart". Put another way, he essentially says, "It's no big deal, so get over it". And David is "very angry" but does...NOTHING! Now Absalom didn't dismiss Amnon's actions outright, as we're told he <u>hated</u> him for what he did, and two years later would exact revenge for his sister by having his men kill Amnon. But David's response? He grieved the loss of his son (2 Sam 13:22-39)!

Add to this his failure to confront the offense – let alone offer her any comfort or support in her suffering was every bit as devastating as the rape itself, as it rendered her desolate.

The English "desolate" fails to capture how the rape affected Tamar, as the original Hebrew word *shamem* means, "stunned, destitute, destroyed, lay in waste". Here you get the idea of a person whose very life has been destroyed. And through this account we can also glean additional insights about the devastating effects of abuse.

Abusive Tendencies Are Passed Down in Families

The effect of parenting – particularly abusive parenting – is hereditary, in that we inherently repeat what we have learned, and are prone to parent in the same way:

> *"...For I, the LORD your God, am a jealous God, visiting the*
> *Iniquity of the fathers on the children to the third and fourth*
> *generations of those who hate Me..." (Ex 20:5; 34:7; Deut 5:9)*

This is seen in the pattern of deception practiced by Israel's patriarchs beginning with Abraham (Gen 12:10-20; 20:18) and repeated by Isaac (26:611) and Jacob (Gen 27:5-29).

It is also seen in Amnon following the example of his father David, who had raped Bathsheba (2 Sam 11:1-27). Other examples include repeating the pattern of yelling or using harsh words when angry or using threats of violence to intimidate others.

Jesus Himself alluded to the effect of childhoods experience in shaping who we become:

> *"For a good tree does not bear bad fruit, nor*
> *does a bad tree bear good fruit.*
> *For every tree is known by its own fruit. For*
> *men do not gather figs from thorns,*
> *nor do they gather grapes from a bramble bush."*
> *(Luke 6:43-44, cf Matt 7:15-20)*[180]

Experiences of abuse shape our perception of what is "normal", "healthy", or "good", and our tendency is to think, feel, and act in the same way as our parents, case in point is how Isaac, Jacob and Amnon repeated the behaviors of their fathers.

Abuse Renders Us Bitter and Resentful

Abuse to the human soul is like the infection that, if untreated, becomes the abscessed tooth that generates a persistent and throbbing pain.[181] Abuse breeds bitterness and resentment for the pain we've suffered, induces heightened sensitivity to the perceived slights we will inevitably experience, and limits our capacity to extend the love, grace, and mercy God has extended to us. If left untreated, the effects of abuse will hinder our ability to have trusting and mutually fulfilling relationships throughout our adult life.

Abuse is a Poison That Affects Us to the Core of Our Being

Perhaps you are suffering from spiritual "cataracts", as something is blurring your vision of your perception of God. You long for that trusting relationship with God others seem to have but are not experiencing. You know the Bible says God loves you, but you don't <u>feel</u> it in your heart. The following may help you understand why.

---

[180] See also Matt 7:24-27 in which Jesus furthered His point through the illustration of a house built on rock or sand.
[181] https://www.webmd.com/oral-health/guide/abscessed-tooth#1

Recall in *Chapter Two* we saw memories are formed in several parts of our brain. While some we draw upon consciously to make decisions throughout the day, others affect our thoughts, feelings – including our perception of ourselves and the trustworthiness of others – at a subconscious level. An example is seen in the effects of food poisoning.

Every year, roughly 48 million – or 1 of every 6 Americans – will suffer from the effects of food poisoning caused by the bacteria, viruses, or parasites in food that is undercooked or poorly packaged.[182] If you've ever had food poisoning, you know it is not a pleasant experience. Within a few hours you start experiencing abdominal pains and cramping, which is soon followed by vomiting and diarrhea. I have had food poisoning twice, both times around 40 years ago, yet to this day I can tell you what I ate, where I ate it – even the fact both incidents occurred after eating lunch on a Friday. And I remember vividly even the thought – let alone the smell or taste – of the food that caused the poisoning generated strong feelings of revulsion for a long time afterwards.

So how does this happen? Well, scientists propose through something called "biological preparedness" we learn to associate the food with the poisoning, which creates a strong dislike for similar foods to protect us from future poisoning and to enhance our chance of survival.[183] This "memory" is stored in the Reptilian part of our brain, which generates the *WARNING* signals you experience viscerally at something that poses a threat to you.

Now the food that caused the poisoning may have been something you've enjoyed many times in the past, and even eaten at a restaurant you've enjoyed on numerous occasions. It may have been that fluke 1 in a 100 experience, yet you found yourself avoiding that kind of food or that particular restaurant for weeks, months – even years – afterwards.

Food poisoning helps us understand the effects of trauma and abuse. These painful, frightening memories become engrained – essentially "encoded" – into the more primitive "lizard" or "dog" parts of our brains as a form of survival mechanism. Another example is the way you instinctively duck or throw up your hands to block an object coming at your head. You

---

[182] https://www.webmd.com/food-recipes/food-poisoning/food-poisoning-causes#1
[183] http://psychology.about.com/od/classicalconditioning/f/taste-aversion.htm

are not consciously thinking or assessing the threat that object represents to your physical well-being. Instead, your brain sub- or unconsciously generates the reflexive reaction to protect yourself.

It is also seen in the "flight, flight, or freeze" reaction generated when threatened. I experienced this in the Fall of 1992 when out on my daily run one nice Minnesota Saturday morning. The route I usually ran took me down a cul-de-sac where some residents had two 100+ pound rottweilers they kept in a large kennel in their back yard. But that Saturday the dogs were out in the yard as the homeowner cleaned the kennel. When they saw me, it was like someone rang a dinner bell, and "Breakfast is served". Before I knew it, one had bitten my left leg and the other my left arm. In reflecting on this I faintly recall learning, "Don't run when a dog is coming after you". But, instead of some kung-fu-like attack/defense response, I simply "froze". It wasn't a conscious, thought-out response but simply a survival-driven reaction.[184]

But these "survival mechanisms that have served human beings through history become debilitating for those who have suffered trauma or abuse through the strong feelings of fear they generate. Anything that reminds the victim of the abuse – a facial expression, a raised hand, yelling or screaming, or sexual intimacy – will generate strong reactions of fear. Even the prospects of making a mistake or being vulnerable and transparent will generate strong feelings of fear and aversion to taking the risk of setting and pursuing goals or developing close, trusting relationships with others, including God Himself.

To experience *WHOLENESS* and the abundant life, we must become like "little children" in letting go of our need to be in control and putting our trust unreservedly into the hands of our heavenly Father (Matt 18:2-3). Yet, those who have experienced insecure attachment or abuse have learned trust and vulnerability exposes one to disappointment, rejection, and pain. And despites all your efforts to use the rational thinking of the higher parts of your brain to apply the Bible verses that tell you that you can trust God unconditionally, you find yourself holding back. And the reason: you are likely being attacked by "fire ANTs".

---

[184] An excellent book to fully understand the effects of trauma is <u>The Body Keeps Score: Brain, Mind, and Body in the Healing of Trauma</u> by Bessel A. van de Kolk, M.D.

BEWARE THE FIRE ANTS!

At some time in your life, you've inevitably encountered ants. For the most part ants are only a nuisance: they get into your house or disrupt your picnic lunch. But for those who have spent time in the desert southwest, there is a particular type of ant – the *Solenopsis saevissima*, or red imported "fire ant" – that is much more than just a nuisance. Fire ants are known for their aggressive behavior (they are notorious for attacking poultry and  small mammals) as well as the burning sensation their sting produces.[185] You will experience their ferocity first-hand if you unknowingly step into a fire ant colony, as before you know it, they are swarming your feet and stinging you repeatedly. And add to the initial pain of their sting is a persistent itch that lasts for days.

Fire ants have a parallel in the field of psychology in what are referred to as "Automatic Negative Thoughts", or "*ANTs*".[186] *ANTs* are negatively framed interpretations of how we perceive ourselves, others, and what is happening in our lives. They are unconscious, habitual, and negatively affect our moods and actions. *ANTs* generate the tendency to assume the worst even if history tells us we have reason to be optimistic. And *ANTs* ultimately are self-sabotaging in that they will prompt us to doubt ourselves when facing an obstacle or challenge – at times to the point we won't even try and simply give up.

Some examples of the effects of *ANTs* include:

- "Catastrophizing", or the tendency to assume the worst, and view situations as "problems" rather than possibilities. An example

---

[185] https://www.britannica.com/animal/fire-ant
[186] The following references are used in this section: http://www.resilient-mindset.com/2012/10/22/negative-automatic-thought/; https://psychologydictionary.org/automatic-thoughts/; https://ahha.org/selfhelp-articles/ant-therapy/; http://www.paulelmore.com/therapeuticprocess/ants/; https://www.therapyinphiladelphia.com/tips/automatic-negative-thoughts-and-core-beliefs/; https://www.therapyinphiladelphia.com/tips/automatic-negative-thoughts-and-core-beliefs/.

might be the student who gets overly anxious about completing an assignment or an upcoming exam despite a history of doing well on similar assignments or exams in the past,

- A tendency towards "always", "never", or "all or nothing" (also referred to as "global") thinking rather than seeing each situation or circumstance uniquely,
- "Fortune telling", or the tendency to expect the worst possible outcome,
- "Mind-reading", or the tendency to assume others are thinking negatively about you – an example being assuming another's silence means he or she is mad at you,
- "Perfectionism", or the tendency to view anything less than "perfect" as unacceptable, and as a result to live in perpetual fear of failing,
- "Shoulding", or the tendency to beat yourself up over what you did wrong or could have done it better while minimizing or flat-out dismissing what you did well; and,
- "Labeling", or the tendency to attach negative labels like "idiot", "failure", "lazy", or "incompetent" to yourself or others. [187]

Those vulnerable to "*ANT*" attacks are prone to experience heightened feelings of anxiousness, fear, hopelessness, and depression. They tend to lack confidence in their ability to overcome obstacles, and doubt others will help them. *ANTs* are a product of what are called negative "core beliefs" about how you subconsciously view yourselves, others, and the world in general. The seeds of the negative core beliefs that produce *ANTs* are usually sown during childhood through insecure attachment experiences (including abuse) with one's parents or primary caregivers but can also develop through a succession of failures or painful experiences through adolescence and into adulthood.[188]

ANTs parallel the experience of food poisoning. You go to a restaurant you've eaten at numerous times without incident. But one day after a typical meal the telltale symptoms of food poisoning begin to set in, and the next 24-48 hours are a living nightmare. And you find yourself

---

[187] I personally am a recovering perfectionist.
[188] See the discussion on Attachment Theory, *Chapter Two*.

visceral
ly repulsed for months or even years at the very thought of going to
that restaurant – despite the fact reason tells you your one bad experience
was a fluke, and it is highly unlikely it will happen again.

"ANTS" BECOME "STRONGHOLDS"

While *"ANTs"* affect us cognitively and emotionally, they are a form of
spiritual attack as well. *ANTs* are referred to as "strongholds" that blind
us to the truth of and about God:

> *"For the weapons of our warfare are not carnal but mighty in God*
> *for pulling down strongholds, casting*
> *down arguments and every high*
> *thing that exalts itself against the knowledge of God, bringing every*
> *thought into captivity to the obedience of Christ…" (2 Cor 10:4-5)*

Strongholds are like the cataracts that form the "scales over our eyes"
that restrict our knowledge and understanding of God, distort our view of
ourselves and others, shape our value system, inflict "stings" to our psyche,
and suck the life out of our souls. And the English "stronghold" is an
appropriate rendering given it is a translation of the Greek *ochuroma*, which
means, "holding safely, a castle". An illustration is seen in the reaction of
the people of Israel when informed by the spies sent into the Promised
Land of the "strongholds" they would have to overcome in conquering
the peoples living there:

> *"Nevertheless, the people who dwell in the*
> *land are strong; the cities are*
> *fortified and very large; moreover, we saw*
> *the descendants of Anak there*
> *… and we were like grasshoppers in our*
> *own sight." (Num 13:28, 33)*

In the preceding verses, we're told the spies informed the people the
land was every bit as bountiful and plentiful as Moses had said it would
be. During the preceding months, they had seen God overcome numerous

obstacles on their behalf by delivering them from Egypt and bringing them to the land. Yet they let what appeared to be insurmountable obstacles blur their vision of what God could do, and resignation crept into their souls.

This is how a deeply engrained stronghold can cloud how you see yourself, and more importantly Who God is and what He can do in your life. You may be in an endless battle with compulsive behaviors you have been unable to break, adding more shame to that which already burdens you. And like the people of Israel facing the fortified cities and the giants inhabiting them, you may be resigned to believing things will never change.

Over the past 25 years in my work as a pastor and addiction therapist I have too often seen the devastating effects of trauma and abuse. Its victims experience strong and rapidly escalating feelings of anxiety and/ or depression, rendering them much more vulnerable to alcohol and/or drug abuse. During the initial assessment process during which I often use the *ACE Questionnaire* and the *Brief Trauma Questionnaire (BTQ)*, I find myself often commenting to the client struggling with alcohol or drug abuse, "With what you've suffered it would be a surprise if you <u>weren't</u> battling addiction".

ATTACKING THE "STRONGHOLDS" AND REMOVING THE "CATARACTS"

Our challenge is to remember Jesus is on our side. He understands as He, too, battled the strongholds Satan tried to put up in front of Him, as He was a victim of all five types of abuse. He was neglected when His closest friends abandoned and denied even knowing Him.[189] He suffered verbal abuse when repeatedly mocked and ridiculed by His false accusers.[190] He suffered the excruciating agony of physical abuse when beaten, scourged, and crucified.[191] He suffered the spiritual abuse of being falsely accused of breaking the Law, being empowered by Satan, and blasphemy.[192] And He

---

[189] Matt 26:56-75; Mark 14:50-72; Luke 22:54-62; John 18:15-18, 25-27.
[190] Matt 26:67-68; 27:29-31, 39-42; Mark 14:65; 15:17-20, 29-32; Luke 22:63-65; 23:35-36.
[191] Matt 26:67-68; Mark 14:65; Luke 22:63-64; John 19:1-2
[192] Matt 9:2-8, 34; 12:1-8, 24; 26:65; Mark 2:1-12, 23-28; ; 3:34; 14:64; Luke 5:17-26; 6:1-5; 11:15.

suffered sexual abuse of being stripped naked and hung on the cross for all to see. Jesus knows all too well knows the pain you have suffered, and the shame you have felt (Heb 2:18; 4:14-16; 5:8).

The construct of God Jesus presented in the Parable of the Prodigal Son would have been foreign to His disciples and other 1st century Jews. Despite Israel's failures to live up to the standards of the Mosaic Law and the resultant discipline God imposed upon her, the people still saw themselves as a nation God set apart to be His holy people (note Ex 19:6; Deut 7:6). And for all their shortcomings, they still recognized the importance of striving to live up to these standards to preserve their collective honor as a nation.

Their response, in what Georges refers to as an "honor-shame" culture, might seem foreign to many of us raised in the more individualistic "innocence-guilt" cultures more common to Western industrialized countries.[193] Americans, for example, might see the consequences the Prodigal brought upon himself as punishment enough. But for 1st century Jews, his actions represented what Nouwen describes as:

> "…a drastic cutting loose from the way of living,
> thinking and acting that had been
> handed down to him from generation to
> generation as a sacred legacy. More than
> disrespect it is a betrayal of the treasured
> values of family and community."[194]

Given this, violating the "code" brought shame not only upon himself, but upon his family and community as well, and strong measures were taken to keep people in line. In their day it was considered shameful for a Jewish man to waste his family's inheritance, particularly if he squandered it amongst the Gentiles (non-Jews), and even more if it involved an immoral woman. Recall the Prodigal had gone to a "faraway country" – presumably a Gentile area – where he blew all his inheritance on indulgent living that, as his brother implies, included engaging with prostitutes (Luke 15:30). The Prodigal had seriously violated all three of these social norms, and

[193] Georges, The 3D Gospel: Ministry in Guilt, Shame, and Fear Cultures.
[194] Nouwen, The Return of the Prodigal Son., p. 36.

the community would have responded firmly and harshly by conducting a *kezazah* ceremony.[195]

According to the tradition of the day, his fellow villagers would have gathered around the Prodigal, broken jars with corn and nuts, and declared him cut off and cast out of their village. And as His disciples are hearing Jesus tell this parable, it is likely that's what they expected to hear. But as we've seen, the Prodigal's father was having none of this.

In a marked break from tradition, he runs out to receive his son before he arrives at the city gates. And in doing this, he not only spares the Prodigal from being shamed by his fellow countrymen but brings shame upon <u>himself</u> as well! In their day it was considered shameful for any Jewish man to run. Add to this the fact it was also considered shameful for a Jewish man to expose his legs, so men wore robes that extended to their ankles. Given this, the father would have had to hike up his robes to enable him to run to his son. Let alone the shame and embarrassment any father would have felt for the Prodigal's grievous errors, the father has sacrificed his own honor by graciously drawing the attention of those ready to bring condemnation upon his son by shaming himself![196]

Through His portrayal of the father in the Parable of the Prodigal Son, Jesus provides a powerful picture of the depths of God's unconditional love and regard for each and every one of us. Jesus wanted to remove the "cataracts" of His audience so they could see God with 20/20 vision. And while a fictitious illustration, it was a precursor of what would become reality a few short months later when Jesus – the Christ, and the Son of the Living God – knowingly and willingly died on the cross for our sins (Matt 16:16; Is 52:13-53:12).

Jesus – Who never sinned and had no reason to suffer shame – essentially became the Prodigal Son in taking on the guilt and shame of the world. He voluntarily departed the perfect purity of heaven, and

---

[195] The following from: https://www.patheos.com/progressive-christian/prodigal-son-alyce-mckenzie-03-04-2013; https://www.thegospelcoalition.org/blogs/trevin-wax/prodigal-son-9-the-running-father/; http://magazine.biola.edu/article/10-summer/the-prodigal-sons-father-shouldnt-have-run/

[196] The following from: https://www.patheos.com/progressive-christian/prodigal-son-alyce-mckenzie-03-04-2013; https://www.thegospelcoalition.org/blogs/trevin-wax/prodigal-son-9-the-running-father/; http://magazine.biola.edu/article/10-summer/the-prodigal-sons-father-shouldnt-have-run/

"journeyed" to the "faraway country" of our fallen world to "bear our griefs", "carry our sorrows", be "wounded for our transgressions", and to be "bruised for our iniquities" (Is 52:13-53:12). But He also became the father through shaming Himself by "running out" to us in our fallen world to save us. Yes, His splendor is arguably best seen in His suffering on our behalf rather than in His sovereignty. And that should render us eternally grateful, and better able to see Him for who He truly is.[197]

Which prompts the question: How do we exterminate the *ANTs* and tear down the strongholds that hinder our ability to experience *WHOLENESS* and the fruit of the Spirit? Recall Adam and Eve's problems began when they listened to Satan's lies and gave in to their desires, which brought shame and resulted in separation from God and each other.

Charles Kraft proposes there are three encounters vital to experiencing freedom and victory in our spiritual lives.[198] These encounters include:

1. The "Truth" Encounter: Realizing this is a battle of the mind.

The Apostle Paul tells us renewal begins in the mind:

> *"And do not be conformed to this world, but be*
> *transformed by the renewing of your mind,*
> *that you may prove what is that good and acceptable*
> *and perfect will of God." (Rom 12:2)*

To which Jesus used the illustration of the foundation of a house to illustrate the renewal that begins in the mind and penetrates deep into the very foundation of our being:

> *"Therefore, whoever hears these sayings of Mine,*
> *and does them, I will liken him to a*
> *wise man who built his house on the rock: and*
> *the rain descended, the floods came, and*

---

[197] Sitter, quoting Wolterstorff, p. 133.
[198] See, Charles Kraft, "What Kind of Encounters Do We Need in Our Christian Witness?"

the winds blew and beat on that house; and it did
not fall, for it was founded on the rock.
But everyone who hears these sayings of Mine, and
does not do them, will be like a foolish
man who built his house on the sand: and the
rain descended, the floods came, and the
winds blew and beat on that house; and it fell.
And great was its fall." (Matt 7:24-27)

The "truth" begins with an accurate understanding of the Person of God. But it also includes an accurate assessment of YOU, and even more importantly how God sees you. Symptoms that reveal areas where the lies of the enemy have a hold on you include:

- Frequent feelings of anger, resentment, anxiety, depression, or hopelessness,
- Feelings of uncertainty or apprehension in new and unfamiliar situations,
- Impatience and/or difficulty dealing with problems,
- A tendency to avoid asking for help or allowing people to get to know you,
- Taking criticism of your performance personally,
- A tendency towards passivity or aggression when in conflict with others; or,
- Coping with the above through compulsive behaviors.

In addressing the psycho-spiritual factors that lead to the development of addiction, psychiatrist Gerald May proposes these tendencies begin when we give up our freedom by "attaching" and becoming "enslaved" to people, objects, substances, or behaviors to cope with stress or feelings of emptiness. Underlying these behaviors is our thinking:

"Another complicating factor is that behavior
is not limited to external physical
activity. Thinking is also a behavior, a 'doing'.
Thus images, memories, fantasies, ideas,

concepts, and even certain feeling states can
become objects of attachment... "[199]

Overcoming problem behaviors begins with overcoming the habitual thought processes rooted in ANTs that become our strongholds. This is the "transformation" Paul wrote of that occurs when our minds are renewed through digging up the faulty foundation that is like the "sand" Jesus referred to. It begins by identifying and putting off the lies and faulty thinking that generates doubt, despair, and distrust in God, our self, and others:

> *"But you have not so learned Christ, if indeed*
> *you have heard Him and have been*
> *taught by Him, as the truth is in Jesus: that*
> *you put off, concerning your former*
> *conduct, the old man which grows corrupt*
> *according to the deceitful lusts, and be*
> *renewed in the spirit of your mind, and that*
> *you put on the new man which was*
> *created according to God, in true righteousness*
> *and holiness." (Eph 4:20-24)*

We put on this new "me" through embracing our new identity as beloved children of God we have the moment we accepted Jesus as our Savior, and the freedom of knowing it is not a product of our successes or failures, but the victory Jesus had on our behalf:

> *"Now the Lord is the Spirit; and where the Spirit*
> *of the Lord is, there is liberty. But we all,*
> *with unveiled face, beholding as in a mirror the*
> *glory of the Lord, are being transformed*
> *into the same image from glory to glory, just as by*
> *the Spirit of the Lord." (2 Cor 3:17-18)* [200]

---

[199] Gerald G. May, Addiction and Grace: Love and Spirituality in the Healing of Addiction. Harper Collins Publishers, New York, 1988, pp 3,
[200] Several passages that define our new identity in Christ are provided in the *Appendix*.

But just as God wants you to see yourself as He sees you, Satan is every bit as desiring to keep you captive to the lies that keep you conformed to that old image.

2. The "Power" Encounter: Engage the Holy Spirit to reveal the lies hindering you.

How much power are we giving the enemy to control our thoughts, feelings, and actions? By listening to the serpent, Adam and Eve gave him the power of influence in questioning God's motives and convincing them they deserved the fruit and there would be no harm in eating it. It might be Satan using lies to convince us we are unworthy or will never measure up, we can't trust others, or we are being cheated out of something we deserve.

These lies can be so deeply engrained in our psyche that we have difficulty identifying them, even if we're aware of how we are reacting to them. And Satan uses them to stir up feelings of fear, powerlessness, and resentment. But this is not what God intends for us:

"For God has not given us a spirit of fear, but of power and of love and of a sound mind." (2 Tim 1:7)

This may include taking the time to process a situation that has caused you distress – whether anger, anxiety, discouragement, or despair – by addressing the following:

- What am I feeling (i.e., anxious, frustrated, discouraged, doubtful, etc.)?
- What is the issue or situation that is causing me to feel this?
- What am I afraid will happen or not happen, and how will it negatively affect me?
- How will God bring good out of this situation if I am willing to trust Him for the outcome (Rom 8:28)? [201]

But it may begin with reconciling any unresolved regrets and the shame that continues to burden you. Our relationship with God begins

---

[201] There are two worksheets provided at the end of this chapter that provide a guide to begin eliminating your *ANTs*.

with the "gospel" (the "Good News") that Jesus died for our sins so we can be reconciled with Him (John 3:16). Consider:

"Surely He has borne our griefs and carried our sorrows; yet we esteemed Him stricken, smitten by God, and afflicted. But He was wounded for our transgressions, He was bruised for our iniquities, the chastisement for our peace was upon Him, And by His stripes we are healed." (Is 53:4-5)

"For to this you were called because Christ also suffered for us, leaving us an example, that you should follow His steps: 'Who committed no sin, nor was deceit found in His mouth'; who, when He was reviled, did not revile in return; when He suffered, He did not threaten, but committed Himself to Him who judges righteously, who Himself bore our sins in His own body on the tree, that we, having died to sins, might live for righteousness -- by whose stripes you were healed." (1 Pet 2:21-24)

Notice the freedom His suffering provides us, the fresh start we can confidently claim, and the resultant joy and abundance we can experience as seen in the following lyrics:

I'm trading my sorrows
I'm trading my shame
I'm laying them down
For the joy of the Lord

I'm trading my sickness
I'm trading my pain
I'm laying them down
For the joy of the Lord [202]

---

[202] http://www.songlyrics.com/darrell-evans/trading-my-sorrows-lyrics/

Through His sacrifice we are justified and declared righteous and have peace with Him (Rom 3:21-28; 5:1-2), and as a result can lay our pain and shame at the foot of His cross, have peace in our souls, and begin to experience the joy that "comes with the morning".

3. The "Commitment" Encounter: Surrendering yourself to a life of discipleship.

The English "disciple" comes from the Greek, *mathetes*, which means, "pupil, learner, to follow". Discipleship requires a commitment to become a student of Jesus, absorbing His words and living them out. It is seen in Paul's exhortation to the Roman believers:

> *"I beseech you therefore, brethren, by the mercies*
> *of God, that you present your bodies*
> *a living sacrifice, holy, acceptable to God, which*
> *is your reasonable service." (Rom 12:1)*

Noteworthy in this passage is the fact discipleship involves "sacrifice": setting aside our interests and desires in service to God. And there is no better example than Paul himself.

THE STEP OF FAITH FROM "SAUL" TO "PAUL"

The year is A.D. 35, and it has been approximately two years since the resurrection of Jesus, the amazing transformation of His disciples, and the events during Pentecost that gave birth to the movement known as "The Way".[203] While Jesus is building His Church, a young and influential Pharisee named Saul, in his determination to crush this movement, is "zealously" persecuting those joyfully proclaiming the good news of the

---

[203] The dates in the narratives addressing the life and experiences of Paul come from Harold Hoehner, *"Chronology of the Apostolic Age"*. Th.D. dissertation, Dallas Theological Seminary, 1965; revised 1972See Acts 9:2. "The Way" was the term used to describe the group of new believers in Jesus who collectively represented His Church (Matt 16:18; Acts 2:47; 5:11.

Gospel.[204] But Saul – like the Perfect Son – saw the God he was so fervently defending through distorted lens. So, Jesus steps in, and gets his attention through afflicting his <u>physical</u> eyesight:

> *"So, he (Saul), trembling and astonished, said,*
> *'Lord, what do You want me to do?'*
> *Then the Lord said to him, 'Arise and go into*
> *the city, and you will be told what you*
> *must do.' And he was three days without sight,*
> *and neither ate nor drank. And*
> *Ananias went his way and entered the house;*
> *and laying his hands on him he said,*
> *'Brother Saul, the Lord Jesus, who appeared*
> *to you on the road as you came,*
> *has sent me that you may receive your sight*
> *and be filled with the Holy Spirit.'*
> *Immediately there fell from his eyes something*
> *like scales, and he received*
> *his sight at once; and he arose and was*
> *baptized." (Acts 9:6, 9, 25-27)*

There are several principles we can draw from this passage in coming to fully believe and internalize the truth of what God says is true about us:

1. Commit to believing it is true!

Up to this point, Saul – who would become known to the world as the evangelist Paul – believed Jesus to be nothing more than a blasphemer and troublemaker.[205] But Saul has come to believe the truth, and in his weakness becomes willing to surrender himself to whatever Jesus wants of him. For

---

[204] This is how the apostle Paul describes himself prior to his coming to believe in Jesus (Phil 3:3-6).

[205] Paul's parents were both Jewish and Roman citizens. While given the Jewish name of Saul, he also had a Greek name *Paulus*, which ironically, means, "small", or "little". Richard N. Longenecker. The Expositor's Bible Commentary: Acts. Frank E. Gaebelein, gen ed. Grand Rapids, MI: Zondervan Publishing House, 1981; http://www.biblestudyinfo.com/paul/biography.shtml

the truth of who you are in Christ to become your truth, you must <u>believe</u> it to be true – regardless of what you, Satan, or others are telling you.

A parallel is starting a diet and exercise program to improve your health. But in doing this we are putting our trust in some "authority" figure who has "proclaimed" a "truth" statement that diet and exercise will improve your health.

Your willingness to change how you eat and commit the time and effort to exercise suggests you trust this will improve your health. And as you begin to implement these changes, you are beginning to <u>live</u> like a healthy person – even though you have not yet <u>become</u> healthy! My point is you will begin to experience *WHOLENESS* simply by <u>trusting</u> you are *WHOLE* positionally while on the journey towards <u>becoming</u> *WHOLE* in practice and purpose.[206]

2. Expect it will require a step of faith on your part.

As we've seen, the book of Exodus tells us how God told the people of Israel He would not only deliver them from bondage but would lead them to something much better: a land "flowing with milk and honey" he would deliver to them from its inhabitants. And this promise wasn't given just once: in fact, God repeated it on several occasions.[207]

Now it would seem those suffering a life of "hard bondage" would leap at the opportunity for freedom, regardless of the risks involved. But consider the *Exodus* Generation had never experienced freedom. From the moment they came out of their mothers' wombs, their lives were completely controlled by the Egyptians. And despite lacking freedom, they did have the <u>certainty</u> of food, shelter, and protection from enemies. Upon walking out of Egypt, however, their "faith" would have to transition from the very visible power of their Egyptian oppressors to the invisible God of their father Abraham. Sadly, it didn't.

They tested God's patience (Ex 17:2) when they "grumbled" and "quarreled" over the seeming lack of water (Ex 15:22-27; 17:7), and

---

[206] A list of the truths about who you are as a believer in Jesus is provided in the *Appendix*.
[207] See Ex 3:8, 17; 13:5; 13:3; Lev 20:24. Note the land is also described as "the place of the Canaanites and the Hittites and the Amorites and the Perizzites and the Hivites and the Jebusites."

amazingly complained they'd rather have "died…in Egypt" where they had "pots of meat" and "bread to the full" (Ex 16:1-3). Yet upon arriving in the Promised Land, they found exactly what God said they would find:

> *"And they went up through the South and came*
> *to Hebron; Ahiman, Sheshai, and Talmai,*
> *the descendants of Anak, were there…Then they*
> *came to the Valley of Eshcol, and there cut*
> *down a branch with one cluster of grapes; they*
> *carried it between two of them on a pole.*
> *They also brought some of the pomegranates and*
> *figs. The place was called the Valley of*
> *Eshcol, because of the cluster which the men of*
> *Israel cut down there." (Num 13:22-24)*

Notice they didn't just find food – they found an <u>abundance</u> of it. The grape clusters were so huge it took two men to carry them on a pole, exactly as God through Moses had promised! But it took a step of faith on the part of the Israelites – including confronting the doubts and fears that arose during their journey through the desert – to realize it.

For the Prodigal, it meant embarking on the long and difficult journey home despite the uncertainty of how his father would receive him. For the man still known as Saul, it meant taking a step of faith to "go into the city". And noteworthy is the uncertainty with which Saul willingly takes that step of faith, because Jesus hasn't told him what to expect, or even if his sight will eventually be restored. Yet go Saul did, with no questions asked.

3. Rest in knowing God understands the challenge of believing.

This is clear in Jesus' interaction with a man whose son was tormented by a "mute spirit":

> *"And often he has thrown him both into the fire*
> *and into the water to destroy him. But if*
> *You can do anything, have compassion on us and*
> *help us.' Jesus said to him, 'If you can*

believe, all things are possible to him who believes.'
Immediately the father of the child
cried out and said with tears, 'Lord, I believe;
help my unbelief!'" (Mark 9:22-24)

A common misconception about faith is we either have it or not: we either trust God in <u>everything</u>, or we don't trust Him at all. The reality is our faith tends to grow (or regress) along the spectrum. In addition, our trust in God may vary depending on the issue, whether our health, our finances, hearing Him through the Spirit, or our very salvation.

Here, the man Jesus encountered tearfully "cries out" that he wants to fully believe, but he has some doubts. Yet, Jesus meets the man where he is in his faith and heals his son.

4. Don't be discouraged if it takes time.

Ever wonder why letters on a keyboard are seemingly arranged randomly rather than alphabetically? The *QWERTY* system was developed nearly 150 years ago due to the fact the type bars on old-fashioned typewriters would frequently jam when typing letters like "a" and "b" consecutively under the "ABC" system.[208] Now it's been over 40 years since old-school typewriters became obsolete, but even today you will find *QWERTY* used on virtually any new keyboard. And the reason: who wants to go through the agony of trying to relearn a skill stored deep into our muscle memory years – or even decades – ago?[209]

While for some healing and renewal is instantaneous, for others it is a process – much like it would be to unlearn the *QWERTY* system. We may also experience spurts of growth followed by periods of no growth. The key question is, "Am I seeing progress?" This is seen in the following two encounters Jesus had with men stricken with blindness:

"When He had said these things, He spat on
the ground and made clay with

---

[208] http://www.geekycamel.com/know-qwerty-system/
[209] I recall learning to type during my junior year in High School (1975). After nearly 50 years using *QWERTY*, I would definitely not want to put in the effort of retraining my brain to learn how to type on an alphabetized keyboard.

> *the saliva, and He anointed the eyes of the*
> *blind man with the clay. And He*
> *said to him, 'Go, wash in the pool of Siloam'*
> *(which is translated, Sent).*
> *So, he went and washed, and came back seeing." (John 9:6-7)*

Here, Jesus gives instructions, the man follows them, and he is instantly healed. Yet the healing process is seemingly more involved for another blind man several months earlier:

> *"Then He came to Bethsaida; and they*
> *brought a blind man to Him, and*
> *begged Him to touch him. So, He took the*
> *blind man by the hand and led him*
> *out of the town. And when He had spit on*
> *his eyes and put His hands on him,*
> *He asked him if he saw anything. And he*
> *looked up and said, 'I see men like*
> *trees, walking.' Then He put His hands on his eyes*
> *again and made him look up. And he was restored*
> *and saw everyone clearly." (Mark 8:22-25)*

Here, Jesus uses two treatments – like an optometrist trying various prescriptions to get the right lens – before the man's sight is fully restored. It is unclear why, but we can assume it isn't a question of Jesus not getting it right the first time.

For Saul, those three days of blindness likely felt like an eternity since he had no idea if Jesus was willing to restore his sight.[210] In fact, it is reasonable to assume Saul – like the Prodigal in his return home – had no expectation, or even hope, Jesus would heal him. Nearly 30 years later, Paul still was humbled by the grace he had received from Jesus:

> *"To me, who am less than the least of all the saints, this*
> *grace was given, that I should preach among the Gentiles*
> *the unsearchable riches of Christ..." (Eph 3:8)*

---

[210] Note in Acts 9:9, we're told Saul "Neither ate nor drank" during those three days.

My point here is soul healing can take time, and it can be uncomfortable – much like the time, commitment and discomfort involved in physical therapy. Your physical therapist will stretch your leg to the point of discomfort to loosen up the scar tissue restricting your movement, but in time your knee will heal as you commit to the process.[211]

Consider how the Israelites responded upon hearing the reports of the spies Moses had sent ahead into the Promised Land. After hearing the land was every bit as bountiful as promised, they are told the land is inhabited with fortified cities occupied by "giants":

So, all the congregation lifted up their voices
and cried, and the people wept that
night. And all the children of Israel complained
against Moses and Aaron, and
the whole congregation said to them, 'If only we
had died in the land of Egypt! Or if
only we had died in this wilderness! Why has
the LORD brought us to this land to
fall by the sword, that our wives and children
should become victims? Would it
not be better for us to return to Egypt'?"
(Num 13:27-29, 32-33; 14:1-3)

Due to their doubt, they were ready to give up the possibility of freedom and abundant life for the certainty of bondage! And the fact people were already living in the Promised Land – and ready to fight to the death to keep it – shouldn't have come as a surprise. After all, this was a land "flowing with milk and honey" – the most desirable place in that part of the world – so if they wanted to have it, they were going to have to FIGHT for it. But they failed to trust that just as God had fought for them before He would again.[212]

---

[211] During the Fall of 2023 I underwent 8 sessions over two months of physical therapy for shoulder impingement. I continue to practice the exercises which essentially involves contorting my arm and shoulder to maximum discomfort.

[212] Note in Ex 3:8, 17, we're told God had already informed Moses the land was fully occupied.

Realize this may happen to you. Perhaps the daily devotion to renewing your mind isn't paying off as quickly as you'd hoped. Or you may find yourself battling the same doubts and fears and begin to question whether you can overcome the obstacles you face. When this happens, remember God is in your corner fighting the "giants" who want to keep you out of the "Promised Land" and experience the abundance He desires for you.

But it begins with taking steps of faith and trusting God will work to produce fruit in your life.[213] It is seen in numerous passages challenging us to "walk in the Spirit".[214] Recall God instructed Moses to first send out spies to the Promised (Num 13:1-2). God knew they would find both the abundance of crops, and the obstacles they would have to overcome. The Israelites were essentially confronted with two questions: "Are we willing to trust "God can overcome this?", and "Are we willing to take a step of faith He will help us do it?"

5. Realize God uses people as part of the healing process.

We're told during those three days Saul is waiting in the city, a "certain disciple" named Ananias shows up, lays hands on Saul, and tells Saul he had been sent by Jesus so Saul would "receive...sight and be filled with the Holy Spirit". Then, "immediately" the scales fall from Saul's eyes, and his sight is restored (Acts 9:17-18).

But this begs the question, "Why didn't Jesus just heal Saul Himself"? Well, two reasons come to mind. First, Jesus wanted to use the giftedness imparted in Ananias to empower and embolden him in the work He had given him to do. But I also believe Jesus wanted Saul to feel accepted among the community of believers, as he would likely be fearful of how he would be received by his former foes/turned fellow believers, in the same way the Prodigal likely doubted his father would be doing backflips upon his return home.

God designed us to love and to experience love in relationships. We cannot realize the sense of *WHOLENESS* God desires for us until we emulate Jesus by extending grace and mercy to others (note Eph 2:8-10).

---

[213] Henri Nouwen. Spiritual Formation: Following the Movements of the Spirit
[214] See, for example, Rom 8:1-4; 2 Cor 12:18; Gal 5:16, 25.

For many, the reality of God's love, grace, and unconditional acceptance becomes real in a visceral way when received from others:

"And let us consider one another in order to stir
up love and good works, not forsaking
the assembling of ourselves together, as is the
manner of some, but exhorting one
another, and so much the more as you see the
Day approaching." (Heb 10:24-25)

We close with two important truths. First, something God through Peter says about us as believers that we hope is becoming increasingly true for YOU:

"But you are a chosen people, a royal
priesthood, a holy nation, God's
special possession, that you may declare the praises of Him who
called you out of darkness into His wonderful light". (1 Pet 2:9)

And second, as much as God wants you to "come home" and know Him more deeply, there is one who is every bit as determined to keep you in that "far away country" alone, defeated, and eating peapods. And that is none other than Satan, the originator of automatic negative thoughts, and the original "Fire *ANT*". And rest assured he is not going to just lie down and let God have victory in your life, as he is armed and ready for a fight!

CHAPTER 6

BUT ONE WHO DOESN'T WANT ME TO TRUST GOD

INTRODUCTION [215]

During the fall of 1970, I took a big step on my journey to adulthood: the transition from elementary to junior high school. Instead of walking the few blocks with my buddies to Hillside Elementary, I now took a bus the 3-4 miles to Park Junior High School where about 65% of the students were new to me. Add to this experiencing the awkwardness of emerging adolescence, and this next step certainly had its challenges.

But if you were to ask me what I remember most about 7th grade, besides getting detention for goofing off in Ms. Stitt's art class, I would say it was the Monday morning ritual of going to Mr. Baxter's biology classroom before school started to watch the weekly feeding of his six-foot boa constrictor. A group of us would gather outside the predator's glass-enclosed cage to see what was on the menu that week: would it be a mouse, a gerbil, or a small chick? Then we'd watch as Mr. Baxter dropped the poor critter being offered up as a sacrifice into the terrarium, and how it would scurry around in an increasing frenzy as it desperately looked for a way to escape.

---

[215] Information regarding the fear of snakes in the *Introduction* derived from https://www.livescience.com/2348-fear-snakes.html; https://www.youtube.com/watch?v=MF3sT97LguU; https://www.pestwiki.com/fear-snakes-science-reasons/

And it's understandable why the mouse, gerbil or chick was so panic-stricken, as it could plainly see that only a few feet away lay a threat to its very existence – its eyes locked in on every movement of its prey. And I felt more than a little of that fear the morning I finally drummed up the courage to let Mr. Baxter drape that snake across my shoulders.

The fear of snakes is one of the most common human phobias – even if one has never encountered a snake, let alone been harmed by one! Researchers have found that while infants and small children tend not to fear small snakes, they are unusually skilled at detecting them, and show a strong predisposition to learn to fear them. Researchers have also found both adults and children can detect images of snakes among a variety of non-threatening objects more quickly than those of harmless things like frogs, caterpillars, or flowers. And this innate predisposition to fear snakes isn't limited to human beings.

In a large outdoor cage holding about 80 Rhesus macaque monkeys, researchers put a fake snake which largely went ignored. But when a real snake slithered in, the monkeys began "mobbing it, and calling out in alarm". This has led scientists to propose the fear of snakes shared by humans and higher primates reflects something "deeply embedded in primate history" as snakes may be the oldest predator of primates. They also propose this has contributed to the superior vision shared by higher primates relative to lower life forms, why humans evolved with an innate tendency to sense and learn to fear things that represent a threat, and acquiring this fear through generations of genetic inheritance provided an advantage in surviving the wild during the early years of human history.

Now one could argue snakes may pose a threat to human beings. Yet images of lions, tigers, or bears OH MY – certainly dangerous predators in their own right – don't generate anywhere near the same reactions of fear in humans as snakes. So, why is this?

Well, some propose cultural factors such as being raised in the Jewish, Christian, Muslim religious traditions may contribute to a general apprehension about snakes, as we are "taught to distrust snakes".

All three traditions accept the first five books of the Bible as part of their Holy Scriptures, and according to the first three chapters of Genesis, everything went downhill the moment Satan shows up in the form of a snake. Or did he?

Have Snakes Gotten a Bad Rap?

In every major English translation of the Bible, Genesis 3:1 begins, "Now the serpent was more...."[216] But the Hebrew word translated "serpent" here is *nachash*, which stems from a root word meaning "to hiss or whisper, prognosticate, divine enchanter, to diligently observe". And while at times *nachash* is translated "snake" or "serpent", there are other Hebrew words that may better translate to reflect the literal physical reptile.[217]

Historically, Satan has been portrayed in a more human yet fearsome form complete with fiery red complexion, horns protruding out of his head, and maybe armed with a pitchfork. Some propose this stems from ancient pagan traditions in which Satan – like other gods – takes on more of a human form but possesses supernatural powers.[218] Yet what we do know is up until Adam and Eve gave in to Satan's temptations, peace reigned throughout creation. From this we can conclude Adam and Eve had never experienced fear, dread, or any sense of threat – even though Adam had encountered every life form he was given the task of naming, including lions, tigers, elephants – perhaps even the dreaded "leviathan", the great monster of the sea (Gen 2:19; cf Job 3:8; 41:1; Is 27:1).

There is no question humans possess cognitive and rational capabilities superior to all other life forms, yet Satan is first introduced as being more "cunning", "crafty", or "subtle" than all the other creatures God had created (Gen 3:1). And if Satan was going to present himself in the form of a living creature, perhaps choosing a snake reveals the shrewdness Adam and Eve encountered that fateful day. After all, they were accustomed to seeing the "beasts of the field" and the "birds of the air" – all creatures who

[216] NKJV, NASM, ESV, ASV, NRS, NIV, NLT, Darby translation.
[217] Examples include *tan* (Ex 7:9-10; Is 27:1; Amos 5:19; 9:3), *sawraf* (Is 14:29; 30:6), *kippoze* (Is 34:15), and *zawkhal* (Mic 7:7).
[218] https://christianity.stackexchange.com/questions/11468/what-is-the-origin-of-the-devils-red-pointy-costume-and-pitchfork.

move about through using their limbs and wings. But then they encounter the "serpent": a creature that quietly slithers along the ground or through the branches of trees.

In *The Passion of the Christ*, Mel Gibson ingeniously chooses not to present Satan as fearsome and frightening, but in the form of an androgynous-looking human being.[219] Perhaps Adam and Eve – their curiosity peaked – were intrigued by the uniqueness of the limbless creature Satan presented himself as that day. Or, perhaps Satan is described as a "serpent" by virtue of his ability to "whisper" and use "enchantment" to ply his gullible victims. Either way, once Satan got their attention, Adam and Eve had more than met their match. Despite living in God's presence and enjoying the abundance He had provided them; Satan was cunning enough to recognize areas of vulnerability he could use to lead them astray.

In *Chapter Five*, we used the fire ant to illustrate how automatic negative thoughts (*ANTs*) hinder our ability to experience the joy and peace God desires for us. Interestingly, fire ants are also called "thief ants", as they are known to rob and steal from other ants. And Satan is certainly the ultimate thief: his sole purpose is to steal, kill, and destroy (John 10:10). He is the roaring lion constantly on the prowl and stalking the prey he seeks to "devour" (1 Pet 5:8). Given this, we will consider what the Bible says about who Satan is, what he is capable of, and how you can avoid becoming another of his victims.

SATAN AND HIS ARMY OF DEMONS [220]

So, who – or what – is this mysterious being named Satan? Well, the name "Satan", which we see nearly 50 times in the Bible, means, "to act as an adversary, to oppose" (note Matt 4:10; 16:23; 1Thess 2:18). And his name is appropriate given everything Satan does is in opposition to God's plans and purposes. This is summed up well by C.S. Lewis:

---

[219] An example can be found at https://www.bing.com/images/search?q=satan+passion+of+the+christ&form=HDRSC3&first=1
[220] Much of the following from: Millard J. Erickson, Christian Theology, 2nd ed. Grand Rapids, MI: Baker Books, 1998

"There is no neutral ground in the universe.
Every square inch and every split
second is claimed by God and counter-
claimed by Satan." – C.S. Lewis [221]

Satan is also given several other names – all descriptive of his character and very being – including *Diabolos* ("devil", "slanderer", "adversary", *Kategor* ("accuser"), the "Enemy", the "Evil One", *Tempter, Beelzebub, Belial* (from a Hebrew word that means "wicked" or "worthless"), the "Father of lies", the "Murderer", and the one who has "sinned from the beginning". He is not "flesh and blood", but one of innumerable spirit beings.[222]

Satan's Origin

Noticeably absent in the creation narrative is any reference to God creating spirit beings. Yet *Chapter Three* opens with the introduction of a being referred to as "the serpent", which begs the question, "Where did Satan come from?"

Well, given creation was "complete" after God created Adam and Eve, it appears God created Satan and all other spirit beings prior creating flesh and blood being (Gen 2:1-3). We come to this conclusion as the Bible tells us spirit beings are immortal (Luke 20:36) and do not reproduce (Matt 22:30), so the same spirit beings that witnessed the creation of the material universe seemingly remain alive today. And there are a <u>lot</u> of them:

"A fiery stream issued and came forth from
before Him. A thousand thousands
ministered to Him; Ten thousand times
ten thousand stood before Him.
The court was seated, And the books were opened." (Dan 7:10) [223]

---

[221] https://www.azquotes.com/quotes/topics/satan.html
[222] Matt 4:1, 3, 5; 8:16; 12:24-27, 45; 13:19, 38, 39; Mark 3:22; Luke 7:21; 8:2; 11:15, 26; John 8:44; Acts 13:10; 19:12; ; 2 Cor 12:3; Eph 6:12; 1 Thess 3:5; 1 John 2:13; 3:8, 12; 5:18; Rev 12:9-10; 16:14.
[223] See also Job 25:3; 2 Kings 6:17; Ps 148:1-7; Matt 26:53; Col 1:16; Heb 12:22; Rev 5:11.

God seemingly created these spirit beings – collectively referred to as angels – for the express purpose of serving Him in the heaven. Angels are described as praising and glorifying God continually.[224] Yet, some – beginning with Satan – chose to rebel against Him:

> *"How you are fallen from heaven, O Lucifer,*
> *son of the morning! How you are cut*
> *down to the ground, you who weakened the*
> *nations! For you have said in your heart:*
> *'I will ascend into heaven; I will exalt my throne*
> *above the stars of God; I will also sit*
> *on the mount of the congregation on the farthest*
> *sides of the north; I will ascend*
> *above the heights of the clouds, I will be like*
> *the Most High'." (Is 14:12-14)*

Interestingly, Satan was originally named "Lucifer", which comes from a Hebrew root word meaning, "Be able, to attain, to have power".[225] The same word is used to describe a temple or palace, or something that is revered. He was the original "son of the morning", and the brightest, most beautiful, and highest ranking of all the angels. He is described as "the seal of perfection, Full of wisdom and perfect in beauty" and given a special role as a cherub with special access to God's presence (Ez 28:12-15). Yet, despite the fact any superiority he possessed over the other angels was solely a product of how God had created him, Lucifer – the original rebel and poster child of the "boastful pride of life" – became full of himself, not only wanting to "be like God", but to usurp God's rightful authority to rule over the heavens as well. Satan then persuaded a significant number of angels to follow him. Given this, he is also referred to as the "prince of demons".[226]

---

[224] See Job 38:7; Ps 103:20; 148:2; Is 6:2-3; Rev 5:11-12; 7:11; 8:1-4.
[225] The Hebrew word is *hay-kawl*. Strong's Exhaustive Concordance.
[226] Matt 12:22-32; Mark 3:22-30; Luke 11:14-23

Their Capabilities

Angels are "personal" beings in that they bear characteristics like those human beings possess. First, they are moral beings, as some ("angels") are described as "holy", while others ("demons") are described as "fallen" and "sinful".[227] Second, they are intelligent beings with the capability of acquiring "wisdom" (2 Sam 14:20; Rev 22:9). And herein lays a major advantage they have over us fragile and fallen human beings.

Angels and demons, like us, have the ability to grow in knowledge and insight by observing and learning about humans.[228] This is significant if you consider as of 2015, the average American will live 79.3 years – not quite 80 years to acquire the knowledge, insights, self-awareness, and wisdom to make the wise choices that lead to a fruitful life while avoiding the bad choices that lead to destruction.[229] Contrast that with demons – all created before Adam and Eve, and therefore thousands, if not <u>millions</u> of years old – that are well-practiced at observing our moods and behavior patterns, learning what irritates, frightens, or appeals to our desires, and attacking us when we're most vulnerable. Given this, they have super-human knowledge they can utilize to manipulate us like puppets.

Demons are also described as being stronger and more powerful than human beings (2 Ps 103:20; 2 Pet 2:11). And we can see from the Bible that Satan and his demons can inflict diseases including deafness and dumbness (Mark 9:17, 25), blindness (Matt 12:22), convulsions (Mark 1:26; 9:20; Luke 9:39), and paralysis or lameness (Luke 13:10-17; Acts 8:7) upon us. In some cases, they even take possession of and control the will of human beings.[230] But their approach is usually more subtle – and dare we say, snake-like.

---

[227] Matt 25:31; Mark 8:38; Luke 1:26; John 8:44; Acts 10:22; 1 John 3:10; Rev 14:10.
[228] See Luke 12:8; 15:10; 1 Cor 4:9; Eph 3:10. Note, demons are limited in their ability to know the future (1 Pet 1:12).
[229] https://en.wikipedia.org/wiki/List_of_countries_by_life_expectancy
[230] See Matt 8:28-34; 12:43-45; Mark 1:21-28; 5:1-20; ; Luke 4:31-37; 8:26-39; 11:14-28; Acts 16:16.

BEWARE THE SERPENT

The devil doesn't come dressed in a red cape and pointy horns.
He comes as everything you've ever wished for... - Tucker Max [231]

In the movie, *The Usual Suspects*, Customs agent Dave Kujan (played by Chaz Palminteri) is investigating the 27 dead men and $91 million in drug money, found on a blown-up ship at a Los Angeles port. The only two survivors are a severely burned Hungarian terrorist, and a low-level conman named Roger "Verbal" Kint (Kevin Spacey).

The clearly terrified Hungarian tells investigators the culprit is none other than Keyser Söze, a mysterious crime-lord unsurpassed in his reputation for using cold-blooded ruthlessness to intimidate his enemies. But Kujan is convinced the mastermind and ringleader is Dean Keaton (Gabriel Byrne), a former policeman-gone-rogue. As Kujan interrogates Kint, he quickly comes to realize how he got the nickname "Verbal", as Kint incessantly wanders off topic in sharing unrelated stories of his past. But Kujan also comes to realize he doesn't have enough evidence to charge Kint and has to release him.

Then just as Kint is walking out of the police station, Kujan receives a facsimile of the police sketch artist's rendering of the Hungarian's description of Söze – and is horrified to realize he is staring at a perfect likeness of Kint. As Kujan reflects on what Verbal has told him during hours of interrogation, he soon realizes he has been completely duped: Kint is in fact none other than Keyser Söze himself! Kujan frantically runs out to catch him, but Kint/ Söze is long gone. The scene then shifts about a block away where Söze is walking toward an awaiting car. As he approaches the car, Söze's pronounced limp disappears, and his crippled hand becomes fully functional. And as Söze gets in the car and drives away, he is heard saying:

"The greatest trick the devil ever pulled was
convincing the world he didn't exist."

Apparently, Satan <u>has</u> been quite successful in convincing the world he doesn't exist. Surveys have found while anywhere from 79-89% of

---

[231] https://www.azquotes.com/quotes/topics/satan.html

Americans believe in God, very few believe in His adversary, the "devil". And in 2009, *Christianity Today* reported only 40% of born-again Christians believe Satan is a real being, and not merely a symbol for evil.[232]

Satan's power and influence are so strong the apostles John and Paul describe him as the "ruler of this world", and the "god of this age".[233] And the fact most Christians – let alone Americans – don't believe Satan even <u>exists</u> renders unbelievers and believers alike vulnerable to his attacks. To Satan, every believer is a soldier in the army of Jesus and a threat to his rule. Given this we are wise to realize he will come at us with everything he's got, including what we refer to as the *Seven Ds of Destruction*, to accomplish his purposes.

1. Deception

Deception is the "act of causing someone to accept as true or valid what is false or invalid".[234] A good example is seen in Paul's second letter to the church in Corinth:

> *"But what I do, I will also continue to do, that*
> *I may cut off the opportunity from*
> *those who desire an opportunity to be regarded*
> *just as we are in the things of which they*
> *boast. For such are false apostles, deceitful workers,*
> *transforming themselves into apostles*
> *of Christ. And no wonder! For Satan himself*
> *<u>transforms himself into an angel of light</u>.*
> *Therefore, it is no great thing if his ministers*
> *also transform themselves into ministers*
> *of righteousness, whose end will be according*
> *to their works." (2 Cor 11:12-15)*

We are vulnerable to deception when offered something we really want, or it confirms something we really want to believe. Noteworthy is

---

[232] http://www.christianitytoday.com/edstetzer/2009/march/barna-how-many-have-biblical-worldview.html; https://news.gallup.com/poll/193271/americans-believe-god.aspx
[233] John 12:31; 14:30; 16:11, 1 John 2:15-17; 5:19; cf Eph 2:2; 2 Cor 4:4; Jam 4:4.
[234] https://www.merriam-webster.com/dictionary/deception.

the <u>intent</u> of deception is rarely pure, as it usually benefits the deceiver at the expense of the deceived.[235] In the Garden of Eden, Satan – the "human whisperer" – approached Adam and Eve in a subtle and tantalizing way. He came as the "good guy" offering them something he led them to believe was better than what God had given them. He was able to deceive Judas Iscariot into betraying Jesus through his self-serving motives and the prospect of financial gain (John 13:2).

Satan entices unbelievers to carry out his will (Eph 2:1-2; 2 Tim 2:2; 1 John 3:8) and to oppose the Gospel and believers (Acts 13:8-10). According to the apostle John, he has been deceiving the "whole world" ever since his encounter with Adam and Eve (Rev 12:9). And even with Jesus ruling over His future Millennial Kingdom from His throne in Jerusalem, Satan will use deception to lead one final rebellion against God (Rev 20:7-8).

2. Distortion

Distortion is, "the act of twisting or altering something out of its true, natural, or original state."[236] Everything that exists is a product of God's creative capabilities, which in the beginning was all good. Satan, on the other hand, is not able to create something from nothing. He is, however, a master of twisting and distorting what God has created for his purposes. And as we've seen, Satan distorted God's command regarding what fruit Adam and Eve were prohibited from eating as well as the reason for that command.

His capacity to deceive believers is evident in the church in Corinth, where Paul worked feverishly to thwart the efforts of the "super apostles", or tools of Satan Paul describes as "angels of light" claiming to teach a Gospel superior to that of Paul's, but in fact was nothing more than a return to the Mosaic Law (2 Cor 11:1-15). Through distortion, Satan "snatches away" the Gospel from the hearts of unbelievers (Matt 13:19) and blinds their minds so they cannot see the light of the Gospel (2 Cor 4:3-4). In his letter to a young pastor named Timothy, Paul warns distorters

---

[235] A noteworthy exception is Rahab's "lie" to protect Israel's spies in Jericho (Josh 2:1-6; cf 6:17-25; Heb 11:31; Jam 2:25).

[236] https://www.merriam-webster.com/dictionary/distortion.

of the truth will lead some to depart from the faith as they "give heed to deceiving spirits and doctrines of demons" (1 Tim 4:1-3).

Satan strives to distort our perception of God to convince us He cannot be trusted, the intent of His laws and standards are merely to keep us from something we might enjoy or are designed to set us up for failure so He can punish us for failing to meet them, with the result we are unworthy of His grace, and He will abandon us when we most need Him.

3. Doubt

"There is nothing like suspense and anxiety for barricading a human's mind against the Enemy. He wants men to be concerned with what they do; our business is to keep them thinking about what will happen to them." –
C.S. Lewis, "The Screw-tape Letters" [237]

Doubt is, "to call into question the truth, to be uncertain of".[238] Once Satan has convinced us God is not the benevolent heavenly Father who cares about our well-being and will never abandon or forsake us, doubt will soon creep in. [239] Throughout the Bible we see instances of God's people doubting His faithfulness and trustworthiness. God repeatedly promised the nation of Israel He would deliver them from bondage to a land "flowing with milk and honey", then demonstrated His commitment to fulfill His promises through His methodical beat-down of Egypt's Pharaoh and their false gods through the ten plagues, His miraculous parting of the Red Sea, and His annihilation of the Egyptian army. Yet the people repeatedly doubted God would provide the food and water they would need on their journey to the Promised Land.[240] And then – despite their spies bringing back evidence the land was as abundant as Moses had promised – they doubted God could give them victory over the inhabitants occupying it (Num 13:26-14:3).

The disciples doubted Jesus could walk on water, concluding He was a

---

[237] https://www.theodysseyonline.com/musing-screwtape-letters
[238] https://www.merriam-webster.com/dictionary/doubt.
[239] See Ps 27:10; 37:28; 94:14; Heb 13:5.
[240] See Ex 15;23-27; 16:2-31; 17:7.

ghost approaching them on the sea (Matt 14:26-33; Mark 6:47-51). They doubted the report He had been resurrected from the dead – despite the fact He had already raised two people from the dead (Luke 7:11-17; John 11:17-44) – and His prediction that He, too, would be resurrected.[241] Even after appearing to over 500 people, some still doubted (Matt 28:17).

4. Distrust

Doubt inevitably leads to distrust, whether of God or of other people. Despite all the blessings God had bestowed upon Adam and Eve, they bought Satan's into lie that God's intentions were self-serving in His command not to eat of the fruit. The Israelites, upon doubting God would in fact give them victory over the inhabitants of the Promised Land, began to "complain against" God's appointed leader, Moses (Num 14:2).

And then there is the blatant distrust exhibited by the disciples towards Jesus. It is seen in that night Jesus is completely relaxed amid what Mark describes as a "great windstorm" while He and His disciples are crossing the Sea of Galilee. As we saw in *Chapter Two*, the fear felt by the disciples is understandable given the "waves beat into the boat" and it was "already filling [up]." (Mark 3:37). But their reaction in seeing Jesus just chilling out and "asleep on a pillow" is arguably not. Mark describes it this way:

> *"And they awoke Him and said to Him, "Teacher, do*
> *You not care that we are perishing?" (Mark 4:38b)* [242]

Now there is no nuance in the English translation of the original Greek here. Let alone the fact Jesus was <u>with</u> them and His well-being was at risk as well, the disciples essentially accuse Jesus of not caring about them! By this time, the disciples had seen Him perform numerous miracles. They had seen Him cast out demons, heal diseases, and raise a young boy from the dead. [243] He had demonstrated His power over nature itself, giving them all the reason to believe He could save His own skin. Yet they seem

---

[241] Mark 16:11; cf John 2:19; Matt 26:61; Mark 14:53

[242] Matt 8:18-27; Mark 4;35-41; Luke 8:22-25

[243] Cheney and Ellisen propose this is the 12th of over 30 miracles that are <u>recorded</u>. The apostle John notes there were numerous other miracles not recorded (John 21:25).

---

to have concluded Jesus would only look out for number one and would abandon them in their time of need.

Distrust breeds fear – the fear our well-being is at stake, and we can't count on God or others to help us in our time of need. As we saw in *Chapter Two*, distrust in others often begins with the neglect or indifference of our parents. We learn that we can't count on others – including God Himself – to be there when we need them. And it can lead to the assumption that not only will others fail to help us, but that their intentions are to <u>harm</u> us. And this will not only disrupt relationships but sow the seeds of <u>dissension</u> as well.

5. Dissension

Dissension is, "partisan and contentious quarreling".[244] Dissension flows out of distrust, and there is plenty of evidence throughout the Bible of Satan's success in disrupting the state of *shalom* present in the beginning. While Adam and Eve enjoyed perfect harmony with God and each other before eating the fruit, it was torn apart once they had sinned. We see how Adam and Eve turned to blaming and finger-pointing to deflect responsibility when confronted by God (Gen 3:12-13). Dissension quickly escalated to the point within one generation Cain had murdered Abel (Gen 4:1-8), and the Israelites had turned on and were ready to stone the leaders God empowered to lead them to the Promised Land.[245]

We are warned repeatedly in the Bible to do everything to avoid disputes, as disputes inevitably lead to dissension. Paul makes this clear in his second letter to Timothy:

> *"But avoid foolish and ignorant disputes,*
> *knowing that they generate strife. And a*
> *Servant of the Lord must not quarrel but be gentle*
> *to all, able to teach, patient, in humility*
> *correcting those who are in opposition, if God*
> *perhaps will grant them repentance, so that*

[244] https://www.merriam-webster.com/dictionary/dissension.
[245] See Num 14:2-10.

they may know the truth, and that they may
come to their senses and escape the
snare of the devil, having been taken captive
by him to do his will." (2 Tim 2:26)

Satan's distortion of the truth prompted the "Judaizers" to demand the Gentile believers in Galatia adhere to the Law by agreeing to be circumcised (Gal 5:6-7). Even church leaders like the apostles Paul and Barnabas succumbed to dissension when they became embroiled in a sharp dispute over whether they should take Mark (writer of the second Gospel) along with them on a trip to visit the churches they had established (Acts 15:35-41). And the apostle James tells us our self-serving egos are the root of "every evil thing":

"For where envy and self-seeking exist, confusion
And every evil thing are there." (Jam 3:16)

And, as Paul says, this opens the door for Satan to do his work:

"Be angry, and do not sin": do not let the sun go down on
your wrath, nor give place to the devil." (Eph 4:26-27)

Satan appeals to our pride, greed, and lust. He sows and waters the seeds of doubt and distrust to stir up dissension as a means of pitting us against one other. This can happen through even the mildest of slights – case in point interpreting another's oversight or failure to recognize your efforts as a willful effort to exclude or minimize your contributions. And the result: the seeds of jealousy, envy, or resentment are sown.

Sadly, Satan has continued to successfully sow dissension among the Church Jesus so selflessly gave of Himself to build. Too often we hear of disagreements that become the conflicts that literally tear a church apart. A win for the kingdom of Jesus, on the other hand, is when two people refuse to let Satan cause division, find common ground, and resolve their differences, and not only mend their relationship, but develop a deeper and more trusting relationship. This occurs when believers humbly practice patience with one another, including being willing to forgive "anything":

*"Now whom you forgive anything, I also forgive.
For if indeed I have forgiven anything,
I have forgiven that one for your sakes in the
presence of Christ, lest Satan should
take advantage of us; for we are not ignorant
of his devices." (2 Cor 2:10-11)*[246]

Satan is clearly alive and well and ruling the world. But Satan doesn't rule through law and order – instead, he rules by sowing chaos and conflict. And one way he accomplishes this is by convincing the world the enemy isn't him, but other flesh and blood human beings. Paul makes this clear in his letter to the Ephesians:

*"For we do not wrestle against flesh and blood, but
against principalities, against powers, against the rulers
of the darkness of this age, against spiritual hosts of
wickedness in the heavenly places." (Eph 6:12)*

For once dissension has been sown, it inevitably leads to denigration.

6. Denigration

Denigration is shifting your attack from the legitimacy of another's concern to their character, specifically to diminish or stain another's reputation. It is seen in the very word "denigrate", which comes from the Latin verb *denigrare*, meaning "to blacken". Job, for example, is described as "blameless and upright – one who feared God and shunned evil" – and was a man of impeccable character. And while Satan attacked Job by destroying his family, wealth, and eventually Job's physical health, his objective was to destroy his character by tempting Job to turn away from God and to turn to sin.

We see a vivid example of this in Satan's attacks on Jesus. Throughout his nearly four-year ministry, Satan continually used those who opposed Jesus to question His character. Instead of seeing His works as evidence of His claim to deity, they attempted to diminish His works (John 7:31),

---

[246] We will address in detail the concept and practice of "forgiveness" in *Chapter Eleven*.

accused Him of being possessed by demons (Matt 9:34; 12:24; Mk 3:24; Luke 11:15; John 8:48), of gluttony and drunkenness (Matt 11:19; Luke 7:34), and being a "deceiver" (John 7:13). And during His trial and execution it only got worse. He was abandoned by His disciples (Matt 25:56; Mark 14:50), denied by Peter numerous times (Matt 26:58-75; Mark 14:54-72; Luke 22;54-60; John 18:16-27), executed in place of a robber and murderer (Matt 27:15-23; Mark 15:6-14; Luke 23:16-22; John 18:39-40), and mocked and spit upon (Matt 27:27-31, 39-43; Mark 15:16-20, 29-32; Luke 23:35-37).

Denigration is the foundation – in fact, the cornerstone – of the strongholds Satan uses to demean and devalue us, and to diminish our effectiveness in serving God. He uses abuse or neglect to suggest you are insignificant, your needs don't matter, and you don't deserve to be valued or treated with the dignity and respect of an image-bearer of God (Gen 1:26-27; cf Jam 3: 7). He leads you to believe your value and worth depends on the position you hold, how well you perform, or how prosperous you are. And he uses your failures or shortcomings to reinforce that nagging sense you are flawed, unacceptable, and God couldn't care less about you. And this leads to discouragement and despair.

7. Discouragement and Despair

After their failure to trust God would give them victory in securing the Promised Land and subsequent rebellion against Him, God sentenced every adult – except for Moses, Joshua, and Caleb – to die while wandering in the desert during the ensuing 40 years (Num 14:26-38). Then God led the "Entrance" generation – those born during the wilderness wandering – back to the Promised Land. Now the *Entrance Generation* faced the same challenge as their fathers in trusting God would give them victory over the inhabitants. And as they camped in the area east of the Jordan, the children of the tribes of Gad and Reuben – content with what they had already received – decided they weren't up to the challenge (Num 32:3-5). To which Moses issued the following challenge:

*"Now why will you discourage the heart
of the children of Israel from
going over into the land which the LORD
has given them?" (Num 32:7)*

In the ensuing verses, Moses – in exhorting the *Entrance* Generation to not make the same mistake their fathers had made – is clear it was discouragement that kept the *Exodus* Generation from taking the Land God had promised He would deliver to them:

*"Thus, your fathers did when I sent them
away from Kadesh Barnea to see the
land. For when they went up to the Valley
of Eshcol and saw the land, they
<u>discouraged</u> the heart of the children of
Israel, so that they did not go
into the land which the LORD had
given them." (Num 32:8-9)*

Satan uses others – like the inhabitants of the Promised Land – as obstacles or barriers to discourage us from what God wants to accomplish through us. Knowing doubt and discouragement were the *Entrance* Generation's biggest enemies, their new leader Joshua repeatedly exhorted them to be of "good courage" and "not be afraid", as they could trust God to help them accomplish what they couldn't possibly do on their own in defeating the inhabitants of the Promised Land.[247] About 900 years later, the prophet Ezra – given the task of leading efforts to rebuild Solomon's Temple – had a similar challenge:

*"Then the people of the land tried to discourage
the people of Judah. They troubled them
in building, and hired counselors against them
to frustrate their purpose all the days of
Cyrus king of Persia, even until the reign of
Darius king of Persia." (Ezra 4:4-5)*

---

[247] Josh 1:9; 8:1; 9:24; 10:25; 11:6.

Notice how Satan entices a full-out assault on God's people by using the inhabitants and counselors to hinder the Israelites' efforts to rebuild the temple and persisting in his efforts "all the days of Cyrus…even until the reign of Darius". Satan will use every trick he can to thwart God by attacking His people through sowing doubt and discouragement. And he knows discouragement often hinders the frequency and fervency of our prayers:

"Satan tries to limit your praying because he
knows your praying will limit him."[248]

Satan even tried using the hostility of those who opposed Jesus to discourage Him in preventing Him from accomplishing the work God had sent Him to do:

"For consider Him who endured such hostility from
sinners against Himself, lest you become weary
and discouraged in your souls." (Heb 12:5)

But Jesus wasn't surprised, and in fact <u>anticipated</u> it. Centuries earlier, Isaiah prophesied of the resilience Jesus would demonstrate despite all Satan's efforts to thwart Him:

"He will not fail nor be discouraged, Till He has established justice
in the earth: And the coastlands shall wait for His law." (Is 42:4)

Satan has been using lies to sow seeds of doubt, distrust, dissension, and discouragement since the beginning, and to denigrate humanity as well. And He will continue to accuse us until He is finally defeated and cast into the lake of fire for eternity (Rev 12:10; 20:10).

Over the years I have had many conversations with people who have doubted whether they could trust God or were even willing to consider <u>believing</u> in Him due to the abuse or traumatic losses they have suffered. It may be the person beaten or sexually abused as a child who wondered aloud, "Where was God when I needed Him?" Or the person trying to

---

[248] Quote by Rick Warren, https://www.azquotes.com/quotes/topics/satan.html

be "honest, open, and willing (*HOW*)" as they consider who or what their Higher Power is as they contemplate *Step Three* of the Twelve Steps of Alcoholics Anonymous but struggles with trusting anyone or anything. I can imagine Satan, lurking in the recesses of his- or her soul, whispering, "You know you can't trust Him". Yet, with all these weapons at his disposal, perhaps Satan's most effective weapon is – are you ready for this – us!

"THE DEVIL WILL HELP YOU DO IT"

"If you haven't met Satan face-to-face, it's because you are running in the same direction" [249]

In the movie, *The Devil's Advocate*, Kevin Lomax (played by Keanu Reeves) is a young, up-and-coming defense attorney in Gainesville, Florida who has never lost a case. After a particularly difficult acquittal in which he has had a crisis of conscience in realizing his client is in fact guilty of child molestation, Kevin is approached by a representative of a large New York law firm offering big money to come work for them. Mystified the firm is even aware he exists, Kevin nonetheless accepts, and soon finds himself living the big life in the inner circle of the firm, which is led by managing partner, John Milton (Al Pacino).

Soon, however, Kevin is given the test of his career: defending a well-known developer who has been charged with murder. As Kevin immerses himself in the case, he neglects his wife Mary Ann (Charlize Theron), who – being tormented by demons – begins falling apart. While preparing a key witness, Kevin faces another crisis of conscience upon realizing the witness is lying and his client is in fact guilty. But Kevin plows ahead and wins the case, only to lose Mary Ann as he helplessly watches her take her own life.

Grief-stricken and tormented by guilt, Kevin is further confronted with the startling truth of the secret his mother has kept from him his whole life: Milton is in fact his father! But Kevin also comes to realize something else: Milton is not just another high-powered, big-city

---

[249] Quote by Zig Ziglar, https://www.azquotes.com/quotes/topics/satan.html

attorney – no, he is in fact Satan himself! Kevin then blames Milton for the choices he has regretfully made, saying, "You made me do it!" To which Milton replies:

> *"I'm no puppeteer, Kevin. I don't make*
> *things happen – it doesn't work like*
> *that. Free will is like butterfly wings: once touched they never get off*
> *the ground. No, I only set the stage: you pull your own strings."*

Satan can't <u>make</u> us do anything: all our actions are the products of the choices we freely make. But Satan certainly gives us a big assist in the choices we later come to regret. He dangles our lusts and desires (note the *Eight Deadly Sins*) in front of us like the red cape a bull-fighter waves to entice a bull to charge head-long to its demise (Gen 3:1-6; cf 1 John 2:16-17). He tantalizes us with the lie we would be so much happier if we had just a little bit <u>more</u>. He sows seeds of dissatisfaction and discontentment by suggesting we <u>deserve</u> more, and that someone – whether others or God Himself – are holding back on us. He gives life to the envy and malice that fuels the dissension and denigration that has afflicted humanity since the days of Cain and Abel. And the satisfaction He receives is reflected in the final scene of *The Devil's Advocate*, when Milton – smiling seductively as he reflects on the devastation he has wrought upon the Lomax family – observes:

> *"Vanity. It's definitely my favorite sin"*

While the human will is the engine that drives us to destruction, it's our lusts and desires that fuel that engine. Whether vanity, pride, or hubris, it's the desire to "be like God" that prompts us to give into temptation and make the decisions we come to regret. While the lust of the eyes and flesh generate the desire to have the things we don't have, it's our ego that tells us we <u>deserve</u> to have them, and to justify taking them.

For all their shortcomings, the people of Israel did have periods during which they humbly surrendered their egos, conformed to the terms of the Mosaic Covenant, and were blessed for their obedience. Israel reached the height of its power from 1010 to 930 B.C. under the leadership of kings

David and Solomon. And this is attributed to the fact both men were humble servants who for the most part surrendered themselves to God. David, for example, is described as a "man after His (God's) own heart".[250] Yet even David and Solomon had moments when they let their egos and desires get the best of them.

For David, it happened after years of fighting to consolidate the twelve tribes of Israel into one cohesive nation committed to serving and honoring God:

> "It happened in the spring of the year, at <u>the
> time when kings go out to battle</u>, that
> David sent Joab and his servants with him, and
> all Israel; and they destroyed the people
> of Ammon and besieged Rabbah. <u>But David
> remained at Jerusalem</u>. Then it happened
> one evening that David arose from his bed and
> walked on the roof of the king's house.
> And from the roof he saw a woman bathing,
> and the woman was very beautiful to
> behold. So David sent and inquired about the
> woman. And someone said, 'Is this
> not Bathsheba, the daughter of Eliam, the wife
> of Uriah the Hittite?' Then David
> sent messengers, and <u>took</u> her; and she came
> to him, and he lay with her, for she
> was cleansed from her impurity; and she
> returned to her house." (2 Sam 11:1-4)

Bathsheba is a married woman: her husband Uriah is a loyal and dedicated commander in David's army. Then David "took" her, or put another way, raped her. Then she becomes pregnant, and David – wanting to cover up his sin – arranges for Uriah to have time with his wife so it will be assumed the child is his. But loyal to a fault, Uriah refuses to abandon his post, so David sends Uriah to the frontlines where he is eventually killed. Yet David isn't in the clear, as God knows the truth (2 Sam 11:5-27).

---

[250] See 1 Sam 13:14; cf 1 Sam 16:7; Acts 13:22.

And then there's Solomon, abundantly blessed and considered the wisest man on earth during the early years of his reign as king when humbly surrendering himself to God's will (1 Kings 4:30). Yet, Solomon threw it all away in pursuing the lust of the eyes, the lust of the flesh, and the boastful pride of life through accumulating wealth, women, and power (1 Kings 10:26-11:11) – despite the warnings God had issued through Moses some 500 years earlier, and of which Solomon certainly would have been familiar:

"When you come to the land which the LORD your God is giving you, and possess it and dwell in it, and say, 'I will set a king over me like all the nations that are around me,' you shall surely set a king over you whom the LORD your God chooses; one from among your brethren you shall set as king over you; you may not set a foreigner over you, who is not your brother. But he <u>shall not multiply horses</u> for himself, nor cause the people to return to Egypt to multiply horses, for the LORD has said to you, 'You shall not return that way again.' Neither shall he <u>multiply wives</u> for himself, lest his heart turn away; nor shall he <u>greatly multiply silver and gold for himself.</u> Also it shall be, when he sits on the throne of his kingdom, that he shall write for himself a copy of this law in a book, from the one before the priests, the Levites. And it shall be with him, and he shall read it all the days of his life, <u>that he may learn to fear the LORD his God and be careful to observe all the words of this law and these statutes, that his heart may not be lifted above his brethren,</u> that he may not turn aside from the commandment to the right hand or to the left, and that he may prolong his days in his kingdom, he and his children in the midst of Israel." (Deut 17:14-17)

Solomon came to realize the folly of his ways, as seen in his later reflections recorded in the Book of Ecclesiastes, in which he repeatedly describes the "vanity" of seeking abundance through power, possessions, and pleasure.[251] And even the disciples of Jesus – after three years of

---

[251] In Ecclesiastes alone, the English "vanity" or "futility" is used over 30 times to describe the emptiness Solomon felt. Note Solomon describes efforts to find fulfillment in power, prosperity, and pleasure as "nothing new under the sun" (Eccl 1:9).

hearing Jesus teach about humbly serving and putting others first, and seeing Him model it through His actions – let their egos get the best of them:

> *"Then He came to Capernaum. And when*
> *He was in the house He asked them,'*
> *What was it you disputed among yourselves*
> *on the road?' But they kept silent,*
> *for on the road they had disputed among*
> *themselves who would be the greatest.*
> *And He sat down, called the twelve, and said*
> *to them, 'If anyone desires to be*
> *first, he shall be last of all and servant of all'."*
> *(Mark 9:33-35; cf Luke 9:46-47)* [252]

The Gospels of Matthew and Luke tell us the <u>first</u> assignment God gave Jesus was a test, as Jesus was led out into the desert to be tempted by Satan.[253] And Satan offered Him everything any person could ever want: power, prestige, possessions, and privilege – complete satisfaction of the lust of the eyes, the lust of the flesh, and the boastful pride of life – in exchange for His worship. But Jesus' response reflects His humility and single-minded determination to put God and His purposes before His own interests:

> *"...Get behind Me, Satan! For it is written, You shall worship*
> *the LORD your God, and Him only you shall serve.'"*
> *(Luke 4:8; cf Matt 16:23; Mark 8:33)*

Now Satan is persistent and doesn't give up. Instead, he bides his time – knowing an opportunity will arise when he can prey upon the frailties and weaknesses of humanity:

> *"Now when the devil had ended every temptation, he*
> *departed from Him until an opportune time." (Luke 4:13)*

---

[252] Amazingly, the disciples raised the same issue during the days before Jesus' arrest and execution (Luke 22:24-27)!

[253] See Matt 4:1-13; Luke 4:2-12. See also Mark 1:13.

As he observed the disciples arguing over "who would be the greatest", Satan knew the disciples were ripe for the picking. But Jesus knew this as well, as shortly before His arrest He warned His "inner circle" (Peter, James, and John) of the dangers of temptation:

"Watch and pray, lest you enter into temptation. The spirit indeed is willing, but the flesh is weak." (Mark 14:38; cf Matt 26:41)

And Peter in particular should have heeded this warning. Throughout the Gospels, Peter is the first to step up and answer the questions Jesus posed to them. While the oldest and informal leader of the Twelve, he generally comes across as the most self-assured. It was Peter that questioned Jesus' suggestion they move to deeper waters to catch fish (Luke 5:1-11; cf Mark 5:31; Luke 8:45). It was Peter who tried to prove his faith by walking on the water, only to falter when doubt overtook him (Matt 14:23-36; Mark 6:47-56; John 6:16-21). It was Peter who spoke for the Twelve in response to Jesus' question if they, too, wanted to leave after hearing some difficult teaching (John 6:59-71), and who was bold enough to ask Jesus to clarify His teaching (Matt 15:1-20; Mark 7:1-23). It was Peter who boldly proclaimed Jesus, "The Christ, the Son of the Living God", but then "rebuked" Jesus for His prediction of His upcoming death – only to have Jesus in turn rebuke him:

"Get behind Me, Satan! You are an offense to Me, for you are not mindful of the things of God, but the things of men." (Matt 16:13-28; Mark 8:27-9:1; Luke 9:18-27).

But Peter's biggest failure – the "opportune time" Satan had anticipated and patiently awaited while biding his time for nearly three years – came shortly after Peter's boldest proclamation of his faith and devotion to Jesus.[254] It is on the Thursday night of Passover Week, and the first day of the Feast of Unleavened Bread when the Passover lamb was traditionally sacrificed (Matt 26:17-20; Mark 14:12; Luke 22:7). Jesus and His disciples are gathered to share the Passover meal when Jesus – knowing He will soon

---

[254] The order of the following events is proposed by Cheney & Ellisen.

become the "Passover Lamb" for all of humanity and knowing Satan had already "put it into the heart of Judas" to betray Him – does something that stuns his disciples: He proceeds to wash their feet (John 13:1-6)! The humility of this action cannot be overstated.

In the culture of their day, a host would have his lowest-ranking servant – usually a slave – remove the sandals of his guests and wash their feet.[255] Now, the streets of Jerusalem were not paved, so their feet would have been covered with dust. Add to this the fact that being Passover week, the streets of Jerusalem would have been packed with Jews who had traveled from all over the Near East for the celebration – along with the donkeys they used for transportation or carrying their supplies, and the lambs they had brought for their offerings. Since 1st century Jerusalem didn't have the street cleaners that keep our roads clean today, you can imagine the animal dung that accumulated during this season of celebration. Yet, there is Jesus, stripped to the waist and washing it off their feet!

Now, Peter – in one of his better moments – objects to His Lord humiliating Himself in such a way. But Jesus insists, and states the reason for this object lesson:

> *"'You call me Teacher and Lord, and you say well,*
> *for so I am. If I then, your Lord and Teacher,*
> *have washed your feet, you also ought to wash one*
> *another's feet. For I have given you an*
> *example, that you should do as I have done to*
> *you. Most assuredly, I say to you, a servant*
> *is not greater than his master; nor is he who is*
> *sent greater than he who sent him. If you*
> *know these things, blessed are you if you do them'." (John 13:13-17)*

Jesus then proceeds to break the bread and share the cup of the Passover – using the elements as symbols of the sacrifice He is about to make on their (and our) behalf. Yet for all His efforts – including washing their feet – to help them understand His point, they incredibly miss it as they let their egos get the best of them <u>again</u>:

---

[255] See, for example, Merrill C. Tenney, <u>The Expositor's Bible Commentary: John, Frank E. Gaebelein, gen ed.</u> Grand Rapids, MI: Zondervan Publishing House, 1981.

WHOLE

*"Now there was also a dispute among them, as to which
of them should be considered the greatest." (Luke 22:24)*

If Jesus was ever going to get discouraged, it would seemingly have
been in this moment. He has spent three-plus years grooming these
men to lead the Church He had come to build (Matt 16:18). He had
repeatedly stressed the importance of humble servanthood and had
just provided a powerful illustration of what it looks like. Yet here they
are – again – bickering about which of them should be "considered the
greatest".

Jesus' patient response is to reiterate – yet again – that greatness is
exemplified through servanthood (Luke 22:25-27). Jesus then commends
them for staying with Him through the trials He had faced up to this
point, and promises they will be <u>rewarded</u> for it:

*"But you are those who have continued with Me in
My trials. And I bestow upon you a kingdom,
just as My Father bestowed one upon Me, that
you may eat and drink at My table in
My kingdom and sit on thrones judging the
twelve tribes of Israel." (Luke 22:28-30)*

But after informing the disciples He had been betrayed and would
soon "go as it was determined" (Luke 22:22) "just as it is written of Him"
(Mark 14:21), Jesus says this:

*"…Now the Son of Man is glorified, and God is
glorified in Him. If God is glorified in
Him, God will also glorify Him in Himself, and
glorify Him immediately. Little children,
I shall be with you a little while longer. You
will seek Me; and as I said to the Jews,
Where I am going, you cannot come, so now
I say to you." (John 13:31-33)*

This leads to Peter's boldest proclamation of his loyalty, and his epic
failure to back it up:

> *"Simon Peter said to Him, 'Lord, where are*
> *You going?' Jesus answered him,*
> *'Where I am going you cannot follow Me now,*
> *but you shall follow Me afterward'. Peter*
> *said to Him, 'Lord, why can I not follow You*
> *now? I will lay down my life for Your sake'.*
> *And the Lord said, 'Simon, Simon! Indeed,*
> *Satan has asked for you, that he may sift*
> *you as wheat. But I have prayed for you, that*
> *your faith should not fail; and when you*
> *have returned to Me, strengthen your brethren.'*
> *But he (Peter) said to Him, 'Lord, I*
> *am ready to go with You, both to prison and*
> *to death'. Jesus answered him, 'Will*
> *you lay down your life for My sake? Most*
> *assuredly, I say to you, the rooster shall*
> *not crow till you have denied Me three times."*
> *(Luke 22:28-34; John 13:36-38).*

While directed at Peter, this warning certainly applied to the other disciples. Yet, when Jesus was arrested a few hours later, they all failed miserably in proving their loyalty:

> *"In that hour Jesus said to the multitudes, 'Have*
> *you come out, as against a robber,*
> *with swords and clubs to take Me? I sat daily*
> *with you, teaching in the temple, and*
> *you did not seize Me. But all this was done that*
> *the Scriptures of the prophets might be*
> *fulfilled.' Then all the disciples forsook Him and*
> *fled." (Matt 26:55-56; cf Mark 14:50)* [256]

Noteworthy is the word choice of both Matthew and Mark in their accounts. The Greek word translated "forsook" is *aphiemi*, which means,

---

[256] Note Ps 88:8, where David was abandoned by all of his friends as well.

"to leave behind, forsake, dismiss, divorce, to yield up".[257] Essentially, they – beginning with Peter – offered up Jesus to save themselves. It is the same word Luke used to describe the disciples' "leaving everything" to follow Jesus some three years earlier (Luke 5:1-11). But just as Peter stood alone in the proclamation of his unconditional loyalty to Jesus, he would stand alone in his failure.

While Jesus predicted Peter would deny Him three times, some theologians propose Peter may have denied Him as many as <u>six</u> times.[258] And his last denial reveals the depths of the fear that overtook Peter in those moments, as he "cursed and swore" in adamantly denying even <u>knowing</u> Jesus (Matt 26:74; Mark 14:71; Luke 22:60). Then this happened:

> *"And the Lord turned and looked at Peter. And*
> *Peter remembered the word of the*
> *Lord, how He had said to him, 'Before the rooster*
> *crows, you will deny Me three times'.*
> *So Peter went out and wept bitterly."*
> *(Luke 22:61-62; cf Matt 26:75; Mark 14:72)*

Peter made three mistakes here. First, he under-estimated Satan's ability to prey upon his weaknesses as he strives to undermine God's plans. Second, he over-estimated his own faith and resilience, which led to his third mistake: failing to heed the warnings of the Man he had declared His "Lord", "Master", and "The Christ, The Son of the Living God". Even when asked to reconsider the bold promise he had made, Peter failed to heed Jesus' warnings, or even inquire about His concerns. And the imagery of being "sifted like wheat" here is powerful. You get a picture of Peter being tossed to and fro, helpless to resist Satan's machinations. And the rest, as they say, is history.

Within hours, Jesus would be tried, convicted, and taken to Golgotha to be crucified where – after being deserted by His closest friends – He would breathe His last breath.[259] And in that moment, it appeared Satan

---

[257] Strong's Exhaustive Concordance.
[258] Matt 26:58, 69-75; Mark 14:54, 66-72; Luke 22:54-62; John 18:15-18; 26-28. This view is proposed by Cheney and Ellisen. Also see https://redeeminggod.com/sermons/miscellaneous/six-denials-of-peter/.
[259] Matt 27:1-50; Mark 15:1-37; Luke 22:66-23:46; John 18:28-19:30

had successfully used his tricks to claim another in a long line of victories. In fact, it seemed Satan could claim a complete shutout and series sweep. He led Adam and Eve to doubt God's words and question His intentions despite all God had given them. He led the people of Israel to doubt God's ability to provide their needs and discouraged them from attempting to conquer the Promised Land. He sowed the seeds of dissension in the disciples and batted Peter around like a human pinball. With their Lord dead, the disciples disappear, and are hiding out of "fear of the Jews" (John 20:19).

Perhaps you would say Satan can add you to his list of victories. You are not experiencing the abundant life, are still battling addictions or other self-destructive behaviors, and doubt whether you will ever overcome them. You are discouraged, are still eating the pea pods of despair you've brought upon yourself through choices you have come to regret and have a hard time believing God will even accept you back let alone be there for you.

Well, it is reasonable to assume the disciples were experiencing more than a little bit of disillusionment – and even despair – in the hours after Jesus was taken down from the cross. And as they are hiding behind locked doors, we can imagine the thoughts going through their minds. After all, they'd left everything to follow Jesus – and had high hopes that He had come to restore Israel to the prominence it had enjoyed under David and Solomon 1,000 years earlier. Yet all their hopes and dreams – including enjoying the positions of prominence He had promised them – appeared to be every bit as broken as the body of Jesus. But in that moment before He breathed His last, Jesus said something that has changed the world as we know it today – and can be a source of hope for you:

"So, when Jesus had received the sour wine, He said, "It is finished!" And bowing His head, He gave up His spirit." (John 19:30)

SATAN HAS BEEN DEFEATED!

In those three short words, Jesus reveals the significance of His death. Rather than what appeared to be a crushing defeat, He had won! In the original Greek, Jesus is declaring He had in fact accomplished the work He had come to do. He had brought an end to Satan's reign and consummated a new era.[260] And this also fulfilled something God told Adam, Eve – and Satan as well – in those moments after Adam and Eve ate the forbidden fruit:

"And I will put enmity between you and the woman,
And between your seed and her Seed;
He (Jesus) shall bruise your head, And you
(Satan) shall bruise His heel." (Gen 3:15)

Here, God declares with universal ramifications what will unfold throughout human history. Yes, Satan will win some battles. He is "more cunning" than anyone us mere mortals – with our fragile egos and insatiable desires – will ever encounter. But he is no match for God. While God's plans to build a nation (Israel) that will be set apart for Him alone (Ex 19:6) and a "light to the Gentiles" (Is 42:60) appeared dashed after Israel failed in her mission and was banished from the Promised Land (2 Kings 25:8-11; 2 Chron 36:15-21), God will one day restore the nation of Israel to unprecedented prominence.[261]

This is due to the fact Jesus is the descendant of Abraham through Whom not only Israel, but people from "all the families of the earth shall be blessed (Gen 12:3). And through His death, Jesus has inaugurated the New Covenant – a covenant in which we are declared righteous and acceptable based on the work of Jesus alone, and not our own efforts.[262]

And that victory is complete (Col 1:20; 2:15). Satan has already been judged (John 16:11), death itself has been overcome (Heb 2:14-15), and it is only a matter of time until that victory will be fully consummated. God will "crush Satan under your feet" (Rom 16:20), and he will be cast into the Lake of Fire for permanent destruction.[263]

In the meantime, while God is allowing Satan to "rule this world"

---

[260] The English "finished" comes from the Greek word *teleo*, which means, "to end, complete, to execute fully, conclude, accomplish, to consummate". Strong's Exhaustive Concordance; William D. Mounce, The Analytical Lexicon to the Greek New Testament, Grand Rapids, MI: Zondervan Publishing House, 1993.

[261] See, for example, Ezekiel chapters 40-48.

[262] See Matt 26:28; Mark 14:24; Luke 22:20; 1 Cor 11:25; cf Jer 31:31-34; Ezek 36:26-32.

[263] Rev 20:10; cf Matt 25:41; Luke 10:18; John 12:31

He is in fact limiting Satan's powers. While God allows Satan to use his tricks, he is being restrained from wreaking the depths of the chaos and destruction he so desires (2 Thess 2:6-7; cf Job 1:12-2:6). He has no claim over believers who are indwelt by the Holy Spirit (Eph 1:13-14; Titus 3:5) and are now part of the kingdom of Jesus (Acts 26:18; Col 1:13). And we can claim victory that we, too, have "overcome him simply by declaring our faith in Jesus:

> "For whatever is born of God overcomes the world. And this is the
> victory that has overcome the world -- our
> faith...and the wicked one
> does not touch him." (1 John 5:4; 18b; cf 1 John 2:13-14; 4:4).

Our challenge is to boldly proclaim and stand upon the truth Jesus did in fact walk out of His tomb. And with all our weaknesses, Satan is every bit as vulnerable to the excesses of his own ego. For all his shrewdness, perhaps the one he has deceived the most is himself! After all, while he vainly and desperately continues to aspire to "exalt his throne above the stars of God" (Is 14:13), it is God who reigns in the heavens today. While Satan may have convinced himself he had won the war, he is nothing more than one of a large cast of characters in a story line that would inevitably lead to Jesus knowingly and willingly being victorious when He became the Passover Lamb for all of humanity.

But in a way this shouldn't have come as a complete surprise, as it was hinted at as many as 1,000 years before by His human ancestor King David, as well as by Jesus Himself.[264] Jesus knew what lay ahead of Him, as at the beginning of His ministry He said to His mother His "hour had not yet come" (John 2:4). At the Passover three years earlier, Jesus predicted he would die, but after three days in the tomb would be resurrected (John 2:19-22). He knew early on the Jewish religious leaders were plotting how they might destroy Him (Matt 12:14; Mark 3:6). On several occasions, He predicted His arrest, crucifixion, and death.[265] He knew six months in advance the "time had come for Him to be received up" (Luke 9:51) and

---

[264] See Psalm 22. See also: http://www.wicwiki.org.uk/mediawiki/index.php/92_Prophecies_of_the_Psalms_Fulfilled_in_Jesus_Christ, which cites 92 passages in Psalms alone containing prophecies about Jesus.
[265] Matt 12:40; 16:21; 20:17; 20:17; 26:28; Mark 8:31; Luke 24:44

knew it would occur during that upcoming Passover (Matt 26:18; Luke 22:15-16; John 13:1).

But Jesus couldn't sacrifice Himself – He needed participants to knowingly and willingly play their parts in falsely accusing and bringing the trumped-up charges that would result in His arrest and execution. And He found that in the Jewish religious leaders: men who resented the praise and worship He received when He rode into Jerusalem on the colt of a donkey during Passover week in proclaiming Himself to be the coming King prophesied by Zechariah over 500 years earlier.[266] Just as God "hardened" Pharaoh's heart in his attempt to resist God's plans some 1,500 years earlier, Jesus "hardened" the hearts of the Jewish religious leaders.[267] And He accomplished this through stoking the fire of the anger, envy, and malice smoldering in their hearts when He called out their hypocrisy and the emptiness of their religious rituals during that fateful Passover week (Matt 23:1-39). And Satan – like everyone else who had a part to play in the dramatic events that unfolded that day – played his part to perfection.

Yet Satan refuses to face the reality of his own inevitable fate. He knows Jesus walked out of the tomb that day to ascend to heaven and is now sitting at the right hand of the throne of the Father (Acts 2:33) – a throne he had attempted but failed to usurp. Satan knows full well that rather than a crowning victory for himself, Jesus' death was a victory for God. And if honest with himself, he knows he cannot win, because the truth is this:

"And I also say to you that you are Peter,
and on this rock, I will build My
church, and the gates of Hades shall not
prevail against it." (Matt 16:18)

And while Satan continues to wage war against God, the reality is the time is ticking until his destruction. And we can say this with confidence, because just as sure as Jesus is alive today, He will in fact build His church through the transformation of believers like you!

---

[266] Matt 21:1-11; Mark 11:1-11; Luke 19:29-44; John 12:12-19; cf Zech 9:9.
[267] See Ex 4:21; 7:3; 8:15, 32; 9:12, 34; 10:1, 20, 27; 11:10; 14:4, 8. The hearts of both the Pharaoh's and Jewish religious leaders who had Jesus executed were already "hardened", and willingly did what God had foreordained for them when their prideful egos were challenged.

CHAPTER 7

RETURNING TO THE FATHER, PART III

INTRODUCTION

There is an old saying we learn more from our failures than our successes. Case in point is the following from Robert F. Kennedy, who once said:

"Only those who dare to fail greatly can ever achieve greatly." [268]

Many highly successful people will tell you they failed miserably before succeeding. Steve Jobs was fired by Apple which he founded in his garage and had to start over and build two successful companies before Apple took him back. Bill Gates, a Harvard dropout, started out by founding Traf-O-Data, which went bust, before starting Microsoft. Henry Ford twice tried his hand in the auto industry only to fail before founding Ford Motor Company. And then there's Thomas Edison, inventor of the lightbulb. Edison failed over 9,000 times before finally getting it right. But all would say there was value in failing, as they learned something that contributed to their later successes. [269] As Ford said:

""The only real mistake is the one from which we learn nothing." [270]

---

[268] https://www.forbes.com/sites/ekaterinawalter/2013/12/30/30-powerful-quotes-on-failure/#1debd6624bd1. Interestingly Bram Stoker, author of the novel, *Dracula*, is given credit for the opening quote.

[269] https://www.wanderlustworker.com/12-famous-people-who-failed-before-succeeding/

[270] https://www.azquotes.com/author/4992-Henry_Ford/tag/failure

Perhaps "failure" is best summed up in the following acronym:

*F*irst

*A*ttempt

*I*n

*L*earning

The disciples "dared greatly" when they went all in and began following Jesus – only to fail greatly in deserting Him during His greatest time of need. Within a day, Jesus is dead and buried in a tomb, and the disciples are hiding in fear behind locked doors (John 20:19-29). Yet, a mere 50 days later, something remarkable happens:

> *"When the Day of Pentecost had fully come, they (the disciples) were all with one accord in one place. And suddenly there came a sound from heaven, as of a rushing mighty wind, and it filled the whole house where they were sitting. Then there appeared to them divided tongues, as of fire, and one sat upon each of them. And they were all filled with the Holy Spirit and began to speak with other tongues, as the Spirit gave them utterance.*

> *"And there were dwelling in Jerusalem Jews, devout men, from every nation under heaven. And when this sound occurred, the multitude came together, and were confused, because everyone heard them speak in his own language. Then they were all amazed and marveled, saying to one another, 'Look, are not all these who speak Galileans? And how is it that we hear, each in our own language in which we were born...we hear them speaking in our own tongues the wonderful works of God.' So they were all amazed and perplexed, saying to one another, 'Whatever could this mean'?" (Acts 2:1-12)*

These same men – who only 50 days earlier were arguing over which is the greatest before deserting Jesus, and Peter denying he even <u>knew</u> Him – are now in "one accord" (i.e., unified in purpose), and speaking in languages they don't even know! As amazing as that is, however, it is <u>what</u> they were saying, not what language they were speaking in, that is noteworthy. In the ensuing verses, Peter boldly proclaims Jesus as the fulfillment of God's promises to Israel, then accuses the Jewish religious leaders of putting Jesus to death and called them to repent of their sins in the name of Jesus – resulting in 3,000 people believing in Jesus and the birth of the Church (Acts 2:16-47). And if that wasn't enough, Peter then heals a lame man (Acts 3:1-9; cf John 5:1-9)! But it's what happened a short time later that reflects the complete transformation of Peter in those 50 days:

> *"And they (Jewish religious leaders) called them*
> *and commanded them not to speak at*
> *all nor teach in the name of Jesus. But Peter*
> *and John answered and said to them,*
> *'Whether it is right in the sight of God to listen*
> *to you more than to God, you judge.*
> *For we cannot but speak the things which we*
> *have seen and heard'." (Acts 4:18-20)*

Peter – who a short time before had cowered before these same Jewish leaders is now boldly standing up to them. And he, along with the remaining Ten, would go on to sacrifice their lives sharing the Gospel.[271] Which begs two questions: What emboldened these men to proclaim the same Jesus they had pretended to not even know? And what empowered them with the ability to speak in foreign languages and to heal the lame?[272]

EMBOLDENED BY THE TRUTH

While Jesus had predicted His death and resurrection, the disciples couldn't comprehend – let alone believe – it would happen.[273] But after

---

[271] Judas Iscariot betrayed Jesus and left during the Last Supper (John 14:21-30), then hung himself (Matt 27:3-5; Acts 1:16-19).

[272] The transformation of the disciples is evidence of Kraft's proposition change occurs through the encounters of the truth about Jesus, empowerment by the Holy Spirit, and a commitment to a life dedicated to serving Jesus.

[273] See John 2:19-22; cf Matt 26:59-61; 27:39-41; Mark 14:58; 15:29; Luke 19:47. See also verses cited in *Chapter Six.*

encountering the resurrected Jesus, they faithfully returned to Galilee to wait as instructed.[274] And while out on a fruitless night of fishing, the disciples experience a repeat of the event that prompted them to "forsake all" some three years earlier (Luke 5:1-11): Jesus again shows up, instructs them to toss their nets one more time, and they catch an abundance of fish. Peter immediately realizes it is Jesus, and joyfully plunges into the water and swims to Him (John 21:1-8).

As the rest slowly row their boat dragging the net full of fish they had just caught to shore, Jesus builds a fire, prepares a meal for them, and invites them to "come and eat breakfast" (John 21:2). But as the Apostle John writes, this meal was undoubtedly quite different from the countless meals they had shared with Him during the past three years:

> *"Yet none of the disciples dared ask Him,*
> *"Who are You?" -- knowing that it*
> *was the Lord. Jesus then came and took the*
> *bread and gave it to them, and*
> *likewise, the fish. This is now the third*
> *time Jesus showed Himself to His*
> *disciples after He was raised from the dead." (John 12:12b-14)*

After his resurrection, Jesus had appeared to His disciples on two prior occasions, but those encounters were seemingly short in duration with the express intent of convincing them He had actually been resurrected.[275] Here, you get a sense they ate in the shadow of an awkward silence. And this is understandable given their last meal together was the Last Supper, after which they all deserted Him, and Peter outright denied Him.

You can imagine the embarrassment – and even outright shame – the disciples, and particularly Peter, were experiencing in that moment. They had committed a grievous offense against their Lord, and a simple, "I'm sorry" likely felt totally inadequate. But then something happens that is

---

[274] See Luke 24:36-43; John 20:19-29; cf Matt 28:10. This is an example of a "movement" (see Nouwen, *Spiritual Formation*) in the disciples positioning themselves in anticipation of what God will do, just as their initial decision to follow Him was.

[275] John 20:19-23; cf Luke 24:36-43; John 20:24-29

arguably the most powerful example of redemption in human history –
and what we propose is the foundation of *shalom* and the abundant life
Jesus offers. After eating, Jesus turns directly towards Peter, and asks him
three questions:

> "…*Simon Peter, 'Simon, son of Jonah, do you love*
> *Me more than these?' He said to Him, 'Yes,*
> *Lord; You know that I love You.' He said to him,*
> *'Feed My lambs.' He said to him again a second*
> *time, 'Simon, son of Jonah, do you love Me?' He said to*
> *Him, 'Yes, Lord; You know that I love You.' He said to him,*
> *'Tend My sheep.' He said to him the third time, 'Simon, son*
> *of Jonah, do you love Me?' Peter was grieved because He*
> *said to him the third time, 'Do you love Me?' And he said*
> *to Him, Lord, You know all things; You know that I love*
> *You.' Jesus said to him, 'Feed My sheep." (John 21:15b-17)*

Notice Jesus addresses Peter by his formal name. It's the only time
Jesus addresses Peter this way, and it carries the formality of a parent
about to reprimand a child. But instead of a reprimand, Jesus asks him
three times if Peter still loves Him. Then after each question, Jesus adds
a command, but with it adds a <u>commissioning</u>. Some eighteen months
earlier, Jesus had referred to Himself as the "Good Shepherd" (John 10:1-
18), a mantle He is now passing on to Peter. But with this mantle Peter
would bear the burden Jesus Himself bore:

> "*Most assuredly, I say to you (Peter), when*
> *you were younger, you girded*
> *yourself and walked where you wished; but*
> *when you are old, you will stretch*
> *out your hands, and another will gird you*
> *and carry you where you do not*
> *wish.' This He spoke, signifying by what*
> *death he would glorify God. And*
> *when He had spoken this, He said to him,*
> *'Follow Me'." (John 21:18-19)*

The price to "follow Me" was big, as Peter would one day die by crucifixion as well.[276] But just like that, Jesus – in a clear demonstration of the fathomless depths of God's love, grace, and mercy – has unconditionally restored Peter to a place of prominence.[277] While repentant and having learned from his failures, Peter has done nothing to warrant such favor. But in that moment Peter learned what only experience can teach, and that's what grace really is. Sure, we get a glimpse of it by reading the Parables of the Prodigal Son or Two Prayers. And Peter had seen it demonstrated in how Jesus engaged and embraced people like the woman he met at the well in Sychar, the woman caught in adultery, and Zacchaeus the tax collector (Luke 19:2-8). But now Peter really understood that grace is "getting what you don't deserve".[278] Through his failures, Peter had come to understand just how undeserving he was of the grace and favor Jesus had once again extended to him.

Now this wasn't a new revelation, and certainly wasn't the first time we see God granting favor through bestowing positions of honor upon far-from-perfect human beings without them having done anything to warrant it, and despite knowing full well they would at one point fail miserably. We can start with Adam – the last created yet given the authority to name every other living creature. And there's Abraham – one of the most well-known names in the Bible and considered the father of the three major world religions (Judaism, Christianity, and Islam) – a mere pagan from the land of Ur when God promises to bless him abundantly simply by "going to a land I will show you". While deemed "righteous" simply for <u>believing</u> God, Abraham also failed by not protecting his wife Sarai, and would fail miserably in jumping ahead of God's timing by having a son (Ishmael) with Hagar.[279]

Then there are David's epic failures. First, God makes him king over Israel, then makes a covenant with him in which David's name would always be remembered and one of his descendants will always sit on the throne of Israel – all the while knowing David would tarnish his name and

---

[276] Early church fathers were unanimous in writing that Peter was crucified in Rome during the persecution of Emperor Nero in AD 64. Some propose Peter insisted in being crucified upside down, though this is less certain. See, for example, http://evidenceforchristianity.org/what-is-the-evidence-that-peter-was-crucified-upside-down-in-rome/

[277] See Matt 17:1-13; 26:36-46; Mark 5:21; 9:2-8; 14:32-42; Luke 9:28-36; 22:40-46.

[278] See Luke 19:2-8; John 4:20-24. See also *Chapter Two*.

[279] See Gen 2:19-20; 12:1-3, 11-20; 15:1-21; 16:1-16; cf Gal 3:5-6; Heb 6:13-14; Jam 2:23.

reputation through his sins against Bathsheba and Uriah. But God also knew how David would respond when confronted by the prophet Nathan:

"So, David said to Nathan, 'I have sinned
against the LORD'." (2 Sam 13:13) [280]

God knew David's repentance was sincere through his unreserved willingness to accept the consequences of his actions: his son Amnon would repeat David's sins by raping his sister Tamar (2 Sam 13:1-39), and his son Absalom would attempt to usurp his authority as king (2 Sam 15:1-12) as well as publicly humiliate him by taking his concubines one at a time into his tent for his own sexual gratification (2 Sam 16:15-23).

This helps us understand an important caveat to the concept of God's grace: while as eternal as His love, it does not come at the expense of justice and righteousness:

"Do not be deceived, God is not mocked; for
whatever a man sows, that he will
also reap. For he who sows to his flesh will
of the flesh reap corruption, but he
who sows to the Spirit will of the Spirit
reap everlasting life." (Gal 6:7-8)

While Jesus represents the perfect expression of God's love and grace, it is important we remember He is also the perfect expression of God's truth:

"And the Word became flesh and dwelt among
us, and we beheld His glory, the glory
as of the only begotten of the Father, full of
grace and truth. John bore witness of
Him and cried out, saying, 'This was He of
whom I said, He who comes after me is
preferred before me, for He was before me.' And
of His fullness we have all received,

---

[280] See Psalm 51 and David's full confession, his regret and remorse, and desire God both forgive cleanse him of unrighteousness.

and grace for grace. For the law was given
through Moses, but grace and truth
came through Jesus Christ." (John 1:14-17; cf Col 1:6; 2 John 1:3)

When we go astray of God's Word, His truth will hit home and "reality will hit you hard, bro" in the form of the pain of unpleasant consequences. Case in point is the Prodigal, who found himself eating pea pods, having to endure that long journey home and humbly confess he had "sinned against heaven and in your sight", and coming to the realization his actions rendered him unworthy of being "called your son" (Luke 15:18-21).

Peter felt the humiliation and remorse of remembering the warning He had ignored, and looking into the eyes of the man he had declared "Lord", but then denied.[281] As Jesus Himself said in the early days of His ministry, He didn't come to destroy the Law but to <u>fulfill</u> it – His point being God's principles still apply, and woe to those who ignore them.[282] And aside from avoiding the pain of "reaping what we have sowed", it is only through realizing our need to fall upon the grace available to us through the perfect life and selfless sacrifices Jesus made on our behalf that we can truly experience abundance in our relationship with God. This is what Peter, and the disciples came to realize as they shared that meal with Jesus on the shore of the Sea of Galilee that morning.

We can't help but wonder if the disciples found themselves reflecting in the days that followed on what Jesus had taught them during their time together. Perhaps it finally sunk in that they had done nothing to earn the favor bestowed upon them when He selected them from among His countless other followers to be members of His Twelve, and empowered them to teach, cast out unclean spirits and heal illnesses (Matt 10:1; Mark 3:14-15; Luke 6:13-16). Perhaps they came to see themselves much like the tax collector who "would not so much as raise his eyes to heaven" in shame while pleading for God's mercy (Luke 18:13), but who in his humility "will be exalted"; or the Prodigal Son, who through disowning and deserting his father came to realize he in fact deserved nothing, yet was blessed by his father when fully restored as a son.

---

[281] Luke 22:61-62; cf Matt 26:65; Mark 14:72

[282] See Matt 5:17-18. See also Rom 6:1-23, where Paul tells us "The wages of sin is death" (v 23).

Perhaps as Jesus called Peter to the center of their circle, they realized He was restoring <u>all</u> of them to the important roles He had prepared them for: that He was healing them spiritually by placing "sandals" of grace upon their feet, dressing them in "robes" of mercy by restoring their relationship with Him, and placing on them the "signet ring" signifying the authority He would bestow upon them on Pentecost. It is in the lowliness of remorse and repentance our hearts are tilled and we become ready to receive the grace of God needed to become the servants Jesus will use to build His kingdom. And it is through the reception of that grace that the willingness to be used for His purposes is planted and takes root. The apostle Paul came to know this as well as he wrote to the Galatians:

"For you have heard of my former conduct
in Judaism, how I persecuted the
church of God beyond measure and tried to
destroy it. And I advanced in Judaism
beyond many of my contemporaries in my
own nation, being more exceedingly
zealous for the traditions of my fathers. But
when it pleased God, who separated
me from my mother's womb and called me
through His grace, to reveal His
Son in me, that I might preach Him among
the Gentiles..." (Gal 1:13-16a)

The former Saul was arguably as undeserving of God's grace as anyone. Before that fateful day on the road to Damascus, we are told Saul "Made havoc" by "dragging off men and women...to prison", and in his zeal to crush "The Way" even giving the go-ahead to the stoning of a faithful disciple named Stephen.[283] But blind, helpless, and with nowhere to turn, a broken Saul became willing, and did what desperate people often do: he prayed. And it was while Saul was praying that God was instructing Ananias to go see Saul. But Ananias is more than a bit resistant, as we see in the account of his interaction with God:

---

[283] See Acts 7:59-8:4. Note in Acts 6:1-6 Stephen is described as a man "full of faith and the Holy Spirit".

"...'Lord, I have heard from many about this
man, how much harm he has done to Your
saints in Jerusalem. And here he has authority
from the chief priests to bind all who
call on Your name.' But the Lord said to him,
'Go, for he is a chosen vessel of Mine
to bear My name before Gentiles, kings, and
the children of Israel. For I will show
him how many things he must suffer for
My name's sake'." (Acts 9:13-16)

Ananias's resistance is understandable: after all, Saul had inflicted significant pain and suffering upon the early Christians, many whom Ananias likely knew personally. But Ananias trusted God and did as he was instructed, and Saul was healed. And the rest is history, as the Pharisee formerly known as Saul would soon become the apostle Paul, and arguably the greatest evangelist in Christian history – his zealousness to persecute Jesus transcended by his zealousness to proclaim Jesus. Through the pressure of love and grace, Jesus transformed a lump of coal named Saul into the diamond named Paul.

While the good memories and warm feelings we experience when blessed in some way often fade over time, Paul never forgot the grace and mercy he had received, as seen in the first letter he wrote to the Corinthians some 20-plus years later:

"For I am the least of the apostles, who am
not worthy to be called an apostle,
because I persecuted the church of God. But
by the grace of God I am what I am,
and His grace toward me was not in vain;
but I labored more abundantly than
they all, yet not I, but the grace of God which
was with me." (1 Cor 15:9-10) [284]

---

[284] This assumes a date of A.D. 35 for Paul's encounter on the road to Damascus, and an A.D. 55 dating of 1 Corinthians.

A few years later he writes the grace he had received – not his vast knowledge, or skills as a lawyer and theologian – as the foundation upon which he proclaimed Jesus:

"To me, who am less than the least of all the saints,
this grace was given, that I should preach
among the Gentiles the unsearchable riches of Christ,
and to make all see what is the fellowship
of the mystery, which from the beginning of the ages
has been hidden in God who created all
things through Jesus Christ; to the intent that now
the manifold wisdom of God might be
made known by the church to the principalities and
powers in the heavenly places, according
to the eternal purpose which He accomplished
in Christ Jesus our Lord, in whom we
have boldness and access with confidence
through faith in Him." (Eph 3:8-12)

And in A.D. 67 – over 30 years since his first encounter with Jesus, and shortly before he would die a martyr's death at the hands of the Roman emperor Nero – Paul remained firmly grounded upon the grace and mercy he had received from God:

"This is a faithful saying and worthy of all
acceptance, that Christ Jesus came into the
world to save sinners, of whom I am chief. However,
for this reason I obtained mercy, that
in me first Jesus Christ might show all longsuffering,
as a pattern to those who are going
to believe on Him for everlasting life. Now to the
King eternal, immortal, invisible, to God
who alone is wise, be honor and glory forever
and ever. Amen." (1 Tim 1:15-17)

Paul never forgot the sins that rendered him "not worthy to be called an apostle". But even more importantly, he never let the burden of his failures and the resultant shame he felt blur the truth he would firmly and unreservedly proclaim to the Christians in Rome:

"There is therefore now no condemnation to those who
are in Christ Jesus, who do not walk according to the
flesh, but according to the Spirit." (Rom 8:1)

Grace is the permanent pardon that sets us free from the guilt and shame of our sins, and allows us to boldly stand in the love and favor of God:

"For I am persuaded that neither death nor life,
nor angels nor principalities nor powers, nor
things present nor things to come, nor height nor
depth, nor any other created thing, shall be
able to separate us from the love of God which is
in Christ Jesus our Lord." Rom 8:38-39)

It is in that moment we place our faith in Jesus that all our failures and shortcomings are set aside (Ps 103:12), and we become a "new creation":

"Therefore, if anyone is in Christ, he is a new
creation; old things have passed away; behold, all
things have become new." (2 Cor 5:17) [285]

And it is in this freedom we can cast aside the guilt and shame of what was, and "reach forward to those things that are ahead" (Phil 3:13). And "those things" are the plans and purposes God has determined for each of us because God doesn't see the problems of our past; instead, he sees the potential in the person we each will become through what He will do in us. And Paul makes this abundantly clear in his letter to the Ephesians:

"For we are His workmanship, created in Christ
Jesus for good works, which God prepared beforehand
that we should walk in them." (Eph 2:10)

---

[285] See also Gal 6:15-16.

No, it is in those moments when we come to realize how far short we fall of the glory and goodness of God that He can begin the "workmanship" He desires to do in us for the good works He has planned and purposed for us.[286] God, like the Prodigal's father, has been anxiously waiting for that moment we return to Him and are ready to do the work He has planned for us. Jesus knew the disciples needed to learn by failing to realize the grace and favor they had received before they would be ready for the mantle of "ambassadors" (2 Cor 5:18-21). But because of their humble acceptance of His much-needed grace, they – as He had told them in the days before His arrest, crucifixion, and resurrection – will one day reign with Him in His kingdom (Luke 22:28-30). Because Jesus uses flawed and fragile human beings like those described in the preceding pages to build His kingdom. People like us, and people like you. And people like Hal Nevitt.

Hal exemplifies much of what we have presented up to this point. Hal grew up in the dysfunction and unpredictability of what he has described as an "alcoholic home" and recalls two memories of his father. The first – one Hal recalls fondly – was the time his dad propped Hal on his lap and turned the reins over to him by letting him steer his car. But the second – the memory of his childhood Hal, now in his '60's still remembers most vividly – was the day at age 5 all dressed up and waiting in anticipation of some quality time with his dad. But as Hal waited – and waited – he finally had to face the truth that was becoming increasingly evident to him: his dad wasn't coming.

As an adolescent and young adult, Hal channeled the pain of his childhood in positive ways. He released his anger as a linebacker in football. He found acceptance, structure, and purpose as a United States Marine, and later as a police officer with the Scottsdale, Arizona police force. In time Hal was assigned to the Special Enforcement Unit as an Undercover Narcotics Detective. Unfortunately, he – like many who grow up in unhealthy homes – fulfilled the prophecy of Moses in following in his father's footsteps.[287] Hal's love for alcohol, and later cocaine, began to take over his life. Eventually it all caught up with him when he was charged and convicted for narcotics offenses and sentenced to seven years in prison (three-and-a-half of which he served) before being released. But

---

[286] See Ps 53:1-5; Rom 3:9-25; Eccl 7:20; Is 64:6; Gal 3:22.
[287] See Ex 20:5; 34:7; Lev 26:40; Num 14:18; Deut 5:9.

as he sat in his prison cell during the early days of his sentence, Hal raged at God Who – like his earthly father – had abandoned him and left him waiting on that doorstep.

Like the Apostle Paul, however, the scales on Hal's eyes soon began to fell away as he began to see the truth that God hadn't turned his back on him; instead, Hal had turned his back on God. And God hadn't abandoned him: instead, God – like the Prodigal's father – had been anxiously awaiting Hal to return home. Hal committed himself to a life of sobriety, and through the stern but relentless guidance of his sponsor in *AA* began to address the wounds and resultant character flaws that had fueled his alcohol and drug abuse. But that left Hal – like the disciples waiting in Galilee – wondering, "What now?"

EMPOWERED BY THE SPIRIT

Something dynamic happened within each of the disciples upon seeing the resurrected Jesus, as the truth of Who He is and what He taught took on a whole new meaning. Once guilt-ridden they were now justified. Once ashamed they had been restored to positions of honor. And having experienced His grace personally they became humble servants ready to serve Him. The debates over who was the greatest had given way to a unity in purpose as they awaited instruction. But it was being empowered by the Holy Spirit that equipped them to become His ambassadors to the world by boldly proclaiming His name and doing the good works He had planned for them. It began with speaking languages they didn't know (Acts 2:4-5) and continued with Paul's healing of a man lame from birth (Acts 3:2-8). But this empowerment wasn't limited to those eleven men that day on Pentecost, as the Bible clearly teaches the Holy Spirit equips every believer in Jesus with abilities that enable every one of us to be ambassadors for Jesus as well.

These abilities – referred to as "spiritual gifts" or "gifts of the Spirit" – are discussed extensively in the New Testament, because without them we are because without them we are incapable of completing the work Jesus has prepared for us.

An Overview of the Spiritual Gifts [288]

The spiritual gifts can be characterized as either "service" gifts or "sign" gifts and are identified in Romans 12:3-8; 1 Corinthians 12:8-10, Ephesians 4:11-12, and 1 Peter 4:10-11.[289] The service gifts include:

Teaching

From the Greek *didasko*, which means "to teach, instruct, or provide direction in a public setting". Jesus was recognized as a "teacher" or "rabbi" for His ability to teach the Jews the correct understanding of the Mosaic Law (Matt 8:19; 9:11; 23:8). And after being empowered by the Holy Spirit, the disciples in turn took on the role of teaching the new believers (Acts 5:42; 13:12; 15:35; 18:11; 28:11). The gift of teaching empowers its bearer to effectively impart biblical truth in a way that enables recipients to better understand the Scriptures, and as a result to experience spiritual growth.

Preaching

While not specifically identified as a spiritual gift, there are 147 references in which some form of the English "preach" can be found in the Bible.[290] In the New Testament these references stem mainly from two Greek words: *euaggelistes*, which means "to effectively declare the good news of the Gospel"; and *kerusso*, which means "to proclaim, make known". The distinction appears as in the former, the message centers on the Gospel of Jesus (the truth of Who He is), while the latter more often refers to life application of His- and the apostles' teachings. An example is seen in one of the early messages of Jesus:

---

[288] Some of this section drawn from Millard J. Erickson, <u>Christian Theology, 2nd ed.</u> Other resources include Strong's Exhaustive Concordance; The Analytical Lexicon to the Greek New Testament; https://mintools.com/gifts-list.htm. Note the order of presentation of the gifts is not ranking them in terms of value or importance.

[289] Note in Ephesians 4:11-12 Paul appears to be presenting the roles or functions in which the spiritual gifts are utilized. We will address this further later on in this chapter. See also 1 Corinthians 12:28.

[290] New King James Version. Note these references are predominately found in the New Testament.

"The Spirit of the LORD is upon Me, Because
He has anointed Me To preach the
gospel to the poor; He has sent Me to heal the
brokenhearted, to proclaim liberty
to the captives and recovery of sight to the
blind, to set at liberty those who are
oppressed; To proclaim the acceptable year
of the LORD." (Luke 4:18-19)

Here, Jesus told His audience He had been anointed to both "preach" (*euaggelistes*) the good news of the Gospel, and to "proclaim" (*kerusso*) the ramifications of what the Gospel means for us. After His ascension, the disciples are seen both preaching and teaching (Acts 5:42; 15:35; 28:31). The distinction may play out in one's calling, as one may be called to be an evangelist or missionary (Eph 3:6-8) to those who have never heard the Gospel; while another may be called as a preaching pastor in areas where the audience is largely familiar with and has accepted the Gospel message, and the message is focused on applying the teachings of Jesus in the believer's life.

Another distinction may be found in the roles of two individuals both gifted in "teaching". The gifted preacher may also be effective at teaching, while the gifted teacher may not be as effective as a preacher. Hence, the "preacher" will prioritize the use of his or her teaching gift in delivering the Sunday morning sermon, while the "teacher" will utilize his or her gift in a classroom, small group, or discipleship setting.

Speaking

From the Greek *laleo,* which means, "to talk, preach, say, tell, address, declare, or announce" (1 Pet 4:11). This is the "gifted speaker" who is effective in inspiring others by engaging them emotionally and experientially when speaking.

Knowledge

From the Greek *ginosko,* which means, "to perceive, understand, know experientially". While all believers have the "knowledge" of Jesus that leads to salvation, spiritual growth requires acquiring the knowledge and wisdom of God (1 Cor 1:4-8; 8:7-13; 2 Pet 1:2-9). God equips some to impart said knowledge to other believers, as seen in the student who effectively incorporates extra-biblical information that enhances the understanding and relevance of Biblical teachings in one's culture (1 Cor 12:8). Paul, for example, was given the gift of knowledge so he could effectively instruct the Ephesians of how to grow in their knowledge and understanding of the "mystery" of the Gospel (Eph 3:1-7).[291]

Paul is clear, however, that the gift of knowledge can be abused, as in Corinth where some became "puffed up" (i.e., "full of themselves"). Hence, those possessing knowledge are challenged to humbly remember the source of his or her giftedness (1 Cor 8:1-2).[292]

Wisdom

Wisdom, from the Greek *sophia,* is where knowledge and experience come together in life application (1 Cor 12:8; cf Jam 3:15-19). The wise person provides enlightenment and insight as to how Biblical truths are applied in the decision-making of everyday life situations. While some are knowledgeable, not all are wise in applying said knowledge.

Chinese philosopher Confucius once said, "Wisdom is knowing what you don't know".[293] Similarly, Greek philosopher Socrates said, "The only true wisdom is in knowing you know nothing".[294] And they were on to something, since the Bible is clear wisdom "comes from above" (i.e., God), and not through natural means (Prov 3:7; cf 2:2-10). In fact, it is "fear (respect) of the Lord, that is wisdom" (Prov 9:10; cf 15:33).

Solomon once wrote, "When pride comes, then comes shame; but with the humble is wisdom" (Prov 11:2). And as we've seen, Solomon learned this the hard way. Wisdom is seen in the person who listens before

---

[291] Ephesus was home to several of the "mystery" cults. Hence, Paul had to be sufficiently knowledgeable about them to contrast Christianity and the Gospel message with these other cults so the Ephesians could grasp the distinction.

[292] Note Paul also warned Timothy to guard against those who think they have knowledge but are nothing more than "idle babblers" (1 Tim 6:18-21). Hence, believers should also scrutinize the words of the "knowledgeable" that they are consistent with the "good fruit" of Jesus and the apostles (note Matt 7:15-27).

[293] https://www.azquotes.com/quote/469963.

[294] https://www.goodreads.com/quotes/9431-the-only-true-wisdom-is-in-knowing-you-know-nothing

speaking – something Peter came to realize the hard way. A common mistake churches often make is calling those successful in business to the position of elder, assuming business smarts translate to the wisdom required for the highest level of church leadership. Sadly, this too often is not the case.

Discernment

Closely related to wisdom is the gift of discernment. From the Greek *diakrisis*, it means, "to discern, distinguish, decide", specifically in distinguishing truth from error, and whether one's intentions, words or actions are from God or Satan (1 Cor 12:10). Old Testament-era Israelites were given instruction as to how they could discern if one was truly a prophet of God (Deut 18:20-22), we are all sufficiently equipped to discern "both good and evil" (Heb 5:14), and believers can increase their ability to discern by growing in their knowledge of Jesus and the Bible (Phil 1:9-10). But those given the gift of discernment will be especially gifted in sensing the spirit and resultant motives of others.

The gift of discernment is addressed in Paul's letter to the church in Corinth where the "sign" gifts (i.e., tongues and prophesy) were seemingly being abused (1 Cor 13:1-14:30). And just as there was controversy in that church during Paul's day, there remains debate as to whether the sign gifts are still active today, and if so, how they are manifested.

Leadership

From the Greek *proistemi*, which means, "to stand in front of, appoint, establish, present". The gift of leadership is seen in those effective in leading, directing, and motivating others in the church (Rom 12:8). Leadership is to be carried out with "diligence" (from the Greek *spoude*, meaning "speed, haste"). The gift of leadership, therefore, is evidenced when the goals and tasks the leader oversees are accomplished efficiently and effectively.

While the Spirit gives life to the Church, structure is needed so the spiritual gifts are used effectively. We see, for example, the apostles demonstrating leadership in the early Church by establishing the office of "deacon" to handle matters that would hinder them from "giv[ing] ourselves continually to prayer and the ministry of the word (Acts 6:1-7).

Noteworthy is the ability to run a successful business does not necessarily mean a person has the spiritual gift of leadership. Conversely, a person who does not own or manage in the business world may be empowered to effectively lead, direct, and motivate others in the church (Rom 12:8).

Administration (Stewardship)

From the Greek *oikonomos,* which means, "to parcel out, distributor, overseer, manager, agent, trustee (estate), holder of commission with responsibility over something he/she doesn't own" (1 Cor 12:28). The gift of administration is closely related to the gift of leadership, but more focused on the process in which the goals or tasks are accomplished through developing and implementing the plan utilized to accomplish said goals.

Another Greek word commonly used is *kubernesis,* which means, "to steer or guide" much like the helmsman assigned to steer a ship. While it may address overseeing functions, it also applies to administrative tasks (secretarial, etc.) or overseeing the church's budget or finances. A skillset of the administrator or steward is a sharp eye to detail.

Exhortation

From the Greek *parakaleo,* which means, "to urge, call alongside, exhort, appeal, console, cheer up". This is the spiritual gift most associated with counseling, and involves coming alongside others with words of encouragement, comfort, consolation, and counsel to help another grow spiritually (Rom 12:8). Noteworthy, however, is to "call alongside" suggests an emphasis on one's spiritual growth (2 Cor 8:7; 12:18; Phil 4:2; 1 Thess 4:10).

Mercy

From the Greek *eleeo* which means, "Compassion, to comfort, the outward manifestation of pity". The gift of mercy complements the gift of exhortation, as while exhortation is forward focused in promoting spiritual growth (Prov 20:5), mercy is directed towards helping others heal from past regrets, injuries or losses that hinder growth (Rom 12:8).

While God's "mercy" is often understood to mean the withholding of judgment or punishment, passages with the English "mercy" more often reflect compassion or pity. God Himself is described as "rich in mercy" born out of His infinite love for us (Eph 2:4; cf Luke 1:72; Rom 15:9; Titus 3:5). This suggests rather than a heavenly Judge impassively choosing to pardon us from our sins and the resultant punishment that we deserve, He also feels the compassion Jesus felt when observing the lost "sheep" of Israel who lacked the direction of the caring Shepherd He came to be for them (Mark 6:34).

The gift of mercy, therefore, is the capacity to see beyond one's bad choices and resultant consequences to the wreckage and resultant pain the "sinner" is suffering. It is seen in the contrast between the compassion felt by the father and the condemnation by the Perfect Son upon the Prodigal's return home. It is also seen in those able to sit with and share in the pain another is experiencing through the loss of a loved one, the disappointment of a series of setbacks, or coming to accept one's illness is terminal, and death is imminent.

A good example of how the gift of mercy is utilized in the church is through *Stephen Ministry*, a ministry founded in 1975 by psychologist Reverend Kenneth Haugk in St. Louis, Missouri. Stephen Ministry provides a structured program including an in-depth training to equip those who have the gift of mercy to provide care for those suffering through the challenges life often presents.[295] It is named after Stephen, a man chosen to oversee efforts to provide care for widows in the early church to free up the apostles to direct their efforts towards "prayer and ministry of the Word" (Acts 6:1-6).

It is vitally important to realize, however, that while mercy is a spiritual gift, it is also a character trait of the mature Christian who has come to understand the depths of grace and mercy he or she has received from God, and in turn is willing to extend it to others.

Jesus, in quoting the prophet Hosea, said on <u>two</u> occasions that God desires "mercy and not sacrifice" (Matt 9:13; 12:7; cf Hos 6:6). And in confronting the self-righteousness of the Pharisees, Jesus described the

---

[295] https://www.stephenministries.org/stephenministry/default.cfm/917?mnb=1

willingness to extend mercy for others as one of the "weightier" (i.e., most important) matters of God's laws (Matt 23:23).

Faith

From the Greek *pistis*, which in the noun form means, "persuasion, credence, conviction, reliance upon", and in the verb form means, "believe, to trust" (1 Cor 12:9). It is seen in the person firmly persuaded of God's promises and power to accomplish His purposes and displays such a confidence in Him and His Word those circumstances and obstacles do not shake that conviction. Like knowledge, all believers have at least some degree of faith as we are saved by faith alone.[296] But the gift of faith is seen in the unwavering trust that God will demonstrate His faithfulness regardless of the circumstance, which inspires and emboldens others who may be wavering in their faith (note Rom 8:28).[297]

Like mercy, faith is not only a gift but a trait all believers are called to cultivate. Like justice and mercy, faith was deemed by Jesus to be one of the most important traits of the mature believer (Matt 23:23). And we are wise to cultivate faith given it empowers patience and perseverance through the most difficult circumstances (2 Tim 3:10-11; Jam 1:2-4), and as a result will lead to a greater sense of inner peace (Rom 5:1-4; 1 Cor 13:13).

Service (Ministering)

From the Greek *diakonia*, which means, "minister, service, help, support, contribution." It is where we get the English "deacon" and is seen in the "attendant" who sees what needs to be done and readily jumps in wherever needed to optimize the church's effectiveness in promoting the Gospel.[298] It is exercised in a spirit of humility in that the person with the gift of

---

[296] Paul painstakingly explains this (Eph 2:8; cf Rom 3:21-31; 5:1; Gal 3:11-29). See also John 3:16; 20:30-31. Throughout the Gospel of John, we're told simply believing (i.e., having faith) in Jesus as our Savior from our sins is required for eternal salvation.

[297] While prior to the coming of the Holy Spirit and His impartation of spiritual gifts to believers, you see powerful examples of unwavering faith in men like Joshua (Num 14:1-9; Josh 1:6-18; 2:5; 10:25), who when others doubted were inspired by his faith that God would fulfill His promises and give Israel victory over her enemies.

[298] Mark 10:43; Rom 13:4, 15:8; Rom 12:7; Gal 2:17; Eph 6:21; Col 1:7, 23, 25; 1 Thess 3:2.

service willingly performs even the most menial of tasks. Also referred to as the gift of "helps", it is seen in those willing to assist others to free them up to work in their areas of giftedness (1 Cor 12:28). It is also seen in what is commonly referred to as the gift of "hospitality" (1 Pet 4:9), which comes from the Greek *philoxenos*, a compound word meaning "love of strangers". And it is an important gift.

Most of us have had a bad experience at a store or restaurant due to poor or slow service.

And while the food may have been good or the store had the items you were looking for, you may not be inclined to go back because your first impression was negative. The same applies to the first impression of the first-time attender at your church.

During most Sunday morning services, those in attendance will not hear the message until anywhere from 30-45 minutes after they've first driven onto the church property. During that time, a church is giving off numerous signals as to how important that first-time attender is: whether good or poor signage, clean or unkempt grounds, how you are greeted, the quality of direction and instruction provided, etc.[299] The gift of service is vitally important to the success of a church, as even the best sermon may not overcome a poor first impression.

Giving

From the Greek *metadidomi*, which means, "to share, give, impart, bestow, bring forth, or commit" (Rom 12:8). This is the person who may have the natural skills or abilities to generate significant income, is imparted with a heart and spirit of generosity, and takes pleasure in sharing his or her resources liberally and cheerfully with others (Luke 3:11;1 Thess 2:8). It is a vitally important gift given operating a church requires the financial resources necessary to maintain a facility and sufficiently compensate staff to enable them to dedicate their energy to serving in their areas of gifting in a full-time capacity. The gift of giving extends to generously sharing with those in need, particularly strangers.

---

[299] https://churchleaders.com/outreach-missions/outreach-missions-articles/312354-8-key-first-impressions-church-dan-reiland.html.

An Overview of the "Sign" Gifts [300]

The sign gifts include:

Tongues

From the Greek *glossa*, which means, "language, tongue, or utterance". In Acts 2:4-11 "tongues" clearly referred to the various languages, spoken by but unknown to the disciples, so the Jews who had traveled from all over the Near East for Pentecost could understand their message. In the church in Corinth, Paul seems to confirm this in stating:

> *"Therefore tongues are for a sign, not to those*
> *who believe but to unbelievers;*
> *but prophesying is not for unbelievers but for*
> *those who believe." (1 Cor 14:22)*

If the Holy Spirit empowers a believer with the gift of tongues, there will always be another believer with the gift of interpretation present so what is said can be understood (see 1 Cor 12:10). Some believers may experience prayer in tongues, though this will typically occur in private, and is specifically for their own edification (1 Cor 14:26-28).

---

[300] The following (from Erickson) is a summary of the positions for and against whether the sign gifts are active today (see also https://www.gotquestions.org/miraculous-gifts.html. Proponents rely heavily on the book of Acts and 1 Corinthians (see also 2 Cor 12:12) in which the disciples/apostles were not only preaching and teaching but healing as well. In addition, proponents point to 1 Corinthians 12:28 to propose God is still appointing apostles and prophets in the church today. Others propose the necessity of the sign gifts ceased with the completion of the apostles' teaching and the writings of the books contained in the Bible (referred to as the "Canon", see 1 Cor 13:8; 2 Tim 3:16-17; Heb 2:3-4), so the "revelatory" gifts are no longer needed. They further propose the office of apostleship was limited to those who witnessed the resurrected Jesus, and that the healings they performed validated their messages as spokespersons for God until the Canon was completed. It is my interpretation that God is no longer appointing apostles and prophets, though some may possess the gifts of tongues or prophecy as will be described.

Prophecy

From the Greek *prophetei*, meaning, "speak forth the message of God to His people, a foreteller, inspired speaker", seemingly with a message that cannot be known by natural means (Matt 26:68). This would include God equipping the Old Testament prophets He appointed to warn the people of Israel of the judgment that would eventually come upon them for failing to live according to the precepts of the Mosaic Law. In the modern-day church, it appears limited to those given insight into what another believer may experience in the future as a means of bolstering the faith of those within the church.

It is easy to see how sign gifts – as well as service gifts such as the gifts of knowledge or preaching – can be abused to "puff" one up and appear super-spiritual. The same can be said of the gift of healing, where "faith healers" have used tricks to convince the vulnerable they can heal them of their diseases or illnesses – often for great financial gain.[301] The Bible tells us God empowered Peter and Paul to heal the sick and lame as a means of validating they had been given the "signet ring" of authority to carry on the work Jesus had started.[302] With that said, I firmly believe God supernaturally heals people today as a means of bringing people to faith, and to strengthen the faith of others.

While I am not one prone to see "God's hand" in every good thing that happens, I can attest to the fact God is still doing miracles today. In 2007, I was informed a 45-year-old woman in otherwise excellent health was in critical condition after experiencing a cardiac event that effectively stopped the flow of blood to her brain. Her prospects were dim, as she was given an 8% chance of surviving, let alone not suffering significant brain damage. The doctors proposed "Operation Standstill" (which none on the hospital staff had performed before), in which they would chill her body down to 60 degrees, repair her heart, then gradually bring her temperature back to normal. Meanwhile, there I was sitting with her husband as their three teenage children slept after a long night at the hospital. So, I listened as he talked about his wife in the past tense, resigned to the fact the love

---

[301] See, for example, the story of Mark Haville at https://thewordonthewordoffaithinfoblog.com/2009/05/26/ex-faith-healer/.

[302] Acts 3:11; 4:14, 22, 29-31; 5:12; 8:7; 14:9-10; 28:8-9, 27.

of his life was gone, and trying to come to grips with the reality of life without her.

Being the "realist" I am, I typically seek the Spirit's guidance to provide the comfort and consolation needed in moments like this. Instead, God gave me a vision: I saw this woman standing in front of our church congregation and testifying to the fact God IS still in the healing business today. And with a confidence I'm still surprised by today, I told him what I believed God had revealed to me. Meanwhile, a prayer chain was actively reaching out to family and acquaintances all over the world, asking God to perform a miracle.

When I went to visit her the next day, I saw a lifeless body, pale and cold to the touch. But the following day, I walked in to see her sitting up in bed and smiling. Within a week she was released, and a few weeks later was telling her story on a Sunday morning in front of our church body – a walking, talking, testimony to the supernatural healing of God.

All this to say God does amazing things through the believers He has empowered with spiritual gifts. Through gifts such as teaching, preaching, leadership and exhortation, He equips the pastors He has called to "feed the sheep" entrusted to them (John 21:16-17).[303]

But He uses each and every believer – equipped by the Holy Spirit with specific gifts and skills – to play an important role in building His church and caring for His sheep.

Principles for Employing the Spiritual Gifts

As you consider what gifts He has imparted to you, the following are some principles you might utilize to guide how you will employ them.

---

[303] The English "apostle" comes the Greek *apostolos*, which means, "to stand, appoint, establish, hold up", specifically the Gospel truths. It is our interpretation apostleship is more a calling to an office than a spiritual gift. We further propose the office of apostleship was limited to those who personally witnessed the resurrected Jesus, including the remaining Eleven originally called by Jesus along with Matthias (Matt 28:16-20; Acts 1:22-26), Paul who encountered Jesus on the road to Damascus (Acts 9:1-9) and was "caught up to the third heaven" (2 Cor 10:1-5) for his anointing, and possibly Barnabas.

1. *The spiritual gifts are distributed by the Holy Spirit.*

The spiritual gifts are distributed by the Holy Spirit "as He wills".[304] While the gifts may include the natural abilities we use outside the church, they are manifested in a unique way within the church. An example is the person good at developing and implementing plans may be given the gifts of administration to be utilized in overseeing ministries.

Noteworthy is the Bible is not clear as to whether the calling and gifting of a believer was present at birth, given after becoming a believer in Jesus, or some of both. One example is the prophet Jeremiah, who proclaimed he was "ordained" to be a prophet before birth:

"Before I formed you in the womb, I knew you;
Before you were born I sanctified you; I ordained
you a prophet to the nations." (Jer 1:1-5)

Yet, Jeremiah was also the son of a priest, and therefore likely would have had more exposure to the holy Jewish Scriptures than other Israelites. Clearly God had a purpose for Jeremiah from the time he was born but may have utilized his upbringing to equip him for his calling. The same can be said of Paul, who in his letter to the Galatians wrote:

"But when it pleased God, who separated me from my mother's
womb and called me through His grace, to reveal His Son in me,
that I might preach Him among the Gentiles..." (Gal 1:15-16a)

Noteworthy is while Jesus spent three years preparing the Eleven to start His Church, it was Paul – who never even <u>met</u> Jesus until after His resurrection – that Jesus used to build His Church by spreading the Gospel throughout the Roman Empire. So, what made Paul better suited for this role than the Eleven? Well, consider their backgrounds.

While the eleven disciples were Jews born and raised in Israel, Paul – the son of a Pharisee (Acts 23:6) – could claim Roman citizenship through his Greco-Roman mother (Acts 16:37; 22:25; 25:11). He spoke Greek, was raised in Tarsus (a major city and "resort of Greek and Roman merchants"),

---

[304] 1 Cor 12:4-11; Eph 2:19-21; 4:11; 1 Pet 4:11

was exposed to the Greco-Roman thinking of his day through his interactions with merchants and traders, and as a result could effectively present the Gospel to them (Acts 17:1-34). But Paul also learned to "work with [his] own hands" to earn a living (1 Cor 4:12) until the churches he established could support him.[305]

Our point is God may equip you with spiritual gifting that employs your natural abilities and life experiences. For Hal Nevitt, the answer to the question, "What now?" was to use his experiences in helping others, and in the ensuing years Hal obtained his bachelor's and master's degrees in social work and became a licensed therapist and substance abuse counselor. But with all his education and training, Hal will say a major factor in his effectiveness in helping others overcome addiction is the fact he can say, "I've been there, done that". Hal can relate to the challenges inherent in overcoming addiction, and with nearly 40 years of sobriety can point to himself as proof others have reason for hope.

An application of this is also seen in ministries such as *Celebrate Recovery*, founded by Saddleback Church in is a Christ-centered 12-Step program that helps people overcome addiction and other behavioral problems.[306] Facilitators of *Celebrate Recovery* are often those who have overcome similar challenges in using their experiences to help others.

2. *There is a diversity in the function of spiritual gifts.*

While there is diversity in the forms of spiritual gifts, there is also diversity in their function. A lead pastor may be gifted at preaching, but not in administration or encouragement. Given this, he (or she) is wise to work in his or her areas of strength, while deferring to others more gifted in the areas where he or she is particularly gifted.

Another distinction might be seen in the gifts of evangelism, teaching, and knowledge. A preaching pastor may develop a diverse team of giftedness, backgrounds, age, and experiences to ensure the message is relevant to all in attendance on Sunday mornings.

---

[305] https://www.britannica.com/biography/Saint-Paul-the-Apostle;   https://www.biblestudytools.com/classics/barnes-scenes-in-life/early-training-of-the-apostle-paul.html
[306] https://www.celebraterecovery.com/

3. *There is a diversity in the roles of spiritual gifts.*

Paul also tells us there is diversity in the utilization of spiritual gifts through the roles each believer holds within the church, specifically how it relates to the hierarchy or structure of the church. In his letter to the Ephesians, for example, Paul writes:

> *"And He Himself gave some to be apostles, some prophets, some*
> *evangelists, and some pastors and teachers,*
> *for the equipping of the saints*
> *for the work of ministry, for the edifying of*
> *the body of Christ..." (Eph 4:10-11)*

These passages suggest Jesus intended there to be a hierarchal structure in the church, as those called to be pastors and teachers are to lead and equip others. Just as Jesus appointed Paul and the Eleven to lead the early Church, Jesus appoints some to roles of leadership in the Church today while appointing others to support their leadership.

4. *All believers are equipped with at least one gift, but none with all of the gifts.*

In the secular world, some (like the CEO or star athlete) are set apart as "indispensable" relative to others. Not so in the Church. In 1 Corinthians 12:14-30, for example, Paul uses the imagery of the human body to emphasize the importance of every gift for the Church to be effective. This is due to the fact while each believer is equipped with at least one spiritual gift, no one has all the gifts, and every church needs every believer engaged in service for that church to accomplish the work Jesus has called it to. And every believer – regardless of his or her role – should be valued and appreciated for the work he or she does. I can recall a vivid example of this in action.

While serving at Moon Valley Bible Church in the North Phoenix area, we undertook renovating about 90% of the interior of our administrative building including moving walls to best utilize the space. I recall one morning – after we had finished tearing out virtually all the sheet rock – just standing and staring at the maze of wiring hanging from the ceiling.

To me, trying to figure out which wire went where and did what was the proverbial "finding a needle in a haystack". But not to a church member named Daniel.

He would be the first to tell you he was the last person you wanted leading a Bible study, and in fact could "hardly read without reading out loud". But being an experienced electrician, Daniel knew exactly where every wire went and what it did. God had not only gifted him with the natural abilities of an electrician, but with the spiritual gift of service to equip him to make a significant contribution to the renovation of the church.

In his letter to the Ephesians, Paul uses the imagery of the Temple building to illustrate the structure needed for a church to thrive:

> *"Now, therefore, you are no longer strangers and*
> *foreigners, but fellow citizens with the saints*
> *and members of the household of God, having*
> *been built on the foundation of the apostles*
> *and prophets, Jesus Christ Himself being the chief*
> *cornerstone, in whom the whole building,*
> *being joined together, grows into a holy temple*
> *in the Lord, in whom you also are being*
> *built together for a dwelling place of God*
> *in the Spirit." (Eph 2:19-21)*

It is clear the church is to be built upon the "foundation" of the apostles and prophets, or the truths of God revealed through the writings of the Old Testament prophets and the New Testament apostles of the early Church. And you can have the best masons lay the smoothest and best-laid foundation, but without carpenters, electricians, sheet-rockers, and painters, you have no building – only a useless foundation simply taking up space.

5. _There is no distinction in the importance of the gifts._

It is a wise and humble pastor who realizes that he (or she) alone isn't the one contributing to the growth a church experiences. That pastor will realize he or she needs the worship team to prepare the congregation to hear his or her message. And the technical team that ensures the sound and visual tools used are ready to go. And the greeters, who through the warm welcome extended to visitors attending for the first time that Sunday morning, ensure his or her first impression is a positive one. And the servers, who come early and prepare the coffee and refreshments visitors will enjoy that morning. And the children's ministry volunteer who lovingly cares for the visitors' children after they have been dropped off in the nursery. And the administrative staff who prepared the bulletins handed out that morning. Without each and every member serving in his or her area of giftedness, the effectiveness of the church is hindered. This leads to our final point.

6. _Spiritual gifts are given to build the Church, not our egos._

God did not impart the spiritual gifts for the gifted preacher to revel in the praise he or she receives from his or her congregants, or for the ministry leader to take pride in the ministry "I" have built. It is through the Holy Spirit we are all "baptized into one body" (1 Cor 12:12-13), and by the grace of God imparted with the abilities to accomplish the work He has called us to. In 1 Corinthians 13:4-7, Paul goes to great lengths to drive home the point that while there are a variety of gifts, they are of the same Spirit, the same Jesus, and the same God. His point: "Remember, you are nothing without the gifting and empowerment of God working through you". Nothing happens without God working through every one of us to give a church life and to promote its growth.

The need to make this point is evident in the remainder of 1 Corinthians, Chapter 12, as Paul addresses those Corinthians who had developed a sense of self-importance and superiority over others in the church. And Paul concludes by challenging them to do all of their work "decently" and "orderly" (1 Cor 14:40).

Sadly, this problem wasn't isolated in the church in Corinth. Paul had to "beseech" the Ephesian believers to walk "worthy of their calling", i.e., to serve with "lowliness and gentleness, with longsuffering, bearing with one another in love, endeavoring to keep the unity of Spirit in the bond of peace" (Eph 4:1-3). The same exhortation was needed in the church in Rome, where Paul beseeches the Roman believers, then presents them with the mindset and approach all believers should employ in utilizing their spiritual gifts:

"…by the mercies of God, that you present
your bodies a living sacrifice, holy,
acceptable to God, which is your reasonable
service. And do not be conformed to
this world, but be transformed by the renewing
of your mind, that you may prove
what is that good and acceptable and perfect
will of God." (Rom 12:1b-2)

Notice Paul begins with the exhortation our service flow out of gratitude for the mercies God has chosen to favor us with. Paul then addresses the spirit in which we are to serve alongside others: one that is loving, affectionate, patient, and giving honor to one another (Rom 12:9-13). Peter succinctly sums up the spirit in which our gifting is to be used:

"As each one has received a gift, minister it
to one another, as good stewards
of the manifold grace of God. *If anyone
speaks, let him speak as the oracles
of God. If anyone ministers, let him do it as
with the ability which God supplies,
that in all things God may be glorified through Jesus
Christ, to whom belong the glory and the dominion
forever and ever. Amen.*" (1 Pet 4:10-11)

Amen to that, which brings us to exploring the giftedness God has imparted to you.

EXPLORING THE GIFTS

So, how can you determine what spiritual gifts God has imparted to you? Well, there are several spiritual gift assessment tools available, but ultimately, you'll need to take that first bold step of faith to confirm it.[307] The following is a process you might employ:

---

[307] An example can be found at: http://firstchristiantemple.org/wp-content/uploads/wagner_modified_houts.pdf.

1. Engage

Before the Prodigal Son could surrender himself to his father, he first had to <u>return</u> to him. For you, it begins with the simple willingness to serve, and to ask how and where you are needed. Trust us, you will always be put to work as the "harvest is plentiful, but the workers are few" (Matt 9:37; Luke 10:1; John 14:35). To begin this process, you might identify the specific days and times you are available to serve.

2. Experience

This may include your work or life experiences. An electrician, mechanic, or plumber can utilize these skills in helping reduce expenses at his or her church or helping others without these skills in his or her congregation. Also consider what work or volunteer experiences you have had that might be helpful in a ministry at your church. Reflect on how your life experiences may help you understand and empathize with circumstances others might be currently suffering. Those who have suffered a painful loss, a divorce, or battled addiction can utilize those experiences by encouraging others. This has been my experience, which led to my leaving banking to work in ministry and as a therapist.

3. Explore

What are the needs at your church? Who might you contact to see what opportunities are available to you? Identify at least one (1) person you can contact to determine how and in what area you can begin serving in your church.

4. Experiment

The only way you will find out if you've accurately determined your spiritual gifts are by <u>using</u> them. Make a commitment for what area in which you will serve, and how long you will try serving said in role or function within your church.

5. Examine

How did you feel serving in that role? Did you feel a sense of purpose, blessing, and accomplishment while serving? Make a list of any positives or negatives you experienced.

6. Evaluate

If you are serving in an area of giftedness, you will be effective. On a scale of 1 (poor) to 5 (very), how effective would you rate yourself? What leads you to this conclusion?

7. Expect

If you are serving in your area of giftedness, expect confirmation from others. You may, for example, feel you were "in way over your head", but hear positive feedback about your potential from those overseeing that ministry. If you are still unsure, seek feedback from others you served with, and evaluate the feedback you receive. Then you might consider how additional training and experience will increase your effectiveness in serving in that area of ministry. In time your area of spiritual giftedness will become clear to you. You will learn when to say "yes" and when to say "no" based on your giftedness.

Employing your spiritual gifts, or what Kraft refers to as the encounter of "commitment", we begin to fulfill the plans and purposes God has for our lives (Eph 2:10). It is then we begin to fully experience the abundant life and joy Jesus offers us.

CONCLUDING THOUGHTS

In the days of His last Passover Week on earth, Jesus said to His disciples:

> "...Have faith in God. For assuredly, I
> say to you, whoever says to this
> mountain, 'Be removed and be cast into
> the sea,' and does not doubt in

his heart, but believes that those things
he says will be done, he will
have whatever he says." (Mark 11:22-23; cf Matt 17:20; 21:11-12)

And during the Last Supper, just hours before His arrest, crucifixion and resurrection, Jesus personalized this message to the disciples:

"Most assuredly, I say to you, he who believes in
Me, the works that I do he will do also;
and greater works than these he will do because
I go to My Father." (John 14:12)

Yes, the disciples would fail miserably. But for all their faults, Jesus saw their potential. And emboldened in faith, empowered by the Holy Spirit, and employing the spiritual gifts the Holy Spirit had imparted to them, the Eleven accomplished amazing things. While many were saved during the three-plus years of Jesus' ministry, the apostles multiplied those numbers many times over during the decades that followed. And it is God's plan that you, too, can do "greater works" if you are willing to "risk failure" by taking a step of faith and seeing what God can do through you.

Case in point is Hal Nevitt. Since taking that first step of faith, Hal has been influential in the healing and life change of literally hundreds whose lives had been devastated by addiction. But Hal is not simply utilizing his life experiences to accomplish this: rather, by the grace he has received, Hal is willingly and powerfully utilizing the spiritual gift of Exhortation in both his professional life and in his service in the church as an elder and respected member of Oasis Community Church. The first to say that he, like Paul, was a "chief sinner" and the "least of all the saints" (Eph 3:8; 1 Tim 1:15), Hal is one example of what God can do with a person emboldened by His love and grace, empowered by the gifts of the Spirit, and willingly employing the spiritual gifts imparted to him in service for the kingdom of Jesus. And Hal is experiencing the abundant life in doing so.

You may be wondering how God could possibly use you. Like the Prodigal Son you may have made more than your share of mistakes. Or you may have tried serving God in the past with no success, or to have it end badly. To which we encourage you to heed the words of Henry Ford – who knew failure all too well himself:

"One who fears failure limits his activities. Failure is only the opportunity to more intelligently begin again."[308]

---

[308] https://www.azquotes.com/author/4992-Henry_Ford/tag/failure

CHAPTER 8

LOVING GOD

INTRODUCTION

While fads come and go, one that has stood the test of time is proclamations of "love". Surveys over the past 50 years have found anywhere from 50-65% of each year's most popular songs are devoted to the subjects of love and relationships.[309] Examine the lyrics, however, and you'll see they often exude those warm, fuzzy, mushy, sappy – or dare we say even needy – feelings of one lost and rudderless apart from the devotee of one's love:

I'm all out of love, I'm so lost without you
I know you were right, believing for so long
I'm all out of love, what am I without you
I can't be too late to say that I was so wrong [310]

But this begs the question, what exactly is "love"? And even more importantly, what does it mean to "love God"? This is an important question since we are called to "surrender our lives to God" and "obey His commandments". And for all the teachings on obedience in the Bible, Jesus summed them all up in the "Great Commandment:

---

[309] From http://news.ufl.edu/archive/2007/05/love-still-dominates-pop-song-lyrics-but-with-raunchier-language.html; https://www.reddit.com/r/theydidthemath/comments/72rq9b/request_what_percentage_of_all_songs_are_love/; https://news.ufl.edu/archive/2007/05/love-still-dominates-pop-song-lyrics-but-with-raunchier-language.html
[310] Lyrics are from the song, "All Out of Love", by Air Supply. https://genius.com/Air-supply-all-out-of-love-lyrics

"Then one of them, a lawyer, asked Him a question,
testing Him, and saying, 'Teacher, which
is the great commandment in the law?' Jesus said
to him, 'You shall love the LORD your God
with all your heart, with all your soul, and with all your mind.
This is the first and great commandment. And the second
is like it: 'You shall love your neighbor as yourself. On
these two commandments hang all the Law
and the Prophets'." (Matt 22:35-40)[311]

Recall in *Chapter Two* we saw the Greek word *agape* translated "love" in these passages means, "love, generosity, kindly concern, devotedness." It is an example of what C.S. Lewis referred to as "Gift-love", or the self-less, sacrificial love reflected in God offering up His one and only Son Jesus so we may have "life in His Name" (John 3:16; 20:30-31), in contrast to the empty, poverty-driven "Need-love" seemingly suggested in the above song lyrics.[312] It is reflected in doing something for the benefit of others that makes them feel good, rather than needing someone to do something for to make us feel good.

So, how do we love God? Well, we propose the answer is seen in the "second" half of the Great Commandment, which we will explore in more detail in *Chapters Ten* and *Eleven*. But for now, we'll focus on the last aspect of the definition of *agape*, or devotion. Consider the definition of "devotion":

"Profound dedication; consecration, earnest
attachment to a cause, person, etc.; an assignment
or appropriation to any purpose or cause".[313]

Devotion – and as a result, *agape* love – is demonstrated when one's heart, soul, mind, and will are in alignment with God's Word, His will, and His ways. It is seen in the transformed disciples who "continued with

---

[311] See *Chapter Three* for Bible Passages on the Ten Commandments and the Mosaic Law. See also Mark 12:28-31; Luke 22:24-27. See also Rom 13:9-10; Gal 5:13-14; and Jam 2:8-10.
[312] C.S. Lewis. The Four Loves. Orlando, FL: Harcourt Brace Jovanovich, Publishers, 1960.
[313] https://www.dictionary.com/browse/devotion. Note the English "devotion" stems from the Latin word *devotus*, which means, "to vow, vote", i.e., to "make a decision".

one accord in prayer and supplication" (Acts 1:14) after Jesus graciously recommissioned them during that breakfast on the beach after His resurrection (John 21:9-21). And it's seen in the early days of the church:

> *"And they continued steadfastly in the apostles' doctrine*
> *and fellowship, in the breaking of bread,*
> *and in prayers. Then fear (reference, respect) came*
> *upon every soul, and many wonders and signs*
> *were done through the apostles. Now all who believed were*
> *together, and had all things in common, and sold their possessions*
> *and goods, and divided them among all, as anyone had*
> *need. So continuing daily with one accord in the temple, and*
> *breaking bread from house to house, they ate their food with*
> *gladness and simplicity of heart, praising God and having*
> *favor with all the people. And the Lord added to the church*
> *daily those who were being saved." (Acts 2:42-47)*

Notice these early believers – like the disciples in the days before Pentecost (Acts 1:14; 2:1) – were living together "with one accord". This was a product of the transformation through the powerful outworking of the Holy Spirit in their hearts, souls, and minds that occurred during the days and weeks that followed upon hearing the proclamation of the Gospel by the disciples, and their response by fully devoting themselves to "loving God". And a byproduct was the "gladness and simplicity of heart" they experienced. Yet the English translation fails to fully capture how Luke describes this in the original Greek.

The Greek word translated "gladness" is *agalliasei*, which means, "exultation, exceeding joy". These early Christians were literally jumping for joy, as they shared *athletes*, or a single purpose of heart![314] And this all seemingly flowed from the deep, heartfelt sense of gratitude they felt upon hearing the Gospel, and experiencing the fruit of salvation and a new-found relationship with God it provides. Given this, we propose experiencing the abundant life and the fruit of the Spirit begin with an attitude of gratitude.

---

[314] Strong's Exhaustive Concordance.

THE ABUNDANT LIFE BEGINS WITH
AN ATTITUDE OF GRATITUDE

In *Chapter Two*, we considered Jim Carrey's character Bruce Nolan in the movie *Bruce Almighty* as a light-hearted example of a man dissatisfied with life, who rather than being thankful for the blessings he was experiencing was consumed with what he <u>didn't</u> have. And while a fictional illustration, *Bruce Almighty* is a fair representation of the problem that all too frequently can creep into our hearts and minds.

Adam and Eve, despite being blessed with everything they needed for the abundant life, became dissatisfied when wanting more (Gen 1:30-31; 3:1-6). David, despite having his own wife, wanted someone else's (2 Samuel 11). Solomon, despite having everything a man could want, became obsessed with accumulating wealth, power, and wives (1 Kings 10:26-11:8). And then there's the example Jesus illustrates through the character of the younger son in the Parable of the Prodigal Son. It is noteworthy, however, that getting more at times only leads to <u>more</u> dissatisfaction – and as a result less gratitude:

Author Mark Manson succinctly sums up research that reveals the "paradox of progress" many throughout the world today are experiencing:

People are more educated and literate than ever before. Violence has trended down for decades, possibly centuries. Racism, sexism, discrimination, and violence against women are at their lowest points in recorded history. We have more rights than ever before. Half the planet has access to the internet. Extreme poverty is an all-time low worldwide. Wars are smaller and less frequent than at any other time in recorded history. Children are dying less, and people are living longer. There's more wealth than ever before....

Yet symptoms of depression and anxiety are on an eighty-year upswing among young people and a twenty-year upswing among the adult population. Not only are people experiencing depression in greater numbers, but they're experiencing it at earlier ages with each generation. Since 1985, men and women have reported lower levels of life satisfaction. Stress levels have risen over the past thirty years. Drug overdoses have hit an all-time high as the opioid crisis has wrecked much of the United States and Canada. Across the U.S., feelings of loneliness and social isolation are up. Nearly half of all Americans now report feeling isolated, left out, or alone in their lives."[315]

Researchers have identified a phenomenon they propose generates the feelings of dissatisfaction, discontentment, envy, and unrest that have plagued the world since the beginning of humanity. This phenomenon, referred to as *Relative Deprivation Theory*, proposes people are generally satisfied if they perceive they are as or at least as well off as others within their social circle; but will begin to become dissatisfied, discontent, envious, and even resentful when they perceive others have more than they have. An example is the employee, initially satisfied with the raise he- or she receives, who becomes disgruntled upon hearing a peer received a bigger raise.[316]

Researchers have also found middle- and upper-income people tend to experience more life satisfaction when they compare themselves to those less-fortunate, but as they climb up the socio-economic ladder the incremental increases in satisfaction become less and less as they compare themselves to those who have the same or more than they have.[317]

While extensive research supports the merits of *Relative Deprivation Theory*, it takes an interesting twist when we consider Adam and Eve and the Prodigal Son. As we've seen, the Bible is clear God gave Adam and Eve

---

[315] Mark Manson. Everything is F...ed. New York: HarperCollins Publishing, Inc., 2019, pp 16-17. Manson cites accomplished researchers and authors such as Andrew Sullivan, Steven Pinker, Klerman and Weissman, C.M. Herbst, and Miller McPherson, Lynn Smith-Loving, and Matthew E. Brashears. Similar conclusions are presented by Gregg Easterbrook in, The Progress Paradox: How Life Gets Better While People Feel Worse. New York: Random House, 2003. Not surprisingly, quite a few of the best-selling books as of the April 9, 2021, edition of *USA*Today are self-help books.

[316] https://study.com/academy/lesson/relative-deprivation-in-psychology-theory-definition.html

[317] David G.Myers and C. Nathan Dewall. Exploring Psychology in Modules, 10th ed. New York: Worth Publishers, 2016, pg 535, citing Gruder, 1977; Suls & Tesch, 1978; Zell & Alicke, 2010. Recall back in *Chapter Three,* envy "rots the bones" (Prov 14:30) and "destroys one's soul" (Job 5:2).

all they needed for satisfying and fulfilling lives (Gen 2:9). But being the only human beings in existence, there was no one better off than them to compare themselves to, and as a result to sow the seeds of "deprivation" – unless they considered their "peer" to be God Himself. After all, they may have grumbled to themselves, "God gets to have the fruit of the Tree of the Knowledge of Good and Evil, so why can't we?" This provided the fertile ground upon which Satan could sow the seeds of discontentment through suggesting God was cheating them out of something.

The Prodigal Son had all he needed for a satisfying and fulfilling life, and he certainly had more and lived better than his father's servants. But once he began to dwell on what his "father" (God) had but wasn't sharing with him, the Prodigal became vulnerable to discontentment and the lie the abundant life is found in what he didn't have.

There is something in our fallen nature that generates a tendency to become bored – and eventually dissatisfied – with the status quo. Whether that shiny new toy you were given for Christmas, the raise or promotion, the dream house, or sadly even the husband or wife who once generated the feelings expressed in one of those love songs; in time the initial joy wears off, it becomes the "same-old", and we become dissatisfied with it.

The fact the Prodigal's inheritance would be only half of his older brother's likely added to his sense of "deprivation". And you can almost see him – the resentment burning in his heart – thinking, "He's no more deserving than I am. He gets <u>twice</u> as much as me just for being born before me." But in this mindset, you also see the glaring absence of something foundational to experiencing the abundant life, and that's <u>gratitude</u> for what he did have.

CULTIVATING AN ATTITUDE GRATITUDE [318]

Perhaps we can turn to none other than the Rolling Stones for a cue in taking the first step to cultivating an attitude of gratitude:

[318] Adapted from, <u>A Neuroscience Researcher Reveals 4 Rituals That Will make You Happier.</u> http://mobile.businessinsider.com/a-neuroscience-researcher-reveals-4-rituals-that-will-make-you-a-happier-person-2015-9

You can't always get what you want
You can't always get what you want
You can't always get what you want
But if you try sometimes well you might
find you get what you need [319]

We've seen that the rates of dissatisfaction, anxiety and depression have been on the rise for decades despite a steady improvement in overall conditions world-wide. Noteworthy is anxiety and depression are direct products of how we interpret the present, and what we expect in the future – whether what is happening or what will happen will be "bad". Given this, the most frequently used therapeutic approach to treat chronic anxiety and depression is *Cognitive-Behavioral Therapy* ("CBT"). Foundational to CBT is the premise:

How you think influences how you
feel and then how you act

Put another way, anxiety and depression may be a product of how you interpret what is happening or will happen in your life, so changing your thinking will alleviate the anxiety or depression you're experiencing, as well as the need for any maladaptive behaviors you're using to cope with it. Noteworthy is while CBT was developed in the last half of the 20th century, its roots go as far back as the philosophies of the Greco-Roman and Eastern thinkers circa 500 B.C., as well as in the Bible itself. Note Paul's words to the Philippians:

"Be anxious for nothing, but in everything by prayer
and supplication, with thanksgiving, let your requests
be made known to God; and the peace of God, which
surpasses all understanding, will guard your hearts
and minds through Christ Jesus. (Phil 4:6-7)

---

[319] http://www.songlyrics.com/rolling-stones/you-can-t-always-get-what-you-want-lyrics/. See also the lyrics of the hymn, "For the Beauty of the Earth". https://www.lyricsmode.com/lyrics/r/religious_music/for_the_beauty_of_the_earth.html

Paul begins by telling us to present our requests with "thanksgiving" for the blessings and favor we have received.[320] This is the very definition of gratitude:

"The quality of being thankful, readiness to show appreciation for and to return kindness. Appreciative of benefits received affording pleasure or contentment. Comfort supplied or discomfort alleviated."[321]

Gratitude alleviates distress and generates a sense of contentment. In fact, an attitude of gratitude can be as effective as medications such as Wellbutrin and Prozac in reducing symptoms of anxiety and depression. These medications work by increasing the levels of neurotransmitters in our brain like dopamine and serotonin that affect our mood. Yet research has found an attitude of gratitude boosts both neurotransmitters, and our mood will improve simply by searching for something to be grateful for.[322] Bottom line: modern science has confirmed the wisdom in Paul's writings nearly 2,000 years ago.

Gratitude is a product of focusing on what we have rather than what we don't have. It is understandable the Prodigal battled discontentment for being destined to receive half the inheritance of his older brother. But just as his brother was no more deserving of a double inheritance than he was, the Prodigal was no more deserving of his birthright and the abundance he stood to inherit than the hired servants who helped produce it. In focusing on what he didn't have, the Prodigal failed to see the divine favor he enjoyed.

Not surprisingly, Jesus addressed our tendency to resent what we perceive to be unfair favor others are receiving in, "The Parable of the Laborers in the Vineyard" (Matt 20:1-16), in which a landowner (like the father in the Parable of the Prodigal Son) hires crews of laborers to work his vineyard. While some start at 6AM, others don't start until 9AM, noon,

---

[320] Strong's Exhaustive Concordance. The English "thanksgiving" comes from the Greek *eucharistia*, which means, "gratefulness or thankfulness for perceived favor one has received".
[321] https://www.merriam-webster.com/dictionary/grateful
[322] A Neuroscience Researcher Reveals 4 Rituals That Will make You Happier. http://mobile.businessinsider.com/a-neuroscience-researcher-reveals-4-rituals-that-will-make-you-a-happier-person-2015-9

WHOLE

and 3PM. While each laborer agrees to the standard pay of a denarius for the day, those who started at 6AM begin to complain, "Not fair!" when they see those who worked a fraction of a day getting the same rate of pay.[323] To which the landowner replies:

> *"Friend, I am doing you no wrong. Did you not agree*
> *with me for a denarius? Take what is yours*
> *and go your way. I wish to give to this last man the*
> *same as to you. Is it not lawful for me to do*
> *what I wish with my own things? Or is your eye*
> *evil because I am good?"' (vv 13-15)*

Instead of being thankful for what they got, they grumbled about what others got. Instead of being grateful for the opportunity to work for a fair wage, they resented seeing others getting the same for less. Sounds like the Perfect Son, doesn't it? Or perhaps you?

Perhaps your challenge is to begin cultivating an "attitude of gratitude" by practicing a daily discipline of determining to see "if there be anything virtuous or praiseworthy", and to "think on these things", focusing on "that which is good, lovely, of a good report" (Phil 4:8). You might begin by taking some time to assess various aspects of your life:

- Your marriage or intimate relationship,
- Your family relationships,
- Your friendships,
- Your job,
- Your skills and abilities,
- Your financial situation and material possessions,
- Your physical health and appearance; or,
- Your relationships at church.

Again, set your thoughts on what is right or good rather than what is wrong or falls short of your hopes or expectations (more on this later). Perhaps you might start each day by identifying at least a few things you

---

[323] A denarius was the standard daily wage for a soldier or laborer. https://www.biblestudytools.com/dictionary/denarius/

are grateful for, and then proclaim the following declaration written by the Psalmist nearly 3,000 years ago:

*"This is the day the LORD has made; We will
rejoice and be glad in it." (Ps 118:24)*

But if you are having a hard time identifying something that is praiseworthy, focus your attention on the One Who is praiseworthy:

*"I will praise You, for I am fearfully and wonderfully
made; Marvelous are Your works, and that
my soul knows very well." (Ps 139:14)*

You might begin with that one most praiseworthy work that stands above all others and is foundational to experiencing the abundant life: the gift of grace through the sacrifice of His Son so you may have life in His name. If there is anything that should generate a sense of gratitude in our souls, it is the fact God cares so much about us He would "run out" to us with a warm embrace and take on the shame and scorn we deserve.

Through this parable, Jesus provides His disciples a powerful picture of the salvation He would soon earn on each of our behalf: Here is God, our Heavenly Father, "running" towards us, His arms outstretched, not only embracing us, but suffering the shame, humiliation, and pain we rightfully should bear.

We feel grateful when blessed or honored in some way, particularly when deep down we know it is undeserved. And therein lies the challenge: going to that deep, dark, place in our soul where we humbly acknowledge we have "sinned against heaven and before you" (Luke 15:19). When we, like David, are no longer "silent", and confess our sins before God who is faithful to forgive us (Ps 32:3-5; cf 1 John 1:8-9).[324] It is only then we can fully experience the blessing God has given us: His willingness to have a relationship with us.

And we might consider while the "measure", or amount, of grace we have received will vary from person to person, it is determined by none other than Jesus Himself:

---

[324] See also Psalm 51.

*"But to each one of us grace was given according
to the measure of Christ's gift." (Eph 4:7)*

And how does Jesus determine this? Seemingly so we don't get too
full of ourselves:

*"For I say, through the grace given to me,
to everyone who is among you,
not to think of himself more highly than he
ought to think, but to think soberly,
as God has dealt to each one a measure of
faith." (Rom 12:3; cf 2 Cor 12:7)*

Now, maybe you've stayed with us up to this point, but have had a
difficult time relating to the Prodigal. You haven't "turned your back"
on God or indulged in every excess imaginable. You have worked hard
and lived within your means. You're a decent person, you attend church,
and perhaps even serve in the church occasionally or regularly. You have
accepted Jesus as your Savior, yet you don't feel particularly "blessed".

Perhaps this is because you have yet to experience in a visceral way
how you, too, are "no longer worthy to be called your son (or daughter)"
and are willing to accept even the role of a "hired servant" (Luke 15:19).
Perhaps you have yet to identify the specific area(s) of your life that fall so
far short of the perfect goodness and righteousness of Jesus. Perhaps you
are more like the Perfect Son, still subtly pleading the case you deserve
favor because you have "never transgressed [His] commandment at any
time" and wonder when God will bless you with a "young goat" so you
can "make merry with [your] friends" (Luke 15:29). Perhaps, like the
Pharisee in the Parable of Two Prayers (Luke 18:10-14), you are quick
to see the "speck in your brother's eye, but slow to consider the plank in
your own eye" (Matt 7:1-5). Or perhaps you resent the "measure of grace"
others have received.

Nouwen cites his own experience as the oldest sibling and "Perfect
Son" who "did all the proper things...complying with the agendas set by
the parental figures in my life", but "didn't have the courage to 'run away'".
He goes on to note the "envy" he felt in "seeing my friends having a good

time doing all sorts of things that I condemn", much like the Prodigal Son.[325] This season of reflection seemingly influenced his proposition that a vital step in one's relationship with God is the transition from resentment to gratitude. While resentment binds us in negative feelings, gratitude allows us to let them go. While resentment renders us a prisoner of our passions, gratitude enables us to transcend our compulsions. And while resentment exhausts us, gratitude gives us a new vitality.[326]

Gratitude begins with realizing just how undeserving we of the gift of God's grace. It is only when we come to acknowledge we are "not righteous" (Rom 3:10), and mere "filthy rags" (Is 64:6) we can fully appreciate this gift.[327] It is the realization Jesus intended in teaching what adhering to the lofty standards of the Mosaic Law really meant in the Sermon on the Mount (Matt 5-7; Luke 6:20-49). Yet in this teaching, Jesus addresses something revolutionary to His disciples. What Jesus wanted them – and us today – to understand is what it means to have a "relationship" with God our Heavenly Father.

REVISITING OUR RELATIONSHIP WITH GOD

From the time their ancestors walked out of Egypt until Jesus began His ministry some 1,500 years later, the people of Israel lived under the Mosaic Law. As we've seen, the 613 tenants of the Law provided the civil, social, and religious rules to govern this emerging nation. But they also provided instruction of how-to-live-in relationship with God.

Noteworthy is the Mosaic Covenant was structured in a format common in the ancient Near East during the times of Israel's exodus from Egypt known as "suzerain treaties". These treaties outlined the expectations between a king and his people and included the stipulations the people were expected to adhere to, the blessings they would receive if they complied, and the "cursings" (or consequences) they would suffer if

---

[325] Nouwen. The Return of the Prodigal Son, p 70.
[326] Nouwen, Spiritual Formation., p. 64.
[327] See also Ps 14:1-3; 53:1-3; Eccl 7:20. Isaiah uses the imagery of a woman's garments stained by her menstrual cycle rendering her unclean and to be separated from the rest of her community (Lev 15:19-24; Ezek 36:17). The point is by virtue of our sin nature each and every one of us, apart from God's grace, is unworthy of even being in His presence.

they failed to comply. And as we've seen, the people all agreed to those terms (Ex 24:3).

Given this, it is understandable that the people of Old Testament Israel tended to view God as that powerful deity Moses had met on Mount Sinai, a god to be feared and obeyed. Missed upon receiving those 613 tenants, however, was God's intent in issuing them:

> *"And let them make Me a sanctuary, that I*
> *may <u>dwell</u> among them." (Ex 25:8)*

> *"I will <u>dwell</u> among the children of Israel and*
> *will be their God. And they shall know*
> *that I am the LORD their God, who brought*
> *them up out of the land of Egypt,*
> *that I may <u>dwell</u> among them. I am the*
> *LORD their God." (Ex 29:45-46)*

Here they received a very different presentation then the "distant" deity that struck terror into them upon Moses' return after receiving the Ten Commandments (Ex 19:15-16). Instead, we see a Benevolent Father wanting to "dwell" with, and have an intimate relationship with, His "children". To fully grasp this, we will draw insight from the definition of the word "relationship". It comes from the Latin *relates*, which means:

> *"The state of being connected, the way in*
> *which two people are connected.*
> *The way in which two or more people regard*
> *and behave toward each other.*
> *A state of affairs existing between those*
> *having relations or dealings." [328]*

This definition suggests two components necessary for a relationship to thrive. First, there is <u>knowledge</u>, including each party's interests, values, and beliefs. But knowledge also reveals what each party's <u>expectations</u> – whether assumed or clearly communicated – of what each will receive

---

[328] https://www.merriam-webster.com/dictionary/relationship

from the other in the relationship. And finally, there must be trust, or the sense each party can reasonably assume the other will strive to meet said expectations. Trust deepens when one strives to meet the expectations of another but will weaken or break down altogether when it is not reciprocated.

Through the Mosaic Covenant, God provided the Israelites the principles of what would produce loving and trusting relationships with Him (the 1st through 4th Commandments) and each other (the 5th through 10th Commandments). Noteworthy is the 613 "laws" provided the action steps of how each of the Commandments are lived out.

But God also wanted them to understand He isn't some insecure, power-hungry tyrant demanding obedience for the sole purpose of stroking His own ego. Instead, He wanted them to see Him as their gracious Heavenly Father simply wanting to provide them with the principles of life they would need to experience *shalom*, that inner peace experienced in the abundant life when a person feels in the depths of his or her soul that each and every day is one the Lord has made and can rejoice and be glad in it (Ps 118:24).

It was His same intent in giving Adam and Eve that one restriction: don't eat the fruit of that one tree (Gen 2:17). It wasn't God saying, "I'm the adult, so do what I say". Instead, it was God in the role of the caring parent, warning Adam and Eve about the consequences of straying from His instructions. God had made Himself known to them, communicated what they could expect of Him, and through His generous provision demonstrated He could be trusted. But Adam and Eve bought into Satan's lies: 1) they didn't really know Him; 2) His expectations of them were unreasonable; and 3) He couldn't be trusted.

The Israelites largely failed to embrace these principles. The Book of Joshua recounts how about 1400 B.C. God delivered the Land He had promised them.[329] In Judges we're told how over the ensuing 325 years, the people of Israel would experience seven seasons marked by periods of obedience and blessings, disobedience, and "discipline" through the

---

[329] Before the *Entrance Generation* under Joshua's leadership conquered the Promised Land, Moses reiterated the terms of the Mosaic Covenant (see the book of Deuteronomy, or the "Second Law"). This was necessary as their parents, the *Exodus Generation* who had been given the Law initially as recorded in the book of Leviticus, had died during the 40 years of wandering.

oppression of enemy nations, and God raising up "judges" to deliver them.[330] Israel would unify and thrive under kings David and Solomon. But upon Solomon's death and the assumption of the throne by his son Rehoboam, the nation split. Over the ensuing 350 years, Israel's disobedience became so severe God found it necessary to "kick His children out of the house".[331] Another 600 years would pass as Israel anxiously awaited their Messiah. And sadly, they never came to see God as their "Heavenly Father".

Yet, God did not write off His children, as evidenced by His issuance of the "New Covenant" in which Jesus through His sinless life atones for the sins of humanity.[332] But Jesus came to do much more than die on the cross to make the New Covenant possible. His mission was to not only clarify the meaning and purpose of the Ten Commandments and the Mosaic Law; but to help the people of Israel see God as their Heavenly Father.

Noteworthy is the fact it was nearly a <u>year</u> into His ministry before Jesus referred to God as His "Father", and it occurred in a subtle and almost happenstance manner during His encounter with not the Jews, but a Samaritan woman at Jacob's well.[333] While the woman attempted to engage Jesus in a theological debate, Jesus had much more in mind:

> *"You worship what you do not know; we know*
> *what we worship, for salvation is*
> *of the Jews. But the hour is coming, and now is,*
> *when the true worshipers will worship*
> *the Father in spirit and truth; for the Father is*
> *seeking such to worship Him." (John 4:22-23)*

Fast forward six months later and Jesus, in the Sermon on the Mount (His first extended teaching), refers to God as "Father" fifteen times. By

---

[330] This is how the writer of the book of Hebrews describes God's punishment of the people of Israel for their disobedience as a means of "making straight the paths of [their] feet (see Heb 12:5-13).

[331] See 1 Kings 12:1-27; 17:1-41; 24:1-27:30.

[332] Jer 31:31-36; Ezek 36:26-27; Matt 26:28; Mark 14:24; Luke 22:20; 1 Cor 11:25; 2 Cor 3:5-6; Heb 4:15; 8:8-13; 9:15; 12:22-24.

[333] Noteworthy as well as according to Jewish tradition, a rabbi would not have engaged in a public conversation with a Jewish woman, let alone a Samaritan woman. Merrill C. Tenney, <u>The Expositor's Bible Commentary: John,</u> Frank E. Gaebelein, gen ed.

the time the disciples are hearing the Parable of the Prodigal Son two years later, Jesus is regularly referred to God as "Father".

Throughout His ministry, Jesus modeled what it looks like to live in relationship with God. In the four Gospels alone, we Jesus addresses God as "Father" 165 times. And it is not surprising the Apostle Paul follows Jesus' example in referring to God as "Father" 40 times in his writings. Yet for the Jews, the idea of referring to God as one's "Heavenly Father" was nothing less than shocking. In the Old Testament, the portrayal of God as "Father" occurs only 15 times. In fact, it was tradition to not even utter the <u>name</u> of God for fear of misusing it and violating the command not to take His name in vain (Ex 20:7).

Paul summarizes the transition from the contractual relationship between a "ruler" and His "subjects" as described in the Mosaic Covenant to a relationship between a "Father" and His "children" in His letter to the Jewish believers in Galatia through referring to God as "Abba, Father!", and them as, "no longer a slave but a son, an heir" (Gal 4:4-7).

What a powerful declaration! Our relationship with God is unbreakable since He has adopted us as His children, the point Jesus wanted to drive home in His presentation of God as a "father" in the Parable of the Prodigal Son. But there was another point Jesus wanted to make, and one He wanted His disciples to fully grasp as well.

A NEW PERSPECTIVE ON "OBEDIENCE"

Recall the English word "prodigal" comes from a Greek word that is the negative of the word to "save". By pursuing "life" through consuming his inheritance, the Prodigal had chosen a path of destruction. But through the errors of his ways, the Prodigal came to realize, "Maybe I should have listened to my father". Put another way, the Prodigal had come to realize something repeated throughout the Bible:

> *"The fear of the LORD is the beginning*
> *of knowledge, But fools despise*
> *wisdom and instruction." (Prov 1:7; cf Job*
> *28:28; Ps 111:10; Prov 9:10; 15:33)*

Noteworthy is the Hebrew word translated "fear" here is *yare*, which means, "to respect, revere, to fear, awe".[334] It is not the sheer terror stemming from the belief God will land on us with both feet if we "disobey" Him, but simply respecting the fact God is the source of wisdom, and heeding His instruction is the first step in ensuring life will go well for us.

Jesus illustrates this in the Parable of the Prodigal Son. Through a life living under the tutelage of their father, his sons had the privilege of gleaning the wisdom of a well-lived life. But the Prodigal failed to see this, and in a clear lack of respect of his father asks for his inheritance early so he can live life his way. And it took "playing the fool" and finding himself alone, destitute, and humiliated for him to come to realize this.

Yet there is also a bit of the "fool" in the Perfect Son as well. While "fearing" his father in "never transgressing his commandments", he still believed the abundant life is found in his father's provisions rather than his principles and his presence, as he too would rather have been "making merry" with his friends (Luke 15:29). Like Adam and Eve, David, and Solomon, there is a part of him that thinks the abundant life is found in power, position, possessions, and pleasure. And like the Prodigal, the Perfect viewed the "blessings" of their father in the form of the material abundance they would one day inherit.

Through this parable, Jesus wanted His disciples to understand God simply wants the best for us. And through the examples of both the Prodigal and Perfect sons, Jesus was holding up a mirror to the people of Israel, as they saw God as the all-powerful being rewarding obedience with prosperity, good health, numerous children, and protection from their enemies; and disobedience with punishment.[335] But they missed something vitally important to experiencing the abundant life, as seen in the following:

> *"The LORD will establish you as a holy*
> *people to Himself, just as He has*
> *sworn to you, if you keep the commandments*
> *of the LORD your God and walk*
> *in His ways. Then all peoples of the earth*
> *shall see that you are called by*

---

[334] Strong's Exhaustive Concordance.
[335] See Ex 23:22-33; Lev 24:4-13; Deut 28:1-14.

> *the name of the LORD, and they shall be*
> *afraid of you." (Deut 28:9-10)* [336]

Notice God didn't instruct the Israelites to simply follow His commandments out of blind obedience, but to "keep" them and to "walk in His ways". And noteworthy is this isn't a one-time statement, as it is repeated several times in the covenant between God and the *Entrance* Generation.[337] Noteworthy as well is the words Moses uses to make this point.

The Hebrew word translated "keep" here is *shamar*, which means, "to hedge, protect, guard, attend to, observe, regard". This suggests principles we embrace and internalize as our own and are diligent in following. And this is seen in the Hebrew word translated "walk" in this passage.[338] God's commandments are more than the means of obtaining rewards and avoiding punishment: they are principles for the abundant life. And through adhering to these principles the Israelites would experience not only His provision and protection, but peace, harmony, and a sense of blessing in their relationships with Him and each other. Bottom line: this is how the people of Israel were to demonstrate their love for God (Ex 20:6).[339] This is seen in something that may come as a surprise to you:

Jesus never commanded us to "obey" Him!

Nowhere in the Gospels does Jesus' command "obedience". In the English translations of the New Testament that most closely provide a literal translation of the original Greek, you will not find Jesus commanding His disciples to "obey" Him.[340] Instead, Jesus said:

---

[336] This passage immediately precedes the blessings and cursings in the covenant between God and the *Entrance* Generation.

[337] See also Deut 5:33; 8:6; 10:12; 11:22; 19:9; 26:17; 28:9; 30:16

[338] Strong's Concordance. The Hebrew word here is *yawlak*, which means, "to walk, grow, to prosper".

[339] See also Lev 22:31; 26:3; Deut 4:2, 40; 5:10, 29; 6:2, 17; 7:9; 8:2, 6; 10:13; 11:1, 22; 13:4, 18; 19:9; 26:17-18; 27:1; 28:9, 45; 30:10, 16.

[340] This includes the NKJV (New King James Version), the KJV (King James Version), the ASV (American Standard Version), the NASB (New American Standard Bible), the RSV (Revised Standard Version). Easier to read versions such as the NIV (New International Version) translate the original Greek to "obey" rather than "keep", but this distorts the meaning of these verses.

"If you love Me, <u>keep</u> My commandments." (John 14:15)[341]

Throughout the Gospels, Jesus challenges us to "keep" His commandments, not to "obey" Now this may appear to be nothing more than an exercise in semantics, but a study of the Greek words commonly translated "obey" or "obedience", and "keep" or "keeping", are insightful to understanding what Jesus intended us to understand.

The Greek word most frequently translated "obey", "obeys" or "obedience" is *hupotasso*, which means "obedience, submission, compliance, to conform to". It is used in the context of a subordinate doing what his or her superior demands.[342] Obedience without buy-in can breed the resentment of the Perfect Son's mindset, "I don't want to, but I <u>have</u> to". It might be obeying traffic laws simply to avoid getting a ticket, having to pay a fine, or spending a Saturday in a driving school class. And the Bible instructs children to "obey" their parents (Eph 6:1), and subordinates to "obey" their bosses (Col 3:22). But again, obedience is encouraged to avoid negative consequences.[343]

There is no hidden meaning in the Greek words translated "commandment" other than contrasting the "rules" or "Law" of God verses the laws, rules, or traditions of human beings. Since the Ten Commandments and the teachings of Jesus and the apostles come from God, they are the standards we are to adhere to. What is critically important, however, is not only how we respond to them, but how we <u>understand</u> them as well.

A good parent or supervisor will tell us not only <u>what</u> to do or not to do, but <u>why</u> their instructions or guidelines are important as well. When God gave Israel the Mosaic Law, it wasn't to give them arbitrary rules to adhere to, but to provide the people with the instructions of how-to live-in <u>relationship</u> with God and each other so Israel would thrive.

---

[341] See Matt 19:17; Luke 11:28; John 8:51-52, 55; 9:16; 12:25; 14:21-24; 15:10, 20; 17:11, 15, 19; 1 John 2:3-5; 3:22-24; 5:2-3, 18,.

[342] The Gospels <u>do</u> say nature "obeys" the commands of Jesus (Matt 8:27; Mark 4:41; Luke 8:25; 17:6), and demons "obeyed" Jesus (Mark 1:27). We propose this distinction is clearly communicated to emphasize the importance of human beings freely and willingly following Jesus out of a response of humble gratitude rather than obligatory compliance.

[343] See Eph 6:5-8; Col 3:21-25; 4:1; 1 Pet 2:13-19. All encourage "obedience" to enhance relationships as well as one's attitude.

Because Israel – like every other culture in human history – <u>needed</u> those instructions.

If you look at the Ten Commandments, the tenants of the Mosaic Law, and the teachings of Jesus and the apostles, you will see they serve to promote the inherent value, dignity, and respect God intends every one of us to experience in our relationships with Him and each other. The Second Commandment prohibits worshipping idols (Ex 20:3-5) as it deprives God of the love and reverence He deserves as our Creator.[344] And the last six Commandments prohibit actions that disrespect and devalue our parents, spouses, or others in our community. Hence, the Law is summed up in the Great Commandment: "Love God and love your neighbor as yourself".[345]

We need these instructions, because as fallen human beings we tend to be self-seeking and self-serving – even if it hurts or devalues others. Without God's Commandments, we are like the person trying to put together an "assembly-required" desk or cabinet from Ikea or Office Max without using the instructions. God didn't want the blind, begrudging obedience of His children in Israel, and Jesus didn't want this out of His disciples. Instead, His hope is we see His Words, and the Bible as a whole, through this simple acronym:

*B*asic
*I*nstructions
*B*efore
*L*eaving
*E*arth [346]

God intended the writings presented in the Bible to be our instruction manual for the abundant life: it provides us principles that we are best served to internalize as our own personal standards. Through this our heart is transformed, and we begin to reflect the character of Jesus so "all will know we are His disciples" (John 13:35).[347]

---

[344] See also Lev 19:4; 26:1.

[345] Rom 13:9-10; Gal 5:14; Jam 2:8-10.

[346] Passages such as Prov 3:5-6 and Jer 17:7 reflect this mindset.

[347] This is the point we believe James is getting at in 2:14-26. We are "justified" as credible witnesses to the Good News of Jesus when our faith is followed by works that manifest the love and grace we have received from God.

To be clear I am not discounting "obedience" in and of itself. The experience of walking in faith is understanding not only what God's instructions are, but why it is in our best interest to adhere to them. An example is "tithing" (giving 10% of income back to God).[348] We may "obey" hesitantly at first, then come to realize the value of acknowledging what God has blessed us with while "serving God not mammon" (Matt 6:24; Luke 16:13).

As we transition from conforming to the "rules" with a merit system mindset to internalizing God's Word as our principles for life, we begin to know Jesus on a personal level. Notice how Jesus drove this point home during the Last Supper:

"If you love Me, keep My commandments" (John 14:15)

"As the Father loved Me, I also have loved you; abide in My love. If you keep My commandments, you will abide in My love, just as I have kept My Father's commandments and abide in His love." (John 15:9-10)

The apostle John also emphasizes this repeatedly in his first epistle:

"Now by this we know that we know Him, if we keep His commandments." (1 John 2:3)

"By this we know that we love the children of God, when we love God and keep His commandments. For this is the love of God, that we keep His commandments. And His commandments are not burdensome." (1 John 5:2-3)

We demonstrate our love for God by keeping His commandments, but this is how we come to know Him in a personal way as well. When John addresses the topic of "knowing God", he uses the Greek word *ginosko*,

---

[348] This principal stems from Abraham giving Melchizedek 10% of the plunder (Gen 14:14-20). Note, some propose Jesus didn't teach a strict "tithe", but "sacrificial" giving (see Mark 12:41-44; Luke 21:1-4; cf 2 Cor 9:5-7).

which means, "To perceive, understand, to know experientially".[349] The more we get to know Him personally, the more we experience the fruit of the Spirit in our lives. And this begins with forging the kind of relationship in which we feel the "oneness" Jesus describes of His relationship with God His Father:

> "...I am the way, the truth, and the life. No
> one comes to the Father except through
> Me. If you had known Me, you would have
> known My Father also; and from now
> on you know Him and have seen Him.... Do
> you not believe that I am in the Father,
> and the Father in Me? The words that I speak
> to you I do not speak on My own
> authority: but the Father who dwells in Me
> does the works." (John 14:6-7, 9b-10)

As we embrace and internalize the commandments of Jesus, we begin to know God in a deeply personal and meaningful way. We will begin to have the "oneness" with Him that Jesus did. And while Jesus will always be our King, He will also become like "kin" to us:

> "Greater love has no one than this, than to lay
> down one's life for his friends. You
> are My friends if you do whatever I command
> you. No longer do I call you servants,
> for a servant does not know what his master is
> doing; but I have called you friends,
> for all things that I heard from My Father I have
> made known to you." (John 15:13-15)

This is what Nouwen terms the fifth movement of spiritual transformation: the movement from "fear to love". It is the transition from apprehension of the consequences of failing to obey His commandments

---

[349] In contrast to *oida*, or "factual" knowledge. This is seen in John 7:27, in which some "knew" factually the city Jesus came from but didn't understand or comprehend where the Messiah would come from.

to an appreciation for and anticipation of what He will do when we keep them. It is in this movement that fear gives way to freedom.[350]

As young disciples of Jesus, John and his brother James were nicknamed the "sons of thunder" (Mark 3:13). One reason for this moniker may have been when they asked Jesus if they should "command fire to come down from heaven and consume" those who failed to receive Him (Luke 9:51-54). Implied is their understanding Jesus was to be obeyed, or punishment was coming. But John came to understand keeping His commandments as the means to experiencing a personal relationship with God, and the abundant life it produces. This is seen in the Gospel and three epistles he wrote as an older, wiser man some 60 years after Jesus' ascension, as John frequently refers to believers in "children", and love as the foundation of our relationship with God our Heavenly Father.[351]

It is John who recounts Jesus saying the abundant life is found in the person of Jesus, not His provisions (John 10:10).[352] And it is John who recounts Jesus telling him and the disciples that their – and our – "joy will be full" as we keep His commandments:

> *"These things I have spoken to you, that My joy*
> *may remain in you, and that your joy may be full."*
> *(John 15:11; cf 1 John 1:4; 2 John 1:12).*

In the Parable of the Prodigal Son, the Prodigal provides us an illustration of the dangers of indulging our senses to excess. But despite his unwavering obedience, the Perfect Son is far from exhibiting the fruit of the Spirit evident in the abundant life himself. While not eating peapods, he is bitter about not being provided the opportunity to live it up with his friends, and resentful of his father's warm welcome of "this son of yours" (v 30). And the reason for this is seen in Jesus' interaction with a wealthy young man a short time later:

---

[350] Nouwen, <u>Spiritual Transformation.</u>
[351] In John's writings alone, you see John use various forms of the word "love" 465 times.
[352] Jesus explicitly addresses this in his interaction with a man who wanted Jesus to command the man's brother to share his inheritance with him. Jesus' reply: "Take heed and beware of covetousness, for one's life does not consist in the abundance of the things he possesses" (Luke 12:13-15).

A NEW PERSPECTIVE ON THE "ABUNDANT LIFE"

There is an old saying, "look out for what you ask for – you just might get it". This was certainly the experience of Adam and Eve, David, Solomon, and the fictional character portrayed in the Parable of the Prodigal Son. It is also seen in the life of a man Jesus encountered who was experiencing the emptiness Solomon seemingly had once felt:[353]

> *"Now a certain ruler asked Him, saying, 'Good*
> *Teacher, what shall I do to inherit eternal*
> *life?' So, Jesus said to him, 'Why do you call Me*
> *good? No one is good but One, that is,*
> *God. You know the commandments: Do not*
> *commit adultery, Do not murder, Do not*
> *steal, do not bear false witness, Honor your*
> *father and your mother.' And he said,*
> *'All these things I have kept from my youth.'*
> *So, when Jesus heard these things,*
> *He said to him, 'You still lack one thing. Sell*
> *all that you have and distribute to the*
> *poor, and you will have treasure in heaven;*
> *and come, follow Me.' But when he*
> *heard this, he became very sorrowful, for he*
> *was very rich." (Luke 18:18-23)* [354]

This young man had everything – and yet nothing. In one sense he was much like the Prodigal: he was blessed with wealth simply for being the son of a wealthy man. Unlike the Prodigal, however, he didn't squander his wealth on excess living. In fact, one could say he was a pretty "good guy" in his diligence in following the commandments. Yet, something was missing, as he, too, equated God's provisions with the abundant life.

---

[353] The chronology of events referenced in this section drawn from Cheney & Ellisen, Jesus Christ: The Greatest life Ever Lived.
[354] See also Matt 19:15-22; Mark 10:17-22.

Here Jesus is proposing a principle for life He was living out Himself. Satan had offered Him everything – the position, and all the power, possessions, and pleasure – a person could ever want. But despite 40 days of going without food while Satan persisted in his efforts to tempt Him, Jesus rejected it all (Matt 4:1-13; Luke 4:1-11). Instead, He chose to find His fulfillment – and His personal sense of "abundance" – in doing the will of God.[355]

Throughout His three-plus year ministry, Jesus essentially lived the life of the homeless. On any given day there was no guarantee He would even have something to eat. He told His disciples that following Him required the willingness to let go of some of the material comforts they had previously enjoyed, and most of us today take for granted.[356] And about a month later, His disciples demonstrated their willingness to make those sacrifices when they "left everything" to follow Him (Luke 5:1-11). Yet in doing so, the disciples missed an important point in the significance of that bold step they took.

Notice the young man begins this interaction by asking Jesus, "What shall I do to inherit eternal life?" Jesus responds, "You know the commandments...", and then rattles off five of the six "loving others" commandments, to which the man states he has kept them all "from my youth".[357] Noteworthy, however, is Jesus leaves out the last of the "loving others" commandments: you shall not "covet" (desire) another's property, before challenging him to sell all and give it to the poor if he wants "treasure in heaven".[358]

Notice this all begins with this man "running up" to Jesus, "kneeling before" Him, and addressing Him as "Good Teacher". While a man of

---

[355] This is seen in His statement to the disciples after his encounter with the Samaritan woman at Jacob's well when He said, "My food is to do the will of Him who sent Me, and to finish His work" (John 4:34).

[356] Jesus said even foxes and birds have a "home", but His followers may not enjoy these comforts (Matt 8:19-20; Luke 9:57-58).

[357] These are the 5th through 9th of the Ten Commandments, or those addressing human relationships (Ex 20:12-17).

[358] Noteworthy in Matthew's account, when Jesus answers, "keep the commandments", the young man responds, "which ones?" suggesting he is aware he has fallen short of meeting at least one of them. Noteworthy as well in Matthew's account, Jesus says "if you want to be perfect...", which is from the Greek word *teleios*, which means, "complete, perfect, whole, mature".

prominence, he was willing to humble himself in seeking Jesus' counsel. Yet sadly, he was unable – or unwilling – to trust Jesus, as he "went away sorrowful".[359] And notice how His disciples respond to all this:

"When His disciples heard it, they were greatly astonished, saying, 'Who then can be saved'?" (Matt 19:25)[360]

The English translation here fails to capture the intensity of their reaction. The English "astonished" comes from the Greek *ekplesso*, which suggests being overwhelmed beyond comprehension. The disciples are flat out stunned and in a state of disbelief. But notice their reaction is not in response to the idea abundance is found in giving away what we have. Instead, they are wondering if they even have a chance of being saved! [361]

Now Jesus' encounter with this wealthy young ruler took place maybe 60 days before His arrest and execution. His disciples had been with Him for the better part of three years, heard numerous teachings including the parables of the Prodigal Son and Two Prayers, and yet they still perceived God's grace and favor were at least somewhat conditional on obedience. And Jesus' reply probably wasn't the clear-cut answer they were hoping for:

"With men this is impossible, but with God all things are possible." (Matt 19:26)[362]

As clearly as He has ever presented it, Jesus is telling them something made clear in the New Covenant prophesied by Jeremiah and Ezekiel some 600 years earlier, and which He would consummate during the upcoming Passover through His death on the cross: that our relationship with God is a product of His grace and favor alone, and not what we have done or

---

[359] Luke 18:18, 23; cf Matt 19:15-16, 22; Mark 10:17, 22.
[360] See also Mark 10:26; Luke 18:26. See Mounce, Analytical Lexicon of the Greek New Testament.
[361] Some today interpret this the same way. In his book, The Gospel According to Jesus: What Does Jesus Mean When He Says, "Follow Me"? (pg 85) John MacArthur writes, "Our Lord gave this young man a test. He had to choose between his possessions and Jesus Christ. He failed the test... salvation is only for those who are willing to give Christ first place in their lives." This would seemingly conflict with the Scriptures stating we are saved by faith alone (John 3:16; Eph 2:8-10, etc.).
[362] See also Mark 10:27; Luke 18:27.

not done. Yet through this encounter as well as that with the Samaritan woman, Jesus also brought clarity to a principle prevalent throughout His teachings:

The Abundant Life is Found in God's Person and Purposes

In His interaction with the wealthy young ruler, Jesus is proposing something He had said to His disciples at some point during His ministry:

> *"And remember the words of the Lord Jesus, that He said,*
> *'It is more blessed to give than to receive'." (Acts 20:35b)*[363]

If we're honest, we all can relate to this. As fallen human beings we are vulnerable to the lust of the eyes in seeking fulfillment through material things, which Jesus addressed when instructing His disciples what "following Him" would require a few months earlier:

> *"Then He said to them all (the disciples), 'If*
> *anyone desires to come after Me, let him*
> *deny himself, and take up his cross daily, and*
> *follow Me. For whoever desires to save*
> *his life will lose it, but whoever loses his life for*
> *My sake will save it'." (Luke 9:23-24)*[364]

In Luke's original writing, the Greek word translated "life" here is *psuche*, which is most frequently translated "soul".[365] If we want to experience the abundant life, we must realize our soul needs the transformation that begins with denying the natural (i.e., fleshly) impulses that govern it. Put another way, we must deny ourselves.

The English "deny" in this passage comes from the Greek, *aparneomai*, which means, "to put away, renounce, reject, deny, disavow". It is internalizing the mindset that joy, peace, and contentment are not found in satisfying the lust of our eyes, flesh, or egos (1 John 2:16). Instead, it

---

[363] While not recorded in the Gospels, the Apostle Paul through Luke the writer of Acts attributes this quote to Jesus.
[364] See also Matt 16:24; Mark 8:34.
[365] Strong's Exhaustive Concordance

reflects the conscious and intentional rejection of the desires evident in our inclination to seek fulfillment through positions, power, possessions, and pleasure.

In some ways Jesus' teaching was not entirely revolutionary. Some 500 years earlier, a wealthy young Indian prince named Siddhartha Gautama experienced the same emptiness the wealthy young ruler was feeling. Shocked by the suffering he saw in the poverty-stricken villages outside the palace walls in which he comfortably lived; he left his life of luxury to find fulfillment. During the ensuing 45 years, Gautama came to believe we "suffer" due to our attachment to and "craving" for pleasure and possessions, and that "enlightenment" (i.e., contentment) comes only by willingly letting go of these desires.[366]

What Gautama – who would become known as the "Buddha" – did not answer, however, is what we are to "attach" our wants and desires to. But Jesus did, as evidenced in His instruction to the wealthy young ruler: sell it all and give it to the poor. In this response, Jesus offered him a sense of purpose. In addition, Jesus provided an application of a principle He had taught His disciples through the Sermon on the Mount:

> *"Therefore I say to you, do not worry about*
> *your life, what you will eat or what*
> *you will drink; nor about your body, what*
> *you will put on. Is not life more than*
> *food and the body more than clothing...*
> *For after all these things the Gentiles*
> *seek. For your heavenly Father knows that*
> *you need all these things. But seek*
> *first the kingdom of God and His righteousness,*
> *and all these things shall be*
> *added to you. Therefore do not worry about*
> *tomorrow, for tomorrow will worry*
> *about its own things. Sufficient for the day is*
> *its own trouble." (Matt 6:25, 31-34)*

---

[366] https://www.thoughtco.com/religion-and-spirituality-4133211. This is also seen in the practice of "stoicism", a philosophy of life that developed in Greece during the Hellenist period. From https://plato.stanford.edu/entries/stoicism/

In this teaching Jesus is telling His disciples 2,000 years ago what research is telling us today: you can't simply stop a bad habit – you must replace it with a healthy habit. [367] Put another way, Jesus is challenging this wealthy young man to make a decision as He had also said while delivering the Sermon on the Mount some two years earlier:

"No one can serve two masters; for either he will hate the one and love the other, or else he will be loyal to the one and despise the other. You cannot serve God and mammon." (Matt 6:24)

Jesus is essentially telling him what "pick up your cross" and "follow Me" will look like for him. Blessed with an abundance of material possessions, he was gifted with the resources to help those in need. But Jesus is also telling His disciples then, and us today, what discipleship is all about. Discipleship begins with embracing His "mission statement:

"Go therefore and make disciples of all the nations, baptizing them in the name of the Father and of the Son and of the Holy Spirit, teaching them to observe all things that I have commanded you; and lo, I am with you always, even to the end of the age." (Matt 28:19-20)

And this begins with the daily decision of, "Who am I going to serve today?" It's the question Joshua posed to his fellow Israelites some 1,400 years earlier as they settled in the Promised Land God had given them:

"And if it seems evil to you to serve the LORD, choose for yourselves this day whom you will serve, whether the gods which your fathers served that were on the other side of the river, or the gods of the Amorites, in whose land you dwell. But as for me and my house, we will serve the LORD." (Josh 24:15)

---

[367] See You Are Not Your Brain: The 4-Step Solution for Changing Bad Habits, Ending Unhealthy Thinking, and Taking Control of Your Life, by Jeffrey M Schwartz, M.D. and Rebecca Gladding, M.D. New York: Penguin Group, 2011. See also James Clear, Atomic Habits: An Easy Way & Proven Way to Build Good Habits & Break Bad Ones. New York: Penguin Random House, LLC, 2018.

And this involves making a decision on how we will utilize the three things He has given us to use in fulfilling the purposes He has for each of us: 1) our time, 2) our talents, and 3) our treasures. In His sovereignty and divine wisdom, God seemingly distributes them in varying amounts: some may receive five "talents" while others receive two or one (Matt 25:14-29), and some may receive ten "minas" while others five or one (Luke 19:13-26). The question, and challenge for each of us on any given day, is whether we will "seek first the kingdom" or satisfy the "flesh". Put another way: will I serve God or me?

Hillel the Elder, a prominent rabbi of their day, pondered:

"If I am not for myself, who will be for me? But if I am only for myself, who am I? If not now, when?[368]

Perhaps this wealthy young man had contemplated these same questions. To which Jesus seemingly provides the answer in challenging him to decide: "Are you willing to deny yourself and follow Me?" But in this Jesus is also challenging him to take a step of faith in proposing by following Him he will experience "treasures in heaven", i.e., a sense of abundance in his life. It was up to him to decide if he was willing to trust Jesus.

Notice Jesus didn't browbeat this wealthy young man for being covetous or greedy, as He knew what He was proposing represented a big step of faith for him. This is seen in His comment to the disciples after the wealthy young ruler walked away sorrowful:

"How hard it is for those who have riches to enter the kingdom of God!' (Luke 18:24; cf Matt 19:23; Mark 10:24)

And it is seen in Paul's reflection about his own personal journey in following Jesus:

"Not that I speak in regard to need, for I have learned in whatever state I am, to be content:

[368] See https://www.aish.com/sp/pg/48893292.html, https://www.chabad.org/library/article_cdo/aid/4042931/jewish/Hillel-the-Elder.htm

I know how to be abased (humiliated, ashamed),
and I know how to abound. Everywhere
and in all things, I have learned both to be full
and to be hungry, both to abound and to
suffer need. I can do all things through Christ
who strengthens me." (Phil 4:11-13)

The English "content" comes from the Greek *autarkes*, meaning, "To be free from care.[369] It is defined as "to be in a state of peaceful happiness and satisfaction."[370] Sounds like the *WHOLENESS* we all desire, doesn't it? But notice the contentment Paul speaks of didn't come naturally or easily, as he had to <u>learn</u> it. And it required him to "deny himself", to "pick up his cross" and devote himself to God's purposes, and to depend on God's power to accomplish those purposes. But once he did, Paul found contentment and inner peace.

The wealthy young ruler was looking for that same sense of contentment and inner peace, and he sought out Jesus for the answers of how to experience it in his life. And in His response, Jesus essentially told this young man that he will experience abundance in doing "the will of Him who sends us" (paraphrasing John 4:34). Sadly, this young man couldn't bring himself to take the step of faith that the answer was in "denying himself" by selling the things he had clung to in hopes they would provide the abundant life. Call it "covetousness", "greed", or simply a lack of faith, it was a bridge too far for him to cross.

The Prodigal Son rejected his father's ways and went HIS way with disastrous results. The question, however, is having returned to his father, will he find the contentment that had been available to him simply by being in his father's presence? With that, we turn to how he we can experience abundance in our daily walk with God our Heavenly Father.

---

[369] International Standard Bible Encyclopedia
[370] Concise Oxford Dictionary

CHAPTER 9

LIVING WITH GOD

INTRODUCTION

Over the past few decades, Americans have become increasingly supportive of living together before marriage due to the belief it will reduce the likelihood of divorce. One survey conducted in 2016 found 65% either strongly or somewhat agree it's a good idea to live with one's significant other before getting married.[371] Unfortunately the opposite is true, as studies have found 50% of cohabiting relationships end within a year, and 90% within five years.[372] Yet, despite these findings, there is some logic to this perception.

Consider the last time you bought a car. You decide on the kind of car you want based on factors such as cost, gas mileage, and overall dependability, and then you negotiate with the dealer on a price. But before pulling the trigger and closing the deal on such a sizeable investment, you take the car out for a test drive to make sure you like it. That, proponents would argue, is why cohabitation before marriage is arguably a smart thing to do.

---

[371] https://www.barna.com/research/majority-of-americans-now-believe-in-cohabitation/. Note this represents a 16% increase over the findings of a 2008 survey conducted by USA Today/Gallup Poll that found 49% believed living together before marriage will reduce the likelihood of divorce.

[372] "Reality Says Cohabitation a Disaster for Marriage but Poll Shows Public Believes Otherwise", by Peter J. Smith. https://www.lifesitenews.com/news/reality-says-cohabitation-a-disaster-for-marriage-but-poll-shows-public-bel

Most would likely agree with the underlying proposition: before we marry someone, we want to make sure we are "right" for each other. And most people probably enter into at least one "dating" relationship before determining they have met their "soul mate" and formalizing their commitment to that person through the covenant of marriage.

Dating, or "courtship", is the process of determining whether we are "compatible", i.e., we share the same values, want the same things, and can compromise in areas we differ. Yet too often a couple begins living together (whether married or not) only to find in the daily grind of work, taking care of household chores, raising kids, and trying to set aside time for fun and/or relaxation that in fact they are not. They find their priorities differ, they are unable to resolve their disagreements, said disagreements grow into full-blown conflicts, and all those warm and fuzzy feelings experienced during the early days of courtship give way to dissatisfaction, disillusionment, disdain, and eventually divorce.

We begin with this discussion as we consider how to experience a more satisfying and fulfilling relationship with God. As we saw in *Chapter Eight*, relationships thrive when needs and expectations are clearly communicated, each person feels respected and valued, and trust is developed. And as we've also seen, God clearly communicated His standards of "compatibility", i.e., the principles through which Israel would experience abundance in her relationships with Him and each other. But while they agreed to His terms, the people of Israel generally failed to live them out. And after God used Babylon to exercise the divine discipline He warned them was coming if they persisted in their disobedience, they then accused Him of being "unfair" (Jer 5:19; 40:3; Ez 18:25).

The breakdown of this relationship happened because the people of Israel disregarded and generally dismissed God's commandments and disrespected Him in the process. Likewise, the Prodigal's problems began when he became disillusioned with his father's ways, disregarded, and dismissed his warnings, disrespected his father through asking for his inheritance early, and deserted him for a life of prodigal living.

Having returned to his father, however, a fair question to the Prodigal might be, "What will be different this time?" Dissatisfied with living his father's ways before his ill-fated excursion to that "far country", why will he now experience "abundance" in living his father's ways, particularly since his inheritance is now gone? It is reasonable to assume his father (again, God in this parable) is not going to change his ways to accommodate the Prodigal any more than God came to the people of Israel to renegotiate the terms of the Moses Law so it would be more to their liking. After all, He is God: all-knowing, perfectly righteous, and just, and like the people of Israel and the Prodigal Son, we certainly are not. Given this, the only way we can expect to experience abundance in living with our Heavenly Father is to become <u>devoted</u> to Him, His will, and His ways.

HALLOWED BE YOUR NAME

In His first major teaching through the Sermon on the Mount, Jesus not only clarified what God's expectations through the Mosaic Law meant, but instructed His Jewish audience on how to pray, or to relate with their Heavenly Father. And He began with this:

> *"In this manner, therefore, pray: Our Father in*
> *heaven, Hallowed be Your name. Your*
> *kingdom come. Your will be done on earth as it*
> *is in heaven." (Matt 6:9-10; Luke 11:2)*

The word "hallowed" comes from the Greek *agios,* which means, "to be pure, set apart, to revere". We begin by "lifting up" God's Name for Who He is: One above and set apart from all of creation. His name is to be exalted above ours, and all God represents – including His plans, purposes and will for us – are to be exalted above ours as well. I can't think of a better way to express this than in the following words of the prophet Isaiah:

> *"Lord, you are my God, I will exalt you and*
> *praise your name, for in perfect*
> *faithfulness You have done wonderful things,*
> *things planned long ago" (Is 25:1).*

On more than one occasion I have heard a person say something to the effect, "It would be a lot easier to trust Jesus if I could see and hear Him like His disciples did". Yet "many" of them – some who had actually seen Him perform miracles – at one point walked away:

> *"Therefore, many of His disciples, when*
> *they heard this, said, "This is a*
> *hard saying; who can understand it?"…From that time many of His*
> *disciples went back and walked with Him*
> *no more." (John 6:60, 66)*

Their expectations seemingly weren't quite in alignment with those of Jesus, and as a result they – like the Prodigal – became disillusioned. The problem, therefore, isn't in how God's plans and purposes are presented to us, but our willingness to accept them at face value. Given this, living with God each day requires personal renewal.

REALIZING ABUNDANCE THROUGH PERSONAL RENEWAL

As the Good News about Jesus spread, churches popped up throughout the areas around the Mediterranean Sea. Yet, a common problem the Apostle Paul found was while "new creations in Christ" (2 Cor 5:17; Gal 6:15), these new believers were still living like their "old" (i.e., sinful) selves. Given this, Paul found it necessary to challenge them to "put on the new man" (Eph 4:17-32) and "walk in the Spirit" (Gal 5:16-26). Put another way, we are challenged to "love God with your heart, soul and mind" through complete renewal.

In his letter to the church in Rome, Paul outlined this renewal occurs:

> *"I beseech you therefore, brethren, by the mercies*
> *of God, that you present your bodies*
> *a living sacrifice, holy, acceptable to God, which*
> *is your reasonable service. And do not*
> *be conformed to this world, but be transformed*
> *by the renewing of your mind, that you*
> *may prove what is that good and acceptable*
> *and perfect will of God." (Rom 12:1-2)*

The Greek word *paristemi* translated "present" means, "to yield, offer up, dedicate". Paul is challenging his audience – and us today – to make the decision presented above to demonstrate our love for God by offering ourselves as "living sacrifices" in serving Him in ways that are pleasing to Him. Before we do, however, we must know what constitutes "holy and acceptable" service in God's eyes. And this begins with renewing our minds.

"Reversing" Our Minds

In August of 2019, I along with other staff members of Oasis Community Church embarked on our second staff retreat floating down a portion of the Salt River. For the most part this is a relaxing 3-4-hour excursion, but woe to the uninformed. Like most rivers the Salt River has its twists and turns, and there are times the currents move along quite quickly over the rocks and into the low-hanging trees jutting out over the water at points along the river. Having learned this the hard way, we came prepared with oars to steer ourselves out of the trees and around the rocks we were helpless to avoid on our first excursion.

The point of this illustration is in a way, the currents of the Salt River represent the desires of our flesh nature that will inevitably take us over the rocks and into the low-hanging trees we want to avoid. Given our thinking influences our emotions and actions, experiencing abundance in our walk with God begins with renewing our "minds".

The Greek word translated "renew" is *anakoisis*, which means "reversal, anew". Recall our minds are naturally "darkened", "blinded", "corrupted", "depraved", and "hostile to God".[373] Further complicating this are the "strongholds" that threaten to bind us:

> *"We destroy arguments and every lofty opinion*
> *raised against the knowledge*
> *of God, and take every thought captive to*
> *obey Christ..." (2 Cor 10:5)*[374]

---

[373] See Eph 4:18, 2 Cor 4:4, Titus 1:5, Rom 1:28, 1 Cor 2:14-15
[374] See *Chapters Three, Six & Seven*

The Prodigal didn't have to be a rocket scientist to come to the realization his idea of the "abundant life" was skewed. For those of you who have not found yourself "eating pea pods" through regrettable decisions and choices, however, it may be a bit more difficult to see the need for a complete "reversal". Realize, however, that our old, unhealthy ways of thinking become deeply engrained in our being. Our minds are like the house in desperate need of a fresh coat of paint, but first needing a thorough scraping of the old paint that is chipped and peeling. Given this, we must "humble ourselves" and become like "little children" to allow the Holy Spirit to reveal the old paint that needs to go.

The battleground for our souls is fought over whether we will serve God or ourselves, and the contestants are Franklin's "reason" versus "passions", and Paul's the "Spirit" versus the "flesh". Recall our self-serving impulses arise out of the limbic part of our brain, while reason and impulse control arises out of the neocortex.[375] The Prodigal's problems began when he let "passion hold the reins" rather than the "reason" imparted by his father, or as St. Augustine proposed he let suggestion give way to his desires which led to consent. Put another way, he let the feeling part of his brain – moved by impulse and immediate gratification – drive his actions. Hitting bottom allowed reason to resurface, prompting the realization he needed to reverse course and return to his father.

The relevance of all this neuroscience stuff is found in Paul's instructions to the Galatians:

"I say then: Walk in the Spirit, and you shall not fulfill the lust of the flesh." (Gal 5:16; cf 5:26; Rom 8:1-6; 2 Cor 12:18).

Here, the Greek word translated "walk" is in what is called the "active" voice, meaning it requires us to proactively engage with the Spirit, and to consciously and willingly allow Him to guide our thoughts and actions. Important to realize, however, is the fact the Holy Spirit guides us through the "truth" found in the Bible, so personal renewal begins with learning God's principles for life, and putting them into practice:

---

[375] See *Chapter Three.*

*"Since you have purified your souls in obeying
the truth through the Spirit in sincere
love of the brethren, love one another fervently
with a pure heart..." (1 Pet 1:22)*

An illustration that comes to mind is driving to an unfamiliar destination using an app like *WAZE* or *Google Maps*. As you drive you hear the automated voice guiding you along and correcting your course if you miss a turn. Your "directions" are the wisdom of God, while the Holy Spirit is the automated voice guiding you along and correcting you if you drift off course.[376] Through this the Spirit "transforms" your neocortex, or the "reason" and judgment portions unique to the human brain, to become aligned with God's Word.

Interestingly, neuroscientists have found when people are engaged in prayer or meditation, these parts of the brain light up like a pinball machine: with neuroimaging you can actually <u>see</u> when a person is encountering God![377] And as we become more "spiritually minded", we begin to experience the fruit of the Spirit:

*"For to be carnally minded is death, but to be
spiritually minded is life and peace." (Rom 8:6)*

John begins his Gospel by referring to Jesus as "the Word": He is the walking and talking manifestation of the truth as He <u>is</u> the truth (John 1:1, 14-17). Our recommendation is beginning by reading the Gospels, contemplating what Jesus taught and how He lived and loved people. In time, His thoughts will become your thoughts.

Redirecting Our Wills

There is a difference between knowing the truths in the Bible and really "knowing" them, which occurs through putting them into practice, and

---

[376] See also John 14:17; 15:26; 16:13; 2 Thess 2:13; 1 John 4:6; 5:6. The Spirit will bring to mind the truths we have already learned but may not immediately recall – particularly in times of stress.
[377] According to D'Aquili, Newberg (<u>Why God Won't Go Away</u>, <u>Why We Believe What We Believe</u>), the frontal lobes are highly active during times of prayer, meditation.

coming to know experientially the validity of their claims. The Apostle James affirms this in this exhortation:

> *"Therefore, lay aside all filthiness and overflow of*
> *wickedness, and receive with meekness the*
> *implanted word, which is able to save your souls.*
> *But be doers of the word, and not hearers*
> *only, deceiving yourselves. For if anyone is a hearer of the*
> *word and not a doer, he is like a man observing his natural*
> *face in a mirror; for he observes himself, goes away, and*
> *immediately forgets what kind of man he was. But he who*
> *looks into the perfect law of liberty and continues in it and is*
> *not a forgetful hearer but a doer of the work, this one*
> *will be blessed in what he does." (Jam 1:21-25)* [378]

If you ask someone, "How do you lose weight?", the answer you will likely get is eat better and exercise regularly. Knowing the instructions then putting them into practice, however, are two different things. Take the Great Commandment, which tells us to love God with "all our heart, soul, mind, and strength" (Mark 12:30; cf Luke 10:27). The Greek word translated "strength" here is *iskuo*, which means "strength, power, or ability". This means using whatever natural skills and abilities God has given us, but even more requires utilizing the spiritual gifts God through His Spirit has empowered us with.

Renewing Our Hearts

David had demonstrated His willingness to surrender his will by serving God. In fact, God told the prophet Samuel he selected David to replace Saul as king of Israel due what He saw in David's heart (1 Sam 16:7). Yet, David still let lust and deceitfulness get the better of him, which begs the question, "Did God misread the condition of David's heart?" [379]

What confirmed God's assessment is how David readily admitted his sins and accepted the consequences for them. The sincerity of his

---

[378] See also Rom 2:12-15.
[379] See 1 Samuel 11.

repentance is seen in Psalm 51, in which David expressed his remorse and desire for God's forgiveness. Then he adds this:

> *"Create in me a clean heart, O God, and renew*
> *a steadfast spirit within me." (Ps 51:10)*

Jesus came to inaugurate a New Covenant first offered to the people of Israel, but now available to us all.[380] It includes the promise of a "new heart", one receptive to God's will and His ways (Ez 36:25; cf 11:19; 18:31). Recall, however, this covenant is not possible without God's grace, which is evident in how Jesus begins the Sermon on the Mount:

> *"Blessed are the poor in spirit, for theirs is*
> *the kingdom of heaven." (Matt 5:3)*

Transformed hearts are cultivated with the attitude of gratitude (see *Chapter Eight)* that springs forth from the realization we've been given something – something we couldn't possibly obtain on our own or earn through our own efforts. That something is God's gracious invitation to join into a relationship with Him despite our unworthiness.

Through this realization comes the willingness to devote ourselves to God's will and His ways, and the good news is God doesn't condition His relationship with us in doing this perfectly. In fact, in those times when we inevitably do fall short, our simple willingness to humbly confess our failures and fall upon His grace (see 1 John 1:9) will enhance our sense of gratitude. The renewal of our hearts, however, occurs in another way as well.

In the example of losing weight, those who exercise regularly will tell you that once they got over the hump of incorporating a regular regimen into their day, they began to experience benefits beyond losing weight. They become more disciplined and resilient in overcoming those not so infrequent days in which they are tempted to skip a workout and sleep in. And they also experience psychological benefits such as a reduction of stress and the boost in mood generated through exerting their bodies.

---

[380] God promised Abraham through his "seed" (Jesus), "…all the families of the earth shall be blessed (Gen 12:3).

In time they become devoted to their daily regimens, as their hearts have followed their minds and their wills.

Another tenant of CBT is the proposition changing our behaviors can change our thoughts and feelings – an example being in "facing our fears". The premise is as we push through fear, we come to realize what we once feared is not as bad as we anticipated (change in thoughts) and will no longer fear (change in feeling) what we once perceived as a threat.

Recall, Jesus said His "food" (i.e., "nourishment") is "doing the will of Him (God) who sent Me, and to finish His work" (John 4:34). Noteworthy is the Greek word translated "food" the writer John chose to employ here. In verse 8, we're told the disciples traveled into town to buy "food": in the original Greek *trophe*, a general word that could include bread, fruit, or meat. But in verse 34 (also see verse 32), we're told Jesus uses the word *broma*, which is better rendered "meat".[381] It is the same Greek word used in the following:

> *"Do not labor for the food which perishes, but for the food which endures to everlasting life, which the Son of Man will give you, because God the Father has set His seal on Him." (John 6:27)*

Recall in Jesus day meat was a luxury enjoyed by the fortunate few, like an expensive cut of meat is for most of us today. For Jesus doing God's will was even more satisfying than "splurging" on a delicacy like filet mignon.

Jesus is essentially describing experiencing the abundant life He offers. As our thoughts become His thoughts and our actions become His actions, our hearts will follow as we begin to want what He wants, and value what he values. In fact, in time our prayers – our very desires and the requests we ask of God – will become aligned with His prayers:

> *"Until now you have asked nothing in My name. Ask, and you will receive, that your joy may be full." (John 16:24)*[382]

What Jesus is saying is the disciples will begin to ask "in [His} name" or ask only what Jesus would ask for. They would desire what Jesus desired,

---

[381] Strong's Exhaustive Concordance.
[382] See also John 14:13-14; 16:16.

i.e., to complete the Father's will by building His kingdom, and in this their "joy [would] be full". It is seen in those early believers, who were "in one accord" with Jesus and each other as they set their minds on the apostles' teaching, enjoyed fellowship with one another, shared their possessions with those in need, and experienced joy in their hearts (Acts 2:41-47).

PERSONAL RENEWAL THROUGH SMART GOALS

The abundant life begins with taking the step of faith that the teachings found in the Bible is God giving us the instruction manual for a blessed life. God does not simply want our blind obedience, but to realize "keeping" His principles is the path to experiencing fellowship with Him. The challenge, however, is overcoming the impulse-driven thoughts, feelings, and actions of our "flesh" nature that come more naturally to us.

Perhaps this has been your challenge, as you've started some kind of "personal renewal" program only to fall short or flat-out fail, leaving you more discouraged than you were when you started. Perhaps you are looking at all the changes you want to make – whether physically, emotionally, and/or spiritually – and they collectively appear to be too big a mountain to climb. To which we turn to someone who might have felt the same way.

The year is 444 B.C. Israel has been under Persian rule since 532 B.C., when Persia under King Cyrus overthrew the Babylonian Empire that had conquered Israel and destroyed the city of Jerusalem in 586 B.C. Nehemiah, an Israelite living in captivity in Persia and serving as cupbearer to King Artaxerxes, is distraught after hearing the 50,000 Israelites allowed to return have failed to rebuild the city walls (Neh 1:3).[383] Artaxerxes grants him permission to go and rebuild the walls (2:1-8), but upon arriving Nehemiah finds the report to be as bad as he had heard: the city "lies in ruins with its gates burned" (2:17). [384]

---

[383] The Book of Ezra tells us Israelites, in 538 and 516 B.C., were allowed to return to Jerusalem to rebuild the temple. While the temple was in fact rebuilt (Ezra 6:15), the returning Israelites and their children did not rebuild the city walls.
[384] Notice Nehemiah recognized God's "good hand" was upon him in being granted this favor by Artaxerxes.

As Nehemiah observes the heaping piles of rubble and considers the daunting task of rebuilding the city, it is reasonable to assume he had moments when he wondered, "How am I ever going to get this done?" After all, there was no way he could do it on his own, and the Israelites living there were seemingly not very motivated to help him. Yet get it done he did. Which begs the question: "How did he accomplish this?"

Well, Nehemiah utilized what behaviorists today refer to as *SMART* goals, which are:

*S*pecific:
W<u>ho</u> is involved, <u>what</u> is the goal I want to accomplish, <u>where</u> it will I do it, <u>why</u> am I doing this (benefits I will realize), and <u>which</u> obstacles will I to overcome to accomplish it?

*M*easurable:
Develop goals that you check off as "yes I did" or "no, I didn't".

*A*chievable:
Is it realistic while at the same represents a meaningful change?

*R*elevant:
Is it worthwhile? Will it help me in achieving bigger goals?

*T*imely:
Set dates of when you'll start and measure progress.

First, Nehemiah had a goal: to rebuild the city walls. Second, he took this monumental project and broke it down into measurable – and achievable – tasks by assigning each family a small section of the wall to rebuild. Third, it was clearly relevant to Nehemiah, as the news of the city's condition had left him in tears (Neh 1:4). To make it relevant to his fellow Israelites, he assigned the portion of the wall sitting "in front of [their] own house", so each family would see the work they had accomplished while experiencing a sense of pride and satisfaction every time they walked out their front door (Neh 3:1-32). Finally, he got it done in a timely manner, as we're told it took only 52 days (Neh 6:15)!

As you consider the changes necessary for you to experience personal renewal, realize your life at this point is essentially a collection of habits: we tend to get up at certain times, eat certain things, and do chores at certain times on certain days. Even our thought processes are habitual in nature, which means to make the changes you have struggled to make in the past you must begin by consciously and proactively challenging and changing your thoughts. Also recall we must replace old habits with new, more desirable habits.[385] This may involve "denying yourself" something that has become comfortable but has hindered you from making the changes you want to make. And you must have a plan as:

"By failing to prepare, you are preparing to fail."
— Ben Franklin [386]

"A goal without a plan is just a wish"
— Antoine de Saint-Exupery [387]

"If you don't know where you are going, you'll
end up someplace else." — Yogi Berra [388]

An example is my experience in taking on the challenge of running the Twin Cities Marathon in Minneapolis/St. Paul, Minnesota in October 1992. As of late June, of that year, I had never run more than six miles at a time, so the thought of running the full 26.2 miles in about 100 days was a daunting proposition. Realizing I needed a plan for how to prepare, I picked up a copy of the latest edition of *Runner's World* magazine, which just happened to include a 100-day daily training regimen to prepare for running a marathon.

I certainly doubted I'd be able to increase my mileage sufficiently to run a marathon. And the added training meant "denying" myself sleep in getting up earlier to train. But I was motivated: I wanted that sense of

---

[385] A great resource on building healthy habits is James Clear's book, Atomic Habits.
[386] http://www.goodreads.com/quotes/tag/planning.
[387] https://www.goodreads.com/quotes/87476-a-goal-without-a-plan-is-just-a-wish
[388] http://www.goodreads.com/quotes/tag/planning

WHOLE

accomplishment. And here's where the wisdom of *SMART* goals came into play: my goal was realistic, as I never had to increase my mileage on any given day by more than two miles. As my mileage increased, my confidence grew with it. And in October of 1992, I successfully completed the Twin Cities marathon.

There's an old saying, "it takes 30 days to change a habit, 90 days to change a lifestyle", which is confirmed in research that shows it takes 30-40 days to develop new habits.[389] And our ability to literally change our brains is seen in the personal experiment conducted by Dustin Sandlin with the "Backwards Bicycle". His curiosity aroused as he taught his pre-school age son to ride a bicycle, Sandlin wondered how long it would take him to "unlearn" the motor skills that had become automatic memory twenty-plus years earlier. Sandlin had a friend design a bicycle that would go the opposite direction the handlebars turned – and quickly found just how difficult it is to unlearn this basic skill. Sandlin says that despite practicing every day, it took him eight months to be able to ride the Backwards Bicycle without falling over.

Having mastered it, Sandlin then attempted to ride a normal bicycle again – only to find himself again falling due to the same balance issues he had when first attempting to ride the Backwards Bicycle. But after about 20 minutes and numerous attempts, he found the old muscle memory suddenly clicked, and he was able to ride a normal bicycle again.[390]

Just as Dustin Sandlin learned to ride the Backwards Bicycle, you can make monumental changes in your body, soul, and spiritual health by identifying the benefits you will experience and developing a realistic plan. Using Nehemiah's *SMART* goal approach, begin by setting a few specific goals – one that targets each aspect of your being:

- *Body: a realistic plan to eat better and exercise regularly,*
- *Mind: a realistic plan to incorporate Bible reading and prayer into your week; and,*

[389] Duhigg, The Power of Habit. See also Jeffrey M. Schwartz, M.D. & Rebecca Gladding, M.D., You Are Not Your Brain: The 4-Step Solution for changing Bad habits, Ending Unhealthy Thinking, and Taking Control of Your Life (2011). NY: Penguin Group (USA).
[390] See Sandlin's experiment at https://ed.ted.com/featured/bf2mRAfC.

- *Will: a plan to explore how you will employ your spiritual gifts by serving in one area of ministry at your church or local non-profit organization.*

One final thought: don't be surprised if you must overcome obstacles in your journey to *WHOLENESS*. At the same time, be encouraged in considering the numerous obstacles Nehemiah had to overcome, which included ridicule (Neh 4:1-6), enemy attacks (4:7-9), discouragement (4:10-12), economic challenges (5:1-5), slander and lies (6:5-9), deceit (6:10-14), and even a plot to assassinate him (6:1-4)! And realize overcoming the most difficult challenges makes it the most rewarding, as Psychiatrist M. Scott Peck proposes:

> *"The truth is that our finest moments are*
> *most likely to occur when we are*
> *feeling deeply uncomfortable, unhappy, or*
> *unfulfilled. For it is only in such*
> *moments, propelled by our discomfort,*
> *that we are likely to step out of*
> *our ruts and start searching for different*
> *ways or truer answers."[391]*

Channel the discomfort or dissatisfaction with where you are in your spiritual life into action steps, but don't try to "build Rome in a day". Take some small steps of faith and watch what God will do in your life!

THE PRACTICES OF "PRAYER" AND "FASTING"

We began this chapter with the example of a committed relationship like marriage to illustrate how we approach loving God: expectations are clearly communicated, we reach agreement about what each will give and can expect to receive within the relationship, we come to share the same values and goals, and trust is developed and deepens as we live out the commitments, we've each made to make the relationship work.

---

[391] https://www.goodreads.com/author/quotes/3061.M_Scott_Peck

Now imagine that relationship when quality time isn't set aside to spend time with each other to talk, share and listen to each other. How would you rate the prospects of that relationship surviving, let alone thriving? Well, it is no different in living in relationship with God. We begin to experience the *WHOLENESS* we all desire through spending time in His presence. And this requires the practice of prayer.

About 3,000 years ago, David provided this insight into a vital component of developing our relationship with God through prayer:

> *"Be still, and know that I am God; I will be exalted*
> *among the nations, I will be exalted in*
> *the earth! The LORD of hosts is with us; The*
> *God of Jacob is our refuge." (Ps 46:10-11)*

Setting aside time to be "still" is vitally important since we don't experience God through our five senses, but "hear" Him through our spirit. This requires eliminating the sensory distractions that hinder our ability to hear Him – something as we've also consider has seemingly becoming increasingly difficult for most Americans.

In his 1986 book, *Amusing Ourselves to Death*, author Neil Postman addressed how even then advancements in technology were impacting not only how we live, but who we are as human beings including our capacity to experience the presence of God in our lives. An example is how the "clock" – invented in the 13th century by Benedictine Monks to signal time for parishioners to practice their spiritual disciplines – was quickly implemented by business owners to regulate work shifts. Fast forward to inventions like the telephone, radio, TV, Internet, and Smartphones, and we now live constantly bombarded with sensory distractions. The impact of technology is aptly summed up by Lewis Mumford:

> *"The clock made us into timekeepers, then time-*
> *savers, and now time servers. In the process, we*
> *have learned irreverence toward the sun and the*
> *seasons, for in a world made up of seconds and*
> *minutes, the authority of nature is superseded…*
> *Eternity ceases to serve as the measure and focus*

of human events...and the inexorable ticking of the
clock may have had more to do with the weakening
of God's supremacy than all the treatises produced
by the philosophers of the Enlightenment."[392]

Something as seemingly insignificant as the clock has weakened our awareness of God more than any of the arguments ever presented to deny His very existence! And this happens when our relationship with God is reduced to the one-way monologue of us telling Him what we want, but never hearing what He wants or is doing in our lives.

Again, the Hebrew word translated "know" in the passage above is *yada*, and it is the same Hebrew word used in Genesis 4:1 to describe how Adam "knew" Eve when she became pregnant![393] Now this certainly describes an intimate, personal knowledge of another person. But it also tells us if we want to truly know God, we need to do more than talk to Him – we need to listen to Him as well. It is the transition from the "monologue" of giving God our wish list, and towards a "dialogue" in which we actively listen as well.

In His aptly titled book, *Prayer: Does It Really Make a Difference?* Philip Yancey proposes we view prayer as the means through which we develop and deepen our relationship with God. Yancey notes, for example, that we might approach prayer in much the same way we engage with those we consider "friends".[394] Yancey doesn't shy away from the challenge in this, as he acknowledges he is prone to approach prayer in much the same way many of us would admit we do: a time for US to tell God what WE want. This is seen in the Greek word *proseuchomai* most often translated "pray". It is a compound word which means, "To turn towards in prayer", and includes one's wishes or desires.[395] Yet Jesus didn't discourage this, and in fact said to pray both hopefully and expectantly:

---

[392] Neil Postman, Amusing Ourselves to Death (New York: Penguin Books, 1986), 11-12; quoting Mumford, *Technics and Civilization*.
[393] Strong's Exhaustive Concordance.
[394] Philip Yancy, Prayer: Does It Make Any Difference? Grand Rapids, MI: Zondervan, 2006, 17.
[395] Strong's Exhaustive Concordance.

*"So, Jesus answered and said to them, 'Assuredly,
I say to you, if you have faith and do not
doubt, you will not only do what was done to the
fig tree, but also if you say to this mountain,
'Be removed and be cast into the sea', it will be
done. And whatever things you ask in
prayer, believing, you will receive." (Matt
17:20-22; Mark 11:23-24)*

*"Then Martha said to Jesus, 'Lord if You
had been here, my brother would
not have died. But even now I know that
whatever You ask of God, God will
give You.' Jesus said to her, 'Your brother
will rise again'." (John 11:21-23)*

An important caveat here is both interactions occurred late in His ministry. He had spent over two years teaching His disciples about the Kingdom He would soon inaugurate. He had taught them the meaning of true discipleship, and modeled servant leadership to them. Put another way, Jesus had clearly communicated His expectations, and what they should expect in serving Him. Then during that fateful Last Supper, after telling them He would soon be leaving them, He encouraged them by telling them He would soon send a "Helper" (the Holy Spirit) to be with them, and to remind them of what He had taught them as well as what they could reasonably request of Him.[396]

Two passages in the Bible affirm that prayer is much more than just checking in with God and telling Him what we want. As we've seen, we begin by "hallowing" (exalting) His name. But prayer also serves to align our will with God's will. Notice what Jesus prays for in the Garden of Gethsemane in those last hours before His crucifixion:

*"...Abba, Father, all things are possible for You. Take this cup
away from Me; nevertheless, not what I will, but what You
will." (Mark 14:36; cf Matt 26:39-44; Luke 22:41-42)*

[396] See John 14:16, 26; cf 15:26; 16:7.

Luke provides the clearest depiction of Jesus' emotional state in that moment: He knows full well the hours of intense physical, psychological, and spiritual torture He is about to undergo are at hand. He is "in agony", praying "more earnestly", and literally sweating blood.[397] While Jesus begins with a request, He knows God's answer will be, "No, You must drink the cup". Yet Jesus made His request known, and He did so without fear.

It is through prayer the Holy Spirit "intercedes" for us by making known to us what we need to be asking for (Rom 8:26-27). As Yancey observes, while prayer can easily become the forum in which we tell God how He should serve us, prayer is the means in which we "raise [our] sight beyond the petty and towards the lofty perspective of God".

Developing the discipline of prayer is what Nouwen considers the second movement of spiritual formation. It is a movement away from the illusion we are in control. But it is also that vital movement of descending from the distractions of our minds and towards the desires of our hearts. It is through prayer our attention moves from what is going on around us – and the doubts and disappointments that stir up unrest in our spirits –and towards the promptings and presence of God. Instead of seeing the "giants" and "fortified cities" that hinder us (Num 13:28) we begin to hear how God will help us overcome them.

Noteworthy is the words "discipline" and "discipleship" both come from the Latin *discipulus*, which means, "pupil, student, follower".[398] Prayer is that precious moment when we metaphorically sit alone at the feet of our teacher. It is what Jesus Himself depended upon throughout His ministry:

> *"Now in the morning, having risen a long*
> *while before daylight, He went*
> *out and departed to a solitary place; and*
> *there He prayed."* (Mark 1:35)

Notice it is "long…before daylight", and Jesus sought a "solitary place". It was in the quiet of the early morning hours when Jesus could get away

---

[397] While extremely rare, "hematidrosis" or "hemosiderosis" is the result of blood vessels rupturing and blood mixing with sweat through "acute fear" and "intense contemplation". https://theologetics.org/2017/07/21/hematidrosis-did-jesus-sweat-blood/.
[398] https://www.etymonline.com/word/discipline.

from the demands already being pressed upon Him for strength and clarity of purpose.[399] Nouwen sums this up well:

"To pray is to walk in the full light of God, and to say simply, without holding back, 'I am human and you are God'."[400]

Prayer is taking time to allow GOD to tell us what we need, which brings us to the challenge of making time to LISTEN to Him. In Psalm 46:10, the Hebrew word translated "be still" is *raphah*, which means, "To cease, slacken, draw toward, leave, let alone."[401] Noteworthy i it comes from the root word *rapha*, which means, "to mend, heal, to make whole." A time of "stillness" enables us to hear Him so He ca bring healing to our souls. For this to happen, however, we must present ourselves to Him willingly, attentively, and openly.

1. We must "cease" ("fast").

Americans are busier – and arguably more distracted – than ever. And while many might blame this on our fast-paced lives, the real problem is arguably not so much busy bodies, but our busy brains. Consider the fact that in 1870, the average American worked over 3,000 hours per year. By 1960 working hours had dropped to 1934, and by 2017 to 1757.[402] Yet Americans often cite how "busy" we are. So, where is all our time going?

Well, a 2017 study found the average U.S. adult spent an average of 123 minutes per day on media devices (laptops or desktops), and 721 minutes (over 12 hours) on all types of media![403] Yet, how many of us would say they have "difficulty making time" for prayer?

---

[399] See Mark 1:36-39; Luke 4:42-44; cf Matt 4:23). While there were many seeking His time and attention, through prayer Jesus was instructed His priority was to go "into the next towns that I may preach there also, for this purpose I have come forth".
[400] Yancey, pp 21-24 and p 34, citing Henri Nouwen, With Open Hands. New York: Ballantine/Epiphany Edition, 1985, 54.
[401] Strong's Exhaustive Concordance
[402] https://ourworldindata.org/working-hours
[403] https://www.statista.com/statistics/276683/media-use-in-the-us/. Social media alone accounts for over 2 hours per day! In the Netflix documentary, *Social Dilemma*, Professor Edward Tufte provides this sobering perspective, "There are only two industries who call their customers 'users': illegal drugs and software".

We can safely speak for God in proposing we cannot speak to Him – let alone <u>hear</u> Him – if we are preoccupied with media devices. To "cease" is not just stopping but involves intentionally "leaving" or "letting alone" the thoughts and activities that preoccupy our attention and prohibit us from connecting with God.

Nouwen proposes prayer is "the intentional, concentrated, and regular effort to create space for God". It is the deliberate effort of becoming "un-busy" and "wasting time" with God.[404] It requires developing the ability to tune out the distractions that preoccupy us and may include the use of daily journaling as a means of centering our thoughts.

Which brings us to "denying ourselves" through fasting or abstaining from something for some time.[405] In the Catholic tradition, fasting is practiced during Lent (the 46 days leading up to Easter). You might make an honest assessment of what keeps you from spending time with God – whether social media, TV, or other distractions – and consider periodic fasts as a means of sharpening your awareness of and attention to Him.

2. We must become "slack", or relaxed.

While prone to condition ourselves to be constantly on the move both physically and mentally, we can also develop the habit of relaxing as well. We can start by setting aside time in a quiet place dedicated to spending time with God and practicing deep breathing or meditation to slow our brains down so we can "hear" God speak through our spirits.

3. We then can "draw toward" God.

Prayer is essentially a conversation with God and as we've seen Jesus took the time to teach His disciples how to pray as seen in the following model (Matt 6:6-14):

---

[404] Nouwen, Spiritual Formation, pp 18-19.
[405] Fasting was introduced as part of the Mosaic Law (see Lev 16:27, 29; 23:27-32; Num 29:7) and affirmed by Jesus in Matt 6:16-18. While the English "fast" comes from the Greek *nesteno*, which means, "without food", the Old Testament word describing the practice of fasting is *aw-nah*, which means, "look down, depress, chasten, pay attention, respond", and is translated "afflict" or "deny". Fasting is also proposed as a means of refraining from a tendency to overindulge (1 Cor 9:24-27; Phil 3:19; 1 Pet 4:3).

- *A*doration – praising God for His love, mercy, grace, and provision.
- *C*onfession – like the Prodigal, addressing specific thoughts or actions (or the lack of actions) that cause us to fall short of what Jesus modeled for us.
- *T*hanksgiving – incorporating gratitude into your relationship with God by identifying specific things that you are thankful for.
- *S*upplication – notice it is only after expressing adoration, confession, and thanksgiving that you present your requests to Him.

Jesus begins by drawing our attention to Who God is, what He has done for us, and how fortunate we are for simply having the privilege of being in relationship with Him before <u>asking</u> Him for anything. And notice this reflects the fruit of "ceasing", through which we "know that (He is) God". As we do this, our prayers – in fact our very hearts and wills – will increasingly begin to mirror that of God's. And this is seen in one subtle condition inserted in Jesus' repeated promises to His disciples that "whatever you ask…I will do":

> *"Most assuredly, I say to you, he who believes*
> *in Me, the works that I do he will*
> *do also; and greater works than these he will*
> *do because I go to My Father. And*
> *whatever you ask <u>in My name</u>, that I will*
> *do, that the Father may be glorified*
> *in the Son. If you ask anything in My name,*
> *I will do it." (John 14:12-14)*

> *"Most assuredly, I say to you, he who believes*
> *in Me, the works that I do he will*
> *do also; and greater works than these he will*
> *do because I go to My Father. And*
> *whatever you ask <u>in My name</u>, that I will*
> *do, that the Father may be glorified*
> *in the Son. If you ask anything in My name,*
> *I will do it." (John 15:12-14)*

"And in that day, you will ask Me nothing. Most
assuredly, I say to you, whatever you ask
the Father <u>in My name</u> He will give you. Until
now you have asked nothing in My name.
Ask, and you will receive, that your joy may be
full.... In that day you will ask <u>in My name</u>,
and I do not say to you that I shall pray the
Father for you..." (John 16:23-24, 26)

To ask "in His name" means to ask what Jesus would ask for: we present our requests, but ultimately surrender our wills to our Heavenly Father, as reflected in the following quote:

"Thy will be done" means you are willing to
submit your goals for your life to Him. It
means you are willing to subjugate your will and
suppress your own desires for His will
and desires for your life. It means, as Elisabeth
Elliot has so eloquently said, "To pray
'Thy will be done' I must be willing, if the answer
requires it, that my will be undone." [406]

Yet, as our wills are "undone", we may find our lives undone through unexpected trials.

GROWING IN FAITH AS WE WALK WITH GOD THROUGH THE TRIALS OF LIFE

Virtually any relationship is easy to maintain when both parties agree things are going well. But even the most committed marriage is challenged by, and at risk of collapsing under the stress and uncertainty of the pressures of life we inevitably will face. The same can happen in our relationship with God.

---

[406] https://complexworldsimplemindset.home.blog/2019/04/01/thy-will-be-done-and-mine-undone/

Those prone to see God as "Authoritative" may see trials as something to suffer through and not question but may resent Him having to go through them. Those prone to see God as "Benevolent" may begin to doubt His intentions, and even His goodness. Those prone to see God as "Critical" may see trials as just one more example of God's displeasure with our failures, and quickness to punish us for them. And those prone to see God as "Distant" may see trials as more evidence they cannot expect God to be there for them.

Instead, trials are something we should expect in life, while not forgetting we can trust God will be there to see us through them. The Bible tells us God will "never leave us or forsake us" (Heb 13:5), nor allow us to experience anything we cannot overcome:

"No temptation has overtaken you except such as
is common to man; but God is faithful,
who will not allow you to be tempted beyond what
you are able, but with the temptation
will also make the way of escape, that you may
be able to bear it." (1 Cor 10:13)

The Bible provides numerous examples of people who endured difficult trials in serving God – case in point Job and Joseph. Then there's Esther, who through putting her life at risk witnessed God working behind the scenes to save her fellow Jews from certain annihilation. And there's prophets like Jeremiah, who God forbid from marrying (Jer 16:2), and Ezekiel, who God forbid from mourning the death of his wife (Ezek 24:15-18). And then there's Hosea, who God commanded to marry the local harlot to experience the humiliation He felt as His "bride" Israel repeatedly "cheated" on Him.

Wisdom writers have proposed we will experience more contentment when we learn to accept the trials life inevitably will bring. In the *Big Book* of *Alcoholics Anonymous*, "acceptance" is considered foundational to those seeking to experience true sobriety:

"And acceptance is the answer to all my problems
today. When I am disturbed, it is because I f some

person, place, thing, or situation – some fact of my
life –unacceptable to me, and I can find no
serenity until I accept that person, place, thing, or situation
as being exactly the way it is supposed to be at this moment.
Nothing, absolutely nothing, happens in God's world by
mistake. Until I could accept my alcoholism [or drug addiction],
I could not stay sober; unless I accept life completely on
life's terms, I cannot be happy. I need to concentrate
not so much on what needs to be changed
in the world as on what needs to be changed
in me and in my attitudes." [407]

In his best seller, *The Road Less Traveled: A New Psychology of Love,*
Traditional Values and Spiritual Growth, Peck proposes suffering is actually
necessary for spiritual growth:

"To proceed very far through the desert, you
must be willing to meet existential
suffering and work it through. In order to do
this, the attitude toward pain has
to change. This happens when we accept
the fact that everything that
happens to us has been designed for our spiritual growth." [408]

It's how Edith Eger chose to embrace the atrocities she suffered in
Auschwitz:

"Our painful experiences aren't a liability –
they're a gift. They give us perspective
and meaning, an opportunity to find our
unique purpose and our strength." [409]

---

[407] Alcoholics Anonymous (4th ed.). New York: Alcoholics Anonymous World Services, Inc.,
2001, p. 417.
[408] M. Scott Peck. The Road Less Traveled: A New Psychology of Love, Traditional values
and Spiritual Growth. New York: Simon & Schuster, 1978.
[409] Eger, Edith.

As we saw in *Chapter Eight*, the apostle Paul wrote he had to "learn" how to be content, and in fact the trials he faced were part of his "schooling":

> *"I know what it is to be in need, and I know what*
> *it is to have plenty. I have learned the secret*
> *of being content in any and every situation, whether*
> *well fed or hungry, whether living in*
> *plenty or in want. I can do everything through*
> *Him who gives me strength." (Phil 4:11-13)*

But the Bible goes beyond acceptance to presenting us with the following challenge: not only should we accept trials, but learn to actually <u>rejoice</u> in them as well:

> *"My brethren, <u>count it all joy</u> when you fall into various trials,*
> *knowing that the testing of your faith produces patience. But let*
> *patience have its perfect work, that you may be perfect and complete,*
> *lacking nothing. If any of you lacks wisdom, let him ask of God,*
> *who gives to all liberally and without reproach, and it will*
> *be given to him. But let him ask in faith, with no doubting,*
> *for he who doubts is like a wave of the sea driven and tossed*
> *by the wind. For let not that man suppose that he will*
> *receive anything from the Lord: he is a double-minded*
> *man, unstable in all his ways." (Jam 1:2-8)*

> *"In this <u>you greatly rejoice</u>, though now for a little*
> *while, if need be, you have been grieved*
> *by various trials, that the genuineness of your*
> *faith, being much more precious than gold*
> *that perishes, though it is tested by fire, may be*
> *found to praise, honor, and glory at the*
> *revelation of Jesus Christ, whom having not*
> *seen you love. Though now you do not*
> *see Him, yet believing, you rejoice with joy*
> *inexpressible and full of glory, receiving*
> *the end of your faith -- the salvation of your souls." (1 Pet 1:6-9)*

Amid the trial that is weighing you down and wearing you out, keep in mind one theme prevalent throughout the Bible is that God is a God of redemption, and can be counted upon to snatch victory out of the jaws of defeat:

> *"And we know that all things work together*
> *for good to those who love*
> *God, to those who are the called according*
> *to His purpose." (Rom 8:28)*

Note we must align our expectations with <u>His</u> purposes and <u>His</u> timing. We will come to see the good God is bringing out of the worst situations if we faithfully and patiently wait to see how He has been at work during them. Examples include people like:

- Dr. Bob and Bill W, founders of Alcoholics Anonymous, who through their spiritual awakenings were transformed from alcoholics to advocates in developing the *Twelve Steps* (which were gleaned largely through wisdom found in the Bible); or,
- Jerry Sittser, who came to see the "good" that came out of his suffering in becoming more compassionate to those going through trials like what he suffered; or,
- Pastor William, who turned the tragedy of his abusive childhood into a triumph for the kingdom, as through his suffering he could speak with experience and understanding to the suffering of those who attend his church; or,
- Dr. Joanne Cacciatore, who after suffering the loss of her child founded the *MISS Foundation*, a Phoenix organization that provides counseling, advocacy, research, and education for families who have suffered the death of her young daughter; or,
- Steve and Celestia Tracy, who through their work with those who have suffered abuse felt compelled by God to start the *Mending the Soul* support groups that help victims of abuse throughout the world experience healing [410]; and,

---

[410] From https://mendingthesoul.org/leadership.

- The numerous survivors who have formed support groups for those who have suffered the loss or incapacitation of a loved one due to various diseases.

Like Andy Dufresne in *The Shawshank Redemption*, each of these individuals made the decision to "get busy living" rather than to concede defeat to the trials they experienced. To a person, they have chosen to watch God "work together for good" amid their suffering, and as a result have redeemed it and found blessing in it, by clinging to the life principal Andy Dufresne of *Shawshank Redemption* never lost sight of, and never let go of:

*"Hope is a good thing, maybe the best of things,
and no good thing ever dies."*[411]

Hope in fact may be the best of things because the Bible itself tells us:

"For we were saved in this hope, but hope that is seen is not hope: for why does one still hope for what he sees?" (Rom 8:24)

None of us have ever actually <u>seen</u> Jesus, yet we believe in who He is and what he did. None of us have seen heaven, yet we believe there is such a place, that Jesus is there, and He is there waiting for us with a room prepared specifically for each of us (John 14:1-3). None of us have seen someone resurrected from the dead, yet we believe the loved ones who have gone before us have been resurrected, and that one day we, too, will exchange the "mortal for the immortal" (1 Cor 15:51-58; cf Rom 8:11). If God can snatch victory from death itself, He certainly can have victory over any of the trials we encounter. Our challenge is simply to trust in Him, and to watch with anticipation of what He will do!

---

[411] https://www.bing.com/images/search?q=andy+dufresne+quote&id=E9D5E95F083A0E26B170CABBF016B97D8CF23DB0&FORM=IQFRBA

JEFF BAUER

FROM THE WORKS OF THE FLESH
TO THE FRUIT OF THE SPIRIT

To understand a concept or principle, it is sometimes helpful to contrast it with what it is not. Paul does this in contrasting the works of the flesh with the fruit of the Spirit:

> *"Now the works of the flesh are evident,*
> *which are: adultery, fornication,*
> *uncleanness, lewdness, idolatry, sorcery,*
> *hatred, contentions, jealousies,*
> *outbursts of wrath, selfish ambitions,*
> *dissensions, heresies, envy, murders,*
> *drunkenness, revelries, and the like..."*
> *(Gal 5:19-21a; cf Eph 4:25-32)*

Notice these "works" reflect the *Eight Deadly Sins* and are all clear indicators we are letting our flesh nature reign. In contrast are the life-giving fruit of the Holy Spirit:

> *"But the fruit of the Spirit is love, joy, peace,*
> *longsuffering, kindness, goodness, faithfulness, gentleness,*
> *self-control." (Gal 5:22-23a; cf Eph 5:8-10)*

The following is an examination of the characteristics of those who live in God's presence and surrender their plans and purposes to His will.[412]

"Love"

Again, from the Greek word *agape*, the sacrificial love born out of concern for the well-being of others, and the sacrificial love God extended to us in sending Jesus to die for our sins (John 3:16). While not explicitly stated, it is our belief Paul begins his list of the fruit of the Spirit with love as the rest are products of love. And our potential to experience the fruit of the

---

[412] Strong's Concordance, The Analytical Lexicon to the Greek New Testament.

282

Spirit is limitless since God is a limitless reservoir of love. In fact, God is love – it is His nature, and the essence of His very being (1 John 4:7-8).

While God is *agape* love, we by nature are certainly not, and must draw upon His love to be able to extend it to others. But when we receive His love through humbly accepting the grace He has extended to us, we become fully capable of showing "all" (whomever we come in contact with) that we indeed are one of His disciples (John 13:35).

"Joy"

From the Greek word *chairo* which means, "Gladness, happiness, joy, to rejoice". Now you might say you are generally "glad" or "thankful": life is going quite well, as you have a job you like, have been blessed materially, and have a healthy family and plenty of friends. But would you still feel "joyful" if you lost your job or suffered another kind of setback?

Trials bring us face to face with what Nouwen proposes is the third movement in spiritual transformation: from sorrow to joy. Trials force us to accept what is painfully obvious: this side of eternity can be hard and flat-out painful. The challenge is how we choose to view losses. As Nouwen writes, this movement involves daring:

> *"...to allow the pain of our sufferings to enter*
> *our hearts, having the courage to let our*
> *wounds [be known and felt], and embracing the*
> *freedom to cry in anguish, or to scream*
> *in protest – and so to risk being led into an inner*
> *space where the joy can be found."[413]*

It is embracing the truth Solomon so painfully came to realize – in life we will have both good times and bad, times we laugh and times we weep, times of new birth and times of death (Eccl 4:1-8). But Solomon prefaces this with one key word in the opening verse:

> *"To everything there is a season, A **time** for every*
> *purpose under heaven..." (Eccl 4:1)*

---

[413] Nouwen, Spiritual Formation, p. 43.

Once we accept life will have its trials, we become capable of realizing God is purposefully at work in even the worst of them as through the testing of our faith we develop patience and become "perfect and complete" (Jam 1:4; cf Phil 1:6). Noteworthy is the English "complete" comes from the Greek *olokleros*, which means "perfect, complete, <u>WHOLE</u>".[414]

"Peace"

From the Greek word *eirene* which means, "Peace, prosperity, blessing, quietness, rest, harmony with others". Jesus came to bring "peace on earth and goodwill toward men!" (Luke 2:14), and it is possible for the peace of God to literally "rule" in our hearts:

> *"For He Himself is our peace, who has made*
> *both one, and has broken down the*
> *middle wall of separation, having abolished in*
> *His flesh the enmity, that is, the law*
> *of commandments contained in ordinances, so*
> *as to create in Himself one new man*
> *from the two, thus making peace, and that He*
> *might reconcile them both to God in*
> *one body through the cross, thereby putting*
> *to death the enmity." (Eph 2:14-16)*

> *"Do not be anxious about anything, but in every*
> *situation, by prayer and petition, with*
> *thanksgiving, present your requests to God. And*
> *the peace of God, which transcends*
> *all understanding, will guard your hearts, and*
> *your minds in Christ Jesus." (Phil 4:7-9)*

Peace is seen in those not easily rattled when facing trials or difficult circumstances. But not only are we called to walk in peace regardless of life's circumstances, but to be peacemakers (Matt 5:9), and "if... possible", to "live peaceably with others" (Rom 12:18).

---

[414] Strong's Concordance, The Analytical Lexicon to the Greek New Testament

"Long-suffering"

From Greek word *makrothumia* which means, "Forbearance, patience, putting wrath far away". It is seen in those who pursue peace in their relationships through developing the ability to listen and seek understanding even when disagreeing. It is putting into practice the exhortation to be "swift to hear, slow to speak, slow to wrath" (Jam 1:19), and seen in those who even when offended persist in pursuing peace. The fact God is "long-suffering" in His relationship with us should inspire us to practice the same with others, regardless of their shortcomings, and even if feeling offended or disrespected.

"Kindness" and "Goodness"

"Kindness" is from the Greek word *chrestotes*, which means, "usefulness, excellence, kindness", while "goodness" is from the Greek word *agathosune*, which means, "goodness, beneficence". While goodness is the inner disposition of wanting the best for others, kindness is its expression through being "useful" in promoting the well-being of others.

Kindness and goodness reflect a gradual shifting of our awareness of and attention from ourselves to others. It is developed through simple acts like complementing or thanking others or opening the door while entering or exiting a building. And it is expressed in its fullness through acts of generosity through giving of our time, talents, and treasures.

"Faithfulness"

From the Greek word *pistis* which means, "Trust, belief, promise, assurance". It is the noun form of the same Greek word that is translated "believe". While love produces the other fruits of the Spirit, faithfulness is what <u>sustains</u> them:

> *"And you, who once were alienated and enemies in your mind by wicked works, yet now He has reconciled in the body of His flesh through death, to*

present you holy, and blameless, and above
reproach in His sight -- if indeed
you continue in the faith, grounded and
steadfast, and are not moved away
from the hope of the gospel which you heard,
which was preached to every
creature under heaven, of which I, Paul,
became a minister." (Col 1:21-23)

When we live grounded in the promises and assurances of God (i.e., in faith), we enable the power of the Holy Spirit as evidenced in the fruit of the Spirit to flow through us.

"Gentleness"

From the Greek word *prautes* which means, "Humility, meekness, mildness". While "meekness" is often confused with "weakness", this couldn't be further from the truth given Jesus described Himself as "gentle (*prautes*) and lowly in heart" (Matt 11:29).

Gentleness flows out of the quiet inner strength and assurance in knowing who we are in Christ. No longer striving to be significant in knowing we already are significant, we willingly become "bondservants" of Christ through selflessly serving others. Gentleness is reflected when one puts to death the pride that compels us to compete with others, and it produces the life that models the example of Jesus (Phil 2:5-11). And it will be rewarded:

"And whoever exalts himself will be humbled, and
he who humbles himself will be exalted."[415]

"Self-Control"

From the Greek word *egkrateia*, which means, "Power or strength against" the self-serving impulses and desires of the flesh. Self-control is also a product of humility and is evidence of our progression towards

---

[415] See Matt 23:12; cf Job 40:11; Luke 14:11; 18:14; Jam 4:6; 1 Pet 5:5.

WHOLENESS and completeness (2 Pet 1:5-8). Self-control enables us to deny our carnal tendencies, to hold our tongue when offended, and to be the beacon of hope and faith Jesus calls us to. But notice Paul begins and ends his discussion of the fruit of the Spirit with the exhortation to "walk in the Spirit":

> *"I say then: Walk in the Spirit, and you shall not*
> *fulfill the lust of the flesh.... If we live in the Spirit,*
> *let us also walk in the Spirit..." Gal 5:16, 25*

And noteworthy is Paul's use of the Greek words translated "walk". While the former might be translated to "stroll along", the latter could be translated to "march" – much like a soldier keeping in step with his commanding officer. Paul appears to be saying the more we walk with the Spirit, the more conformed we become to the leading of the Spirit.

Finally, notice virtually all the fruits of the Spirit involve how we interact with and relate to others, as Jesus outlined in the second half of the Great Commandment:

> *"This is the first and great commandment. And the second is like it:*
> *'You shall love your neighbor as yourself.'*
> *On these two commandments*
> *hang all the Law and the Prophets." (Matt 22:38-40)*[416]

In the original Greek, the English "the second is like it" means, the second "is the same thing": we love God by loving others. So how do we "love others"? Well, read on…

---

[416] See also Mark 12:28-31; Luke 22:24-27; cf Rom 13:9-10; Gal 5:13-14; Jam 2:8-10.

CHAPTER 10

LOVING OTHERS

INTRODUCTION

Imagine a world in which there is perfect harmony – a world in which all acknowledge God as Lord and live according to His commandments. A world not divided by borders, walls, ethnicity, or politics, and a world in which people trust one another, and care for others in need. That is the world God created and declared "very good" (Gen 1:31).

That world disappeared once Adam and Eve bought into Satan's lies, determined to "be like God," and took what they wanted. What was once good was corrupted by the sin virus, a virus that affects not only humanity but all of creation (Rom 8:22), and so deadly that within one generation it had generated envy, malice, and the first murder (Gen 4:8).

And the sin virus is thriving today. It alienates us from God and manifests itself in *The Eight Deadly Sins*. We are prone to conflicts with even those we love the most. In my 65+ years, the only time Americans have not been at odds with each was right after 9/11 when we stopped pointing fingers at each other, and towards our BIGGER enemy.

Satan is presently the "ruler of this world" (John 12:31; 14:30; 16:11), and being the master of sowing doubt, distrust, and dissension has succeeded in stirring the conflict and chaos we see in our world today.[417] But God sent His "only beloved Son" Jesus to redeem us so we can be set free and experience the abundant life (John 8:32; 10:10).

---

[417] See John 12:31; 14:30; 16:11; cf Eph 6:12.

The play book Jesus gave us to help Him establish His kingdom on earth is quite simple and is summed up in one word: love. It is seen in the Great Commandment, in which we are to "Love God with all our heart, soul, mind, and strength."[418] But this begs the question, "How do I show my love for God in a way that is meaningful to Him?"

While teaching a Bible study class one Sunday I posed that question. In the moments that followed there was an awkward silence. Eventually someone offered "pray," and another, "read the Bible." And while important components of the abundant life, they only equip us to love God, as seen in the second half of the Great Commandment:

> *"And the second, like it, is this: You shall love*
> *your neighbor as yourself. There is no*
> *other commandment greater than these." (Mark*
> *12:31; cf Matt 22:39; Luke 10:27)[419]*

Note the phrase, "like it."[420] The Second Commandment is the same as the first: you love God by loving your neighbor. You can't love God without loving your neighbor. And this wasn't anything new to Jesus' audience, as it was a central tenant of the Mosaic Law:

> *"You shall not take vengeance, nor bear any*
> *grudge against the children of your*
> *people, but you shall love your neighbor as*
> *yourself: I am the LORD." (Lev 19:18)[421]*

Jesus came to bridge the divide between God and humanity caused by sin. Love is the antidote to the sin virus. We love God by loving others. To which we'll take a more in-depth look at what "love" looks like as it is expressed in our relationships with others.

---

[418] Mark 10:30; cf Matt 22:37; Luke 10:27
[419] This is paraphrased by Paul (Rom 13:9-10; Gal 5:14) and James (Jam 2:8-10) in their summations of the meaning of the Law.
[420] From the Greek word *omoios*, which means, "Of the same nature, like". Strong's Exhaustive Concordance.
[421] See Rom 13:9-10; Gal 5:14; Jam 2:8-10. See also Deut 6:5.

WHAT IS "LOVE": A CLOSER LOOK

In their 1984 #1 hit song, *Foreigner* expresses a common sentiment:

> *I wanna know what love is*
> *I want you to show me*
> *I wanna feel what love is*
> *I know you can show me*[422]

Safe to say Jesus answered that question for us. Yet just as there are several Hebrew words translated "God" in the English to describe His various attributes, there are several Greek words translated "love" in the English found in the Bible, and how it is expressed in our various human relationships.[423] C.S. Lewis provides an insightful overview of each.[424]

- ***Eros: The "Erotic" Love***

In Greek mythology, the Greek god Eros was the god of romantic or sexual desire. While the Greek word *eros* is not actually found in the Bible, it is seen in Adam's response upon first laying his eyes upon Eve (Gen 2:24-25), in the romantic expressions between Solomon and his Shulamite bride in the Song of Solomon, and in the healthy sexual union of a husband and wife (1 Cor 7:1-5; cf Eph 5:23-33). *Eros* love is a husband and wife openly sharing themselves with each other.

- ***Storge: The "Affectionate" Love***

Storge is the affection felt between two people: a husband and wife, a parent and child, or close friends. While *eros* is the "love" that draws a man and woman together, *storge* is the mutual appreciation and a growing awareness "we're made for each other." It is also the care and concern exhibited by a mother to her child, or two close friends.

Affection breeds acceptance, and in turn tolerance. We become more

---

[422] https://www.azlyrics.com/lyrics/foreigner/iwanttoknowwhatloveis.html
[423] See, for example, https://foundinantiquity.com/2013/08/17/greek-words-for-love-in-context/
[424] C.S. Lewis. The Four Loves.

accepting of the shortcomings or less desirable qualities in another due to his or her good qualities.

- ### *Philia: The "Friendship" Love*

Philia is the product of *storge* love deepening over time into true companionship. It is seen in the unity of those who share common beliefs, values, interests, or causes. It is the least "jealous" of the loves, as while one may feel threatened when the object of one's affection begins to express affection towards a third party, *storge* gladly welcomes others to the "pack." Jesus expressed this to His disciples in the hours before His arrest:

> *"Greater love has no one than this, than to lay*
> *down one's life for his friends. You are*
> *My friends if you do whatever I command you.*
> *No longer do I call you servants, for a*
> *servant does not know what his master is doing;*
> *but I have called you friends, for all*
> *things that I heard from My Father I have*
> *made known to you." (John 15:13-15)*

A good example is seen in the "gladness and simplicity of heart" the early Christians experienced as "the Lord added to the Church daily" (Acts 2:46-47).

- ### *Charis: The "Generous" Love*

Finally, there is *charis* or love expressed through generosity towards those in need. *Charis* is the most selfless and sacrificial of the four loves and seen in those who graciously extend favor to others out of a concern for their well-being. It is seen in the Apostles' numerous exhortations to their readers to live out the example of Jesus through patiently and lovingly caring for the needs of others.[425] It is the purest expression of love in that

---

[425] See Is 58:10; Matt 5:42; 6:1-4; 25:35, 40; Luke 10:35; 11:41; 12:33; 14:13; 18:22; 19:8; Acts 9:36; 10:2-4, 31; Rom 9:15-18; 11:30-32; 12:10; 14:15; 1 Cor 8:1; 13:1-8, 13; 14:1; 16:14; 2 Cor 9:6-7; Gal 2:10; Eph 4:28; Col 3:14; 1Thess 3:6;2 Thess 1:3; 1 Tim 1:5;2:15; 3:16; 4:12; 2 Tim 2:22; 3:10; Titus 2:2; 1 Pet 4:8; 5:14; 2 Pet 1:7; 1 John 3:17; 3 John 6.

joy is experienced simply through the act of giving to others (John 15:11, Acts 20:35).

The above are examples of what Nouwen referred to as "Gift-love." For us fallen, fragile human beings prone to selfishly prioritize our wants and needs, however, it is impossible to "Gift-love" – whether *eros, storge, philia,* or *charis* – in the sacrificial *agape* love of how God loved us apart from Him. But Jesus tells us how this becomes possible:

> *"As the Father loved Me, I also have loved*
> *you; abide in My love." (John 15:9)*

The Greek word translated "abide" here is *meno,* which means, "to dwell, remain, be present, continue, remain, endure." It requires regularly drawing near to God our Father, the endless reservoir of "Gift-love" we must draw upon to love others unconditionally. And Jesus made this unequivocally clear to His disciples a moment earlier:

> *"I am the true vine, and My Father is the*
> *vinedresser. Abide in Me, and I in you. As*
> *the branch cannot bear fruit of itself, unless it*
> *abides in the vine, neither can you,*
> *unless you abide in Me. I am the vine; you are*
> *the branches. He who abides in Me,*
> *and I in him, bears much fruit; for without Me*
> *you can do nothing." (John 15:1, 4-5).*

Like the branches in the vineyard Jesus and His disciples observed on their way to the Garden of Gethsemane where Jesus would soon be arrested, our efforts to be fruitful will be in vain unless nourished with the grace and mercy we have received from Him.

SO, WHERE'S THE LOVE?

The hippie movement of the late 1960's embraced the themes of "peace" and "love". Advocates lived in "communes" and shared their possessions. But while proclaiming Jesus, peace and harmony was more the product of indulging in alcohol and other mood-altering substances than the work of the Holy Spirit.

While love was evident in the early days of the Church it did not last, as within one generation the Apostle Paul observed a glaring absence of love. Instead, the "works of the flesh" ran amok.[426] Sadly, the works of the flesh were prevalent in the other churches as well.[427] So, Paul confronted the self-centeredness and disregard for others he observed:

"Be kindly affectionate to one another with brotherly love, in honor giving preference to one another..." (Rom 12:10)

"Do not be overcome by evil but overcome evil with good." (Rom 12:21)

"We then who are strong ought to bear with the scruples of the weak, and not to please ourselves. Let each of us please his neighbor for his good, leading to edification." (Rom 15:1-2)

Paul is essentially asking, "Where's the love?" And he might ask many people in the Church today the same question. Instead of *philia* being expressed in loving, mutually respecting marriages, he would find the more "Need-driven" *eros* love expressed in sexual relationships outside marriage, or in its full expression through sexual addiction.

He would find *storge* expressed in the enmeshment of a mother whose identity is realized through her children, or the father pushing his son or daughter too hard out of his need to be "made proud".[428] He would observe friendships fractured by envy, jealousy, or resentment through some perceived offense, or the pseudo-*storge* evident in the "co-dependent" relationship in which affection is conditional on the other reciprocating through affirmation or attention, and in which desires have become demands.

And he would find *philia* corrupted through an "us vs them" mindset

---

[426] See Gal 5:19-21.

[427] See 1 Cor 3:1-3; Eph 4:20-32; Jam 4:1-6.

[428] It is seen in Paul's warning to fathers to not "provoke" their children to wrath or discouragement (Eph 6:4; Col 3:21).

that discounts, dismisses, or outright denigrates "those" who differ ethnically, politically, or spiritually. Instead of loving others, he would find united fronts against those considered a threat.[429]

And Paul would find acts of *charis* love tarnished through the failure of recipients to express gratitude for the favor they have received, or the resentment felt by the giver driven more to receive the "glory of men" (Matt 6:1-4; 1 Thess 2:6) than the "well done good and faithful servant" (Matt 25:21, 23; Luke 19:17). Which begs the question, "Why do we too often fall short in extending to others the love we have received from God?

Well, we propose there are two reasons for this. First, while "reborn" and made "new creations" through the indwelling of the Holy Spirit, the sin nature remains alive and well and at work within us. It is the battle between the flesh and the Spirit we will fight until the day we die.[430] And at the heart of this battle is pride, the first of *The Eight Deadly Sins*. It is pride that, even as we acknowledge our inadequacy before God, directs our attention away from our shortcomings and towards those of others.[431]

Along with this is the challenge of overcoming the "merit system" mindset we begin to learn and internalize in early childhood: if you do "good" you receive favor, but if you do "bad" you will be punished. But then Jesus came and turned this all upside down.

"DESERVES" AIN'T GOT NOTHING TO DO WITH IT

It is approximately 1400 B.C., and the *Entrance* Generation of Israel is looking across the Jordan River at the Land promised their parents after God delivered them from Egyptian bondage 40 years earlier. Before conquering the land, however, Moses gives them a little history lesson. In the first three chapters of Deuteronomy, we see him recount all the favor God has granted the people of Israel through the miraculous works He had done to bring them to this moment. Moses then instructs them of the terms and conditions under which they could earn the opportunity

---

[429] Arguably a good example is seen in the Evangelical Church uniting with Conservatism against Liberal causes.
[430] See Gal 5-6; Eph 4-5; Rom 7-8.
[431] Hence Jesus' warning about judging others (Matt 7:1-5).

to prosper in this land. And he begins with "The Commandment," or Commandment *Numero Uno:* "Fear the Lord your God…and keep all His statutes and his commandments…" (Deut 6:1-2), after which he reminds them of something vitally important to experiencing the abundance God is offering them:

> *"For you are a holy people to the LORD your*
> *God; the LORD your God has chosen*
> *you to be a people for Himself, a special treasure*
> *above all the peoples on the face*
> *of the earth. The LORD did not set His love on*
> *you nor choose you because you were*
> *more in number than any other people, for you*
> *were the least of all peoples; but because*
> *the LORD loves you, and because He would*
> *keep the oath which He swore to your*
> *fathers, the LORD has brought you out with a*
> *mighty hand, and redeemed you from*
> *the house of bondage, from the hand of Pharaoh*
> *king of Egypt." (Deut 7:6-8)*[432]

There was nothing special about the nation of Israel: in fact, Moses describes them as the "least of all peoples". Yet, God chose to bless them, and as the book of Joshua details God gave them favor in having victory over the inhabitants of the Promised Land.[433]

Upon conquering the Land, God then provided instruction as to how it was to be divided up equitably among the twelve tribes so each Israelite would have the opportunity to grow crops, feed their herds, and raise their families.[434] What should not have been lost upon them was any prosperity they experienced would be a product of what God had arbitrarily chosen to give to them. Put another way, "deserves had nothing to do with it."

---

[432] The *Entrance* Generation, born during the desert wandering, had not heard Moses issue the Mosaic Law (Ex 19:1-23:30; Leviticus). Deuteronomy records Moses issuing the *Entrance* Generation the instructions their parents had heard 40 years prior.

[433] Note in Joshua 10:1-15, God caused the sun to "stand still", i.e., He preserved daylight until Israel was victorious.

[434] See Josh 14:1-21:45.

You would think the people of Israel would have been grateful for the blessings God had extended to them and demonstrated it through humbly loving God and each other. Yet, they weren't, and didn't. While claiming to be "obedient" through their prayers, fasting, sacrifices, and tithes, they consistently failed to uphold the "weightier" matters of the law such as mercy, justice, and care for the poor and powerless. And God let them know it:

> *"To what purpose is the multitude of your*
> *sacrifices to Me?" says the LORD. "I have*
> *had enough of burnt offerings of rams and the*
> *fat of fed cattle. I do not delight in the*
> *blood of bulls, Or of lambs or goats. "When you*
> *come to appear before Me, Who has*
> *required this from your hand, to trample My*
> *courts?... Learn to do good; seek justice,*
> *rebuke the oppressor; Defend the fatherless,*
> *Plead for the widow. (Is 1:11-12, 17)*[435]

In fact, the Old Testament prophetic books reveal the two major reasons God rejected Israel was: 1) idolatry, and 2) social injustice.[436] The people were guilty of the same works of the flesh that emerged in the churches Paul founded over 1,500 years later.

In the ensuing years after conquering the Promised Land, it is easy to understand how those who prospered had difficulty drumming up any compassion towards those who struggled. Israel was the true "land of opportunity," as each tribe was granted a portion of the Land upon which to live and work. Add to this God even instituted laws such as no-interest loans, debt-forgiveness, and the Year of Jubilee to "help" (bail-out?) those who through poor choices got into trouble.[437] Given this, if you struggled – or flat-out failed – you had no one to blame but yourself. Not

---

[435] Recall Jesus quoted the prophet Hosea in stating, "I desire mercy and not sacrifice" (Matt 9:13; 12:7; cf Hos 6:6). Also note Micah 6:9, in which God's requirements were: 1) do "justly"; 2), love mercy; and 3) "walk humbly with your God".

[436] See for example Is 1:1-6:13; Jer 3:6-6:30; Ezek 20:1-24:27; Hos 4:1-13:16; Amos 1:1-2:16; Micah 1:1-2:13; Zeph 1:1-3:8; Hab 1:1-15; Zech 7:1-8:23; Mal 2:18-4:6).

[437] See, for example, Lev 25:8-17; Deut 23:19-20.

surprisingly, "mercy" was short in supply. Yet, God challenged the Israelites to be merciful to even the least deserving, just as he challenges us today, redeemed and declared righteous, to extend grace mercy to others.

You may recall, *"Grace is getting what you don't deserve, Mercy is not getting what you do deserve."* Foundational to Christianity is the fact God was willing to give us what we don't deserve (grace), and having Jesus take our place in bearing the punishment we so deserve (mercy). Yet too often we struggle to extend the same mercy God has extended to us.

We see this in the Perfect Son's response to his Prodigal brother's return home (Luke 15:28-32). And while his father pleads with him to share in the celebration, what he is really doing is challenging the Perfect to extend mercy to his brother. Put another way, the father (again, God) is saying, "deserves ain't got nothing to do with it".

We have all encountered "Prodigals," or those we feel don't deserve any favor. It could be the person who has made ill-advised (i.e., "senseless") choices, and is asking for a handout. It could be the co-worker who isn't pulling his or her weight, or the person who thinks he or she is above the rules. Yet Jesus says, "Love 'em anyway," as love is demonstrated in extending favor even to the most undeserving. And we might remember our assessment of who deserves mercy – i.e., our sense of "justice" – is often skewed.

As fallen human beings, we are prone to what is called *Fundamental Attribution Error.*

Researchers have found we tend to be harsher critics of others than ourselves. Research has also found while we are prone to blame circumstances for our mistakes or failures, we tend to point our fingers at another's character for their mistakes or failures.[438]

In a way this is "being like God" in deciding who is "deserving" and who isn't. It also reflects our fallen human tendency to persist in proving our worthiness, at times by putting others down. When we hold contempt towards someone like the Perfect Son felt towards the Prodigal, we are essentially playing God. But in this we are failing to "love others," as well as failing to love God Himself.

---

[438] David G. Myers, Exploring Psychology, 9th ed. New York: Worth Publishers, 2014, pp 458-9, citing several research studies on *Attribution Theory* and *Fundamental Attribution Error.*

WHO IS MY "NEIGHBOR?"

God's standards as reflected in the Mosaic Covenant are certainly high. And the difficulty of meeting them became even more palpable through a parable Jesus shared in response to a Jewish lawyer seemingly wanting to limit what constitutes one's "neighbor":

> *"But he (the lawyer), <u>wanting to justify himself,</u> said*
> *to Jesus, 'And who is my neighbor?' Then*
> *Jesus answered and said: 'A certain man went down*
> *from Jerusalem to Jericho, and fell among*
> *thieves, who stripped him of his clothing, wounded*
> *him, and departed, leaving him half dead. Now*
> *by chance a certain priest came down that road. And*
> *when he saw him, he passed by on the other*
> *side. Likewise, a Levite, when he arrived at the place,*
> *came, and looked, and passed by on the other*
> *side. But a certain <u>Samaritan,</u> as he journeyed, came to where he*
> *was. And when he saw him, he had compassion. So, he went to him*
> *and bandaged his wounds, pouring on oil and wine; and he set him*
> *on his own animal, brought him to an inn, and took*
> *care of him. On the next day, when he departed,*
> *he took out two denarii, gave them to the innkeeper, and said*
> *to him, 'Take care of him; and whatever more you spend,*
> *when I come again, I will repay you. So, which of these*
> *three do you think was neighbor to him who fell among the*
> *thieves?' And he said, 'He who showed mercy on him.'*
> *Then Jesus said to him, 'Go and do likewise'." (Luke 10:29-37)* [439]

If asked, "Who is your 'neighbor,'" you will likely include people you know, get along with, would gladly help, and assume would return

---

[439] While all four Gospels record Jesus summarizing His teaching in "The Great Commandment", it appears He stated this on several occasions. Cheney and Ellisen propose this interaction occurred about nine months before the Passover and Jesus' death and resurrection, while His interaction with other Jewish religious leaders recorded in Matthew 22 and Mark 12 occurred sometime during the Passover Week. John (13:34-35; 15:1-13) records Jesus teaching a variation of this during the Last Supper.

the favor. This would have been the norm in 1ˢᵗ century Israel. Their communities small and the people often related, they knew those they encountered. Given this, failing to help a neighbor in need would have brought the scorn – if not an outright black-listing – by others in his- or her community.

To which Jesus seems to say, "Not so fast: your neighbor is <u>anyone</u> you come in contact with." And in this Jesus also confronted our tendency to show favoritism, or "partiality," towards those we like. Throughout the Bible we are told God is "righteous" and "just".[440] He is always fair, and never shows partiality or favoritism.[441] And the fact the exhortation to not show favoritism is repeated frequently tells us it is an important issue to Him.[442]

Recall "love" upholds the dignity and worth inherent in every human being, and if you've ever been dealt with unjustly, you know how much it hurts. And it is serious enough to God that it was a major factor in His judgement of Israel:

> *"They have grown fat, they are sleek; Yes,*
> *they surpass the deeds of the*
> *wicked; They do not plead the cause,*
> *The cause of the fatherless; Yet.*
> *they prosper, And the right of the needy*
> *they do not defend." (Jer 5:28)*

> *"Therefore, I also have made you contemptible*
> *and base before all the people,*
> *because you have not kept My ways but have*
> *shown partiality in the law." (Mal 2:9)*

---

[440] See, for example, Gen 18:25; Deut 32:4; Job 38:12; 40:2, 8; Ps 19:8; Is 45:19; Rom 3:25; 9:20-21.

[441] See Ex 23:3; Deut 1:17; 10:17; 16:19; 2 Chron 19:7; Job 34:19; 37:4; Prov 18:5; 24:23; 28:21; Acts 10:34; Rom 2:11; Eph 6:9; Col 3:25; Jam 2:1-10; 3:19; 1 Pet 1:17. Note the Bible writers at times questioned God's "justness" (Job 13:8-10; Ps 82:1-4). Note also even those who despised Jesus respected the fact He didn't show "favoritism" (Luke 20:21).

[442] See, for example, Ex 23:3; Lev 19:15; Deut 1:17; 16:19; Prov 18:5; 24:23; 28:21; Jer 5:28; Mal 2:9; 1 Tim 5:21; Jam 3:17.

299

And this is seen in the strong rebuke by the Apostle James of the believing Jews in the church in Israel – people who would have been very familiar with the above passages:

> *"My brethren, do not hold the faith of our Lord*
> *Jesus Christ, the Lord of glory, with*
> *partiality. For if there should come into your*
> *assembly a man with gold rings, in fine*
> *apparel, and there should also come in a poor man*
> *in filthy clothes, and you pay attention*
> *to the one wearing the fine clothes and say to him,*
> *"You sit here in a good place," and say*
> *to the poor man, "You stand there," or "Sit here at my footstool,"*
> *have you not shown partiality among yourselves, and become*
> *judges with evil thoughts? Listen, my beloved brethren: Has God*
> *not chosen the poor of this world to be rich in faith and heirs of the*
> *kingdom which He promised to those who love Him? But you have*
> *dishonored the poor man. Do not the rich oppress you and drag*
> *you into the courts? Do they not blaspheme that noble name by*
> *which you are called? If you really fulfill the royal law according*
> *to the Scripture, "You shall love your neighbor as yourself," you do*
> *well; but if you show partiality, you commit sin, and are convicted*
> *by the law as transgressors. For whoever shall keep the whole law,*
> *and yet stumble in one point, he is guilty of all. (Jam 2:1-10)*

James is confronting the human tendency to favor those we hope will in turn return the favor or can help us through their power, positions, or possessions. And James is simply reiterating to his audience what Jesus taught in the Sermon on the Mount:

> *"For if you love those who love you, what*
> *reward have you? Do not even the tax*
> *collectors do the same? And if you greet your*
> *brethren only, what do you do*
> *more than others? Do not even the tax*
> *collectors do so?" (Matt 5:46-47)*

Extending favor to those we expect will return the favor doesn't make us "good" or "righteous", as even the worst sinners will do this. And noteworthy is this interaction didn't occur until about two years after Jesus preached the Sermon on the Mount. While we can't be certain the lawyer was aware of this teaching, we do know his motive: "to justify himself". Put another way, he is trying to lower the bar of the Law so he can declare himself "righteous." But Jesus knows this, and through His response ups the ante in a way that shocked His listeners, as the hero in the parable was a <u>Samaritan</u>.

The animosity between the Jews and Samaritans dated back to Assyria's conquest of northern Israel in 722 B.C., after which the Assyrians intermixed the Israelites with people from other countries around Samaria. The result was a group of people only part Jewish biologically and culturally. Complicating this was the fact the Samaritans developed a religious system comprised of a mix of the Mosaic Law and the polytheistic systems of the surrounding nations the Jews considered a perversion of their Law.[443]

Now none of this would have happened if Israel hadn't failed to live up to the terms of the Mosaic Covenant and brought God's judgment upon herself. Given this, the Jews had no one to blame but themselves for the existence of the Samaritans and their "corrupted" form of Judaism, and every encounter with a Samaritan was a reminder of this fact.

In using a Samaritan as the model of obedience, Jesus subtly poked at Israel's refusal to humbly acknowledge her collective shortcomings and deflection of her guilt through her animosity towards and contempt for the Samaritans. But in doing so, Jesus also used a poignant illustration of something else He had said in the immediately preceding verses:

> "You have heard that it was said, 'You shall love
> your neighbor and hate your enemy.'
> But I say to you, love your <u>enemies</u>, bless those
> who curse you, do good to those who

---

[443] See 2 Kings 17. The Assyrians did this to dilute the cultures of the people they had conquered to reduce the likelihood of revolution. Further exacerbating the tension was the Samaritans' resistance to Israel's rebuilding efforts under Nehemiah (Neh 4:1-2; cf Is 44:28-45:1). Note in John 4:4, we're told Jesus "had" to go through Samaria when He encountered the woman at the well. Jews traveling between the northern and southern parts of Israel would typically travel around Samaria – even if it extended their travel time by several days – to avoid having contact with Samaritans!

hate you, and pray for those who spitefully
use you and persecute you, that you
may be sons of your Father in heaven; for He
makes His sun rise on the evil and
on the good and sends rain on the just and
on the unjust." (Matt 5:43-45)

Recall under the Mosaic Law, the Jews were commanded, "… you shall not take vengeance or bear grudges but love your neighbor as yourself (Lev 19:18)". There is nothing there – or anywhere else in the Mosaic Law for that matter – about hating your enemy.

Now some speculate this saying developed as a means of lowering the standards of the Mosaic Law. [444] But Jesus not only rejected this interpretation, He raised the standard even higher through His use of the Greek *exthros*, which means, "enemy, foe, adversary, those opposed to us, or those disfavored."[445] Given this, your "enemy" could be:

- That irritating family member,
- The neighbor who makes too much noise or doesn't take care of his or her yard,
- The co-worker who doesn't carry his or her load, or causes problems at work,
- Someone who has wronged you or hurt you through their actions or words; or,
- People of differing ethnicities, nations of origin, political, or religious views.

Jesus once again turned to none other than Peter himself as his object lesson. Peter had come a long way from the time he denied even knowing Jesus to boldly proclaiming His Name.[446] Yet, Peter could not comprehend Jesus came to save Gentiles as well as Jews. So, Jesus, as with the former Saul (Acts 9), chose to pay Peter a "visit" as well.

---

[444] See, for example, https://www.defendinginerrancy.com/bible-solutions/Matthew_5.43.php

[445] Strong's Exhaustive Concordance.

[446] Matt 26:58, 69-75; Mark 14:54, 66-72; Luke 22:54-62; John 18:15-18; 26-28; Acts 4:13-22.

It is approximately eight years after Jesus' resurrection and the transformation of Peter during the ensuing Pentecost.[447] A "God-fearing" Roman centurion named Cornelius has a vision during which an angel of God instructs him to send men to find Peter and bring him to Cornelius (Acts 10:1-8). The next day Peter, while praying, has his own vision, and:

> "...saw heaven opened and an object like a great
> sheet bound at the four corners, descending to
> him and let down to the earth. In it were all kinds of
> four-footed animals of the earth, wild beasts,
> creeping things, and birds of the air. And a voice came to
> him, 'Rise, Peter; kill and eat.' But Peter said, 'Not so, Lord!
> For I have never eaten anything common or unclean.' And
> a voice spoke to him again the second time, 'What God has
> cleansed you must not call common.' This was done
> three times. And the object was taken up into
> heaven again." (Acts 10:11-16). [448]

The rest of Acts *Chapter Ten* tells us as Peter is trying to wrap his head around the meaning of this, Cornelius' men show up and take him to Cornelius at which time Peter realizes the creatures in the vision represent non-Jews: God actually loves Gentiles, too!

And one could argue this shouldn't have been a surprise to Peter. Throughout the Mosaic Law and the words of the Prophets we see repeated commands to welcome and not mistreat the "stranger" or "alien".[449] And he had heard Jesus Himself, in arguably the "closing arguments" of His presentation of God's Law in the days immediately preceding His arrest and execution, reaffirm this (Matt 25:31-46). Yet somehow Peter missed it.

Whether those who have offended us, or with whom we differ ethnically, politically, or religiously, Jesus challenges us to see them as

---

[447] See Harold Hoehener; *"Chronology of the Apostolic Age"*, Th.D. dissertation, Dallas Theological Seminary, 1965; revised 1972. Hoehener proposes Jesus' ascension occurred the spring of 33 A.D., and the events described in 40-41 A.D.

[448] This suggests creatures deemed unclean and therefore not to be eaten according to the Mosaic Law (Lev 11; Deut 14).

[449] Ex 22:1; 23:9; Lev 19:10, 33-34; 23:22; Deut 10:18-19; 14:29; 23:7; 24:19-22; 27:19; Jer 7:5-7; 22:3; Ezek 22:7, 29; Mal 3:1.

God does, and to love them by extending the same grace He extended to us. It reflects the humble acknowledgement that regardless of where we are from or what we believe, we are no different in that we are all flawed and fallen human beings.

Psychologist Lawrence Kohlberg proposed six stages of moral development, the final in having developed a "Universal Ethical Principle" orientation. Those who reach this stage do not show partiality or seek approval, and seek the greater good in one's decisions and actions.[450] Drawing from Kohlberg, James Fowler proposed "Stages of Faith", in which the sixth and final stage is seen in a "Universal Faith" reflected in an increasing awareness of and compassion for those experiencing injustice, as demonstrated by people including Dietrich Bonhoeffer, Mahatma Ghandi, Mother Theresa, and Martin Luther King.[451]

Nouwen's sixth movement of spiritual formation is from exclusion to inclusion. An example is the care the Good Samaritan extended to a "stranger" in the person of the injured Jew (Heb 13:2). Common in all three is mature faith, which few reach, and is seen in appreciating our commonality as human beings rather than our differences.

I cite these theorists as they all reflect the spirit of Jesus' teaching and John's writings:

> *"By this we know love because He laid down*
> *His life for us. And we also ought to lay*
> *down our lives for the brethren. But whoever has*
> *this world's goods, and sees his brother in*
> *need, and shuts up his heart from him, how does*
> *the love of God abide in him? My little*
> *children, let us not love in word or in tongue, but*
> *in deed and in truth." (1 John 3:16-18)*

And it is the capacity to love one's "enemies" that is the epoch of the *WHOLENESS* we desire, and evidence of the work God wants to complete in each of us:

---

[450] https://www.britannica.com/science/Lawrence-Kohlbergs-stages-of-moral-development
[451] James W. Fowler. Stages of Faith: The Psychology of Human Development and the Quest for Meaning. New York: HarperCollins Publishers, 1981.

*"Therefore, you shall be perfect, just as your Father
in heaven is perfect." (Matt 5:48)*[452]

Recall at the end of *Chapter Nine*, we considered the fact we were once His enemies (Col 1:21-22). And it is likely no coincidence Paul used the same Greek word translated "enemies" as Matthew records Jesus used. To which I propose the following principle:

*Your love for God is seen in how much you
love the person you like the least.*

Jesus left this principle for us to grow His kingdom. His business plan is short and to the point: love God and love others. Love is the only cure for the chaos and conflict that permeates our world. Yet, as we all too well know, it isn't always easy.

Dr. Peck provides these descriptions of the kind of love Jesus is describing here:

*"When we love someone, our love becomes
demonstrable or real only through our
exertion - through the fact that for that someone
(or for our self) we take an extra
step or walk an extra mile. Love is not effortless.
To the contrary, love is effortful."*

*"Genuine love is volitional rather than emotional.
The person who truly loves does
so because of a decision to love. This person
has made a commitment to be loving
whether or not the loving feeling is
present. ...Conversely, it is not only possible
but necessary for a loving person to avoid acting on feelings of love."*

And Peck adds this about the impact acts of love have on both us and the recipient:

---

[452] See Col 1:19; 2:9.

"I define love thus: The will to extend one's self for the purpose of nurturing one's own or another's spiritual growth."[453]

In the same way working out at the gym strengthens our physical muscles or studying strengthens our mental muscles, extending love strengthens our "spiritual" muscles. Love is the antidote to the symptoms of hate caused by the sin virus. Extending grace and mercy to the "undeserving" is the way we demonstrate our love for the same God who sent His Son to bring peace to a world torn apart by conflict and chaos (Luke 2:14). But Peck wisely adds this caveat – and warning – about the cost involved:

"Love always requires courage and involves risk[454]

Loving sacrificially comes with a cost – and that cost is seen in the willingness to "lose."

WINNING BY LOSING

It is a Thursday evening in the spring of the year A.D. 33, and the streets of Jerusalem are bustling with Jews who have traveled from all over the Middle East to celebrate Passover. Jesus and His disciples have gathered in the upper room of a home to share the Passover meal. What His disciples didn't know, but Jesus was acutely aware of, was the fact His "hour had come" (John 13:1). In a few short hours He will suffer abandonment, betrayal, false accusations, mocking, beatings, scourging, and crucifixion. Yet, it is in this moment He uses a powerful illustration to hammer home what "loving others" really means:

*"Jesus, knowing that the Father had given all things
into His hands, and that He had come from*

---

[453] M. Scott Peck, The Road Less Traveled: A New Psychology of Love, Traditional Values, and Spiritual Growth. From https://www.goodreads.com/author/quotes/3061.M_Scott_Peck
[454] Ibid

God and was going to God, rose from supper and
laid aside His garments, took a towel and girded
Himself. After that, He poured water into a basin
and began to wash the disciples' feet, and to
wipe them with the towel with which He was girded.
Then He came to Simon Peter. And Peter
said to Him, 'Lord, are You washing my feet?' Jesus
answered and said to him, 'What I am
doing you do not understand now, but you
will know after this.'" (John 13:3-7)

Jesus – Lord of Lords and King of Kings – has taken on the demeaning role of a slave by washing the dirt and dung off the feet of the very men who would soon abandon and betray Him! Jesus knew this lesson was necessary, as He had graciously tolerated the following interchange amongst His disciples that would occur just moments later:

"Now there was also a dispute among them,
as to which of them should be
considered the greatest. And He said to them,
'The kings of the Gentiles exercise
lordship over them, and those who exercise
authority over them are called
benefactors. But not so among you; on the
contrary, he who is greatest among
you let him be as the younger, and he who
governs as he who serves. For who
is greater, he who sits at the table, or he
who serves? Is it not he who sits at
the table? Yet I am among you as the One
who serves'." (Luke 22:24-27)

For three years Jesus had modeled humble servanthood to His disciples. Yet here they are, arguing over who is the greatest! In *CHAPTER EIGHT* we saw *WHOLENESS* begins with something counter-intuitive in that we lose our life by holding onto it but save our life by "letting go" of it (Luke

9:23-24). We love God by denying ourselves and choosing to put His plans and purposes before ours through loving others.

But our fragile egos often get in the way. Pride and self-centeredness generated the "hatred, contentions, jealousies, wrath, selfish ambitions, dissensions, and envy" in the church in Galatia (Gal 5:19-21). And pride fueled the dispute over "who is the greatest."

Contrast this with Jesus' response when His accusers come to arrest Him. After Peter draws his sword and lops off the ear of the high priest's servant, Jesus calmly says, "Please allow Me," and proceeds to heal the servant's ear before subtly explaining why He is not resisting or fighting back. First, the only reason His accusers could arrest Him was His willingness in allowing them to, as in a simple word He could have brought a literal army of angels to defend Him. But second – and more importantly – He had a mission to fulfill. And that mission? To "drink the cup" His Father had given Him to drink.[455]

In the ensuing hours, Jesus would endure the most painful physical, psychological, and spiritual torture human beings in our wretchedness have ever concocted to inflict hate upon another. Yet, through it all, Jesus simply said – nothing![456] In fact, all He said was to affirm that, yes, He is the Son of God.[457]

Jesus had every reason to defend Himself, but that would have undermined His mission and purpose in coming – and something Paul challenges us to always remember:

"Let this mind be in you which was also in Christ Jesus, who, being in the form of God, did not consider it robbery to be equal with God, but made Himself of no reputation, taking the form of a bondservant and coming in the likeness of men. And being found in appearance as a man, He humbled Himself and became obedient to the point of death, even the death of the

---

[455] Matt 26:49-54; Mark 14:43-50; Luke 22:47-52; John 18:1-11.
[456] Matt 26:63; 27:12-14; Mark 14:61; 15:3-5; Luke 23:9-10; John 19:9.
[457] Matt 26:63-64; Mark 14:60; Luke 22:70-71.

WHOLE

*cross. Therefore, God also has highly exalted Him
and given Him the name, which is above
every name, that at the name of Jesus every knee
should bow, of those in heaven, and of
those on earth, and of those under the earth,
and that every tongue should confess
that Jesus Christ is Lord, to the glory of
God the Father." (Phil 2:5-11)*

Jesus didn't demand approval or affirmation because He didn't <u>need</u> it. And He didn't "lose" that day in allowing Himself to be executed, as in doing so He achieved the greatest victory in the history of humanity by defeating death itself!

*"So, when this corruptible has put on incorruption,
and this mortal has put on immortality,
then shall be brought to pass the saying that is
written: 'Death is swallowed up in victory. O
Death, where is your sting? O Hades, where is your victory?'
The sting of death is sin, and the strength of sin is the law.
But thanks be to God, who gives us the victory through
our Lord Jesus Christ. Therefore, my beloved brethren,
be steadfast, immovable, always abounding in the
work of the Lord, knowing that your labor is not
in vain in the Lord." (1 Cor 15:54-58)*

While Jesus has already won the war, we remain engaged in the daily battles for our very souls. We can choose to fight to win in defense of our fragile egos, or we can concede and seek peace and unity as a powerful testimony to what Jesus is doing in our lives!

CULTIVATING THE HEART OF JESUS

As His disciples and "friends" (John 15:11-15), we model the example of Jesus by being cultivators of peace. We are called to "be peaceable," to "live

309

in peace," and to "pursue peace".[458] And Paul "beseeches" us to "keep the unity of the Spirit in the bond of peace":

> *"I, therefore, the prisoner of the Lord, <u>beseech</u>*
> *you to walk worthy of the calling*
> *with which you were called, with all lowliness*
> *and gentleness, with longsuffering,*
> *bearing with one another in love, endeavoring*
> *to keep the unity of the Spirit in the*
> *bond of peace. There is one body and one*
> *Spirit, just as you were called in one*
> *hope of your calling; one Lord, one faith,*
> *one baptism; one God and Father*
> *of all, who is above all, and through all,*
> *and in you all." (Eph 4:1-6)*

And the challenge to be at peace with others clearly extends to those <u>outside</u> the church as well, including the "neighbors" we may encounter as we go about our days:

> *"If it is possible, as much as depends on you, live*
> *peaceably with <u>all</u> men." (Rom 12:18)*

It is through the work of the Holy Spirit in our hearts that "brings forth good" (Luke 6:34; Matt 12:35). And it is the fruit of the Spirit – lowliness, gentleness, longsuffering, and bearing another in love – that enables us to "live peaceably" with others.

After 900 years, it was clear the Mosaic Law and the promises of prosperity, progeny, and protection was not enough for the people of Israel. So, God sent prophets like Jeremiah and Ezekiel to announce the coming of the New Covenant – a covenant of peace in which God would forge in its participants a new heart (Jer 31:31-34; Ezek 36:26; 37:26-28):

> *"I will give you a new heart and put a new spirit*
> *within you; I will take the heart of stone out*

---

[458] Titus 3:1-2; 2 Cor 13:11; Heb 12:14.

of your flesh and give you a heart of flesh. I will
put My Spirit within you and cause you
walk in My statutes, and you will keep My
judgments and do them." (Ezek 36:26-27)

This New Covenant was possible due to the sacrificial life and death of Jesus. While the "new heart" God desires to cultivate within us is the product of the work of the Spirit, it doesn't happen unless we "walk in the Spirit".[459] And this takes place as we apply the teachings in the Sermon on the Mount, beginning with the Beatitudes (or, "Be-attitudes"):

Matt 5:3 "Blessed are the poor in spirit, for
theirs is the kingdom of heaven.

Matt 5:4 Blessed are those who mourn, for they shall be comforted.

Matt 5:5 Blessed are the meek, for they shall inherit the earth.

Matt 5:6 Blessed are those who hunger and thirst
for righteousness, For they shall be filled.

Matt 5:7 Blessed are the merciful, for they shall obtain mercy.

Matt 5:8 Blessed are the pure in heart, for they shall see God.

Matt 5:9 Blessed are the peacemakers, for
they shall be called sons of God.

Matt 5:10 Blessed are those who are
persecuted for righteousness' sake,
For theirs is the kingdom of heaven.

The following are the action steps of how we "walk in the Spirit", and in the process allow God to cultivate this new heart – one that models the heart of Jesus – within us:

---

[459] See Rom 8:1-5; 2 Cor 12:18; Gal 5:16, 26.

1. Acknowledging our spiritual bankruptcy (Matt 5:3-4)

We usually don't fix something until we realize it is broken. In the Parable of the Prodigal Son, Jesus begins with the Prodigal, a "sinner" (in the Greek, a "spiritual beggar") who confesses and humbles himself before his "father and heaven." In contrast there is the Perfect, the "good person," who sees no fault in himself, and therefore no need for change.

To "mourn" is to feel the regret and remorse that leads to the repentance demonstrated by the Prodigal. We develop the capacity to love and the willingness to live peaceably with others when we see them just as we see ourselves: flawed and imperfect, yet every bit as deserving of God's love, grace, and mercy as we are (Rom 3:10-12; cf Is 64:4).

Yet as uncomfortable as it is to take the proverbial look in the mirror, examine our hearts, and see how far short we fall in comparison to Jesus, the result is a profound sense of "blessing." This comes from the Greek *makarios*, which means, "Fortunate, happy, well-off, having received divine favor."[460] It is through the humble process of reflection and repentance that we fully grasp the grace and mercy Jesus wants us to extend to others.

2. Practicing humility by putting peace first (Matt 5:5-6)

Humility is seen in the quiet inner strength of those grounded in their identity in Him yet are aware of and actively working to overcome shortcomings. It is expressed by having gratitude for God's love and grace and finding abundance in serving God's purposes.

Humility isn't cultivated by winning an argument or demanding one get his- or her way, but desiring righteousness prevails. "Righteousness," from the Greek *dikainosune*, means, "dealing equitably with others, pursuing justice, integrity, generosity." We walk in righteousness when our thoughts and actions are like those of Jesus. Humility chooses to defer rather than demand or defend– even to one's own detriment – to achieve peace.

And notice the reward is a sense of "fullness," from the Greek *kortadzo*, which means, "contentment, satisfaction and self-fulfillment." Sounds like abundant life, doesn't it?

---

[460] Through confession we experience: 1) the freedom of God's forgiveness, and 2) intimacy in our relationship with Him.

3. Become a "Bleeding Heart" (Matt 5:7-8)

If you're unfamiliar with the term "bleeding heart", it is used to describe those who are "dangerously softhearted", and "excessively sympathetic to those who claim to be exploited or underprivileged".[461] It is often used condescendingly to describe those who are too "soft" or "easy" when extending favor to those who are perceived as undeserving.

The English "merciful" comes from the Greek *spagchnon*, which means "pity or sympathy, inward affection, mercy." It comes from a compound word that refers to the spleen or intestines and describes the gut-wrenching sensation of feeling another's pain.[462] It is feeling empathy for another even if he or she has offended you in some way. Instead, you choose to seek to understand what happened that generated the irritability and resultant Uzi blast you just received. Mercy is felt as well as given.

This is seen in Paul's exhortation that we put on "bowels" of mercy (Col 3:12). This is an interactive process requiring both the work of the Spirit and our willingness to allow Him to accomplish it. And let's face it: there are some we will have difficulty feeling empathy for, let alone extending mercy towards. Whether obnoxious, demanding, inflexible, or belligerent there are those who will test our patience, leaving us to decide: "Am I going to let my flesh – and Satan – win? Or am I going to win one for the kingdom of Jesus"?

Put another way, "Am I going to choose mercy, or malice?" One man challenged with this decision was the Prophet Jonah. It is about 760 B.C., and Assyria has become a world power. Advanced in both culture and the sciences, the Assyrians are also known for their cruelty.[463] Enter God – Who in another example of His unending grace – is willing to give the Assyrians a chance to repent, and calls Jonah to go to their capital city

---

[461] https://www.bing.com/search?q=bleeding%20heart%20meaning&FORM=PRHP HI&refig=25589f7143e04b2185e19d2ecdfc0b6b&httpsmsn=1. https://www.audioenglish. org/dictionary/bleeding_heart.htm

[462] It is the same Greek word describing the father's feelings upon seeing the ragged state of the Prodigal. Another example is seen in Jesus weeping uncontrollably at Lazarus's funeral (John 11:35).

[463] Examples included flaying the skin of victims with knives or on a threshing sled; impaling them on a stake; crushing their skulls with a mallet; mutilating them through cutting off their ears and noses, blinding them with hot irons, plucking out their tongues by the roots; or leading them around with fishhooks pulled through their lips.

Nineveh to warn them of His impending judgment. So, Jonah does what any godly man or woman would do: he gets on the first boat he can find headed for Tarshish – a city in what is modern-day Spain, and about 1,000 miles in the opposite direction!

Now Jonah's rejection of God's calling is understandable given what we know about the Assyrians of that time. Jonah is clearly having difficulty feeling any compassion for them, and in fact deep-down wanted to see God punish them. But in the end, Jonah relented: perhaps assuming any exhortation will be ignored, God will punish the Assyrians, and Jonah can say, "Oh well, I tried." But then this happens:

> *"Then God saw their works, that they turned from their evil way; and God relented from the disaster that He had said He would bring upon them, and He did not do it. But it <u>displeased Jonah exceedingly, and he became angry</u>. So, he prayed to the LORD, andsaid, 'Ah, LORD, was not this what I said when I was still in my country? Therefore, I fled previously to Tarshish; for I know that You are a gracious and merciful God, slow to anger and abundant in lovingkindness, One who relents from doing harm'." (Jonah 3:10-4:2)*

As a prophet of God, Jonah understood <u>nobody</u> deserves God's favor, regardless of how "good" a person he or she is. Yet, Jonah is "angry" and "exceedingly displeased" when God relents and extends mercy to the Ninevites. His response suggests he is thinking, "I know You are gracious and merciful, but are You really willing to forgive <u>them</u>?"[464]

Mercy flows out of the humble and grateful awareness that I am completely undeserving of God's grace. This in turn renders us capable of "keeping" the commandments of Jesus as our own personal standards rather than simply "obeying" them as rules, because:

Obedience grounded in grace breeds compassion, but obedience without grace breeds contempt

---

[464] Jonah Chapters 3-4. See also Habakkuk 1:1-2:1 in which Habakkuk first bemoans the fact God has not judged the "wicked" in Judah but is then stunned when God replies He will use the wicked Babylonians to judge Judah.

Compassion is a product of grace. A humble heart softened through the tilling of God's grace and mercy produces compassion and the willingness to initiate peace – even to the most "unlovable." When we fully acknowledge the grace and mercy we have received, we in turn become able and willing to extend grace to others, as:

An attitude of gratitude produces latitude.

Acknowledging our need for grace also implies one – like the Prodigal – has undertaken painful self-reflection and come to realize the "impure-fections" of his- or her heart.

4. Purify your heart.

The English "pure" comes from *katharos*, which means to be "clean, pure, innocent, free of guilt, sincere, upright." Recall in the Bible our "heart" refers to our inner thoughts and desires. A pure heart, therefore, is one free of the desire for position, power, possessions, and pleasure" (1 John 2:16-17), which leads to disputes and strife:

> *Flee also youthful lusts; but pursue righteousness, faith,*
> *love, peace with those who call on the Lord out of a*
> *pure heart. But avoid foolish and ignorant disputes,*
> *knowing that they generate strife. (2 Tim 2:22-23)*

A pure heart clears up our spiritual "vision" and enables us to "see" God, which in the original Greek means, "To understand, perceive, to know." The purer our thoughts and motives, the greater our sense of connectedness with Him, and the more inner peace and sense of *WHOLENESS* we will experience.

5. A peacemaker is not a "pushover," but may be a "pacifist" (Matt 5:9-12)

"Peacemaker" comes from the Greek *eiranopos*, which means to "be disposed to seek peace, quietness, rest, blessing and good wishes towards others." It describes the person who wants the best for others and prioritizes peace over winning. It is the person who refuses to stoop to the level of those who don't fight fairly and may try to take advantage of you. It is the example of Jesus who – in the face of false accusations – was "silent" (Mark 14:55-61). He refused to fight back and defend himself because He understood that in the end, His heavenly Father would fight His battle and that righteousness would prevail.

Yet Jesus is not telling us to be the "pushover" who retreats out of fear, intimidation, or insecurity – but one who stands strong as one of God's redeemed and justified:

> *"Who shall bring a charge against God's elect?*
> *It is God who justifies." (Rom 8:33)*

An illustration of a person going through this transformation is a former client of mine, a man who after a serious accident was unable to work, lost his sense of self-worth, got addicted to prescription painkillers and later crystal methamphetamine, lost his family, and found himself homeless and living on the streets. He told me how one night a man – also in the throes of addiction – became agitated and challenged him to a fight.

My client says his first impulse was to do what he had too many times done in the past: defend his pride and ego, and "kick his [butt]," which my client was confident he could have done. But instead, "I just laughed and walked away." A female friend observing this was shocked and challenged him to defend his honor. But my client just laughed again and said, "Not worth it." What he was beginning to realize was even if he would have won the physical fight between two men, he would have lost the spiritual battle for his soul.

The peacemaker rests in the quiet inner strength emanating from the knowledge that despite his or her unworthiness, he or she is blessed with the grace and favor of God through the redeeming work of Jesus. The peacemaker is motivated by righteousness rather than "rightness" and wants a win for the kingdom rather than a win for his or her ego. An example is Paul's exhortation to refrain from eating certain foods others found offensive (1 Cor 8:4-13). Put another way, Paul challenges us to defer to our Lord rather than defend our liberty. Paul himself modeled this in the example Paul he set for them:

316

"For though I am free from all men, I have made
myself a servant to all that I might win
the more; and to the Jews I became as a Jew,
that I might win Jews; to those who are
under the law, as under the law, that I might
win those who are under the law; to those
who are without law, as without law (not being without law
toward God, but under law toward Christ), that I might win those
who are without law; to the weak I became as weak, that I might
win the weak. I have become all things to all men
that I might by all means save some. Now
<u>*this I do for the gospel's sake*</u>*, that I may be*
partaker of it with you." (1 Cor 9:19-23) [465]

As believers in Jesus, we are justified on the merits of what Jesus did for us, and therefore are "free" from the Law.[466] But our freedom does not give us the right to impose our liberties or standards upon others. Like the pacifist – guided by a higher principal in his or her refusal to fight or defend him or herself – the peacemaker sets aside his or her agenda in deference to the greater purpose of winning others to Jesus.

In 2020-2021, during the worst of the COVID-19 pandemic, health officials urged the public to wear masks and limit public gatherings. While some Christian churches saw this as an attack on our personal and religious freedoms, I would argue we better served Jesus by setting aside our freedom in choosing to wear masks and limit gatherings as a means of loving others and not being a "stumbling block" to those in our communities.[467]

Noteworthy is peacemakers will be called "sons" (or "daughters") of God – arguably the highest compliment we can receive from Jesus. The peacemaker is a "chip off the old block" in manifesting the love, grace, mercy and very person of Jesus in his or her life:

---

[465] See also Rom 12:19-23, in which Paul addressed a similar source of conflict in the church in Rome. Note this comes right after his admonition, "…as much as depends on you, live peaceably with <u>all</u> men." (Rom12:18b)

[466] See Rom 3:20-28; 4:2-3; 5:1-10; 8:2; 1 Cor 6:11; 9:1; Gal 2:16-17; 3:11, 24; 5:1-4.

[467] Note Paul setting aside his freedom and challenge to not offend the "weaker" brother (Rom 14:1-15:2; 1 Cor 8:7-13; 9:19-23).

*"By this all will know that you are My disciples, if
you have love for one another." (John 13:35)*

Our desire and number one priority should be to help build His kingdom by winning hearts for the Gospel (Matt 28:19-20) through living out the principles of the Beatitudes:

- We develop the capacity to truly "love" others by cultivating a humble heart that desires righteousness, is merciful, and demonstrates it through acts of kindness,
- We take the lead in "pursuing" peace, not waiting for others to initiate it,
- We not only pray for our enemies, but seek <u>peace</u> regardless of the cost; and,
- We promote peace by being "longsuffering" (or patient) as God was with us.[468]

Yet Jesus warns this may come with a price, as we may become targets of persecution:

*"Blessed are those who are persecuted for righteousness'
sake, for theirs is the kingdom of
heaven. Blessed are you when they revile and
persecute you and say all kinds of evil
against you falsely for My sake. Rejoice and be
exceedingly glad, for great is your reward
in heaven, for so they persecuted the prophets
who were before you." (Matt 5:10-12)*

Jesus is referring to the prophets who were generally ignored, rejected, and downright ostracized for confronting the idolatry and social injustices prevalent in Old Testament Israel.[469] Put another way, the prophets challenged their fellow Israelites to get their acts together, and to start living up to the standards of righteousness of the Mosaic Law.

---

[468] See, for example, Ex 34:6; Num 14:18; Ps 86:15; Rom 2:4; 9:22.
[469] See Hebrews 11:36-40.

The following are examples of Christians experiencing persecution for their beliefs. Jack Phillips, owner of Masterpiece Cakeshop, charged with discrimination by the Colorado Civil Rights Commission after turning down a request to prepare a wedding cake for two men, citing his unwillingness to use his talents to "convey a message of support" for same-sex marriage which is "at odds with his religious faith." Phillip's case went all the way to the Supreme Court, which in its reversal of a prior ruling determined the Colorado Commission's ruling "had been infected by religious animus."[470]

Then there is Scott Warren, a volunteer with *No More Deaths*, an advocacy group based in Arizona whose mission is to end the deaths of undocumented immigrants crossing the United States-Mexico border. In 2018, Warren was charged with one felony count of conspiracy to transport and harbor, two felony counts of harboring undocumented immigrants, and faced up to 20 years in prison for providing aid to two men who were experiencing chest pains and exhibiting signs of dehydration after crossing the border illegally. In response to the charges, of which he was eventually acquitted, Warren's attorney argued, "Scott Warren never committed anything but basic human kindness."[471]

Two men charged with violating state or federal laws for living out their faith by applying the teachings of the Bible. Which begs the question, are these legitimate examples of suffering persecution for "righteousness' sake"? After all, aren't we called to obey the law and "subject" ourselves to governing authorities (Rom 13:1-3; 1 Pet 2:13-17)? Yet, we are also to "do what is good" (Rom 13:3) as "bondservants: (slaves) of God (1 Pet 2:16). So, what does righteousness look like when it seemingly conflicts with societal laws?

Throughout history, philosophers and ethicists have debated what constitutes morality, or "goodness." Most (like Kohlberg and Fowler)

---

[470] https://www.nytimes.com/2018/06/04/us/politics/supreme-court-sides-with-baker-who-turned-away-gay-couple.html

[471] https://www.cnn.com/2019/06/03/us/trial-scott-warren-no-more-deaths-volunteer-migrants-arizona-invs/index.html. A similar decision was reached on 2/3/20 when a federal judge in Tucson, Arizona overturned the convictions of four found guilty of leaving food and water for migrants who crossed in Arizona. The judge based her decision on the fact the "defendants met their burden of establishing their activities were exercises of their sincere religious beliefs, and the Government failed to demonstrate that application of the regulations against Defendants is the least restrictive means of accomplishing a compelling interest."

would certainly agree not breaking the law (i.e., robbing a bank or killing someone) is a good thing, as theft or murder come at the expense of others. Yet both would argue conforming to the law is not necessarily "goodness" or the *agape* love Jesus calls us to, as in a way it is self-serving through avoiding scorn or the negative consequences disobedience brings upon us.[472]

In Kohlberg's "Universal Ethical Principal Orientation" and Fowler's "Universal Faith", "goodness" is seen in the person guided by principles that promote social justice and uphold the inherent worth and dignity of another human being – even if it requires breaking a law and suffering the resultant consequences.[473] But what does the Bible tell us? Put another way, there is the proverbial *WWJD*, or "What would Jesus do?"

Well, there's Paul, imprisoned for preaching the Gospel in Jerusalem (Acts 21:27-36). And then there are Peter and John, emboldened by the resurrection of Jesus and the filling of the Holy Spirit, who when "commanded not to speak at all nor teach in the name of Jesus," explained their "lawlessness" this way:

"Whether it is right in the sight of God to listen
to you more than to God, you judge.
For we cannot but speak the things which we
have seen and heard." (Acts 4:18-20)

And of course, there is Jesus, repeatedly accused by the Pharisees (for what they would consider "righteousness" sake) of breaking the law only to have Jesus turn the legitimacy of their complaints inside-out. Two examples include His defense of His disciples for picking grain to eat (Matt 12:1-8) and healing a man with a withered hand (Matt 12:9-14; Mark 3:1-6; Luke 6:6-11) – both deemed violations for working on the Sabbath.[474]

---

[472] Recall Jesus agreed in saying, "do not even the tax collectors do the same?" (Matt 5:46)
[473] Myers & DeWall, Exploring Psychology, 10th ed., pg 150; https://www.acpeds.org/kohlbergs-theory-of-moral-development.
[474] See also Mark 2:23-3:6; Luke 6:1-11. As stated by the writers of the commentators of Matthew, Mark, and Luke in The Expositor's Bible Commentary, the Jewish religious leaders had established 39 categories of activities considered "work" and therefore considered violations of the Law prohibiting work on the Sabbath (Ex 20:8-10; 31:15; 34:21; Num 15:30-36).

Noteworthy in this parable is how Jesus contrasts the Samaritan with a priest and Levite, who "passed by on the other side" of the road rather than stopping to help a fellow country man. While some argue their refusal to stop and provide aid could be justified as adherence to the Mosaic Law through avoiding touching a "dead body" and becoming ritually unclean (Lev 21:1, 10-12; Num 6:6; 19:11), Jesus argues righteousness is better served through breaking the law of the day if a greater good is at stake, particularly if that greater good is upholding the dignity, worth, and well-being of another human being.[475]

Jesus accepted His arrest, conviction, and execution for "breaking the law." Peter and John boldly stared down the Jewish religious leaders and whatever consequences their refusal to heed their warnings might bring upon them. Paul not only accepted his imprisonment, but saw how God used it for good, as it resulted in an opportunity for Him to share the Good News of Jesus with the very guards responsible for watching him (Phil 1:12-14).[476]

And Paul is clear of his motive in accepting the persecution he suffered for serving Jesus:

"For to me, to live is Christ, and to die is gain." (Phil 1:21)

Paul's ultimate motivation was to glorify Jesus, regardless of what it cost him. And this should be our motivation in pursuing the causes we engage in for "righteousness' sake." Jesus makes this clear in the verses that immediately follow the Beatitudes where He tells us to be "salt" and "light", i.e., to have our "good works" generate a thirst for God, and to "glorify Him" by being the light that helps others find their way to Him (Matt 5:13- 16). Put another way, consider, "Will this help lead people to Jesus?" (John 13:34-35).

Recall the Beatitudes begin with "blessed are the poor in spirit" (Matt 5:3). Whatever we do should come from a humble heart absent a spirit of judgment or spiritual superiority and born out of a concern for those

---

[475] This seemingly supports Warren's efforts to care for the needs of "illegals" crossing the border for a better life in America.

[476] Note Paul's instructions to his letter to Philemon. While instructing Onesimus, a runaway slave, to obey the law and return to his master Philemon, he also challenged Philemon to receive Onesimus as a "brother" and grant him his freedom.

affected by our actions. Before "speaking the truth in love" (Eph 4:15), we might remember Jesus led with grace before truth (John 1:14-16). We might consider if our "obedience" comes at the expense of another's well-being. And we might consider if our motive is to build ourselves up by condemning the sin of others, like the Pharisees ready to stone a woman accused of adultery. Note Jesus' response:

> *"He who is without sin among you, let him*
> *throw a stone at her first." (John 8:7)* [477]

As we have seen, Jesus and the apostles summed up all their teachings on Christian morality through the Great Commandment. That laws or ethical principles should always promote the value and dignity inherent in all human beings is seen in Jesus' version of the "Golden Rule," which emerged in various forms as many as 2,000 before His teaching:

> *"Therefore, whatever you want men to do to you,*
> *do also to them, for this is the Law and the Prophets."* [478]

And this would certainly mean promoting the most important (i.e., "weightier) matters of the Law: justice, mercy, and faith (Matt 23:23), but in a way that reflects the love of Jesus. A powerful example is the life of Nelson Mandela.

In 1961, Mandela led a campaign against apartheid, then was charged and convicted for conspiring to overthrow the state. He served 27 years under horrible conditions during which he contracted tuberculosis. Fast forward to 1990, he won election as South Africa's first Black president. During his presidency, Nelson recounts his "Golden Rule" moment:

> *"I asked…some members of my close protection to stroll with*
> *me in the city and have lunch at one of its restaurants. We*
> *sat in one of the downtown restaurants and all of us asked*
> *for some sort of food. After a while, the waiter brought us our*

---

[477] Also recall the Parable of Two Prayers (Luke 18:9-41). Paul writes we are to only judge those in the church who have accepted God's truth their ethical standards (1 Cor 5:12-13) and leave judgment to those outside the church to God (John 16:8-11).
[478] https://philosophyterms.com/golden-rule/; Matt 7:12; Luke 6:31.

*requests, but I noticed that there was someone sitting in front
of my table still waiting for his food.*

*I told one of the soldiers, 'Go and ask that person to join us
with his food and eat with us.' The soldier went and asked
the man to do so. The man brought his food and sat by my
side, as Mandela had asked, and began to eat. His hands
were trembling constantly until everyone had finished their
food and then the man left. The soldier said to Mandela,
'The man was apparently quite sick. His hands trembled
as he ate!'*

*'No, not at all,' Mandela said. 'You see, this man was one of
the guards of the prison where I was jailed. Often, after the
torture I was subjected to, I used to scream and ask for a little
water. The very same man you saw eating with me today
used to come every time and urinate on my head instead. So,
I found him scared, trembling, expecting me to reciprocate
now ... either by torturing him or imprisoning him as I am
now the president of the state of South Africa'.*[479]

When we love others like Jesus loved us, we are one step closer towards
WHOLENESS, as it takes us one step closer to being like Jesus. And then
there is the impact it has on our OWN sense of self, as described by C.S.
Lewis in his book, *The Screwtape letters:*

> *"When they have really learned to love their
> neighbors as themselves, they
> will be allowed to love themselves (emphasis
> added) as their neighbors."*[480]

Loving others – particularly when it involves a healthy dose of grace
and mercy when every fiber of our being screams, "they don't deserve"
it – can be a powerful testimony to others about the love of God and the

---

[479] Arizona Republic. 7/11/20.
[480] https://www.azquotes.com/quotes/topics/screwtape-letters.html

hope they, too, can have in Jesus. This is evident in the testimony of Dr. Don Worcester, a counselor in Scottsdale, Arizona.

In August of 2018, Don was the headline speaker at the annual *Thrive* Men's Retreat in Williams, Arizona. During one of his presentations, Don shared a story of his experience as a teenager 40 years earlier. He recounts going out one night with a friend who was driving his parents' car and doing "foolish things" that resulted in damage to the car.

Several days later, Don was invited by his friend's parents for dinner. Don recalls being more than a bit apprehensive about their intent in extending the invitation, and what they would say during their time together. But instead of a lecture, Don received love. Nothing was said about the car; instead, they simply engaged him in conversation in what Don felt was a sincere effort to simply get to know him. Don summed it up this way:

"I've never felt less deserving and more welcome."

We will all experience the challenge to "love our neighbor as ourselves" at one point in our lives. Sometimes, it will occur through a random event or chance encounter. But often, it is in the day-by-day encounters with the spouse, family member, neighbor, or co-worker – someone we are not particularly fond of, but are part of our lives, nonetheless. With that, we turn to learning how to live with the "neighbors" we are challenged to love, even when it is particularly difficult.

CHAPTER 11
LIVING WITH OTHERS

INTRODUCTION

Imagine you are a first century Jew born and raised in Israel, a nation that has lived under the civil, social, and religious standards of the Mosaic Law. You know the commandment, "love your neighbor as yourself" (Lev 19:18), as well as the teaching that precedes it:

> *"You shall do no injustice in judgment. You shall not be partial to the poor, nor honor the person of the mighty. In righteousness you shall judge your neighbor. You shall not go about as a talebearer among your people, nor shall you take a stand against the life of your neighbor: I am the LORD. You shall not hate your brother in your heart. You shall surely rebuke your neighbor, and not bear sin because of him. You shall not take vengeance, nor bear any grudge against the children of your people, but you shall love your neighbor as yourself: I am the LORD." (Lev 19:15-18)*

No partiality or playing favorites. No talking behind someone's back, bearing grudges, or harboring ill-will towards others. To further complicate this, Moses uses two Hebrew words translated "neighbor" throughout this passage: one meaning one's countryman, the other more directly referring to those we encounter in our day-to-day lives.[481] Yet by

---

481 Strong's Exhaustive Concordance.

Jesus' day, it had morphed into "love your neighbor and hate your enemy" (Matt 5:43).[482]

Jesus clearly rejected this in challenging the Jews to "love your enemies" as well as your neighbor (Matt 5:44) and is clear your "neighbor" means anyone you encounter. And while "hate" is a strong word, Jesus extends this to anyone we dislike, let alone "hate":

> *"You have heard that it was said to those of old,*
> *'You shall not murder, and whoever*
> *murders will be in danger of the judgment.' But*
> *I say to you that whoever is angry with*
> *his brother without a cause shall be in danger of*
> *the judgment...Therefore if you bring*
> *your gift to the altar, and there remember that*
> *your brother has something against you,*
> *leave your gift there before the altar and go your*
> *way. First be reconciled to your brother,*
> *and then come and offer your gift. Agree with*
> *your adversary quickly, while you are on*
> *the way with him, lest your adversary deliver*
> *you to the judge, the judge hand you*
> *over to the officer, and you be thrown into*
> *prison. Assuredly, I say to you, you will*
> *by no means get out of there till you have paid*
> *the last penny." (Matt 5:21-26)*

Add to this Jesus expands the meaning of "murder" to include being angry at another "without cause". We naturally feel anger when hurt, offended, or betrayed in some way. The problem, however, is our standard of justice is often skewed to satisfy our egos and desires, and we are prone to create "cause" to justify our anger. Whether overlooked for a promotion or pay raise, taken for granted by our spouse or a friend, or disrespected at a

---

[482] Some point to Deut 25:19, in which the *Entrance* Generation was instructed to "blot out the remembrance of Amalek" (a false god) through the annihilation of the Canaanites inhabiting the land as the basis for this interpretation. https://newtheologicalmovement.blogspot.com/2011/02/whoever-said-thou-shalt-hate-thy-enemy.html

retail checkout counter, we are prone to take offense when feeling slighted or devalued. And our anger will certainly escalate if we think the person did it intentionally.

When offended, Jesus challenges us to stop and consider whether our anger is justified (i.e., "righteous") anger. Put another way, humbly consider if we were wronged according to God's standards, or if our "cause" is nothing more than a wounded ego, or not getting what we want. And then there are those who "get on our nerves" simply for who they are.

LEARNING TO LIKE THE "UNLIKEABLES"

Let's face it: there are some we don't like, let alone get along with. It could be those who "talk all the time", are "always late", or "disorganized". And there are those who insist you "follow the rules", or those who go by the principle "every rule is made to be broken". While they haven't committed a severe offense, they just "bother" you. They don't intend to offend you, and if the roles were reversed, they wouldn't be offended or feel you have failed to "love your neighbor as yourself". This stems from the fact that while we are all "fearfully and wonderfully made" (Ps 139:14), God chose to create us uniquely and distinctly as seen in what is referred to as our "temperament", or "personality type".

For over two millennia, philosophers and social scientists have studied how people differ personality-wise, and concluded people fall into one of four general personality types. Psychologist and former Cal State University Professor David Kiersey provides an in-depth description of each personality type, which we'll briefly summarize.[483]

---

[483] David Keirsey, Please Understand Me II: Temperament, Character, Intelligence (Del Mar, CA: Prometheus Nemesis Book Co; 1998), 18-21; See also H. Norman Wright, Communication: Key to Your Marriage (Ventura, CA: Regal Books, 2000), 149-205. These are based on the Myers-Briggs Indicator Test (MBIT) personality indicator originally developed by psychologist Carl Jung, Katharine Briggs, and Isabel Briggs Myers. An example of the test can be found at http://www.humanmetrics.com/cgi-win/jtypes2.asp. We've also provided the names for each type based on the Hippocrates, DISC, and Smalley-Trent descriptions.

- *The "Artisan" ("Sanguine", "Expressive", or "Otter")*

Artisans are spontaneous, live for the moment, and like to have fun. Stifled by structure and routines, they are drawn to what is new and different. Artisans are the most creative, good at "thinking outside of the box", and most comfortable taking risks. But Artisans are not good planners, as they would rather "figure it out as we go along". And they are often seen as "impulsive", "disorganized", and "inconsiderate", as they are prone to be "late".

- *The "Guardian" ("Phlegmatic", "Amiable", or "Golden Retriever"):*

In stark contrast to the Artisan, Guardians like routines, structure, and predictability. They want clear-cut instructions, and like tasks and to-do lists. Guardians don't like change, will be on time, will "do the right thing" (i.e., follow the rules), and are considered "good team players" as they strive to be "responsible". But Guardians are also the hardest on themselves and most critical of others – particularly those who won't follow or want to change the rules. In addition, Guardians are most prone to resent when they feel their sacrificial efforts aren't appreciated, or when others aren't carrying their weight.

- *The "Rational" ("Choleric", "Driver", or "Lion"):*

Rationals are driven, calculating, and analytical: there are always mountains to climb or goals to achieve, as well as a more efficient and effective way of achieving those goals. Rationals are the most logical when solving problems but are also good at "thinking outside the box" therefore best suited to devise a plan to achieve the goal at hand. There are no "sacred cows", so Rationals will question – and often challenge – the status quo, frustrating the Guardian who "likes things the way they are". In addition, they will value efficiency and effectiveness over emotion, at times putting them at odds with the Idealist.

- *The "Idealist" (or "Beaver"):*

Idealists are "contemplators" and most likely to ask "why", particularly when evaluating the merits of a "rule", why a biblical commandment or moral principle is "good". Idealists are the most empathetic and compassionate, strive for cooperation and how the greater good can be achieved, and the most diplomatic in finding a way to bring people together.

Rather than seeing things as "black" or "white", Idealists tend to "live in the grays", seeing the merits of seemingly conflicting propositions. While generally willing to "go along", Idealists will take a stand against dogmatic assertions – whether rules, policies, or procedures – they believe may hurt others, and will accept them only if they protect the vulnerable. Given this, if the Idealist cannot see the good in some rule or standard, he or she will willingly break it if in his- or her mind said rule comes at the expense of others.

While not stated explicitly, we see indications of the four personality types in the Bible. Ezekiel saw humankind embodied in "four living creatures" with "four faces" (Ez 1:5-15; 10:14-21; cf Rev 4:6-9). The Apocalypse will be executed by four horsemen (Rev 6:1-8). And God chose four men to write four Gospel accounts to tell the world about Jesus.

Matthew, a "Guardian", has by far the most references to the "rules" of the Mosaic Law. Mark, an "Artisan," presents an action-oriented, fast-paced, emotion-laden account that jumps from one scene to the next with the least reference to the Law. Luke, a "Rational", presents the most precise, detail-laden account in stating specific names, locations, titles, and years of the events he addresses (Luke 3:1-2). And John, the "Idealist" and last of the Gospel writers, uses the most symbolism and metaphors while being the only writer to reflect and contemplate on the deeper meanings of the things Jesus said.[484]

Noteworthy is while "fearfully and wonderfully made", David also suggests God was at work in shaping who we are before we were even born (Ps 139:13).[485] We don't "choose" our personality types or traits; rather, they are virtually hard-wired into us and influence how we function most naturally and comfortably at a subconscious level.

---

[484] See John 2:19-20; 3:2; 13:30; 20:8-10. Dr. Kiersey writes early church father Irenaeus, when asked why the Gospels were not integrated into one account, responded "Living Creatures are quadriform...the Gospel also is quadriform". The Gospels seemingly reflect how God created us with different personality types.
[485] See also Jer 1:5; Gal 1:15.

These differences are a breeding ground for conflict. Yet, God's wisdom in creating us uniquely and distinctly is seen in how we complement each other. When looking at the positives of each personality type, you can see how each is vital to the success – and even survival – of an organization. In our increasingly fast-paced and changing business world, a company needs Artisans and Rationals to reinvent itself through developing, marketing and efficiently producing new products. But you also need Guardians to oversee production as well as ensuring it is done in compliance with federal regulations. And finally, you need Idealists to ensure employee needs are tended to.

And just as God seemingly chose four men to tell the story of Jesus in their own unique style, God wants us to realize He created us to complement each other and to use our unique strengths to help Him build His kingdom. To which, in paraphrasing Jesus:

"Learn to like your neighbor as yourself".

Which brings us to an application in what is the most committed and intimate human relationship: marriage.

"YOU CALL THAT LOVE?"

In 1992, Gary Chapman published, "The Five Love Languages", which has been translated into over 50 languages and over 20 million copies have been sold.[486] While his principles are quite simple and straight-forward, churches 30 years later continue to offer small groups in which husbands and wives seek to apply these principles in the hope the quality of their marital relationship will grow.

Foundational is Chapman's premise we have differing "love languages": what makes one feel loved may not be as meaningful to another.[487] A brief overview is as follows:[488]

---

[486] https://5lovelanguages.com/store/the-5-love-languagese
[487] Chapman proposes we each will have one primary and one secondary love language.
[488] The following from: https://www.webmd.com/sex-relationships/features/love-timeline#2. To discover your love language, see https://www.5lovelanguages.com/quizzes/.

- *"Words of Affirmation"*

The "tongue" is powerful as words give "life or death".[489] Some feel most loved through kind words that affirm, encourage, and build them up. Husbands, including me, tend to score themselves highest on words of affirmation. Psychologist John Gottman proposes a "magic ratio" of at least five positive interactions for every negative one.[490] Even when disagreeing we are challenged to humbly choose to be affirming in making "requests" rather than "demands" and refusing to resort to criticisms and put-downs.

- *"Quality Time"*

"Quality" time is giving your spouse your undivided attention: the TV is paused or turned off, and he- or she is not competing with whatever task you might be engaged in. It might include going for walks and being intentional about arranging date nights. While affirming words focus on what you are saying, quality time focuses on listening.

And a word of advice to husbands: pause before giving advice. When your wife shares the events of her day – particularly something that was frustrating or discouraging – she simply wants your attention. If she wants advice as to how to solve a problem, she'll ask.

- *"Gifts"*

For some a gift means, "You were thinking about me". And realize the value of a material gift may be more about getting something meaningful than how much it cost. For husbands it could be the card or flowers you surprise your wife with. The key is being proactive and intentional about giving gifts, and for those prone to forget important dates like birthdays or anniversaries, you might put notes in your calendar as a reminder.

- *"Acts of Service"*

While the former are gifts through your words, attention or material resources, acts of service are gifts of action. An example is Jesus humbly washing His disciples' feet (John 13:1-9). As we've seen, the significance of His actions wasn't lost on Peter. For some, the sacrifice of your time and effort is the powerful demonstration of your love.

- *"Physical Touch"*

Finally, there is "physical touch". It extends beyond sexual intimacy to hugs, holding hands, or a casual caress. Noteworthy is while Jesus was able to heal from a distance (an example being His healing of a "noble" man's son, John 4:46-54), He most often included some form of physical touch to those deemed "unclean" as part of the healing process.[491]

Couples often come to realize they have differing love languages when one or both express some frustration over not feeling "loved" or "appreciated". And beyond the fact we are prone to first think of "me" rather than "we" or "you", we are prone to love our spouse in ways that are meaningful to us.

But this is where an obstacle can become an opportunity: when your husband or wife realizes you have mindfully taken the time to love him- or her in a way that doesn't come naturally for you, it is a greater and more meaningful expression of love.

A Sixth Love Language?

A quick internet search revealed several suggestions of a sixth love language, including "distance," "social media," and even "tattoos." But one, while it might not fit Chapman's definition of a formal "love language," it is certainly a powerful expression of love.

Elaine Mansfield shares the following in reflecting on her marriage with her late husband Vic, who she cared for during his valiant two-year battle with lymphoma:

> *"I would add a sixth language of love: Tolerance. I could be*
> *irritable and anxious. He could be testy and rushed. I got*
> *tired of his need for mothering and the demands his career. He*

---

[491] See, for example, His healing of the blind man we considered in *Chapter Five* (Mark 8:22-25).

became exasperated by my lack of self-confidence and excess of complaints. I was exhausted from the last two years of caretaking. But he rarely forgot how hard it was to care for a dying man. Our intolerances were replaced by love and sorrow.[492]

Tolerance (or, "long-suffering", Gal 5:22-23; Eph 5:8-10), reflects the fruit of the Spirit actively working in our hearts. It is an example of what C.S. Lewis referred to as "Gift-love". Instead of seeing another's "problems", choose to see his- or her "potential" in being every bit as fearfully and wonderfully made as you. This begins with surrendering our egos and choosing to serve Jesus by submitting ourselves to each other as well.

LIVING IN MUTUAL SUBMISSION

We love God by "loving others as our self," regardless of our relationship with them. In the New Testament, there are three main passages that instruct husbands and wives how to develop the most intimate and meaningful marriage.[493] But notice in the immediately preceding verses, these instructions are prefaced with the challenge to "submit to one another in the fear (reverence) of God"; to "put on love"; to "let the word of Christ dwell in you richly", "whatever you do in word or deed do in the name of the Lord Jesus"; and, to "do good and suffer, patiently, for this is commendable before God".[494]

Regardless of the relationship – whether the lifelong commitment of marriage, the next-door neighbor, or an encounter in the checkout line at the grocery store – we are to strive to be the example of Jesus by doing whatever we can to live peaceably with all others.[495]

Late in His ministry, Jesus had what must have been a difficult conversation for Him with two of His disciples (John and James) after they posed the following question to Him:

---

[492] https://goodmenproject.com/featured-content/there-are-actually-6-love-languages-not-just-5-hlg/
[493] See Eph 5:25-33; Col 3:18-19; 1 Peter 3:1-7.
[494] See Eph 5:21; Col 3:14-17; 1 Pet 2:19-20.
[495] Rom 12:18; cf Matt 5:9.

*"Teacher, we want You to do for us whatever
we ask…Grant us that we may sit,
one on Your right hand and the other on Your
left, in Your glory." (Mark 10:35, 37)*

You can imagine Jesus saying to Himself, "Are you kidding me"? He had spent nearly three years teaching and modeling servanthood to His disciples, and in just a few weeks He would die a horrible death on their (and our) behalves. To which He replied:

*"'You know that those who are considered rulers
over the Gentiles lord it over them, and their
great ones exercise authority over them. Yet it shall
not be so among you; but whoever desires
to become great among you shall be your servant.
And whoever of you desires to be first shall
be slave of all. For even the Son of Man did not
come to be served, but to serve, and to give
His life a ransom for many." (Mark 10:42-45; cf Matt 20:25-28)*

While our fallen egos want to "rule it over" others by insisting things go our way and in our time, in Jesus' kingdom the "humble are exalted, but the proud are humbled".[496] The humble defer to others to model the example Jesus set for us. It is seen in how Jesus loved those disciples who later abandoned Him, and the grace and mercy God extended to us.

Submitting to others doesn't come naturally to us – in fact, it usually goes against every fiber of our being. But as we choose to love others as Jesus loved us, we become His "friend," and begin to experience the "joy" He promised us (John 15:11-15).

This is the *WHOLENESS* the new believers described in Acts 2:42-47 experienced, and like them we, too, will experience harmony and unity when we mutually submit to one another. This begins with the mindset we "win by losing", and willingly deferring to whenever possible. But there's an important caveat in this: when we do so <u>willingly</u>.

---

[496] See Luke 14:11; 18:14; cf Prov 28:5; Matt 23:12; Jam 4:6; 1 Pet 5:5.

But what if we're not given a <u>choice</u>? Put another way, what if someone is imposing their will upon us? After all Jesus did say, "Love your neighbor <u>as</u>...", not <u>before</u> yourself. Needless to say, this is a recipe for conflict, which brings us to how we respectively ask others to value us in the same way Jesus challenges us to respect and value them.

FROM CONFLICT TO COLLABORATION

In the 1972 movie *The Godfather*, mafia chieftain Vito Corleone is shot and nearly killed in an assassination attempt orchestrated by narcotics trafficker Virgil "the Turk" Sollozzo. Vito's oldest son Sonny, known for his volatile temper, is angrily pacing back and forth muttering, "I want to kill that..." But Michael, who had wanted nothing to do with the family "business," calmly lays out a plan: he'll meet with Sollozzo and the corrupt police captain protecting him over dinner, during which "I'll kill 'em both". Sonny, laughing hysterically at the idea of his "college boy" brother killing someone, says, "You're taking this personally," To which Michael replies, "It isn't personal Sonny, it's strictly business."

As fallen human beings, we will inevitably get caught up in conflicts, as even the most dedicated followers of Jesus found themselves in conflict with one another. One example is the conflict between the Apostle Paul and another apostle named Barnabas:

> *"Then after some days Paul said to Barnabas, 'Let us now go back and visit our brethren in every city where we have preached the word of the Lord and see how they are doing.' Now Barnabas was <u>determined</u> to take with them John called Mark. But Paul <u>insisted</u> that they Should not take with them the one who had departed from them in Pamphylia and had not gone with them to the work. Then the <u>contention</u> became so sharp that they parted from one <u>another</u>. And so Barnabas took Mark and sailed to Cyprus; but Paul chose Silas*

and departed, being commended by the brethren
to the grace of God." (Acts 15:36-40)

Safe to say they had a "conflict", isn't it? When you see words like a "contention" that became "sharp", it is clear things got heated to the point they went their separate ways.[497] But how could two godly men – two apostles – let something escalate to this point? Well, apparently it "got personal" for Paul. And a closer look helps us understand why.

Barnabas is determined (from the Greek *boulomai*, "to will") to take his cousin Mark (Col 4:10) with them. And Barnabas is seemingly trying to impose his will upon Paul, who is having none of it since Mark had "departed" (from the Greek *apochorizo*, "to go away, leave") while with Paul on an earlier missions' trip to Pamphylia (Acts 13:13). But as Paul recounts it, Mark not only left, but "deserted" Paul (Acts 15:39).[498] And Paul's feelings of betrayal, coupled with Barnabas's "determination" to take Mark with them, became the emotional equivalent of pouring gas on a smoldering fire, and as they say, "it was on".

Paul and Barnabas had some history. It was Barnabas who first accepted and validated the newly converted Saul to the still-skeptical apostles (Acts 9:26-27), then took Saul to teach the new believers in Antioch (Acts 11:25-26). And it was Barnabas who, along with Paul, confronted the Judaizers demanding Gentile believers be circumcised (Acts 15:1-12). Yet Paul had to confront Barnabas as well as Peter for "playing the hypocrite" when they avoided associating with Gentiles out of fear of those same Judaizers (Gal 2:1-16).

Like Paul, Barnabas underwent a name change. Formerly Joses, the apostles renamed him upon recognizing he exemplified the gift of encouragement (Acts 4:32-36). Perhaps this is why he saw Mark's departure as a learning opportunity rather than the failure Paul saw it to be. Either way, Paul and Barnabas disagreed, and a few definitions of "conflict" are revealing as to how their disagreement escalated into full-blown warfare:

"To be different, opposed, or contradictory: to fail to be in
agreement or accord; to content in warfare."[499]

---

[497] Note the word "sharp" comes from a Greek word referring to a "god". Winning became almost a "god" to each of them!

[498] Here the author Luke uses the Greek word *ephistemi,* which means, "To desert, revolt").

[499] https://www.merriam-webster.com/dictionary/conflict.

"A disagreement through which the parties involved
perceive a threat to their needs, interests, or concerns."[500]

Conflicts begin with a simple disagreement that escalates when we are unable to achieve resolution. And there are three reasons for this, which the Bible has plenty to say about.

WHAT ARE WE FIGHTING ABOUT IN THE FIRST PLACE?

Virtually all conflicts are fueled by the "lust of the eyes, the lust of the flesh, and the boastful pride of life" (1 John 2:16) as manifested in *The Eight Deadly Sins*:

> *"But if you have bitter envy and self-seeking in your*
> *hearts, do not boast and lie against the truth. This wisdom*
> *does not descend from above, but is earthly, sensual,*
> *demonic. For where envy and self-seeking exist, confusion*
> *and every evil thing are there." (Jam 3:14-15)*

Simple disagreements get personal and escalate when we let envy and our self-seeking passions "take the reins" (recall Ben Franklin) and bring "confusion" (doubt, distrust, and dissension). But disagreement gives way to peace when we allow the Spirit to guide us:

> *But the wisdom that is from above is first pure, then peaceable,*
> *gentle, willing to yield, full of mercy and good fruits, without*
> *partiality and without hypocrisy. Now the fruit of righteousness*
> *is sown in peace by those who make peace." (Jam 3:16-18)*

And we are wise to proactively turn to someone we trust to discern the "wisdom from above," as numerous Scriptures encourage us to seek the counsel of others:

---

[500] https://www.ohrd.wisc.edu/onlinetraining/resolution/aboutwhatisit.htm

*"Counsel in the heart of man is like deep water, but a
man of understanding will draw it out." (Prov 20:5)*

*"By pride comes nothing but strife, but with
the well-advised is wisdom." (Prov 13:10)*

*"A wise man will hear and increase learning, and a man
of understanding will attain wise counsel," Prov 1:5)*

*"Listen to counsel and receive instruction, that
you may be wise in your latter days." (Prov 19:20)*

*"The way of a fool is right in his own eyes, but a
wise man is he who listens to counsel." (Prov 12:15)*

The "wise" person will help us sift out ways in which we might be deceiving ourselves about the merits – or very validity – of the issue we're in conflict over:

*"The heart is deceitful above all things, and
desperately wicked. Who can know it?" (Jer 17:9)*

Bottom line: "Does fighting over this issue honor God?" If not, righteousness must supersede "rightness," and seeking a mutually agreeable resolution our objective.

TAME THE TONGUE, BUT DON'T BE TONGUE-TIED

Ever say something in the heat of the moment you regret, and wish you could take back? Well, join the club, because we've all been there. While sticks or stones (and fists) can break our bones, James proposes it is our tongues – what he describes in the original Greek as an "insignificant body part" – that can unleash the very fire of hades itself.[501]

---

[501] "Little member" from the Greek *micron melos*. Strong's Exhaustive Concordance. Also see Prov 18:21.

"Even so the tongue is a little member and boasts
great things. See how great a forest
a little fire kindles! And the tongue is a fire, a world
of iniquity. The tongue is so set among
our members that it defiles the whole body, and
sets on fire the course of nature; and it is
set on fire by hell. For every kind of beast and
bird, of reptile and creature of the sea, is
tamed and has been tamed by mankind. But no
man can tame the tongue. It is an unruly
evil, full of deadly poison. With it we bless our
God and Father, and with it we curse
men, who have been made in the likeness of
God. Out of the same mouth proceed
blessing and cursing. My brethren, these things
ought not to be so." (Jam 3:5-10)

James is describing the use of verbal aggression to get one's way and win the fight, including yelling, cutting statements, or the verbal Uzi-blast unleashed to flat-out pound another into submission. Or it might be in the form of more subtle passive-aggressive, sarcastic statements such as, "If only you …," "well THAT'S fine", or "I'm glad YOU'RE satisfied". And then there's the "silent treatment" or withdrawing altogether and refusing to engage as a means of punishing the other. James condemns such actions as "evil" and "full of deadly poison", as they serve one purpose: to denigrate those we are angry at.

Now you might be thinking, "Well, I don't do any of that"! You might be more the "go along, get along" person who would rather surrender than "confront" someone. Put another way, you are prone to passivity, which usually reflects a discomfort with conflict coupled with a desire to be liked or thought of as a "good person". But consider this:

Being "nice" isn't the same as loving your neighbor.

I say this as while avoiding conflict and keeping others happy, those prone to passivity often find themselves frustrated and resentful. This inevitably leads to grumbling – and then "gossip" – which is one of seven "abominations", or the most grievous of sins:

> *"These six things the LORD hates, yes, seven are*
> *an abomination to Him: A proud look,*
> *A lying tongue, Hands that shed innocent blood,*
> *A heart that devises wicked plans,*
> *Feet that are swift in running to evil, A*
> *false witness who speaks lies, And*
> *one who sows discord among brethren." (Prov 6:16-19)*[502]

By now I trust you have come to realize how poisonous unresolved resentment can be. While gossiping about those we resent may provide a form of primal release, it is like throwing gas on a fire (Prov 26:20-22) while corrupting us to the very core of our being:

> *"The words of a whisperer are like delicious morsels;*
> *they go down into the inner parts of the body." (Prov 18:8)*

Gossip inevitably leads to slandering the target of our anger (Ps 105:5; cf Ps 34:13), and one needs only to consider how social media platforms such as Facebook, TikTok and Instagram can expand the range of our outbursts. To which we are wise to remember we will have to "give an account" for what we say on that day we meet Jesus Himself:

> *"I tell you, on the day of judgment people will give account*
> *for every careless word they speak..." (Matt 12:36)*

Recall when angry, Jesus challenges us to go and seek reconciliation (Matt 5:21-26). And Paul warns about the danger of letting bitterness and resentment fester:

> *"Be angry, and do not sin": do not let the sun*
> *go down on your anger" (Eph 4:26)*

---

[502] See also Prov 11:13; 16:28; 20:19; 25:23; 1 Tim 5:9-15.

This comes on the heels of Paul telling us to "speak the truth in love" (Eph 4:15). He also offers these thoughts on how to resolve differences, so they don't escalate:

"Let no corrupting talk come out of your mouths,
but only such as is good for building
up, as fits the occasion, that it may give grace
to those who hear." (Eph 4:29)

"To speak evil of no one, to avoid quarreling, to be gentle, and to
show perfect courtesy toward all people." (Titus 3:2)

Be direct, but in a gentle and respectful way. Proverbs offers wisdom on how this is done:

"When words are many sin is not lacking, but
whoever restrains his lips is wise." (Prov 10:19)

"Whoever restrains his words has knowledge, and he who
has a cool spirit is a man of understanding." (Prov 17:27)

"The heart of the wise makes his speech judicious
and adds persuasiveness to his lips." (Prov 16:23)

"Whoever belittles his neighbor lacks sense, but
a man of understanding remains silent. (Prov 11:12)

Principles we can draw from these and the other passages we've considered include:

1. Cool off before confronting (Prov 17:27)

Take time to cool down and calm yourself before confronting those who have offended you. Any "confrontation" to address a perceived slight or offense should be pursued with a goal of seeking reconciliation, not retribution.

2. Avoid attacking (Prov 11:12)

Avoid any statements that attack, demean, or belittle the recipient in any way.

3. The fewer words the better (Prov 10:19; 16:23)

A few well-thought-out words are most "persuasive." Take the time to process what you want to say shortly and succinctly: identify the issue, why it is important to you, and how it can realistically be resolved. The goal: minimize resistance and maximize reception.

When our message is not well thought out, we are prone to overwhelm the recipient with too many words, which increases the likelihood the recipient will feel you are imposing your will upon him- or her. Paul challenges us to ensure our every word edifies others (Rom 14:19). This includes communicating your respect for and desire for peace with others. Put another way, Paul is telling us to be better, not bitter. Which brings us to the most important component to resolving disagreements, and that's learning to listen.

"HE WHO HAS EARS": USE THEM!

Jesus encountered two types of people: those who listened and received what His teachings, and those unwilling to listen and rejected Him. But this didn't surprise Jesus – in fact, He anticipated it – as it was the same reaction the Old Testament prophets received when warning the people of Israel of God's impending judgment:

> "Who is blind but My servant, or deaf as My
> messenger whom I send? Who is
> blind as he who is perfect, And blind as the
> LORD's servant? Seeing many things,
> but you do not observe; opening the ears, but
> he does not hear." (Is 42:19-20)

God wanted His "servant" Israel to be His messenger. If Israel adhered to the Law God would bless her obedience, and surrounding nations would embrace the true God. Instead, Israel rejected His commandments, and refused to heed the prophets warning of judgment.

While speaking directly and succinctly during His first year of ministry, Jesus began to speak in "parables" to illustrate the principles He was teaching. But at the end of the Parable of the Sower, Jesus concluded with the following:

WHAT DID JESUS MEAN WHEN HE SAID, "HE WHO HAS EARS TO HEAR"?

Source: www.gotquestions.org

"He who has ears to hear, let him hear!"
(Matt 13:9; Mark 4:9; Luke 8:8)[503]

And when asked why He was teaching in parables, Jesus said:

"...Because it has been given to you to know the mysteries of the kingdom of heaven, but to them it has not been given. For whoever has, to him more will be given, and he will have abundance; but whoever does not have, even what he has will be taken away from him. Therefore, I speak to them in parables, because seeing they do not see, and hearing they do not hear, nor do they understand." (Matt 13:11-13)[504]

Jesus realized He would encounter some who while "listening" wouldn't "hear" Him. To "hear" goes beyond simply listening to what someone says, to understanding what he or she means, and accepting it as valid. Realize effective communication involves four steps:

---

[503] The Parable of the Sower (Matt 13:1-8; Mark 4:1-8; Luke 8:4b-7). See also His explanation of the parable (Matt 13:18-23). The Greek word translated "hear" in every one of these passages is *akouw*, which means, "to understand, comprehend, accept".
[504] See also Mark 4:11-12; Luke 8:9-10

1. *What you want to communicate to the other person.*
2. *The words you actually speak to the other person.*
3. *What the other person hears you say.*
4. *What the other person thinks you mean.*

There is ample opportunity for misunderstanding – particularly if one is resistant to hearing what the other is saying, or either of you feels offended – and a disagreement escalates into conflict. We might heed the advice of Greek Stoic philosopher Epictetus:

> *"We have two ears and one mouth so we can listen twice as much as we speak."*[505]

Dr. Peck offered this in addressing the challenge of truly <u>listening</u> to what one is saying:

> *"You cannot truly listen to anyone and do anything else at the same time."*[506]

The point here is we must be both deliberate and determined to really <u>listen</u>. And this summarizes what numerous Proverbs say about the importance of listening:

> *"He who answers a matter before he hears it, it is folly and shame to him." (Prov 18:13)*

> *"Even a fool is counted wise when he holds his peace. When he shuts his lips, he is considered perceptive." (Prov 17:28)*[507]

Unfortunately, our tendency is to "speak first and ask questions later", prompting James to propose a principle that is foundational to resolving, let alone avoiding, conflicts:

---

[505] https://www.coolnsmart.com/?s=we+have+two+ears+and+one+mouth
[506] M. Scott Peck, <u>The Road Less Traveled: A New Psychology of Love, Traditional Values and Spiritual Growth.</u>
[507] See also Prov 16:32; 18:2; 21:23; 29:20.

So then, my beloved brethren, let every man be
swift to hear, slow to speak, slow to wrath;
for the wrath of man does not produce the
righteousness of God. (Jam 1:19-20)

Being "swift to hear" requires the willingness to set aside what we want to say, while striving to ensure we understand both what the other wants and why it is important to him or her. It may include asking clarifying questions or repeating back what you understand the other is saying or requesting of you. And it may require sifting through the onslaught of an "untamed tongue", as seen in this principle on receiving criticism:

"In the midst of the Uzi blast, seek to hear the pellet of truth"[508]

There will be times when it will get "personal", as something said to you will hurt. But we are challenged to be "wise" in seeking to hear pellets of truth amid the Uzi blast:

"He who keeps instruction is in the way of life,
But he who refuses correction goes astray." (Prov 10:17)

"Open rebuke is better than love carefully concealed." (Prov 27:5)

"For whom the LORD loves He corrects, just as a
father the son in whom he delights." (Prov 3:12)[509]

These principles provide the foundation of what is called an "assertive" approach to conflict resolution. While some may conflate assertiveness with "aggression", it is what Paul had in mind in his exhortation for peace and unity among the believers in Ephesus:

"…but, speaking the truth in love, may grow up
in all things into Him who is the head
-- Christ – from whom the whole body, joined
and knit together by what every joint

---

[508] Principle stated in a sermon by Dr. Steven Tracy.
[509] See also Prov 9:8-9; 15:10.

> *supplies, according to the effective working*
> *by which every part does its share,*
> *causes growth of the body for the edifying*
> *of itself in love." (Eph 4:15-16)[510]*

Assertiveness is striving for an "I win/You win" outcome. It fulfills the call to love your neighbor <u>as</u> yourself in valuing the needs of both parties with a goal of realizing a mutually agreeable resolution. It requires "collaboration," or the exchange of thoughts and feelings, which requires an equal balance of assertiveness and cooperation. Assertiveness requires taming our tongues and learning to listen effectively.

Like death and taxes, we will experience conflict in life. But conflicts don't have to end badly – in fact, conflicts can actually be <u>good.</u> Which leads to this important principle:

See conflicts as a <u>clarifier</u> rather than a crisis.

When conflicts are successfully resolved, both parties experience two things: first, they gain a better understanding of each other; and second, the level of trust and respect mutually felt will deepen. Peck captures this well in the following statement:

> *"The overall purpose of human communication is – or*
> *should be – reconciliation. It should ultimately serve to lower*
> *or remove the walls of misunderstanding which unduly*
> *separate us human beings, one from another."[511]*

Our challenge in being the peacemaker Jesus calls us to be is to lead with a willingness to listen first by standing in our position as a redeemed child of God. This renders us less sensitive to any hurtful things said or

---

[510] See also 1 John 3:18; 2 John 1:1-3; 3 John 1:1. Note Jesus is described as "full of grace and truth" (John 1:14-17).
[511] <u>Different Drum: Community Making and Peace</u> from https://www.goodreads.com/author/quotes/3061.M_Scott_Peck.

done to us and presents a powerful testimony to the good work God is completing in us. As we extend the same grace and mercy we have received, we can profoundly impact those who have yet to accept Jesus as their Savior:

> *Bless those who persecute you; bless and do not*
> *curse. Rejoice with those who rejoice,*
> *and weep with those who weep. Be of the same*
> *mind toward one another. Do not set*
> *your mind on high things, but associate with the*
> *humble. Do not be wise in your own*
> *opinion. Repay no one evil for evil. Have regard*
> *for good things in the sight of all men.*
> *If it is possible, as much as depends on you, live*
> *peaceably with all men. Beloved, do*
> *not avenge yourselves, but rather give place to*
> *wrath; for it is written, 'Vengeance is*
> *Mine, I will repay,' says the Lord. Therefore "If*
> *your enemy is hungry, feed him; If he*
> *is thirsty, give him a drink; For in so doing*
> *you will heap coals of fire on his head.*
> *Do not be overcome by evil but overcome*
> *evil with good." (Rom 12:14-21)*

We honor Jesus as we move from combativeness to collaboration through the mindset of the peacemaker desiring to love God and others. We refuse to take things "personally," instead, choosing to humble ourselves in serving Jesus through doing whatever we can to "live peaceably with all men" (Rom 12:18). But this leaves one factor that is necessary for peace to be possible – and for us to experience the abundant life – and that is forgiveness.

UNDERSTANDING AND EXTENDING FORGIVENESS

"Everyone thinks forgiveness is a lovely idea until
he has something to forgive." CS Lewis [512]

We have considered some daunting challenges to living out the Christian life: extending mercy to those for which every fiber of our being screams, "They don't deserve it!" and being a "peacemaker" in the face of harsh words or unreasonable expectations. And then there are the relationships devastated by false accusations, betrayal, rejection, and abuse.

If you have experienced any of the above, you have likely felt anger, hurt, and resentment: feelings so strong you find yourself reliving them over and over in your mind.[513] You may have even wanted to see the offender suffer in some way, and "seeking peace" is the farthest thing from your mind. But then we're reminded to "forgive" as God forgave us:

"As far as the east is from the west, so far has He
removed our transgressions from us." (Ps 103:12)

"I, even I, am He who blots out your transgressions for
My own sake: And I will not remember your sins." (Is 43:25)

While you may be familiar with at least the concept of forgiveness, it is a fairly complex issue that must be properly understood as we contemplate extending it to others.

What Does "Forgive" Actually Mean?

In the Hebrew of the Old Testament and the Greek of the New, the words translated "forgive" can mean "forgive, pardon, send away, spare, release, abandon, cancel, tolerate, accept, desire, to respect." Just considering this range of meaning gives you an idea of how complex the concept of forgiveness is, as well as the process it may entail.

---

[512] https://www.goodreads.com/quotes/198171-everyone-thinks-forgiveness-is-a-lovely-idea-until-he-has

[513] The English "resentment" comes from the old French *resentir*, or "to feel again". https://www.etymonline.com/word/resent.

To "pardon," "release", or "cancel" means to eliminate the charge and forgo any punitive or disciplinary actions. But words like "tolerate", "accept", "desire" and "respect suggest something more: not only is the offense set aside, but there is a willingness to resume the relationship disrupted by the offense as well, as seen in the following Bible passages:

> *"For if you forgive men their trespasses, your*
> *heavenly Father will also forgive you.*
> *"But if you do not forgive men their trespasses,*
> *neither will your Father forgive*
> *your trespasses. (Matt 6:14-15; cf Mark 11:25-26; Col 3:13)*

> *Then Peter came to Him and said, "Lord, how*
> *often shall my brother sin against me,*
> *and I forgive him? Up to seven times?" Jesus*
> *said to him, "I do not say to you,*
> *up to seven times, but up to seventy times seven. (Matt 18:21-22)*

Now this isn't as difficult if someone has hurt you but has come to see the error in his ways, apologized, and made things right with you.[514] Unfortunately, this isn't always the case, as too often the offender refuses to acknowledge, let alone apologize, for the offense.[515] But Jesus challenges us to forgive not only unconditionally, but repetitively – up to "seventy times seven" times – and regardless of the offense! To which you might be wondering, "Does God really expect me to just let it go as if it never even happened?" Well, the answer seems to be both "yes" – and "no" – as we consider forgiveness is not:

- *Letting someone "off the hook" from any consequences,*
- *Forgetting it ever happened,*
- *Condoning, excusing, or justifying why he/she did it,*
- *Letting time heal the wound,*
- *Thinking positively instead of negatively,*

---

[514] We will refer to the offender in the male gender throughout the remainder of this session for the sake of simplicity.

[515] This is common in cases of sexual abuse, particularly when the victim is a child.

- *Making a decision to forgive; or,*
- *Accepting what happened.*[516]

Seem like a lot of conditions for something that's supposed to be "unconditional"? Notice:

> *"Take heed to yourselves. If your brother sins against you, rebuke him; and if he repents, forgive him. And if he sins against you seven times in a day, and seven times in a day returns to you, saying, 'I repent,' you shall forgive him." (Luke 17:3-4; cf 2 Cor 2:7-10)*

Jesus is clear forgiveness isn't just a one and done deal. But notice He qualifies this with the Greek equivalent of the English word "if" is three times, suggesting forgiveness is <u>conditional</u> on the offender's repentance.[517] This seeming contradiction is reconciled in recognizing three elements of "forgiveness."[518]

1. "Judicial" Forgiveness:

While God alone has the right to execute justice and exact vengeance (Is 61:1-2; Rom 12:19), He does use human government authorities to restrain evil and render justice.[519] The challenge, however, is we may still suffer the hurt, anger, sense of betrayal, and loss of trust sin inflicts upon us. Which brings us to the second element of forgiveness.

2. Psychological Forgiveness

A sin against us is a blow to our sense of worth, and if left unresolved may fuel an almost obsessive desire to see the offender suffer. And while our

---

[516] In Is 43:25, the Hebrew word *machah* translated "blots out" means "smoothed out, erased". This suggests more a debt excused then forgotten. See also: Enright, R.D., & Fitzgibbons, R.P. (2000). *Forgiveness* (Video). American Psychological Association.

[517] Strong's Concordance defines the Greek root word *ei* as, "a particle of conditionality".

[518] Steven R. Tracy, <u>Mending the Soul: Understanding and Healing Abuse</u>. Grand Rapids, MI: Zondervan, 181-193.

[519] Gen 9:6; Rom 13:1; 1 Pet 2:13-16. This doesn't mean one won't suffer consequences, as David experienced (2 Sam 11:1-12:13).

tendency is to minimize the severity of our wrongdoings, we are prone to exaggerate those done against us. And the angrier we get, the more skewed our sense of justice and fairness will get as well.

In the ancient Near East, "revenge" was often confused with "justice", as the offended exacted "two deaths for one death, and five teeth for one tooth".[520] In His effort to reign in this distorted view of "justice", God gave Israel the principle of "an eye for an eye and a tooth for a tooth".[521] But then Jesus came along, and challenged us to not only forego our desire for revenge, but to set aside our demand for justice as well.[522] And in doing this, Jesus provided one of the best therapeutic interventions in the history of psychology.

In 2013, the city of Phoenix – and much of America as well – was captivated by the trial of Jodi Arias, who was charged with murdering her estranged lover Travis Alexander. The defense readily acknowledged early on that Arias had in fact killed Alexander, so the jury's role in executing "justice" was to determine what her punishment would be.

Alexander's family members were present throughout the trial, and the pain they felt was evident on their faces. When interviewed, it was clear their view of justice was along the lines of "an eye for an eye", as they wanted to see Arias executed. They would soon be severely disappointed, however, when Arias was sentenced to life in prison.

The Arias trial renewed the decades-long debate over the merits of the ultimate form of an "eye for an eye." Proponents have argued capital punishment is not only "fair" but provides "closure" for family and friends who have lost a loved one. But research has found otherwise. In one study, less than 7% of survivors of victims reported executing the offender had or would at some point bring "closure".[523] In another study, 20.1% reported no closure, while 4% reported it actually hindered their ability to heal. Of the 41% who did experience some closure, it was attributed to the offender

[520] R. Laird Harris, Expositor's Bible Commentary: Leviticus. Grand Rapids, MI: Zondervan Publishing House, 1990.
[521] Ex 21:23-25; Lev 24:19-20; Deut 19:21; (cf Gen 9:6). Jesus did not advocate for a criminal's life to be spared (Luke 23:39-43).
[522] See Matt 5:38-40.
[523] Mowen, T.J., & Schroeder, R.D. (2011). Not in my name: An investigation of victims' family clemency movements and court appointed closure. Western Criminology Review, 12(1), 65-81.

being found guilty, their suffering validated, and knowing the offender was no longer a threat.[524]

Researchers in fact have found "healing", "moving on" in life, and the capacity to regain a sense of wholeness and experience joy again requires three things: 1) "judicial closure" in which a guilty verdict is rendered and justice is served; 2) "psychological closure", in which rituals are performed to honor and remember the loved one; and, 3) "emotional forgiveness", in which the survivors let go of the anger felt toward the offender.[525]

Put another way, modern research has affirmed the wisdom in Jesus' teaching: while getting even through seeing an offender suffer may provide a sense of primal satisfaction, it will not bring back the deceased, nor will it erase the offense suffered. Instead, the only way to regain some sense of life and vitality is through psychological forgiveness.

Psychological forgiveness is the conscious and deliberate process of casting off the anger and bitterness that, like a straight-jacket or set of handcuffs, binds, and hinders our ability to experience joy in life again. It doesn't mean the offense didn't occur or wasn't hurtful, the offender "deserves" your forgiveness, or you deserve anything less; instead, it's determining to no longer let another's actions steal your joy and inner peace.

Psychological forgiveness is the refusal to accept the lie another's actions determine your value and worth, and your offender must suffer or make things right before you can experience the abundant life. And psychological forgiveness facilitates restoring broken relationships. This brings us to the final element of forgiveness: relational forgiveness.

3. Relational Forgiveness

Relational forgiveness – the restoration of a relationship shattered by sin – is conditional on the offender repenting of his offense. Sadly, some will refuse to repent, yet will persist in demanding you just "forget" it, "let it

[524] Vollum, S., & Longmire, D.R. (2007). Co-victims of capital murder: Statements of victims' family members and friends made at time of execution. *Violence and Victims, 22*(5), 601-619; Armour, M.P. & Umbreit, M.S. (2006). Exploring "closure" and the ultimate penal sanction for survivors of homicide victims. *Federal Sentencing Reporter, 19*(2), 105-112.
[525] Armour & Umbreit. We inject Tracy's terms here as accurate reflections of what is described in the research studies.

go," and resume your relationship as if it never happened. This is what a friend of mine named "Amy" experienced.[526]

As a young girl, Amy's father abused her in about every way imaginable. As an adult, Amy severed their relationship, and had no contact with him for years until he began reaching out in hopes of restoring their relationship. Through years of counseling and the work of the Holy Spirit in her life, Amy experienced healing and felt compelled to forgive him. Yet, every time he reached out to her, she was torn between her desire to forgive him, and a gnawing sense that something wasn't quite right.

Through the counsel and efforts of church leadership to mediate reconciliation, it became clear while he was experiencing regret for what his actions had cost him through the loss of their relationship, he was not remorseful in his unwillingness to acknowledge what he had done to her – let alone repent and make amends to her. While "forgiving" him by letting go of her desire he suffer for his actions (judicial forgiveness) and experiencing freedom from her pain through psychological forgiveness, she wisely refused to offer relational forgiveness until he repented. And in late 2018, Amy's diligence bore fruit.

Amy's father – burdened by the pain and destruction he had inflicted upon Amy and their relationship – finally relented. He acknowledged all he had done, and tearfully apologized. Since then, Amy and her father have had several conversations in which she has seen evidence of his remorse and repentance. As of late-2020, they have continued to talk, and there is hope that one day they can have a meaningful relationship.

Forgiveness begins with the decision to "let go" of the offense and a willingness to resume a relationship if the offender repents. Sincere repentance is seen in those who readily accept the "rebuke" of truth "spoken in love" (Luke 17:3; Eph 4:15), acknowledge their wrongdoings, are sorrowful for the harm inflicted said actions inflicted, and are willing to do what it takes to make things right (2 Cor 9:9-10). Dr. Tracy offers the following:

- *He has acknowledged and taken full responsibility for his actions,*
- *He has accepted the consequences for his actions without complaining,*

---

[526] "Amy" is not her actual name. Her story illustrates how confusing and challenging this can be for victims of abuse. This is particularly common when the abuser is the parent and the victim a child.

- *He has acknowledged the damage he has done, and is remorseful for it,*
- *He is willing to make restitution for the harm done to you,*
- *He has taken active steps to change his behavior; and,*
- *He wants you to experience healing and is willing to help facilitate it.*[527]

The following is a principle you might utilize in extending relational forgiveness:

Be willing but watchful!

This brings us to a process you can implement to facilitate the healing and restoration of wholeness you can experience in forgiving someone who has harmed you:

1. Identify (specifically) the offense that has harmed you.

When wronged, we may be overwhelmed with strong feelings of anger, confusion, fear, and resentment. To mitigate the impact of these emotions, utilize the "Five W's":

- **W**hat happened,
- **W**ho is/are the offender(s),
- **W**hen it happened,
- **W**here it happened; and,
- **W**hy you consider it an offense (how it has harmed and affected you)

2. Deliberately let go of your right to "get even", or see the offender suffer.

Practice "judicial" forgiveness in letting God "get vengeance" in His time and in His way to render justice. This is the first step in letting go of the hurt, anger, hatred, and/or bitterness that can fester and become a poison in your soul.

---

[527] Steven and Celestia Tracy. By His Wounds: Trauma Healing for Africa. Note the example of David, 2 Sam 12; Ps 1.

3. Take into consideration the offender's humanity and extend appropriate grace.

Like you, the offender is an imperfect human being with his own fears and insecurities and may in fact have suffered abuse himself. You might consider asking yourself, "How does God want me to model the same grace and mercy He has given me?"

4. Determine what it would take for the offender to "make things right."

After making the decision to set aside your "right" to be judge, jury and executioner, identify what the offender can do to make things right with you. This might include:

- Acknowledging the offense to you (and others if applicable),
- Making an apology and appropriate changes in his behavior; and,
- Making restitution for material losses you've suffered (counseling expenses, etc.).

If the offense is serious, this may take time to heal. Getting input from a trusted friend, pastor, or therapist will help you do this wisely, objectively, and thoroughly.

5. Confront the offender.

"Confrontation" is often understood to mean an aggressive, in-your-face assault on another. Instead, hold off on confronting the offender until you can do it in a matter-of-fact manner that includes the specifics of the offense outlined above. Inform the offender you have something important you need to address with him and arrange a specific time and place where you will meet. This will help reduce any interruptions and distractions and make the issue the focus of your discussion. With the input of counsel, also consider if having a third party to mediate would be appropriate.

6. Establish necessary boundaries.

Relational forgiveness suggests an unresolved offense warrant stepping back from the relationship until it is clear the offender is repentant and has at least begun taking the steps to demonstrate his repentance is real. This might include putting any form of relationship on hold until the issue is resolved.

By refusing to resume a relationship, your actions speak loudly to the fact: 1) the offense has created a barrier in your relationship; and 2) the offender needs to do something to remove the barrier to restore your relationship. If the offender fails to respect your boundaries, he is essentially telling you he isn't ready to restore your relationship.

7. Be determined to get on with your life and grow from the experience.

To preserve our sense of dignity and worth, we tend to hold onto wrongs committed against us. It may seem by "letting go" of our anger and indignation, we are in effect saying, "It wasn't that big a deal," or "I don't deserve to be treated any better."

Letting go of emotional pain is an action you DO matter. It allows you to take your life back and facilitates the process of humbly assessing anything YOU need to learn and change to prevent something similar from happening again. Self-assessment doesn't mean you did anything wrong or deserved what happened but may reveal an area of weakness that made you vulnerable to the offense. A principle you might consider is:

*While he may not deserve my forgiveness, I
deserve freedom from his offense!*

Edith Eger, despite all she suffered at the hands of the Nazis in Auschwitz, came to realize any desire for vengeance or seeing her offenders suffer would only hinder her quest to experience joy and fulfillment in life again:

*"You can live to avenge the past, or you
can live to enrich the present."*

In fact, holding on to a desire for vengeance only kept her in her own virtual prison:

> *"The worst prison is not the one the Nazis put me in.*
> *The worst prison is the one I built for myself."*

Remarkably, Eger came to realize she could see her painful experiences as a gift:

> *"Our painful experiences aren't a liability—*
> *they're a gift. They give us perspective*
> *and meaning, an opportunity to find our*
> *unique purpose and our strength."*

And as Eger found, we can only come to comprehend such a profound perspective on suffering when we choose to forgive those who have wronged us:

> *"Time doesn't heal. It's what you do with*
> *the time. Healing is possible when*
> *we choose to take responsibility when we*
> *choose to take risks, and finally,*
> *when we choose to release the wound, to*
> *let go of the past or the grief."*[528]

If someone has hurt you deeply, our encouragement is to begin by talking about it with a trusted person. Peck describes it this way:

> *"How strange that we should ordinarily feel*
> *compelled to hide our wounds*
> *when we are all wounded! Community*
> *requires the ability to expose our*
> *wounds and weaknesses to our fellow*
> *creatures. It also requires the ability*

---

[528] Edit Eger. https://www.goodreads.com/work/quotes/51302181-the-choice

to be affected by the wounds of others...
But even more important is the
love that arises among us when we share,
both ways, our woundedness." [529]

One benefit of living in the community of a church body is receiving the support and encouragement of others. The process of sharing the hurt and pain of our wounds is therapeutic in the same way a person recovering from a surgical procedure relies upon a physical therapist to facilitate healing. Paul challenges us to "bear one another's burdens", as this is one way to live out the commandment to "love others as ourselves" (Gal 6:2).

BUT HOW DO I KNOW IF I'VE REALLY "FORGIVEN" SOMEONE?

My hope is this provides clarity in understanding the role of forgiveness in helping you overcome hurts you have suffered. But this brings us to one final question: "How do I know if I have really forgiven someone"? Well, just as love builds up relationships, sin – particularly abuse – tears down and destroys relationships. And just as we must grieve the loss of a relationship severed by death, we must grieve the loss of a relationship destroyed by sin or abuse.

Grief is a process, since we don't just "get over" the loss of a loved one by having a nice memorial service. The process of grieving is described in the "Five Stages of Grief" first articulated by Elisabeth Kubler-Ross in her 1969 book, *On Death and Dying*.[530] These stages include: 1) denial and isolation, 2) anger, 3) bargaining, 4) depression, and, 5) acceptance.[531] The

[529] M. Scott Peck. https://www.goodreads.com/author/quotes/3061.M_Scott_Peck

[530] See https://psychcentral.com/lib/the-5-stages-of-loss-and-grief/. This process is seen in Jerry Sittser's experience of overcoming the shocking loss of his wife, mother, and daughter in his book, *A Grace Disguised: How the Soul Grows Through Loss*.

[531] Some propose seven stages in the grief process including: 1) shock & denial, 2) pain & guilt, 3) anger & bargaining, 4) depression, reflection, loneliness; 5) the upward turn; 6) reconstruction and working through; and 7) acceptance & hope. https://www.recover-from-grief.com/7-stages-of-grief.html. In his book, *On Grief and Grieving*, David Kessler proposes a sixth stage of finding "meaning" in one's loss. We propose this reflects discovering how God will use it for good (Gen 50:20; Rom 8:28).

process of working through each stage varies from person to person, and you may find yourself cycling back through stages in working through them. But there are two components that are critical to knowing if you have truly forgiven someone.

First, your anger is gone. You are no longer wrestling with the question of why he- or she did it or wishing ill will towards him- or her – in fact, you now pray for, and perhaps even wish the best for the person (Matt 5:44). This gives way to the second component – depression – better described as "sadness" for your loss. It may be remembering with at least some fondness the good things you experienced in your relationship with that person. There is "acceptance" (in the absence of repentance) that the relationship is now over, or joy (if there is repentance) you have been able to renew the relationship. Either way you have moved on and are able to experience abundance again.

WHAT ABOUT ME?

We have given considerable attention to the issue of forgiveness, as it is foundational to experiencing abundant life. With that we now turn to those of you who may be the "Prodigal Son": it is you that was the offender, you doubt whether God has really forgiven you, or you have been unable to forgive yourself. Perhaps this describes how you feel:

> For my iniquities have gone over my head;
> Like a heavy burden they are too
> heavy for me. My wounds are foul and festering
> Because of my foolishness. I am
> troubled, I am bowed down greatly; I go
> mourning all the day long. For my loins
> are full of inflammation, and there is no
> soundness in my flesh. I am feeble and
> severely broken; I groan because of the
> turmoil of my heart. (Ps 38:4-8)

To which we return to the example of Paul. If anyone had difficulty forgiving himself, it would have been Paul. Recall in *Chapter Six* we saw that before accepting Jesus as his Savior, he had persecuted Christians and approved of the stoning of Stephen. Yet, while readily considering himself the "least deserving" of the saints, he embraced the promises of God and was able to let go of his guilt by placing it at the foot of the cross:

> *"Brethren, I do not count myself to have apprehended;*
> *but one thing I do, forgetting those*
> *things which are behind and reaching forward*
> *to those things which are ahead, I press*
> *toward the goal for the prize of the upward call*
> *of God in Christ Jesus." (Phil 4:13-14)*

If Paul can proclaim this, so can you. But there is one step you may still need to take to experience this in a meaningful and life-changing way:

> *"He who covers his sins will not prosper, but whoever*
> *confesses and forsakes them will have mercy."*
> *(Prov 28:13; cf Ps 51:6-7; 1 John 1:8-9)*

Ask God to help you spiritually "clean house". You might consider utilizing *Steps 4-9* of the *Twelve Step* programs, which is the process of transitioning from rationalizing, justifying, or blaming others to identifying our wrong-doings and taking full responsibility for what we have done. It is only then that we can release our regrets, experience the freedom God desires for us, and for Him to complete the good work He promises to do in us.[532]

LEARNING FROM THE EXAMPLES OF PAUL AND BARNABAS [533]

With this we return to Paul and Barnabas, who after their "contention" have parted ways, with Barnabas and Mark sailing off to Cyprus and Paul and

[532] See Phil 1:3-6; 2 Tim 3:16-17; Heb 13:20-21; Jam 1:4; 1 John 1:9.
[533] Insights in this section adapted from Bob Deffinbaugh, "When Division Becomes Multiplication: Acts 15:3-16:10. https://bible.org/seriespage/24-when-division-becomes-multiplication-acts-153-1610

Silas traveling throughout Syria and Cilicia to "strengthen the churches" (Acts 15:39-41). But their story doesn't end there, and we can learn from the examples of these two imperfect and humble servants of Jesus.

First, while their conflict may have gotten personal, they kept it private, as we see no evidence they bore resentment towards one another, gossiped, or involved others. Second, they didn't let their disagreement become disruptive within the Church; instead, it became a catalyst for duplication as they embarked on two missionary ventures rather than one, with Barnabas retaining Mark while Paul added Silas to his team.[534] Third, while Mark's "departure" may have felt like a betrayal, Paul didn't let it become a barrier, as years later we see he came to see Mark as "profitable" in his ministry" (2 Tim 4:11).[535]

And most importantly, Paul allowed His Lord to use this painful experience as an exercise in "pruning" (John 15:2) so he would be even more fruitful in his ministry. Perhaps for Paul, the "pellet of truth" amid the "Uzi blast" of Mark's desertion was laying hands on Mark too quickly for something he wasn't yet prepared for (1 Tim 3:10; 5:22). Or, maybe he learned from the example of Barnabas (the "Son of Encouragement", Acts 4:36) to see the "failure" of a disciple or mentee as a "first attempt in learning".[536]

And maybe Barnabas experienced some "pruning" through this experience as well. Perhaps Barnabas – in his enthusiasm to encourage potential – was a bit guilty of laying hands on Mark too quickly. And Barnabas may have been guilty of both a bit of nepotism (recall Mark was his cousin) and failing to be sensitive to the slight Paul felt. Either way while not expressly stated, we can assume they had forgiven each other and put their conflict behind them as they carried on in the work Jesus had given them.

CONCLUDING THOUGHTS

The greatest demonstration of God's love is seen in His grace and mercy. We mirror this through "denying ourselves" and "picking up our crosses" by extending grace and mercy as we strive to be at peace with others.

---

[534] Note Jesus sent his disciples out in pairs (Luke 10:1). More on this in *Chapter Twelve*.
[535] From the Greek word *euchrestos*, which can be translated, "useful, beneficial, profitable".
[536] Recall the discussion of "fail" as a "first attempt in learning" in the *Introduction* of *Chapter Seven*.

It is living out the saying, "kill 'em with kindness," just as God chose reconciliation over retaliation with us once "alienated" and "enemies in [our] minds and works" (Col 1:21-23). This is captured in "The Prayer of St. Francis":

Lord, make me an instrument of Your peace;
Where there is hatred, let me sow love;
Where there is injury, pardon;
Where there is doubt, faith;
Where there is despair, hope;
Where there is darkness, light;
And where there is sadness, joy.

O Divine Master,
Grant that I may not so much seek
To be consoled as to console;
To be understood, as to understand;
To be loved, as to love;
For it is in giving that we receive,
It is in pardoning that we are pardoned,
And it is in dying that we are born to Eternal Life.[537]

But as we live out the example Jesus set for us, something else occurs. Instead of seeing His teachings as "commands" to be "obeyed", we begin to see them as the guide to experiencing the abundant life. Notice how David came to understand the Mosaic Law:

"Taste and see that the LORD is good; Blessed is
the man who trusts in Him!" (Ps 34:8)

"How sweet are Your words to my taste, Sweeter
than honey to my mouth! Through
Your precepts I get understanding; Therefore, I
hate every false way." (Ps 119:103-4)

---

[537] https://www.ourcatholicprayers.com/the-prayer-of-st-francis.html

Writer and lecturer Dale Carnegie once said this about the power of extending kindness:

"Years ago when I was a barefoot boy walking
through the woods to a country school out in
northwest Missouri, I read a fable about the sun and the wind.
They quarreled about which was stronger, and the wind said, 'I'll
prove I am. See the old man down there with a coat? I bet I can
get his coat off him quicker than you can'. So, the
sun went behind a cloud, and the wind blew
until it was almost a tornado, but the harder it blew,
the tighter the old man clutched his coat to
him. Finally, the wind calmed down and gave up, and then the sun
came out from behind the clouds and smiled kindly on the old man.
Presently, he mopped his brow and pulled off his coat. The sun
then told the wind that gentleness and kindness
were always stronger than fury and force." [538]

Perhaps our most difficult challenge in following Jesus is responding graciously and mercifully to those who disregard, disrespect, or degrade us in some way. But in those moments, when the insult cuts deep into the core of our souls, we might choose to see it as merely a test God wants to use to build our character:

"And not only that, but we also glory in tribulations,
knowing that tribulation produces
perseverance; and perseverance, character;
and character, hope." (Rom 5:3-4)

As we put into practice the teachings of Jesus by "loving our neighbors", our hearts will begin to mirror the character qualities of Jesus Himself. More and more we become "sons (or daughters) of God" (Matt 5:9), and in each of those moments we will hear the subtle "well done good and faithful servant" in our souls (Matt 25:21-23; Luke 19:17).

---

[538] https://www.uexpress.com/harvey-mackay/2019/6/24/the-power-of-kindness. Gregory the Great once said: "the punishment of those who hate is their own hatred which consumes them". https://www.quora.com/What-does-the-quote-kill-them-with-kindness-mean

In his 1993 commencement speech to the graduates of Citadel Military College in South Carolina, former President Ronald Reagan had this to say about character formation:

> *"The character that takes command in moments of crucial choices has already been determined. It has been determined by a thousand other choices made earlier in seemingly unimportant moments. It has been determined by all the little choices of years past — by all those times when the voice of conscience was at war with the voice of temptation, whispering the lie that it really doesn't matter. It has been determined by all the day-to-day decisions made when life seemed easy and crises seemed far away — the decisions that piece by piece, bit by bit, developed habits of discipline or of laziness, habits of self-sacrifice or self-indulgence, habits of duty and honor and integrity — or dishonor and shame. Because, when life does get tough, and the crisis is undeniably at hand — when we must, in an instant, look inward for strength of character to see us through — we will find nothing inside ourselves that we have not already put there."[539]*

And this is articulated beautifully as well in the song, *The Garden*, by one of my favorite bands, the Canadian Hall of Fame band Rush:

> *The measure of a life is a measure of love and respect*
> *So hard to earn, so easily burned*
> *In the fullness of time*
> *A garden to nurture and protect*
>
> *The treasure of a life is a measure of love and respect*
> *The way you live, the gifts that you give*
> *In the fullness of time*
> *It's the only return that you expect* [540]

---

[539] https://www.startribune.com/the-gift-of-character/600014609/
[540] https://www.rush.com/songs/the-garden/. I used these lyrics to describe Barton Bauer, a man I was blessed to have as my dad, in my eulogy during his memorial service on June 30, 2022.

As we allow God's grace and mercy to work in our hearts, we become the "good ground" that yields a bountiful crop for the kingdom of Jesus (Matt 9:3-9; Mark 4:3-9; Luke 8:5-8), and in turn experience a virtual bumper crop of the fruit of the Spirit in our lives as well.

CHAPTER 12

A LIFESTYLE OF WHOLENESS

INTRODUCTION

There is a saying, "Life is a journey, not a destination". While attributed to essayist Ralph Waldo Emerson, it is more a principle drawn from something else Emerson wrote:

> *"To finish the moment, to find the journey's*
> *end in every step of the road, to live the greatest*
> *number of good hours, is wisdom."*[541]

Regardless of its origin, many have recognized and expanded upon the wisdom in these words. Rabbi Sidney Greenberg, for example, proposes, "Happiness is not 'there' but here, not 'tomorrow', but today."[542] The relevance is found in two sayings you will see posted prominently on the walls of an *AA* or other 12-Step recovery group meeting room:

> *"One day at a time", and "Easy does it"*

But is it true? Is life more about the journey than the destination? Should we really stop and smell the roses, relish the moment, and not worry about tomorrow? For those of us task-oriented, get-the-job-done (i.e., get to the "destination") types, it may be a helpful principle to remember,

---

[541] https://quoteinvestigator.com/2012/08/31/life-journey/
[542] https://www.azquotes.com/quotes/topics/life-is-a-journey.html

and certainly one I learned first-hand on a family trip taken over 30 years ago from our then-home in Minneapolis to Yellowstone National Park.

To me, the logical route would have taken us straight west through southern Minnesota, South Dakota, and Wyoming into Yellowstone. But my wife Mary, on a tip from an old friend, had other ideas. She proposed we enter Yellowstone by going through Beartooth Pass in Montana, a drive the late CBS News Correspondent Charles Kuralt once called, "the most beautiful drive in America".[543] To  me, however, it would only add another 150 miles to the 1,038-mile trip that already lie ahead of us.

Of course, Mary persisted, and being the "peacemaker", I conceded. So off we went to Beartooth Pass, and I can say with all sincerity the extra 150 miles and 3-4 additional hours of travel time were well worth it, as the twelve miles of zigzags and switchbacks through the mountains is one of the most beautiful drives I have ever partaken.

Learning to be still, to breathe, to live in the moment and be thankful for what we have is a critically important step to experiencing God's presence in our lives. Yet, as we saw in the quotes of Berra, Franklin, and de Saint-Exupery, a journey without a destination may be a recipe for failure, if not outright disaster. Knowing not only where we are going, but why we are going there may be the difference in pushing through the obstacles we will face in getting there and overcoming the doubts that will inevitably come with them.

This is seen in the lyrics of Aerosmith's hit song, *Amazing*, written by singer Steven Tyler and collaborator Richie Supa during their journeys out of the depths of drug addiction:

> *"It's amazing with the blink of an eye you finally*
> *see the light. It's amazing when the moment arrives*
> *that you know you'll be alright. It's amazing and I'm*
> *saying a prayer for the desperate hearts tonight."*

---

[543] https://en.wikipedia.org/wiki/Beartooth_Highway

I share these lyrics from a rock band you likely won't see at the next Christian music festival in how they capture the experience of us Prodigal Sons and Daughters who have finally seen the light, been welcomed home by our loving Father, and cling to the hope we'll be alright if we just surrender our lives to Him. But Tyler and Supa add this caveat:

"Life's a journey not a destination
And I just can't tell just what tomorrow brings"[544]

So, the answer appears to be – are you ready for this – YES! Life is not just a destination, but neither is it just a journey. A life well-lived involves <u>both</u> enjoying the journey while keeping an eye on our destination. And therein lays the challenge of living the abundant life: learning to weather the challenges of life by embracing the blessings of the moment, while never losing sight of where we are headed. We cannot lose sight of the fact we will inevitably "have tribulation" (John 16:33) and will "fall into" and be "grieved by" various trials (Jam 1:2-4; 1 Pet 1:6-9).[545] This lesson is evidenced numerous times in the Bible.

The destination of the *Exodus* Generation was the Promised Land, and their journey began when God fulfilled His promise to free them from bondage in Egypt.[546] Yet, they lost sight of their destination when confronted with a lack of water and food, and then with the seemingly insurmountable challenge of conquering the inhabitants occupying the Land. And while the *Entrance* Generation didn't make the same mistakes as their predecessors, they failed to remember the question Joshua posed to them (Josh 24:15).

Am I going to serve Jesus, or am I going to serve ME? Am I going to be led by the Spirit or my fleshly desires (Gal 5:16-25; cf Rom 8:1-11)? Am I going to put on the new me, or let the old me reign (Eph 4:17-24; Col 3:9-14)? It's the question God posed to Adam and Eve in the Garden of Eden. It's the question Joshua posed in asking the people of Israel if they were going to seek abundance in God's presence or through His provisions, and if they would fulfill their destination of becoming the "holy people" set apart, "high above" all other nations (Deut 26:15-19), and a "light onto the Gentiles" (Is 42:60).

---

[544] https://www.oldielyrics.com/lyrics/aerosmith/amazing.html
[545] See also Mark 4:16-17; Rev 2:10.
[546] Ex 7:14-11:10.

It's the question David and Solomon seemingly failed to ask themselves in those critical moments, and the question implied when Jesus said, "seek first the Kingdom of God" as "the day is its own trouble" (Matt 6:33-34), and reframed into their mission statement: "Go, therefore, and make disciples of all nations…" (Matt 28:19-20). Through these words, Jesus is essentially establishing the destination He has for the lives of all of us disciples.

As we "choose for ourselves" who we will serve each day, our decision begins with our perception of how we will experience the abundant life: Will I be satisfied with a life of living in the grace and presence of my Heavenly Father? Or will I – like Adam and Eve and the Prodigal Son – be led astray by dissatisfaction, disappointment, and disillusionment? And how will I choose to utilize the time, talents, and treasures He has gifted me with? Sadly, for the people of Israel – and the believers in the early Church – it was the latter.

Recall how those early believers chose to live "with one accord". Facing persecution, they chose – to quote Tyler and Supra – to live in "amazement" rather than acrimony. Yet, Paul's letters suggest this didn't last, as soon they were at each other's throats.[547] Having lost sight of their destination and no longer "enjoying the journey", they let dissatisfaction, disappointment, disillusionment, and denigration creep into their hearts.

Now as you've been reading this, you may have felt I've been too hard on the Israelites and the early Christians. My intent is not to be critical, but to assess what lessons we can learn from their mistakes that we can apply in our lives today.[548] Living a life devoted to the plans and purposes God has for each of us can at times be like enduring a marathon:

"Do you not know that those who run in a race
all run, but one receives the prize?
Run in such a way that you may obtain it. And
everyone who competes for the prize
is temperate in all things. Now they do it to
obtain a perishable crown, but we for an

---

[547] See the Epistles of Romans, 1 & 2 Corinthians, Galatians, Ephesians, and Colossians.
[548] Note Paul, Peter, and the writer of the book of Hebrews essentially scolded their audiences for acting like little children in saying, to paraphrase, "You're not ready for big-boy food yet" (1 Cor 3:1-3; Heb 5:12-14; 1 Pet 2:1-5).

imperishable crown. Therefore, I run thus: not
with uncertainty. Thus, I fight: not as
one who beats the air. But I discipline my body
and bring it into subjection, lest, when
I have preached to others, I myself should become
disqualified." (1 Cor 9:24-27)[549]

Paul never lost sight of his destination: the recognition and reward of the faithful. Paul never lost sight of the fact life is a journey with times of plenty and times of need (Phil 4:11-13), yet persevered when trials came his way. And it certainly wasn't easy:

"...I speak as a fool -- I am more: in labors more
abundant, in stripes above measure,
in prisons more frequently, in deaths often.
From the Jews five times I received forty
stripes minus one. Three times I was beaten with
rods; once I was stoned; three times
I was shipwrecked; a night and a day I have been
in the deep; in journeys often, in perils
of waters, in perils of robbers, in perils of my own
countrymen, in perils of the Gentiles,
in perils in the city, in perils in the wilderness,
in perils in the sea, in perils among
false brethren; in weariness and toil, in
sleeplessness often, in hunger and thirst,
in fastings often, in cold and nakedness --
besides the other things, <u>what comes</u>
<u>upon me daily: my deep concern for all</u>
<u>the churches</u>." (2 Cor 11:23-28)

---

[549] See 1 Tim 6:12; 2 Tim 4:6-7, in which Paul challenges Timothy to run the race and "fight the good fight" so as to be "blameless" before Jesus at His Second Coming. Paul challenged the Philippians to "work out their salvation with fear and trembling" in living their lives a way that wouldn't shame the name of Jesus (Phil 2:12-13). The apostle John challenges believers to abide in Him, so we may approach His throne in confidence rather than shame for a life not worthy of His sacrifice on our behalves (1 John 2:28).

Despite all his suffering, Paul's biggest burden was his concern for his flock.[550] But, this begs the question, "How did he find the deep sense of purpose to <u>want</u> to persevere"?

Well, I propose it flowed out of a deep sense of gratitude that produced an unwavering devotion to God's plans and purposes. And it involved a daily discipline of the following:

- *Experiencing God's Presence*
- *Expressing Your Love for God Through Worship*
- *Embracing God's Plans and Purposes for Your Life*
- *Entering the Battle Fully Armed*
- *Enduring Doubt, Dissatisfaction, Disillusionment, and Despair*

Throughout the remainder of this chapter, we will explore each of these.

EXPERIENCING GOD'S PRESENCE

As we saw in *Chapter Nine*, we cannot experience God's presence unless we take the time and make the effort to "be still" (Ps 46:10). But due to the fact God created us uniquely and distinctly, we may best experience Him in unique and distinct ways.[551]

1. The "Naturalist": Loving God Out of Doors

Naturalists encounter God in the beauty and majesty of His creation and experience Him through the calming influence of nature when hiking in the mountains, spending time at a lake, or tending a garden. Hagar,

---

[550] Note the Greek word translated "concern" is *merimna*, which means, "apportion, bestow, to share, distribution". Here Paul is describing his responsibility for the churches as a burden given him by Jesus, and one that brought him anxiousness and worry.
[551] Gary Thomas. Spiritual Pathways: Discover Your Soul's Path to God. Grand Rapids, MI: Zondervan, 1996. An assessment tool you can use to identify your spiritual pathway can be found at https://northpoint.org/spiritual- pathways-assessment. See also Dr. Myra Perrine, What's Your God Language? Connecting With God Through Your Unique Spiritual Temperament. Carol Stream, IL: Tyndale House Publishers, Inc., 2007.

Abraham, Jacob, Moses, John the Baptist, and Jesus met God in the desert, on a mountain or at a river crossing, and even in a burning bush.[552]

2. The "Sensate": Loving God with Senses

Sensates experience God in the stimulating effects of a beautifully decorated sanctuary, music, and incense. Ezekiel vividly described encountering God in the winds he felt, the slashing lightning and brilliant light he saw, and the roaring waters he heard.[553]

3. The "Ascetic": Loving God in Solitude and Simplicity

Ascetics experience God while in prayer and may find service needs and fellowship groups as distractions from your desire to spend time alone with God. Rather than filling your life with activities you prefer the simple life and are most likely drawn to fasting as a means of encountering God much like John the Baptist: a loner sustained by a simple diet of locusts and honey who came out of the desert wearing camel's hair clothing.[554]

4. The "Traditionalist": Loving God through Ritual and Symbol

Traditionalists encounter our eternal and unchanging God through the rituals of the faith and history of tradition. In contrast to Sensates, you experience God in the disciplines of the Christian life, and value continuity and predictability in your worship experience.

5. The "Activist": Loving God through Confrontation

Activists encounter God when confronting evil and fighting for justice and experience Him more fully through time alone in prayer or when involved in prayer marches. You are inspired by the example of Jesus cleansing

---

[552] See Gen 21:14ff; 22:1ff; 32:14ff; Ex 3:2ff; 19:3ff; Matt 3:1; 4:1ff; 5:1ff; 13:1ff; Mark 3:7ff; 5:13, 21; Luke 3:2; 4:1ff.
[553] See Ezek 1:4, 6; 3:1-15; 43:2. See also John's vivid descriptions in Rev 1:10-14, 17.
[554] See Matt 3:4; Mark 1:6. See also the Nazirites, Num 6:2; Judg 13:5-7. Other names include Jerome and St. John of the Cross.

the temple, or men like Moses, Elijah, Habakkuk, and John the Baptist confronting the wrongdoings of their fellow Israelites.[555]

6. The "Caregiver": Loving God by Loving Others

In contrast to the Activist and his- or her passion for confronting "evil", Caregivers experience God by doing "good" in living the example of the humble servant through giving of themselves to those in need (note Matt 25:34-45).

7. The "Enthusiast": Loving God with Mystery and Celebration

Enthusiasts are drawn to the "mystery" of God, waiting expectantly to see how He will respond to our prayers, and most apt to expect to see or hear Him through dreams, visions, or other sign languages. Enthusiasts are inspired by joyful celebration, as simply knowing the Bible is inadequate if not accompanied by a moving experience.

8. The "Contemplative": Loving God through Adoration

Contemplatives encounter God emotionally through words like "enjoy" or "love", are most apt to describe God as "my loving Father" or "friend" and are drawn to the imagery seen in Song of Songs or the Psalms.

9. The "Intellectual": Loving God with the Mind

Intellectuals encounter God through comprehending who God is and how He engages with the world. "Faith" is something understood as much as experienced and learning and seeking understanding (Prov 1:1-9; 2:3-4) is foundational to developing character.

We will find ourselves drawn to certain approaches to experiencing God. The problem, however, is it may come at the exclusion of – and even contempt for – other approaches.

---

[555] See Ex 2:11-12; 17:5; 1 Kings 18-19; 2 Kings 8:11; Hab 1;2-4; Matt 3:1ff; 21:12ff; Mark 1:4ff; 11:15ff; Luke 3:1ff; John 2:19ff.

- Naturalists may be prone to isolating themselves from others (Heb 10:24-25), worshipping creation over its Creator, or "hearing" God in the form of insights or inspirations that merely reflect your own thoughts or desires,
- Sensates may be prone to prioritizing emotions over educating themselves biblically, and worshipping the experience over encountering His Person,
- Ascetics may be prone to overemphasizing the importance of personal piety, and seeking God's favor through "suffering" in the form of acts of self-denial,
- Traditionalists may be prone to equating serving God with experiencing Him, deifying rituals, overlooking the call to care for the needs of others and judging practices you deem "inappropriate" or "disrespectful" to God,
- Activists may be prone to considering yourself holier than your less-active peers, and judging others before judging your own motives and actions (Matt 7:1-5),
- Caregivers may be prone to judging others for their lack of concern for the poor, serving others to be affirmed or appreciated, and neglecting family and friends through giving your time, talents, and treasures to the "stranger",
- Enthusiasts may be prone to equating emotional highs with quality worship, and avoiding the fellowship and accountability of other believers (Heb 10:24-25),
- Contemplatives may be prone to seeking "encounters" while ignoring fellowship with others, and prioritizing intense spiritual experiences while minimizing the importance of service and developing a righteous mind and pure heart; and,
- Intellectuals may be prone to stirring up conflicts by correcting "inaccurate" doctrine, prioritizing "knowing" over "doing", and becoming prideful of your biblical knowledge (1 Cor 8:1).

Since our spiritual pathway(s) are those that provide us the most meaningful experiences with God, our tendency is to limit our encounters to those we find the most rewarding.

Thomas wisely advises us to be intentional in diversifying our spiritual experiences by practicing the other pathways. What is vitally important is that we ensure we prioritize regular time to experience and hear God. But experiencing *WHOLENESS* is not just a product of spending time with God, but our mindset in how we approach Him as well.

EXPRESSING YOUR LOVE FOR GOD THROUGH WORSHIP

In one short verse, Paul pretty much sums up the "storyline" of the Bible:

> *"For as in Adam all die, even so in Christ all*
> *shall be made alive." (1 Cor 15:22)[556]*

And it is seen in the contrast of how each responded when tempted by Satan. Adam and Eve were created in a state of *WHOLENESS*, lived in His presence, and had everything they needed for the abundant life. Yet, when tempted with more than what God had given them, they bought Satan's lie and sought abundance through God's provisions over His presence and purposes for them. Contrast that with how Jesus responds when tempted:

> *"Again, the devil took Him up on an exceedingly*
> *high mountain, and showed Him all*
> *the kingdoms of the world and their glory. And*
> *he said to Him, 'All these things I*
> *will give You if You will fall down and*
> *worship me.' Then Jesus said to him*
> *'Away with you, Satan! For it is written,*
> *you shall worship the LORD your*
> *God, and Him only you shall serve'." (Matt 4:8-10; cf Luke 4:1-8)*

Note Jesus is quoting the exhortation of Moses to the people of Israel 1,500 years earlier:

---

[556] See also Rom 5:14-17; 1 Cor 15:45.

"You shall fear the LORD your God and serve Him,
and shall take oaths in His name." (Deut 6:13)

Even Jesus actively sought God's presence through spending time alone in prayer. Yet in His response, we see two key elements to experiencing WHOLENESS: 1) approaching God through a mindset of worship, and 2) living it out in a life committed to serving Him.

When you think of "worship", what may come to mind is singing songs of praise for and appreciation of God during a Sunday Morning service. But worship is much more, as it involves expressing our love for God with "all our heart, mind, soul, and strength".[557] The Greek word most frequently translated "worship" is *proskuneo*, which means, "To kiss the master's hand, to prostrate oneself in reverence to, to adore". Satan wants Jesus to pay Him homage through bowing down and worshipping him, but Jesus firmly refuses in declaring His devotion, affection and service would be given to God alone.

And noteworthy is Jesus quoting a passage exhorting the people of Israel to "fear" God, which as we saw in *Chapter Ten* is just what it means.[558] Case in point is Adam and Eve, who could have used a healthy dose of fear before disregarding God's warning of eating the forbidden fruit; the consequences the Prodigal Son suffered in failing to "fear" his father; or those Jesus encountered who were suffering the consequences for not heeding God's commands.[559] But notice the verse that immediately follows this exhortation:

"You shall not go after other gods, the gods of the
peoples who are all around you." (Deut 6:14)

Now we may not create idols like the golden calves the people in Moses' day worshipped, but like Adam and Eve and the Prodigal Son, we are every bit as vulnerable to serving the "gods" of position, power, possessions, and pleasure. And while we do not live under the terms of

---

[557] Mark 12:30; cf Matt 22:37; Luke 10:27; cf Deut 6:5.

[558] In Deuteronomy 6:13, the Hebrew word translated "fear" is *yare*, which means, "to fear, revere, dread, to be afraid".

[559] Case in point the Samaritan woman Jesus encountered at Jacob's well (John 4), or the woman caught in adultery (John 8:3-11).

the Mosaic Covenant, the principles of the Ten Commandments remain every bit as applicable as the means of living in relationship with God as they did in Moses' day.[560]

This begins with remembering it is the same God who delivered Israel from the bondage of the Egyptians (Deut 6:5) who delivered us from the bondage of our sins. Given this, we will not experience *WHOLENESS* unless we place Him on His rightful place on the throne through gratitude and reverence. This might include exalting His name as David did:

> *"I exalt You, my God, the King, and praise your*
> *name forever and ever. I will praise You*
> *Every day; I will honor your name forever and*
> *ever. I Yahweh is great and is highly*
> *praised, His greatness is unsearchable. One*
> *generation will declare Your works to*
> *the next and will proclaim Your mighty acts.*
> *I will speak of Your splendor and*
> *glorious majesty and Your wonderful works.*
> *They will proclaim the power of*
> *your awe-inspiring acts, and I will declare*
> *Your greatness." (Ps 146:1-6)*

The same sentiment is captured beautifully in the lyrics of the *Revelation Song*:

> *Worthy is the Lamb who was slain, holy, holy is He*
> *Sing a new song to Him who sits on heaven's mercy seat*
> *Worthy is the Lamb who was slain, holy, holy is He*
> *Sing a new song to Him who sits on heaven's mercy seat*
>
> *Holy, holy, holy is the Lord, God Almighty*
> *Who was and is and is to come*

---

[560] As we saw in *Chapters 4, 8-11*, through the Sermon on the Mount (Matt 5-; Luke 6:20-49), Jesus essentially ratifies the principles of the Ten Commandments as the means to experiencing *WHOLENESS* and the fruit of the Spirit of the abundant life.

With all creation I sing praise to the King of Kings
You are my everything and I will adore You, I will adore You [561]

The abundant life begins with revering God because He alone is worthy, and worshipping Him out of gratitude for Who He is and what He has done for us through:

Giving God Our Affection

Express your affection for God, Who longs to spend time with you and hear your heart. An example is the psalmist's longing to experience God's presence:

"As the deer longs for streams of water, so I long for You,
O God. I thirst for God, the living God." (Ps 42:1-2)

"How lovely is your dwelling place, Lord Almighty! My soul yearns,
even faints, for the courts of the Lord; my heart and
my flesh cry out for the living God." (Ps 84:1-2)

Giving God our respect

God, in His infinite grandeur and majesty, is deserving of our reverence. Recognizing His greatness keeps Him in His rightful place as the Lord of our lives, and invokes the humble acknowledgement He is worthy of us willingly surrendering to His will and ways:

"Therefore, having these promises, beloved,
let us cleanse ourselves from all
filthiness of the flesh and spirit, perfecting holiness
in the fear of God." (2 Cor 7:1)[562]

---

[561] https://www.bing.com/search?q=revelation+song+lyrics&form=PRUSEN&mkt=en-us&httpsmsn=1&refig=c1f3c6effe234ab8a51bad68f00dc186&sp=-1&pq=revelation+song+lyric&sc=8-21&qs=n&sk=&cvid=c1f3c6effe234ab8a51bad68f00dc186. See also the lyrics to, *Here I am to Worship.*
[562] See also Eph 5:18-22; 1 Pet 2:17.

"Therefore, my beloved, as you have always
obeyed, not as in my presence only, but
now much more in my absence, work out your
own salvation with fear and trembling;
for it is God who works in you both to will and to
do for His good pleasure." (Phil 2:12-13)

While challenged to cleanse ourselves of any "filthiness" and work out our salvation with "fear and trembling", it should not come from a fear of punishment, but reverence and respect so our lives reflect those of our Savior. It is reflected in the willingness to follow Jesus by "denying our self" and "picking up our cross" and is demonstrated as we present our bodies as "living sacrifices" through devoting ourselves to His plans and purposes.[563]

EMBRACING GOD'S PLANS AND PURPOSES FOR YOUR LIFE

Just as God chose Israel to set her apart to be a "light onto the Gentiles" (Is 42:60), Jesus has left us with a mission: to go and make disciples (Matt 28:19-20). His purpose for us is is to be "salt and light" to the world (Matt 5:13-16), and to do our part to help Him "build His kingdom" by helping the lost come to know the true Living God:

"For by grace you have been saved through
faith, and that not of yourselves,
it is the gift of God, not of works, lest
anyone should boast. For we are
His workmanship, created in Christ Jesus
for good works, which God
prepared beforehand that we should
walk in them." (Eph 2:8-10)

These "good works" are the fruit of our efforts as we willingly present our bodies as living sacrifices for His purposes. As we saw in *Chapters Seven*

---

[563] See Matt 16:24; Mark 8:34; Luke 9:23-24; Rom 12:1-2.

and *Nine*, it is vital that each and every believer is serving in his- or her area of giftedness. Whether serving refreshments, greeting attenders, working with children, praying for others, or simply helping set up for Sunday morning services, your church needs you to be at its best. Any lead pastor will tell you how dependent upon and appreciative of he- or she is for the collective church body in accomplishing the mission and vision God has given that particular church. Jesus is counting on you to step into the role He has uniquely gifted you to fill.

Jesus and the apostles were quite clear we can only experience the abundant life and fruit of the Spirit by "forsaking all" and surrendering ourselves to His purposes, which begins with a bold step of faith not unlike that made by the disciples (Luke 5:1-11). While it may not mean something like quitting your job and joining the mission field, it does mean embracing a missional mindset and prioritizing the use of your giftedness.

And as Nouwen insightfully observes, it is seen in the transformation from the rebellious Prodigal or the resentful Perfect to becoming "sons" (and "daughters") of God. It is the transition from operating out of "Need-love" to exhibiting the "Gift-loves" through the patience, kindness, and gentleness the father extended to his sons. But as you boldly take that step of faith, prepare yourself for the challenges that will inevitably come your way, the first being the spiritual attacks the enemy will inevitably mount against you.

ENTERING THE BATTLE FULLY ARMORED

Here's a sobering reality: the closer we walk with Jesus and the more committed we are to His purposes the more Satan and his army take notice. C.S. Lewis describes this well:

> *"Do not be deceived, Wormwood. Our cause is never more*
> *in danger than when a human, no longer desiring, but still*
> *intending, to do our Enemy's will, looks round upon a universe*
> *from which every trace of Him seems to have vanished,*
> *and asks why he has been forsaken, and still obeys."* [564]

---

[564] C. S. Lewis, The Screwtape Letters. https://www.goodreads.com/work/quotes/2920952-the-screwtape-letters

Given this, the more we move towards the frontlines of the spiritual battlefront, the bigger a target we become for Satan and his army as they ramp up their attack upon us:

"The moment you enlist in the army of
God, you personally become a
target. You need to remember that if you're
living for and walking with
Jesus Christ, the powers of darkness are aligned against you." [565]

The term "spiritual warfare" is particularly appropriate given Satan seemingly has organized his demons into an army-like structure comprised of the legions, cohorts, and centurions of the 1st century Roman army Paul's readers would have been familiar with:

For we do not wrestle against flesh and blood, but
against principalities, against powers, against the rulers
of the darkness of this age, against spiritual hosts of
wickedness in the heavenly places. (Eph 6:12) [566]

Paul draws from his knowledge of the Roman army, the armor and weaponry utilized by the soldiers, and the strategies the generals commonly employed. In movies like *Gladiator*, you see two armies comprised of hundreds or even thousands of soldiers collectively marching towards each other, locking eyes, and engaging in hand-to-hand combat as the two sides collided.[567] It is not this way in the spiritual battles we engage in, however, as demons won't confront us head-on. Instead, they are like snipers – watching and waiting for an opportunity to pick off an unsuspecting foe. Like Satan, the weapons demons utilize are their remarkable powers of deception, distortion, and dissension. And like Satan successfully used

---

[565] Walter Martin. https://www.azquotes.com/quotes/topics/satan.html

[566] http://www.preteristarchive.com/Rome/Military/index.html. The terms "principalities", "powers", and "rulers" suggest various ranks like the legate, centurion, and prefect that commanded the various units of the Roman army. Note there appears to be a similar hierarchy among God's faithful angels with Michael, the "archangel", seemingly the commanding officer (1 Thess 4:16; Jude 9; cf Dan 10:10-22).

[567] See also *Troy*, *Braveheart*, and *The Patriot*.

---

these weapons to appeal to tempt Adam and Eve (Gen 3:1-6), he and his army have continued to systematically deceive and destroy people ever since.

The influence of Satan powers will reach its zenith in the End Times, as prophesied in the Book of Revelation, particularly *Chapter 13*, when the Antichrist rules over the world. Incredibly, he will not need to exert force to obtain this power – instead, it will gladly and willingly be <u>given</u> to him! And this seems to be the product of his ability to win over vulnerable human beings through our desire for power, prosperity, and pleasure:

> *"For all the nations have drunk of the wine*
> *of the wrath of her fornication,*
> *the kings of the earth have committed fornication*
> *with her, and the merchants*
> *of the earth have become rich through the*
> *abundance of her luxury." (Rev 18:3)*[568]

But Satan's ability to ascend to ruler of the world is articulated in how he and his demonic minions work to sow the seeds of doubt, disillusionment, dissatisfaction, despair, and denigration in the hearts of human beings, one at a time, as articulated in the lyrics of the song, *Sympathy for the Devil*, by the Rolling Stones:

> *Please allow me to introduce myself*
> *I'm a man of wealth and taste*
> *I've been around for a long, long years*
> *Stole many a man's soul and faith* [569]

Now it may seem God has left us to fend for ourselves in a proverbial "David vs Goliath" mismatch, since demons are virtual "giants" who have been battle-tested through millennia of conflict. But history tells us that just as Goliath had his limitations, demons – and Satan as well – have theirs. While they may be able to afflict us, they cannot

---

[568] Upon Jesus' final defeat of Satan, the world (particularly the wealthy and powerful) will mourn his defeat and the destruction of the "Great City" Babylon and its riches (Rev 18:9-23), validating the "love of money is a root of all kinds of evil" (1 Tim 6:10).

[569] https://genius.com/The-rolling-stones-sympathy-for-the-devil-lyrics.

possess believers indwelt by the Holy Spirit (Titus 3:5), and "sealed" as a possession of God (Eph 1:13; 4:30; cf Rev 9:4). The imagery of the "seal" is prevalent throughout the Bible, as it was utilized by rulers as a symbol of their power and authority, whether to claim ownership or validate an official decree. Examples are the hot wax indented by the emperor's signet ring to seal official documents, the seal (likely clay) affixed upon Jesus' tomb, and the seven seals securing the scroll to be revealed during the Tribulation.[570]

It is as simple as this: what God owns, Satan is powerless to possess. And recall Satan and his demons cannot create or give us thoughts or desires we aren't already prone to have. While it is wise to not minimize how deceptive demons can be in tempting us with power, pleasure, and possessions, any actions we choose are simply that – our choice. Given this, we are challenged to reject the proverbial, "the devil made me do it", and to acknowledge, "The devil suggested I do it, but I chose to do it, so it's on me".

And keep in mind God has not left us to fight this battle alone. Just as Satan has an army of demons attacking us, God has an army of angels actively defending us:

"Bless the LORD, you His angels, Who excel
in strength, who do His word,
Heeding the voice of His word. Bless the
LORD, all you His hosts, You
ministers of His, who do His pleasure.
Bless the LORD, all His works,
In all places of His dominion. Bless the
LORD, O my soul!" (Ps 103:20-22)

Even Jesus Himself had angels to care for Him:

"Then the devil left Him, and behold, angels
came and ministered to Him." (Matt 4:11)

---

[570] Regarding Jesus' tomb see Matt 27:62. Regarding the scroll's unsealing during the Tribulation see Rev 5:1; cf Dan 9:24; 12:4.

And then there is the fact God puts limits on what Satan and his demons can do to us. In *Chapter Five* we saw while God allowed Satan to "test" Job in about every way imaginable, He set a limit with these simple words: "…only do not lay a hand on his person" (Job 1:12). So, we can rest in the knowledge we can in fact have victory when he attacks us:

> *"Therefore submit to God. Resist the devil and*
> *he will flee from you." (Jam 4:7)*

> *Resist (oppose) him, steadfast in the faith,*
> *knowing that the same sufferings*
> *are experienced by your brotherhood in the world. (1 Pet 1:9)*

This is due to the fact God has given us not one, but <u>six</u> weapons to fight back with:

> *"Therefore, take up the whole armor of God*
> *that you may be able to withstand in*
> *the evil day, and having done all, to stand. Stand*
> *therefore, having girded your waist*
> *with truth, having put on the breastplate of*
> *righteousness, and having shod your feet*
> *with the preparation of the gospel of peace; above*
> *all, taking the shield of faith with*
> *which you will be able to quench all the fiery*
> *darts of the wicked one. And take*
> *the helmet of salvation, and the sword of the*
> *Spirit, which is the word of God;*
> *praying always with all prayer and supplication*
> *in the Spirit…" (Eph 6:13-18a)*

1. Buckle up for battle with the belt of truth.

To prepare for battle, a Roman soldier would first buckle on the "belt of truth". The truth is the weapon we use to defend us against the strongholds Satan will attack us with.

2. Strap on the breastplate of righteousness.

The Roman soldier wore a breastplate that extended from his neck to his thigh and wrapped around his back to protect his vital organs. We need our backside protected, as Satan won't attack us in ways we expect; instead, he will blindside us with the "arrows" of the lies and other forms of deception he uses that we least expect and don't see coming at us. Our "breastplate" is the fact we are declared righteous by virtue of what Jesus has done for us, and as a result can rest in the knowledge God is with us and will protect us from anyone who comes against us (Rom 8:31). At the same time, it is important we live righteously so we don't give Satan an opening he can use to attack us (1 John 2:28-29).

3. Walk in peace.

The Roman soldier wore boots called *caligae* studded with sharp nails to ensure firm footing on even the most rugged terrain. We are called to walk in the peace we have through Jesus, and to strive to be at peace with others (Matt 5:9; Rom 12:18). But expect things will get "rocky" as you become more fruitful for the kingdom of Jesus.

4. Stand behind the shield of faith.

As we march ever more boldly and confidently in *WHOLENESS*, expect the enemy will escalate his attacks in both frequency and intensity. A common tactic utilized by the Roman army was dipping arrows in a flammable concoction before firing them at their opponents. Expect a full-out assault through the lies, deceptions, or appeals to your desires you are most vulnerable to including:

- Attacking your sense of value and worth, or resurrecting old fears and self-doubts,
- Reminding you of the pleasure or relief you got from alcohol and/ or drugs; and,
- Raising doubt about the motives of family or co-worker, causing dissension.

5. Receive the helmet of salvation.

While the breastplate and shield protect our "hearts", the helmet of salvation protects our minds from Satan's lies and distortions. Noteworthy is while a Roman soldier would put on his sandals and belt and pick up his shield, the helmet was often handed to him by an attendant or armor bearer. Salvation is the gift earned by Jesus and "handed to" us by God, and it is in this hope we are sustained while amid the battle (1 Thess 5:8).

6. Swing the sword of the Spirit.

Roman soldiers used the *gladius*, a short, double-edged sword with which they could both slash and thrust while fighting in tight quarters. The truth is both a defensive and offensive weapon, and one employed prayerfully through the Holy Spirit (Heb 4:12).

The spoken word of God is so powerful it brought all there is into existence and is such a powerful weapon that in the End Times Jesus will overthrow Satan and all opposed to Him simply through His words (Rev 19:15-21). While we must fight this battle in our lives today, we can draw upon the truth that the war in fact has already been won:

> *"And you, being dead in your trespasses and the uncircumcision of your flesh, He has made alive together with Him, having forgiven you all trespasses, having wiped out the handwriting of requirements that was against us, which was contrary to us. And He has taken it out of the way, having nailed it to the cross. Having disarmed principalities and powers, He made a public spectacle of them, triumphing over them in it." (Col 2:13-15)*[571]

Notice this in the past tense: there is no "if" or "maybe" – it is done! It is like watching a pre-recorded football game of which you already know the outcome only to see how it played out. Sure, the opposition will get some

---

[571] See also John 12:31; Col 1:19-23; Heb 2:14-15; 1 John 3:8; 4:4; Rev 12:11.

first downs and score some points, but in the end, you know your team ultimately won. With this we know that when drawing upon the Holy Spirit we are virtually invincible, as summed up in the following quote:

> *"Satan trembles when he sees the weakest*
> *saint upon their knees."*[572]

At the same time, we are wise to heed Paul's closing thoughts: Be diligent in always being prayerfully dependent upon God. The moment we become self-reliant is when we – like Peter – will be "sifted like wheat" (Luke 22:31). Which brings us to the enemy that brought down Adam and Eve in the Garden of Eden, and the *Entrance* Generation of Israel once they conquered the Promised Land – an enemy that is every bit as dangerous, and one Satan has enlisted to attack humanity ever since the beginning – and that's ourselves.

ENDURING DOUBT, DISSATISFACTION, DISILLUSIONMENT AND DESPAIR

In 2016, momentous changes occurred in the world of politics. Americans elected Donald Trump, a man with no political experience, as its 45th president. Meanwhile across the pond, Brits shocked experts in voting for "Brexit", Britain's exit from the European Union after over 40 years of participation. And while products of "populist" movements, the motivating factor seemingly underlying these decisions was the growing dissatisfaction and disillusionment felt towards the political leadership of their respective countries.[573]

This certainly wasn't the first-time people expressed dissatisfaction with their country's leadership, and certainly won't be the last. Human beings are prone to not only use, but at times blatantly abuse the power given to them. And you, at one time or another, have likely become dissatisfied or disillusioned with "leaders" you were serving under.

---

[572] William Cowper. https://www.azquotes.com/quote/66363
[573] https://www.forbes.com/sites/johnmauldin/2016/07/05/3-reasons-brits-voted-for-brexit/#793831c91f9d

Many – whether presidents, prime ministers, CEOs, or even pastors – may not deserve the loyalty of those he or she is leading. But God – the Alpha Omega, Creator and Heavenly Father, whose intentions are always good, and will "never leave or forsake us" (Heb 13:5) – certainly does. Yet the Bible provides numerous accounts of people experiencing doubt, dissatisfaction, disillusionment, and despair even under God's leadership.

Overcoming Doubt, Dissatisfaction, and Disillusionment

About a year after leaving behind everything to follow Jesus (Luke 5:1-11), Peter and his fellow disciples are crossing the Sea of Galilee one night when a violent storm erupts. But then they see Jesus – walking on the sea towards their boat! Now the disciples had witnessed Jesus calm a similar storm, but are terrified nonetheless, and conclude they are seeing a ghost.[574] After Jesus assures them it is, in fact, Him, Peter tries to prove his faith:

> "...'Lord, if it is You, command me to come to
> You on the water'. So, He said, 'Come'.
> And when Peter had come down out of the boat,
> he walked on the water to go to Jesus.
> But when he saw that the wind was boisterous,
> he was afraid; and beginning to sink he
> cried out, saying, 'Lord, save me!' And immediately
> Jesus stretched out His hand and
> caught him, and said to him, 'O you of little faith,
> why did you doubt'?" (Matt 14:28-31)[575]

Notice at first Peter is doing just fine, as with his eyes locked in on Jesus, he, too, is walking on the water! But then his attention is drawn away from Jesus, and towards the winds and the waves that threaten to drown him. And as doubt sets in, he begins to sink.

This event provides an insightful illustration of how trials affect our ability to faithfully persevere in following Jesus. First, trials draw our attention away from Him and towards our concerns. We may

---

[574] Matt 8:18-27; Mark 4:35-41; Luke 8:22-25.
[575] See also Mark 6:47-56; John 6:16-21.

"catastrophize" or anticipate the worst possible outcome. And then as doubt becomes disillusionment, we begin to bemoan our poor fortune, perhaps question God, and begin to "sink".[576] And instead of waiting expectantly to see how God will "snatch victory from the jaws of defeat" (Rom 8:28), we give up and walk away.

Like any exercise program that pushes us to the limit physically, God uses trials to strengthen our resilience both psychologically and spiritually. We cannot develop the spiritual fruits such patience, faith, and wisdom without trials. And note "faith" is not something you either have or don't have; instead, like physical strength or conditioning, it is something that develops only when tested. Given this we are challenged to view trials as an opportunity to grow in our faith. And instead of bemoaning our misfortune, we might choose to practice gratitude, as seen in the words of the psalmist:

"This is the day the LORD has made; We will rejoice and be glad in it." (Ps 118:24)

Instructive, however, are the words in the immediately following verse:

Save now, I pray, O LORD; O LORD, I pray, send now prosperity." (Ps 118:25)

Insightful is the fact the English "prosperity" comes from the Hebrew *tsalach*, which means, "To push forward, to go through, make progress, succeed, to prosper". We take this to mean we are to ask not so much for the outcome we want, but the strength to push forward, to persevere, and to see us through the trial we are facing in anticipation of the good God will bring out of it. Instead of becoming disillusioned and turning away from God, turn towards Him in fervent prayer, and ask that He send "prosperity" your way.

There is application in this as well for us followers of Jesus. He regularly maintained a discipline of seeking God's guidance and strength through regular times in prayer. And Luke's Gospel tells us when Jesus sent out seventy disciples on a mission of evangelism, He did not send them alone:

[576] See *Chapter Nine.*

instead, He sent them out in <u>pairs</u> (Luke 10:1).[577] And Jesus Himself took Peter, James and John to be with Him in the Garden of Gethsemane when facing the trial of His life (Matt 26:36-46).[578] The point is we are encouraged to draw upon the support of believers in the midst of trials (Gal 6:2), and in fact are challenged to actively participate in the fellowship for this express purpose (Heb 10:24-25).

Peck offers these thoughts regarding the trials of life we will inevitably encounter:

"It is in the whole process of meeting and solving problems that life has meaning. Problems are the cutting edge that distinguishes between success and failure. Problems call forth our courage and our wisdom; indeed, they create our courage and our wisdom. It is only because of problems that we grow mentally and spiritually. It is through the pain of confronting and resolving problems that we learn."

"To proceed very far through the desert, you must be willing to meet existential suffering and work it through. In order to do this, the attitude toward pain has to change. This happens when we accept the fact that everything that happens to us has been designed for our spiritual growth." [579]

Don't be surprised – and in fact, <u>expect</u> – you will experience trials that will test your faith, and can chip away at your desire to continue following Jesus. But also realize the trial may come from within in the form of temptation. In the Parable of the Sower, the third seed Jesus described is that which fell among thorns that "choked it" and hindered its growth. These "thorns" can be any or a combination of the *Eight Deadly Sins*: the wounded or unfulfilled pride that fuels feelings of envy and malice towards

---

[577] See also Matt 22:1; Mark 6:7; 11:1; 14:13; Luke 9:2; 19:29; cf Acts 9:38; Eccl 4:12.
[578] See also Mark 14:32-42; Luke 22:40-46.
[579] https://www.goodreads.com/author/quotes/3061.M_Scott_Peck

others; seeking fulfillment through materialism, excess eating or the use of alcohol or drugs; or the apathy that leads to an unwillingness to work, serve, or live in fellowship with others.

Satan is a master at generating doubt about God's intentions. Adam and Eve chose to eat the fruit after Satan stirred up doubt about God's motives. Israel doubted God would provide the food and water they needed to survive their journey to the Promised Land and doubted He could help them conquer the "giants" occupying the fortified cities once they got there. But there was something within Adam and Eve and the people of Israel that provided the fertile ground upon which the seeds of doubt Satan sowed could take root and grow into the dissatisfaction and disillusionment that fueled their decisions to turn away from God. This is seen in the Parable of the Sower Jesus used to teach His disciples:

"Listen! Behold, a sower went out to sow. And
it happened, as he sowed, that some seed
fell by the wayside; and the birds of the air came
and devoured it. Some fell on stony ground,
where it did not have much earth; and immediately
it sprang up because it had no depth of earth.
But when the sun was up it was scorched, and
because it had no root it withered away. And
some seed fell among thorns; and the thorns grew
up and choked it, and it yielded no crop.
But other seed fell on good ground and yielded
a crop that sprang up, increased
and produced: some thirtyfold, some sixty, and
some a hundred." (Mark 4:3-8)[580]

The "seed" represents the Gospel, and the "ground" four types of people. The first reject the Good News about Jesus. The second (the "stony" ground) represent the new believer "on fire for the Lord" who, once scorched by the trials of life, "withers" and becomes disillusioned due to the lack of the strong "root system" of a battle-tested faith that empowers us to persevere through trials. A case in point is none other than, again – Peter.

---

[580] See also Matt 13:3-8, 18-23; Mark 4:14-20; Luke 8:5-8

Dissatisfaction takes root in the perception God is not blessing us in some way. For Adam and Eve (and the Prodigal Son), it was a preoccupation with what they <u>didn't</u> have rather than gratitude for what they did have. For the Rich Young Ruler, it was his unwillingness to part with his wealth that led him to walk away from Jesus and the abundant life he sought.[581] And in the End Times, seeking abundance through the "lust of the eyes, the lust of the flesh, and the boastful pride of life" will lead the world to give the Antichrist authority to rule over the world (Rev 18:11-20), as well as during the final rebellion against King Jesus during His 1,000 year rule on earth after His Second Coming.[582]

Preoccupation with material satisfaction and personal comfort "chokes" the work of the Spirit in our lives, to which Jesus proposed to experience the abundant life we must be willing to let go of the "wants" that hinder us spiritually. It is practiced in choosing not to worry about material things but seeking first His kingdom and trusting God will provide all we need (Matt 6:25-33). And notice the key word here is "need", not "want". When we, unlike Adam and Eve, can accept that what we have is sufficient for the abundant life, we will be like the fourth seed in the Parable of the Sower – a "fruitful" seed:

> *"But other seed fell on good ground and yielded*
> *a crop that sprang up, increased*
> *and produced: some thirtyfold, some sixty, and*
> *some a hundred." (Mark 4:8)* [583]

The step of faith we are all challenged to take is to trust that if I'm all in for Jesus, I'll have all I need to experience the abundant life seen in those early believers in Acts *Chapter Two*. And for all his failures, it is none other than Peter who provides the example for us.

---

[581] See Matt 19:15-26; Mark 10:17-27; Luke 18:18-27. In Ecclesiastes, Solomon – through his own experiences – declares he has gained the wisdom that one cannot experience abundance living a life "apart from him (God)" (Eccl 2:25-26; 3:12-15, 18; 6:1).

[582] Luxury is considered one form of idolatry (Ezek 27:30-35), and those mourning Jesus' defeat of the Antichrist are those who have relished the abundance of wealth the Antichrist has provided. This assumes a Pre-millennial interpretation of Revelation.

[583] See also Matt 13:8; Luke 8:8

It is literally within a few days after his failed attempt in following Jesus by walking on the water (John 6:22, 59-60), and Jesus is speaking to a large crowd of His followers. But Jesus is using metaphors many found difficult to comprehend:

> *"'I am the living bread which came down from*
> *heaven. If anyone eats of this bread, he*
> *will live forever; and the bread that I shall*
> *give is My flesh, which I shall give for*
> *the life of the world.' The Jews therefore*
> *quarreled among themselves, saying,*
> *'How can this Man give us His flesh to eat'?"*
> *(John 6:51-52, cf vv 59-60)*

It is understandable this confused His audience. Eating pork or certain sea foods was deemed "unclean" according to the Mosaic Law, and what sounded like "cannibalism" certainly would present a test for His disciples (John 6:60).[584] But Peter's reaction:

> *"From that time many of His disciples went back*
> *and walked with Him no more. Then*
> *Jesus said to the twelve, 'Do you also want to go*
> *away?' But Simon Peter answered Him,*
> *'Lord, to whom shall we go? You have the words*
> *of eternal life. Also we have come to*
> *believe and know that You are the Christ, the*
> *Son of the living God'." (John 6:66-69)*

Peter certainly had his shortcomings, but if there is one thing we can commend him for it was his absolute loyalty to Jesus. He had not only left behind, but "forsaken" <u>everything</u> to follow Him.[585] And in that moment

---

[584] See Lev 11:1-47; Deut 14:3-21. In the rest of the passage (John 6:49-58), Jesus is contrasting the "bread" (manna) God provided the Israelites on their journey from Egypt to the Promised Land to sustain them physically (see Ex 16:31-35; Num 11:6-9; Deut 8:3-20), with the spiritual sustenance available through faith in Jesus. See also Gen 9:4.

[585] See discussion in *Chapter Six* of the Greek word translated "forsook" or "forsaken" in Luke 5:11 (cf Matt 26:55-56; Mark 14:50).

of doubt and confusion, any temptation for Peter to "walk with Him no more" was simply no longer an option.

As we saw in the example of the man who "cried out…with tears, 'Lord, I believe; help my unbelief'", we will have moments of doubt and uncertainty.[586] This testing of our faith is what produces patience and the "perfect work" that produces "completeness" (Jam1:2-4).

Our ability to overcome the trials that stir up doubt, dissatisfaction and disillusionment is strengthened through two things. First, it involves a conscious decision evidenced in the form of some resolute action step in which we, like Peter, "leave behind" some aspect of our life. It is seen in Billy and Dawn Claudio's decision, upon hearing the unmistakable calling to plant what would become Oasis Community Church, to resign their positions in South Caroline, sell their home, and move their family to Arizona. It is seen in those who have left a former career to become fulltime pastors or move to a faraway country to join the mission field. It is that action step of "burning the bridges" of one's former life to the point there is no turning back. While you may not sense such a significant calling, it will involve giving up something you value, and leaving it behind once and for all.

But notice in his moment of confusion and uncertainty, Peter turned to the truth about what He had come to believe about Jesus.[587] It is that same truth that kept him and his fellow disciples waiting expectantly until the Holy Spirit came upon them on Pentecost, and inspired their bold proclamation of the Good News of Jesus in the presence of the same Jewish leaders they hid in fear from 50 days earlier (Acts 2:1-47; John 19:19, 26).

In the Parable of the Prodigal Son, Jesus abruptly ends with gently but firmly confronting his "perfect" son's lack of joy upon his Prodigal brother returning home safely, and the underlying dissatisfaction hindering his capacity to feel it. And, at least for me, we're left wondering, "So what happened afterwards?" Did the Prodigal, having learned from his regrettable decision to diss his father to go "make merry" in a life on indulgence, remain grateful and appreciative for the privilege of living with and learning from his father?

---

[586] See Mark 9:24, and discussion towards the end of *Chapter Five*.
[587] See also Matt 16:15-16; John 20:19-29, in which the disciples' belief was confirmed upon seeing the resurrected Jesus.

I pose this question as the obvious answer would seem to be a resounding "Yes". You would think, for example, the person – after "hitting bottom" and "eating peapods" due to the devastating effects of his- or her alcohol and/or drug abuse – would never drink or use drugs again. Yet research shows – and sadly I've seen it too many times in my work as an addiction therapist – that 40-60% of people relapse within a year after completing treatment.[588] And those who relapse often point to some form of trial that triggered the craving to drink or use drugs again. But researchers have found it is not so much the trial that causes the relapse, but a growing dissatisfaction or disillusionment with sobriety and the resultant drifting away from the practices necessary to maintain one's sobriety (AA meetings, prayer, self-care, fellowship with and serving others) that leads to relapse.[589]

In the Parable of the Prodigal Son, we get hints of how "spiritual relapses" can occur. First there's "only seeing the negatives" (i.e., dissatisfaction). All both sons had to do was look at the blessings they enjoyed simply by being sons of the "father" and the positional and prosperous lives they enjoyed because of it and compare it to the lives of their servants. And perhaps at one time one or both did. But then they lost sight of it.

For the Prodigal it is reasonable to assume for at least awhile he will experience what those in the addiction recovery world refer to as the "pink cloud", or the "euphoria and extreme joy, hopefulness, peacefulness and optimism" those in early recovery often feel when the physical, emotional, and relational devastation wrought by addiction begin to ease.[590] In time, however the relief begin to wane, and the "same old…" erodes the joy, apathy begins to set in and one begins to wistfully remember only the "good times" of using, leading to relapse. In *Chapter Eight* we considered how generations of Israelites cycled through this seven times over about 400 years as recorded in the book of Judges.

---

[588] https://www.psychologytoday.com/us/basics/relapse

[589] The following is from Lewis, Dana, & Blevins, p. 156; http://alcoholism.about.com/od/relapse/a/relapsesigns.htm;http://www.promises.com/articles/relapse-prevention/7-warning-signs-you-are-heading-for-a-relapse/;http://www.addictionresearch.com/treatment_articles/article/addiction-relapse-warning-signs?223.html;https://www.discoveryplace.info/3-serioous-warnings-signs-relapse.

[590] A good description of the "Pink Cloud" can be found at https://www.healthline.com/health/pink-cloud#signs.

In a way, it is easier to see how the Perfect could be vulnerable to dissatisfaction. He had never suffered the misery of eating peapods and being lost and desperate. He simply fell prey to that all-to-human tendency that started with Adam Eve by wanting more than he had been given. And failing to practice gratitude.

By simply reading the daily news we can be jolted out of the subtle sense of "feeling deprived" by considering those who are "less fortunate" than us: those suffering poverty, life-threatening illness, or the ravages of war like the Ukrainians, the residents of the Gaza Strip, or other war-torn areas in the world. But as we have also considered the "I've got it better than…" can easily get lost by comparing ourselves to those who have it "better" than me (recall "Relative Depravity", *Chapter Eight*).

We are reminded of the importance of the regular practice of "being still" and spending quality time talking with and listening to God through time in humble reflection of the "state of our soul" to remember – or for some to realize in the depths of your souls for the first time – just how undeserving we are of His grace and favor.

As I've pondered the Parable of the Prodigal Son, something dawned on me: in a way, the Prodigal Son, for all his selfishness and disrespectful disdain of his father, was at least honest. He didn't want his father's ways, he only wanted his father's wealth, and he boldly asked for it. In contrast, the Perfect Son was lying to both his father and himself in his postering as the "obedient" and "good son". But deep in his soul his conscience was tormenting him. This is seen in the Apostle Paul's words to the Roman believers:

> *"…who show the work of the law written in their*
> *hearts, their conscience also bearing witness,*
> *and between themselves their thoughts accusing or*
> *else excusing them) in the day when God*
> *will judge the secrets of men by Jesus Christ,*
> *according to my gospel." (Rom 2:15-16)*

In an interaction with Jewish leaders, who a short time later He accused repeatedly of being "hypocrites", Jesus shared the following parable:

*"A man had two sons, and he came to the first
and said, 'Son, go, work today in
my vineyard.' He answered and said, 'I will
not,' but afterward he regretted it
and went. Then, he came to the second and
said likewise. And he answered and
said, 'I go, sir,' but he did not go. Which of
the two did the will of his father?
They said to Him, 'The first.' Jesus said to
them, 'Assuredly, I say to you that tax
collectors and harlots enter the kingdom of
God before you'." (Matt 21:28b-31)*

When we fail, ignore, or simply refuse to acknowledge our shortcomings, we are prone to prop ourselves up by stepping on and over those we consider to be "worst" sinners than us. Instead of exhibiting the love, compassion and concern Jesus expressed to the "lost" of His day, we treat them with the same disdain the Perfect Son expressed towards His brother. And instead of experiencing the joy of being a blessed child of God we become critical, cynical, and condemning towards others – and like the Perfect Son – God Himself!

Notice in *v 28*, the Perfect – being informed his father has thrown "this son of yours" a party – is angry and becomes critical not only at the Prodigal but his father as well. He refuses to join the party, withdrawing as well. For us today, this might manifest itself into a temptation to "go away" (John 6:66-67) in passively withdrawing from our calling to "go make disciples" (Matt 28:19-20), or becoming "Christian soldiers" in fighting "flesh and blood" for God's causes while failing to recognize the enemy we are really fighting are the "principalities...powers, ruler of the darkness of this age and spiritual hosts of wickedness" once again stirring up dissension – and hate – amongst us (Eph 6:12).

Overcoming Despair

While doubt, disappointment and disillusionment will chip away at our faith, even those fully committed to serving God may experience unexpected setbacks that can crush our resolve and plunge us into the depths of despair. This can happen to the best of the best and the most faithful of the faithful, as seen in the experience of the prophet Elijah.

During the 9th century B.C., Ahab is king over the northern kingdom of Israel.[591] Arguably the worst king to rule over Israel, Ahab instituted idol worship and rejected prophets like Elijah and Micaiah that God had sent to warn him.[592] I Kings 18 tells us Elijah challenged 400 prophets of Baal to a "battle of the gods" to see whose god will "answer by fire" (1 Kings 18:24). After the impotent gods of the prophets of Baal go MIA during their day-long appeals, Elijah instructs them to soak the wood three times, and then – with a mere few words – the pile of wood bursts into a raging fire! The God of Israel has won, and after executing the 400 false prophets, Elijah waits expectantly for his people to turn away from their false gods and towards the one true God. But his hopes are soon crushed:

> *"And Ahab told Jezebel all that Elijah had done,*
> *also how he had executed all the prophets*
> *with the sword. Then Jezebel sent a messenger*
> *to Elijah, saying, 'So let the gods do to*
> *me, and more also, if I do not make your life*
> *as the life of one of them by tomorrow*
> *about this time.' And when he (Elijah) saw*
> *that, he arose and ran for his life,*
> *and went to Beersheba, which belongs to Judah,*
> *and left his servant there. But he*
> *himself went a day's journey into the wilderness,*
> *and came and sat down under a*
> *broom tree. <u>And he prayed that he might*
> *die, and said, 'It is enough! Now,*
> *LORD, take my life, for I am no better*
> *than my fathers!'</u> (1 Kings 19:1-4)*

---

[591] See *Chapter Eight* for the history leading up to Ahab's rule.

[592] See 1 Kings 16:30-33, in which he is described as doing "more evil than all who were before him", did "more to provoke the Lord God of Israel to anger than all the kings…before him", and sin was a "trivial thing for him to walk in". During his reign, Israel worshipped false gods (Baal and Asherah), and practiced child sacrifice (Jer 19:5). See also 1Kings 18:17; Lam 4:9-10.

In this passage we get a clear picture of the despair Elijah felt, as he is virtually suicidal! No spiritual slouch, Elijah was in fact a devoted prophet, and one of only <u>two</u> men God spared from having to suffer death itself.[593] Yet, in the ensuing verses, we're told God sends angels to tend to Elijah as he recovers from this overwhelming setback. Then after regaining his strength, he travels by foot to meet God at Mount Horeb (the "mountain of God" 1 Kings 19:5-10). Upon arriving, God tells Elijah to stand on the mountain, where he is met by "great and strong" winds, an earthquake and a fire (vv 11-12). And then...

> "...after the fire a still small voice. So it was,
> when Elijah heard it, that he wrapped
> his face in his mantle and went out and stood
> in the entrance of the cave. Suddenly
> a voice came to him, and said, "What are you
> doing here, Elijah?" (1 Kings 19:12b-13)

God has, to quote Maximus in *Gladiator*, unleashed "[hades]". Yet, Elijah – unlike Peter – has the spiritual strength and fortitude to stand firm and hear the "still, small" voice of God in the midst of nature's onslaught. And then we're given the reason for his despair:

> "...'I have been very zealous for the LORD
> God of hosts; because the children
> of Israel have forsaken Your covenant, torn
> down Your altars, and killed Your
> prophets with the sword. I alone am left; and
> they seek to take my life." (1 Kings 19:14)

Elijah has taken the ultimate risk in giving everything to serve God in hopes Israel will turn back to Him, yet nothing has changed except he now has a death sentence hanging over his head. He is shocked and confused, and his despair seemingly stems from his inability to comprehend what has happened. Yet rather than packing it in and walking away, Elijah

---

[593] In 2 Kings 2:11, we're told God took Elijah up in a "chariot of fire" in a "whirlwind into heaven". The second was Enoch, who unlike others seemingly never died but was "taken" by God (Gen 5:24).

turns <u>towards</u> God – and in fact walks for <u>forty days</u> seeking answers.[594] And through this experience, Elijah grows in his ability to persevere in the journey while not losing sight of his destination: to be a faithful and dedicated prophet of his Lord.

Facing the Fire

When you think of "trials", what probably comes to mind are the unforeseen turn of events in which you, like Andy Dufresne in *The Shawshank Redemption*, have the "bad luck" of being in the "path of the tornado". There's Job, the "blameless and upright" man (Job 1:1) God allows Satan to torment to the point he questions God's fairness. And there's Joseph, whose only "fault" is doing the right thing yet end his "reward" is ending up in prison for it. And then there are the present-day examples of people like Pastor William and Jerry Sittser, who experienced the kind of pain and suffering that leads one to utter the words of despair Jesus Himself cried out:

> *"My God, My God, why have You forsaken Me?" (Matt 27:46)*[595]

While humbled by these examples, we can be encouraged by the fact that if given a choice they – and even Jesus Himself – would just as soon have had the "cup" of suffering pass them by (Matt 26:39, 42).[596] If given a chance, they'd just as soon not have to wait to see how God will use it for good (Gen 50:20; Rom 8:28). Rather than walking into the raging fire that threatens to consume us, we'd just as soon walk – if not run – in the opposite direction. Yet it is in midst of the most intense heat that we – like Jonah "hopping a ship to Joppa" and sailing 1,000 miles in the opposite direction God was pointing him to go – that we may discover what French poet Jean de La Fontaine poignantly states:

---

[594] In the ensuing verses we're told God's purpose for Elijah was for him to serve as an instrument of the justice God would eventually render upon Israel. God then gives Elijah his new marching orders, which he faithfully carries out.

[595] See also Mark 15:34; cf Ps 22:1.

[596] The Garden of Gethsemane shortly before His arrest and eventual execution (see Matt 26:39, 42; Mark 14:35; Luke 21:46).

*"A person often meets his destiny on the
road he took to avoid it"* [597]

We may struggle to comprehend what God is doing amid the trials we are facing. Yet, for all the miracles He performed and the wise teachings He imparted, what we appreciate most is how Jesus humbly bore the shame of our sins by willingly sacrificing Himself for us. And what really makes this meaningful is the fact He knew <u>exactly</u> what was coming yet chose to go through it anyway.[598] And remarkably in the moments before His arrest, Jesus tells His disciples that for Him, His suffering will be worth it because of the joy He will experience because of it:

> *"These things I have spoken to you, that My joy may remain in you, and that your joy may be full." (John 15:11)*

Fast forward to Pentecost, and these same disciples – who had deserted Him – are now boldly declaring His name. Yet, when confronted by the Jewish leaders demanding they cease <u>speaking</u> His very name (Acts 4:18), their response is essentially, "Uhm, don't think so", as they could not help but boldly proclaim the good news![599]

Their refusal came out of the same single-minded loyalty to Jesus, they had seen Him demonstrate in choosing to serve His Father. They had taken on the "steadfastness" and resolute mindset Jesus demonstrated during His journey to Jerusalem and the fiery trial He knew lay ahead for Him when He "steadfastly set His face" to go to Jerusalem (Luke 9:51-52).[600] He would not be deterred; instead, He "fought the good fight and finished the race" (2 Tim 4:17). He found strength in knowing the good it would accomplish and the joy He it would bring Him. It is this same joy Paul found in his suffering (Phil 4:1) and hoped to further experience if His hearers would follow his example (Phil 2:2).

---

[597] https://www.goodreads.com/author/quotes/82948.Jean_de_La_Fontaine
[598] Note John 2:19-21, in which Jesus predicts His death and resurrection three years before it happens! See also Matt 16:21; 17:22-23; 20:18-19; Mark 8:31-32; 9:31; 10:33-34; Luke 9:22; 43-45; 11:29-30; 18:31-34.
[599] From the Greek *dunamai*, also translated "power". Peter and John simply couldn't help themselves from speaking Jesus' name!
[600] From the Greek *sterizo* which means, "To strengthen, make firm, resolve, fix".

Our challenge is to accept that the joy and abundant life in living a life devoted to serving Jesus will have its ups and downs. We will have seasons when we feel God is blessing us tremendously, as well as times we may wonder if He has abandoned us. and in those moments of testing, we choose to press on and wait expectantly to see how He will take what was "meant for evil" and use it for good (Gen 50:20; cf Rom 8:28). And just those who refused to walk away, we too will choose to give our lives in serving the King who has suffered everything we will ever suffer and understands the temptations we face. We revisit what Peter wrote for his readers, but perhaps as a reminder to himself as well:

"For to this you were called because Christ also
suffered for us, leaving us an example,
that you should follow His steps: Who committed
no sin, nor was deceit found in His
mouth"; who, when He was reviled, did not revile
in return; when He suffered, He did
not threaten, but committed Himself to Him
who judges righteously; who Himself
bore our sins in His own body on the tree,
that we, having died to sins, might
live for righteousness -- by whose stripes you
were healed." (1 Pet 2:21-24) [601]

THE JOURNEY TOWARDS YOUR
DESTINATION: THE ABUNDANT LIFE

It is with this mindset we will begin to experience *shalom*: the peace and contentment of the abundant life. As we saw in *Chapter Eight*, Paul learned that when drawing upon the strength available through Jesus, he experienced a sense of abundance regardless of his circumstances. And something to keep in mind: Paul himself readily acknowledged that while he had learned to experience the abundant life, he by no means had mastered it, and was in fact still a work in process (Phil 3:12). To which

[601] See also Heb 2:18; 4:14-16; 5:8.

we again turn to Dr. Peck, who sums up well the answer to the question we posed at the beginning of this chapter:

> *"All my life I used to wonder what I would become when I grew up. Then, about seven years ago, I realized that I was never going to grow up—that growing is an ever-ongoing process."*[602]

The abundant life – like life itself – is <u>both</u> a journey and a destination, and the challenge of "growing up" is fully embracing what Jesus said to His disciples during those last few hours before His arrest and execution:

> *"These things I have spoken to you, that in Me you may have peace. In the world you will have tribulation; but be of good cheer, I have overcome the world." (John 16:33)*

Jesus is straight and to the point: during our respective journeys, we can expect we <u>will</u> experience tribulation. Yet, amid our troubles, we can still experience the abundant life and the fruit of the Spirit if we don't lose sight of our destination, and that is to "seek first the kingdom of God and His righteousness". In this, we are assured that all we will ever need will be given to us (Matt 6:33). May this be your experience in your journey to the destination He has for you.

---

[602] https://www.goodreads.com/author/quotes/3061.M_Scott_Peck

EPILOGUE

INTRODUCTION

My purpose in writing this book is my hope that in some small way it will help you on your journey to realizing the abundant life Jesus promises us through experiencing more of the fruit of the Spirit in our lives (John 8:32; 10:10; Gal 5:22-23; cf Eph 5:9-10). I've proposed *WHOLENESS* flows out of living in a loving relationship with God in which we "keep" His commandments as our own principles for life rather than serving Him through obedience to His "laws". Given this, the abundant life is realized through:

- *Living with the Person of God through a lifestyle of prayer*
- *Living through the Power of God by utilizing the spiritual armor; and,*
- *Living for the Purposes of God by seeking first His kingdom.*

This happens through the daily decision to follow the example of Jesus Himself, the Suffering Servant (Is 52:13-53:12), who in the hours before His death on the cross, said:

> *"If you keep My commandments, you will*
> *abide in My love, just as I have kept*
> *My Father's commandments and abide in His*
> *love. These things I have spoken to*
> *you, that My joy may remain in you, and that*
> *your joy may be full." (John 15:10-11)*

The fruit of embracing and living out His words in our lives leads to the kind of deep and meaningful relationship we all desire to have with Him:

> *"You are My <u>friends</u> if you do whatever I command*
> *you. No longer do I call you servants,*
> *for a servant does not know what his master is*
> *doing; but I have called you friends, for*
> *all things that I heard from My Father I have*
> *made known to you." (John 15:14-15)*

What a powerful statement and promise for us today! Despite all our shortcomings, Jesus promises that if we embrace and live out His teachings, He will consider us His friends! This is the abundant life He offers that we hope will become your reality.

THE WAR HAS ALREADY BEGUN: CAN HE COUNT ON YOU?

In 1917, the United States – with World War I raging throughout Europe – declared war on Germany. To build up our military and drum up volunteers, recruiters developed the "Uncle Sam wants you" poster, of which over 4 million copies were distributed throughout the country. This same image has been used during subsequent wars to stir up the patriotic spirit that prompts young men to risk their lives defending our country and protecting the freedom we all enjoy. Noticeable is the image of "Uncle Sam" looking towards and pointing his finger directly at the viewer. And while directed  at any young American, it becomes highly personal with the message, "I want <u>YOU</u>". And as history tells us, this campaign logo has been successful, as many have responded to the call.

World War I would prove to be the deadliest war in human history to date, with total casualties estimated at 37.5 million.[603] While America and her allies fought their flesh-and-blood enemies represented in the Triple Alliance, however, the world collectively found itself in another war with a silent, invisible, and more deadly enemy. By the time the Spanish Flu pandemic had subsided, it had claimed as many as 100 million victims.[604]

Fast forward 100 years, and the world found itself in a similar war – one which our unending international tensions pale in comparison to, and one for which American political leaders found a way to come together on an unprecedented $2 trillion stimulus bill to overcome it. And while vaccinations developed have been effective in combating the devastating effects of the Coronavirus, variants rendered it a continuing threat worldwide.

For all this ominous news, however, there is another virus – one that is much more deadly – that continues to afflict the world. This virus is 100% lethal, and it attacks the body, soul, and spirit. It has plagued humanity since the Garden of Eden, and one for which there is only one cure: the blood of the Lamb, Jesus Christ.[605] It is the sin virus.

Like Uncle Sam's petition 100 years ago to join in the cause of World War I, Jesus – our Commander-in-Chief – is petitioning you to join in the battle for the souls of humanity. And it is a battle in which you will have victory if you hold on to the following promises.

GOD HAS BEEN WORKING FOR YOU

God desires no one perish, and all are saved (2 Pet 3:9). He loves each and every one of us and wants us all to be part of His team. But this isn't the desperate, last second, "we're at war with the Germans and we need your help" sort of plea proclaimed 100 years ago. Instead, He has plans and purposes He determined before He even created all that exists:

"Blessed be the God and Father of our Lord
Jesus Christ, who has blessed us

---

[603] https://www.historyhit.com/facts-about-world-war-one-casualties/
[604] https://www.history.com/topics/world-war-i/1918-flu-pandemic
[605] John 1:29; 1 Pet 1:9; Rev 7:14; 12:11.

with <u>every spiritual blessing</u> in the heavenly
places in Christ, just as He <u>chose us in</u>
<u>Him</u> <u>before the foundation of the world</u>, that
we should be <u>holy and without blame</u>
before Him in love, having <u>predestined</u> us to
adoption as sons by Jesus Christ to
Himself, according to the good pleasure of
His will, to the praise of the glory of
His grace, by which He has made us accepted
in the Beloved." (Eph 1:3-6)

"For whom He <u>foreknew</u>, He also <u>predestined</u>
to be conformed to the image of
His Son, that He might be the firstborn among
many brethren. Moreover whom
He predestined, these He also <u>called</u>; whom
He called, these He also <u>justified</u>;
and whom He justified, these He also
<u>glorified</u>. What then shall we say to
these things? If God is for us, who can
be against us?" (Rom 8:29-31)

Think about this: God not only planned but <u>predestined</u> you for adoption into His family with a role designed specifically for you! And unlike Uncle Sam's appeal that <u>you</u> sacrifice your life for your country, God sent Jesus to sacrifice <u>His</u> life on your behalf! The bottom line: you have value, you are significant, and you will always matter to Him. You have been declared "holy and blameless", and in His eyes you are *WHOLE*!

GOD IS WORKING THROUGH YOU

But God didn't send Jesus just to save us – He also sent the Holy Spirit to <u>sanctify</u> us. If you're unfamiliar with this theological term, it means to be "cleansed, or set apart" for His purposes with a role designed specifically for <u>you</u>. You may recall the following passage:

*"For You formed my inward parts; You covered me in
my mother's womb. I will praise You, for I am fearfully
and wonderfully made; Marvelous are Your works, and
that my soul knows very well." (Ps 139:13-14)*

You matter because God has uniquely equipped you to fulfill a role
He has designed specifically for you to fill. Through your natural skills
and abilities as well as the spiritual gifts He has imparted to you, God has
prepared you to do something significant for His kingdom. And as we saw
in *Chapter Seven*, while there is diversity in the types of spiritual gifts, there
is no difference in the <u>importance</u> of the function each serves:

*"But now indeed there are many members, yet one body. And
the eye cannot say to the hand, 'I have no need of you'; nor
again the head to the feet, 'I have no need of you.' No, much
rather, those members of the body which <u>seem to be weaker
are necessary</u>. And those members of the body which
we <u>think to be less honorable, on these we bestow greater honor;</u> and
our unpresentable parts have greater modesty, but our presentable
parts have no need. But God composed the body, having given
greater honor to that part which lacks it, that there should be no
schism in the body, but <u>that the members should have the same
care for one another. And if one member suffers, all the members
suffer</u> with it; or <u>if one member is honored, all the
members rejoice with it.</u>.... But earnestly
desire the best gifts. And yet I show you a more
excellent way.... And now abide faith,
hope, love, these three; but the <u>greatest of these
is love</u>." (1 Cor 12:20-26; 13:13)*

Notice Paul goes to great pains to emphasize the importance of even
the "weaker" or "less honorable" (i.e., those less visible and often less
recognized) gifts, as just as each part of the human body is necessary for
us to survive and thrive, <u>all</u> gifts serve an important role in accomplishing
the purposes Jesus has for us in building His kingdom.

In drawing from the example of the Uncle Sam poster, consider the fact historians believe "Uncle Sam" is named after none other than Sam Wilson, a meatpacker who stamped the initials, "U.S." on each barrel of meat he sold to the army during the War of 1812. Sam Wilson – not a general or "hero" who bravely gave his life on the field of battle – but just your everyday meatpacker. Yet his name has been preserved in history because of the contributions he made on behalf of his fellow Americans.[606] In the same way, Jesus will remember you as a "good and faithful servant" for the contributions you make for the cause of His kingdom if you faithfully serve Him in the role He has called you to.[607]

One final note: God will not only use your natural skills and spiritual gifts, but your life experiences – whether good or bad, and whether joyful or painful – in preparing you for His purposes. Joseph came to realize God was able to use the abuse, the false charges and resultant imprisonment he suffered to save the nation of Israel (Gen 50:20). In the same way He will redeem the failures, regrettable choices, and any pain and suffering you have experienced – just as He redeemed those of men like Peter – for His purposes as well:

> *"And we know that all things work together for*
> *good to those who love God, to those who are the*
> *called according to His purpose." (Rom 8:28)*

Like Uncle Sam, God wants you – He graciously and mercifully made the sacrifice to save you, but for purposes He wants to fulfill through you:

> *"For by grace you have been saved through*
> *faith, and that not of yourselves,*
> *it is the gift of God, not of works, lest*
> *anyone should boast. For we are*
> *His workmanship, created in Christ Jesus for*
> *good works, which God prepared beforehand that*
> *we should walk in them." (Eph 2:8-10)*

---

[606] https://www.history.com/this-day-in-history/united-states-nicknamed-uncle-sam
[607] Note, for example, Matt 25:14-30; cf Luke 19:11-27.

If you have any lingering doubts that you can actually accomplish "greater works" than Jesus (John 14:12), we offer the following examples. First, there's Saul – renamed Paul –who would go on to writer much of the New Testament and become arguably the greatest evangelist in Christian history. And then we offer Rahab, a woman whose story – while lesser known – is in some ways no less impactful.

Rahab's role in God's redemptive story begins around 1405 B.C. God has delivered Israel from Egyptian bondage but has wandered in the desert for 40 years after failing to trust He could deliver the Promised Land to them. Moses has died, and Joshua is to lead the *Entrance* Generation into the Promised Land where with God's help Israel will overcome the "giants" and fortified cities occupying the Land at that time (Num 13:1-14:35).

In Joshua 2:1-24, we're told Joshua sends two spies into the city of Jericho. The spies encounter a woman named Rahab – a known prostitute – who has heard how the God of Israel has given her victory over her enemies. The king of Jericho hears there are spies in his city, that Rahab is helping them, and orders Rahab to "bring out the men". So, Rahab is confronted with the ultimate test of her faith: "Do I obey the king and ignore what the God of Israel has done, or do I believe in Him – even if I have to risk my life in doing so?"

Rahab chooses the latter: she believes God will give Israel victory despite Jericho's seemingly insurmountable walls, and she and her family will be spared. She proceeds to help the spies escape and her faith is confirmed: God brings down the walls of Jericho and the people of Jericho are slaughtered, but Rahab and her family are spared (Josh 6:17-25).

Rahab – a mere prostitute – is remembered for her act of faith.[608] But she is remembered for another reason as well: Rahab happens to be an ancestor of none other than Jesus Himself (Matt 1:5)! And she is just one example of God using the most unlikely people to accomplish great things for His purposes. All Rahab had to do was to take a step of faith.

---

[608] See Heb 11:31; Jam 2:25.

GOD WILL FINISH THE WORK HE HAS STARTED IN YOU

What will probably come as no surprise to you is exercising more and eating better were the top two New Year's Resolutions for 2023 (53% and 50% of respondents, respectively.[609] And many likely acted on their resolutions initially by joining a gym or buying some exercise equipment. The question, however, is what percentage of those respondents will be still sticking with those resolutions by the end of the year.[610]

You may have heard the old sayings, "talk is cheap", and "actions speak louder than words". These certainly have merit, as the Bible says a lot about not only knowing God's Word but putting it into practice as well. And critically important is realizing this isn't simply a matter of "being obedient" or avoiding "disappointing God", but God giving us direction as to how we can begin experiencing the abundant life:

> *"But be doers of the word, and not hearers only,*
> *deceiving yourselves. For if anyone is a*
> *hearer of the word and not a doer, he is like a man*
> *observing his natural face in a mirror,*
> *for he observes himself, goes away, and immediately*
> *forgets what kind of man he was.*
> *But he who looks into the perfect law of liberty*
> *and continues in it and is not a forgetful l*
> *hearer but a <u>doer of the work</u>, this one will be*
> *<u>blessed in what he does</u>." (Jam 1:22-25)*

> *"Now may the God of peace who brought up*
> *our Lord Jesus from the dead, that*
> *great Shepherd of the sheep, through the blood*
> *of the everlasting covenant, make*
> *you <u>complete in every good work to do His will</u>,*
> *working in you what is <u>well pleasing</u>*

---

[609] https://www.usatoday.com/story/life/reviewed/2023/01/13/most-popular-new-years-resolutions-2023/11044163002/

[610] I finished my final editing of this book on December 30, 2023.

---

in His sight, through Jesus Christ, to whom be
glory forever and ever." (Heb 13:20-21)

Throughout this study I have emphasized the promise of Jesus that we can experience the abundant life evidenced by the fruit of the Spirit (John 10:10; Gal 5:22-23). This will increasingly become your experience if you choose each day who you will serve (Josh 24:15). But as with any of His promises we want to see fulfilled in our lives, it requires we pause and consider if we truly believe God will do what He has promised to do:

"...being confident of this very thing, that He who
has begun a good work in you will complete it
until the day of Jesus Christ..." (Phil 1:6)

And it requires patience, as like anything worth having it will take time to realize it:

"But let patience have its perfect work, that you may be perfect
and complete, lacking nothing. If any of you lacks wisdom,
let him ask of God, who gives to all liberally and without
reproach, and it will be given to him. But let him ask in
faith, with no doubting, for he who doubts is like a wave
of the sea driven and tossed by the wind." (Jam 1:4-6)

Finally, we must take the same step of faith required in following the rehabilitation plan given us by a doctor or physical therapist after a major surgery: that if we follow their instructions, we will in fact recover and be restored to health. Put another way, we live and move forward in the belief we will be made *WHOLE*, which in turn leads to us actually becoming WHOLE:

"Not that I have already attained, or am
already perfected; but I press on, that I
may lay hold of that for which Christ Jesus has
also laid hold of me. Brethren, I do
not count myself to have apprehended; but one
thing I do, forgetting those things which

are behind and reaching forward to those
things which are ahead, I press toward
the goal for the prize of the upward call of
God in Christ Jesus." (Phil 2:12-14)

And as we follow the example of Paul and "press toward" this goal, we too will be transformed into becoming more and more like Jesus, and as this occurs, we will be given a glimpse of the unveiled glory of the Lord (2 Cor 3:17-19).[611]

But as these passages tell us, the blessing we hope to experience comes when we respond in faith through carrying out the works God has planned specifically for each of us. And it all boils down to this: we can only really know God – we can only have the deeply personal and meaningful relationship with Him that we all desire – if we love others in the same way God loved us:

"But whoever keeps His word, truly the love of God is perfected
in him. By this we know that we are in Him." (1 John 2:5)

"No one has seen God at any time. If we love one another,
God abides in us, and His love has been perfected in us. By
this we know that we abide in Him, and He in us because
He has given us of His Spirit." (1 John 4:12-13) [612]

My prayer and hope for you is that you will believe God will complete the good work He has started in you, and that you will take the steps you've identified to fulfill His purposes for you. And with that, I close with Paul's words to the Ephesians, as well as my prayer that you experience a profound sense of His blessing in your life:

"Peace to the brethren, and love with faith, from God the Father
and the Lord Jesus Christ. Grace be with all those who love
our Lord Jesus Christ in sincerity. Amen." (Eph 6:23-24)

---

[611] See discussion in *Chapter Five*.

[612] Again, the Greek word translated "know" in these passages is *gynosko*, which means the experiential knowledge we gradually gain as we get to know a person by being in relationship with him or her. It extends beyond the factual head knowledge to the knowledge of fondly knowing someone in our hearts.

"The Lord bless you and keep you; the Lord make His face shine upon you and be gracious to you; the Lord turn His face toward you and give you peace." (Num 6:24-26)[613]

And may that blessing include more love, joy, peace, patience, kindness, goodness, faithfulness, gentleness, and self-control (Gal 5:22-23) in your life! Amen.

---

[613] See also Rom 1:7; 15:33; 2 Thess 3:16; 1 Tim 1:2; 2 tim 4:22; Heb 13:20-21; 1 Pet 5:14; 2 Pet 1:2; Rev 1:4-5.

APPENDICES

CHAPTER TWO: WHO IS GOD? [614]

Complete the survey with the most honest answer based on how you feel rather than what you think is the "right" answer (ranging from 5 for "very well", 1 for "not at all"):

God's Judgment: How well do you feel each of the following words describe God?

	Very Well	Somewhat Well	Undecided	Not Very Well	Not at All
1. Loving	5	4	3	2	1
2. Critical	5	4	3	2	1
3. Punishing	5	4	3	2	1
4. Severe	5	4	3	2	1
5. Wrathful	5	4	3	2	1
6. Angered by human sin	5	4	3	2	1
7. Angered by my sin	5	4	3	2	1

God's Engagement: How well do you feel that each of the following words describes God?

	Strongly Agree	Agree	Undecided	Disagree	Strongly Disagree
1. Distant	1	2	3	4	5
2. Ever-present	5	4	3	2	1
3. Removed from world affairs	1	2	3	4	5

---

[614] Drawn from and used by permission by Paul Froese & Christopher Bader. <u>America's Four Gods" What We Say About God & What That Says About Us.</u> New York: Oxford University Press, 2010.

4. Removed from my affairs	1	2	3	4	5
5. Concerned w/ well-being of world	5	4	3	2	1
6. Concerned w/ my well-being	5	4	3	2	1
7. Directly involved in world affairs 5	4	3	2	1	
8. Involved in my affairs	5	4	3	2	1

Total up your scores as follows:

- God's Judgment: total of answers for questions 1-7 _____
- God's Engagement: total of answers for questions 8-15 _____

The following reflect how you perceive God:

God's Judgment Score		God's Engagement Score	Your God
Low (6 – 17)	AND	High (32 – 40)	Benevolent
High (18 – 30)	AND	High (32 – 40)	Authoritative
High (18 – 30)	AND	Low (8 – 31)	Critical
Low (6 – 17)	AND	Low (8 – 31)	Distant

Questions:

- Did the description you chose match the results from your answers to the survey?
- Which description do you feel best represents God as you understand He is presented in the Bible, and therefore is the "right" answer? Briefly explain why.

_____

_____

- How much do you think your answers were influenced by what you think is the "right" answer?

_____

_____

The four types of attachment are as follows:

1. *Secure: Confident Connection*

> ➤ My parents were consistently available and approachable when I was upset or needed help (never irritated or bothered for being "interrupted",

> ➤ I was comfortable in getting help, assurance, and comfort from my parents and as a result, always felt they were good, cared about me, and were willing to help me,

> ➤ I find it relatively easy for me to become emotionally close to others,

> ➤ I am comfortable in depending on others and having others depend on me,

> ➤ I don't worry about being alone or having others not accept me.

Question: On a scale of 1 (not at all) to 5 (very much), how much does this describe you? _____

Write out some reasons or examples of why you answered as you did:

_____

_____

_____

2. *Insecure-Preoccupied: Anxious/Ambivalence:*

> ➤ My parents were not always available nor approachable when I was upset or needed help,

> ➤ I often felt anxious or angry when my parents weren't available to me,

> ➤ I tend to get anxious about asking for help because I don't want to be a burden, or doubt whether they'll make time for me,

---

[615] Drawn from <u>Safe Haven Marriage: Building a Relationship You Want to Come Home To,</u> by Drs. Archibald D. Hart and Sharon Hart Morris (Nashville, TN: Thomas Nelson Publishers, 2003), 57-66.

➤ I want to have close relationships with others, but I am not sure I can trust that others will consistently be there for me, or even want to be close with me,

➤ I tend to doubt my ability to get the help I need from others

Question: On a scale of 1 (not at all) to 5 (very much), how much does this describe you? _____

Write out some reasons or examples of why you answered as you did:

_____

_____

_____

3. *Insecure-Fearful: Anxious-Disorganized*

➤ My parents tended to get angry or frustrated with me when I needed help,

➤ I tended to be careful not to upset my parents,

➤ I tend to not ask others for help because I assume it will bother them,

➤ I tend to be uncomfortable getting too close to others,

➤ I'm afraid I'll get hurt if I let others know too much about me.

Question: On a scale of 1 (not at all) to 5 (very much), how much does this describe you? _____

Write out some reasons or examples of why you answered as you did:

_____

_____

_____

4. *Insecure-Dismissive: Anxious-Avoidance*

➤ My parents were both unavailable and emotionally unapproachable when I needed help. I was taught to "stand on my own two feet",

➤ I tend to avoid close relationships with others,

➤ I tend to be independent, driven, and at times prone to perfectionism,

➤ I tend to feel I am on my own, and it's up to me to take care of myself,

➤ I cannot trust others to be there for me when I need them.

Question: On a scale of 1 (not at all) to 5 (very much), how much does this describe you? _____

Write out some reasons or examples of why you answered as you did:

_____

_____

_____

CHAPTER FIVE: WHAT'S MY ACE SCORE?

Prior to your 18<u>th</u> birthday:

1. Did a parent or other adult in the household **often** or **very often**...
    Swear at you, insult you, put you down, or humiliate you?
    Or
    Act in a way that made you afraid that you might be physically hurt?
    Yes   ***No***   If yes, enter "1" _____

2. Did a parent or other adult in the household **often** or **very often**...
    Push, grab, slap, or throw something at you?
    Or
    Ever hit you so hard that you had marks or were injured?
    Yes   ***No***   If yes, enter "1" _____

3. Did an adult or person at least 5 years older than you **ever**...
    Touch or fondle you or have you touch their body in a sexual way?
    Or
    Attempt or actually have oral, anal, or vaginal intercourse with you?
    Yes   ***No***   If yes, enter "1" _____

4. Did you **often** or **very often** feel that...
    No one in your family loved you or thought you were important or special?
    Or
    Your family didn't look out for each other, feel close to each other, or support each other?
    Yes   ***No***   If yes, enter "1" _____

5. Did you **often** or **very often** feel that...
    You didn't have enough to eat, had to wear dirty clothe, and had no one to protect you?
    Or
    Your parents were too drunk or high to take care of you or take you to the doctor if you needed it?
    Yes   ***No***   If yes, enter "1" _____

6. Was a biological parent **ever** lost to you through divorce, abandonment, or other reason?

Yes   *No*   If yes, enter "1" _____

7. Was your mother or stepmother:
   Often or **very often** pushed, grabbed, slapped, or had something thrown at her?

   Or

   Sometimes, often, or **very often** kicked, bitten, hit with a fist, or hit with something hard?

   Or

   Ever repeatedly hit over at least a few minutes or threatened with a gun or knife?

   Yes   *No*   If yes, enter "1" _____

8. Did you live with anyone who was a problem drinker or alcoholic or who used street drugs?

   Yes   *No*   If yes, enter "1" _____

9. Was a household member depressed or mentally ill or did a household member attempt suicide?

   Yes   *No*   If yes, enter "1" _____

10. Did a household member go to prison?

    Yes   *No*   If yes, enter "1" _____

Now add up your "Yes" answers: _____   This is your ACE Score

CHAPTER FIVE: WHO I AM IN CHRIST

I AM ACCEPTED

- *I am God's child (John 1:12)*
- *I have been washed clean of my sins (John 15:3)*
- *I am a friend of Jesus (John 15:15)*
- *I have been justified (Rom 5:1)*
- *I have been bought with a price and belong to God (1 Cor 6:17-20)*
- *I am a part of Jesus' Church – His body of believers (1 Cor 12:26-27)*
- *I am established, anointed, and sealed as a child of God (2 Cor 1:21-22)*
- *I have been chosen by God and adopted as His child (Eph 1:3-8)*
- *I have been redeemed and have direct access to God through the Holy Spirit (Col 1:13-14)*
- *I am complete in Jesus (Col 2:9-10)*
- *I have direct access to God through Jesus Christ (Heb 4:14-16)*

I AM SAFE

- *I am forever free from condemnation (Rom 8:1-2)*
- *I am assured that all things work together for God's good (Rom 8:28)*
- *I am free from any condemning charges against me, and cannot be separated from the Love of God (Rom 8:31-34)*
- *I can approach God with freedom and confidence (Eph 3:12)*
- *I can be confident the work God has begun in me will be completed (Phil 1:6)*
- *I am a citizen of Heaven (Phil 3:20)*
- *I can be free from fear because God has given me a spirit of power, love, and self-control (2 Tim 1:7)*
- *I can find grace and mercy to help in time of need (Heb 4:16)*
- *I have been re-born of God and the evil one cannot reach me (1 John 5:18)*

I AM IMPORTANT

- *I am the salt and light of the earth (Matt 5:13-14)*
- *I am a branch of the true Vine and a channel of His life (John 15:1, 5)*
- *I have been chosen and appointed to bear the fruit of Jesus (John 15:16)*
- *I am a personal witness of Jesus (Acts 1:8)*
- *I am God's temple (1 Cor 3:16)*
- *I am God's workmanship (Eph 2:10)*
- *I may approach God with freedom and confidence (Eph 3:12)*
- *I am confident God will complete the good work He has started in me (Phil 1:6)*

CHAPTER FIVE: AUTOMATIC THOUGHT RECORD

Automatic Thought Record

An Automatic Thought Record (ATR) takes an event and breaks it down into automatic negative thoughts, emotions and behaviors. Then, it challenges your initial negative reactions to the inciting event. With practice, an ATR can have a huge positive impact on how we interpret and react to situations.

Situation	Automatic Negative Thought (ANT)	Emotion	Challenge ANT	New Balanced Thought	Emotion
Recall the problematic situation	The first negative thoughts in reaction to the situation	What were you feeling? How intense was each emotion? Scale 1- 10	What do you know about yourself and the situation that could challenge the ANT	The more balanced thought after challenging ANT	How intense are the previously stated emotions? What new emotions are you feeling?
I waved at my friend on the street but did not wave back when he saw me wave.	Why did he ignore me? He must be mad at me He must not like me He must have pretended to be my friend	Angry- 9 Sad- 9 Confused- 10 Embarrassed- 7 Frustrated- 9 Concerned- 10	This is a busy street; he may have not realized it was me. I am dressed in work clothes; maybe he did not recognize me. Maybe he is deep in thought	He and I have been friends for some time now, it is not like him to ignore me. There must be a reasonable explanation for this. The next time I see him I will ask if he noticed I was waving at him.	Angry- 5 Sad- 3 Confused- 7 Embarrassed- 5 Frustrated- 6 Concerned- 5 Relief - 7

Trigger	Automatic Thought	New Thought
EXAMPLE: I made a mistake at work.	"I'm probably going to be fired. I always mess up. This is it. I'm no good at this job."	"I messed up, but mistakes happen. I'm going to work through this, like I always do."

ACKNOWLEDGEMENTS

While the genesis of this book dates to late 2017, the seeds were planted back in late 1986 when I attended the Saturday Nooner's AA meeting at the Fridley Alano Club in Fridley, Minnesota for the first time. Thanks to all those men and women, who of course remain anonymous, that I would see each Saturday who gave me hope and introduced me to the *Twelve Steps of Alcoholics Anonymous.*

Thanks to my sister-in-law Patty Kelley and her husband Jim, through whom I saw Jesus at work and inspired me as I began contemplating *Step Three* and making the decision to "... *turn [my] will and [my] life over to the care of God as [I] understood Him.*"

To all my brothers and sisters in Christ from Elim Baptist Church in "Nordeast" Minneapolis, my first church family. Special mention to Ruth and Brian Hill, who invited my wife Mary to Elim, as well Roger Dahl and Paul Pennoyer, who warmly welcomed me the first time I visited Elim in spring of 1987, and Don Heide, who led the Friday morning Men's group I learned so much from.

To the leadership of Shiloh Community Church, particularly Pastor Tom Garasha, who saw the spiritual gift of encouragement in me and invited me to join their Elder Board in 1995.

To Pastor Bob Kerrey, then Associate Pastor at Shiloh and through Shiloh's support would plant what became Moon Valley Community Church, for inspiring me to begin my seminary studies at Phoenix Seminary, recommending me for my first pastoral position at Moon Valley, and providing encouragement in taking that big leap in walking away from a 20-year career in banking into full-time ministry.

To the professorial staff at Phoenix Seminary, circa 1997-2001, who nurtured my theological and spiritual growth. Special thanks to Dr. Steve Tracy through whom I became keenly aware of the prominence of the call for social justice in the Scriptures, and whose knowledge and insights are referenced frequently in this book. Special thanks to Dr. Fred Chay, my mentor during my seminary studies who gave me the privilege of being his teaching assistant during the spring of 2000, his mantra "Leaders are readers" which inspired my passion for learning and as a result is partly to blame for the library that fills the office in our home, and provided input on the writing of this book and encouraged me to publish it. And thanks to Dr. Kem Oberholtzer, my first theology professor, and Dr. Norm Wakefield in whom I saw the heart of a true spiritual "shepherd".

To the leadership and staff at Oasis Community Church in Scottsdale, Arizona, for the opportunity to take the lead and, particularly Pastor Dawn Claudio, provided input in developing the spiritual growth curriculum that became the foundation for this book.

To my dad Barton Bauer and my mom Shirley Bauer for teaching and modeling for me the life skills including hard work, responsibility and persistence that have served me well in life.

To my daughters, Jill and Kristin and their husbands Jason and Emmett and our four grandchildren, Lilly, Artemis, Sydney, and Lucas (I'll spare them including the nicknames I've lovingly given each of them 😊), who are such a blessing to me.

But most of all I need to thank two people: first, Dr. and Reverend James D Smith III who I first met 37 years ago at Elim, my dear friend and who will always be "Pastor Jim" to me. Thank you for your wisdom, insights, recommendations for this book, but most importantly your friendship and spiritual guidance through all these years after helping me meet and get to know Jesus as my Savior. And finally, my wife Mary, my life partner, who despite my idiosyncrasies, or as Robin Williams in *Good Will Hunting* would say, my peccadilloes, has been patient and supportive as I wrote this book and encouraged me to step out and publish it. You all have been a blessing to me, and I am grateful for you all!

BIOGRAPH

Jeff Bauer is a licensed therapist specializing in helping people overcome addiction to alcohol and drugs. After 19 years in banking, Jeff sensed God leading him in a new direction, and began his studies at Phoenix Seminary from which he graduated with his master's in divinity degree in 2002. Over the past 25 years Jeff has served in the church as a pastor and elder, and as an adjunct professor taught General Psychology and Bible Survey classes at Arizona Christian University from 2006-2019. Jeff obtained his master's in social work from Arizona State University in 2014. He and his wife Mary have two daughters, two sons-in-law and four grandchildren, and along with their cat Archie reside in Phoenix, Arizona, where in his free time Jeff enjoys time with his family, sports, music, movies, and of course reading!

Printed in the United States
by Baker & Taylor Publisher Services